HOKE SMITH

and the Politics of the New South

Hoke Smith

and the Politics

of the New South

DEWEY W. GRANTHAM, JR.

Louisiana State University Press

FOR VIRGINIA

Acknowledgments

It is a pleasure to acknowledge the assistance I have received from numerous individuals and institutions in the completion of this biography. I am especially indebted to Professor Fletcher M. Green, who first aroused my interest in Hoke Smith. Professor Green's understanding of the Southern past, his rare gifts as a teacher and critic, and his friendly counsel have benefited me at every turn. I should like to think that this book maintains the high standards of his famous seminar at the University of North Carolina.

I am grateful to the following friends and fellow-historians for reading portions of the manuscript at an early stage in its development: Dean Judson C. Ward of Emory University, Professor Cecil Johnson and Dr. James W. Patton of the University of North Carolina, and Professor and Mrs. Carl Sutton of North Texas State College. I owe an especially heavy debt to my friend and colleague, Henry L. Swint, who generously read the manuscript in its entirety and offered many valuable suggestions for its improvement.

The interest and encouragement of many friends and professional colleagues have helped sustain me in the work on this project. I particularly want to express appreciation to Professors Harold W. Bradley and Herbert Weaver, and to Dean Leonard B. Beach of Vanderbilt University; to Dr. William C. Binkley of Tulane University; to Professor E. Merton Coulter of the University of Georgia; and to Dr. J. Isaac Copeland of George Peabody College for Teachers. I shall always be grateful to Professor Howard K. Beale for the critical judgment and sound scholarship he demanded in his courses on recent American history at the University of North Carolina. My obligations to other scholars in the field of recent Southern history are too numerous to list here. The illuminating studies of C. Vann Woodward and Arthur S. Link have been particularly helpful.

I want to express my thanks to the Institute of Research and Training in the Social Sciences at Vanderbilt University, Dr. George W. Stocking, Director, for a generous grant to assist in the publication of the book. I am also grateful to the Research Committee of the Graduate Council, North Texas State College, for a summer grant which allowed me to complete some of the research for the biography.

My labors have been lightened by the help of many libraries and librarians. Special thanks are due the staffs of the Southern Historical Collection and the University of North Carolina Library, the Joint University Libraries of Nashville, the University of Georgia Library, the Duke University Library, the Georgia Department of Archives and History, and the Manuscripts Division of the Library of Congress. I am indebted to Mrs. Callie Hoke Smith Thornton and to Mr. Hoke Smith II for kindly permitting me to use certain Smith materials not in the Smith Collection at the University of Georgia. Miss Ruth Blair, Executive Secretary of the Atlanta Historical Society, and Mrs. Mary G. Bryan, Director of the Georgia Department of Archives and History, generously assisted in securing most of the illustrations used in the book. T. Harry Williams, editor of the *Southern Biography Series*, and the efficient staff of the Louisiana State University Press deserve a special word of appreciation from the author for their co-operation, patience, and good humor throughout the book-making process. I would also like to thank Mrs. J. W. Swingley, secretary of the Department of History, Vanderbilt University, for the cheerful and skillful manner in which she typed the manuscript.

Finally, I want to acknowledge the great debt I owe to my mother, Ellen H. Grantham. She and my mother-in-law, Louella T. Burleson, have facilitated the work from beginning to end. I am indebted most of all to my wife, Virginia Burleson Grantham. She has helped me in every phase of the undertaking, and has been a constant source of inspiration.

D. G.

Contents

HOKE SMITH

and the Politics of the New South

Carolina Boyhood

The boy was too young to play a part of any consequence in the Civil War and Reconstruction, but the events of that era left an indelible imprint upon his mind. Despite his youth, he was a part of the war generation, and however vicariously, he participated in the drama of a nation's birth and experienced the slow agony of its death. He knew at first hand the dark postwar years of sectional subservience and economic hardship. In later years a fellow Southerner referred to him as "a son of the Confederacy," [1] and even when the boy himself had become an old man he would sometimes say rather proudly that he had been "raised with great respect for brigadier generals." His early heroes were men like his Uncle Robert F. Hoke, a major general in the Confederate Army, and Zebulon Baird Vance, wartime governor of North Carolina. He never forgot the visits that Zeb Vance made to his father's house in Chapel Hill. [2] Such experiences deepened Hoke Smith's Southernism, but for all his devotion to the Southern cause and his admiration for Confederate heroes, he could not forget that many of his relatives were Northerners, his father a Yankee.

His father was a New Englander, born in Deerfield, New Hampshire, in 1820, the son of William True Smith, a farmer, and his wife, Martha Ambrose. Hildreth Hosea Smith could name as his direct forebears two Smiths who served in the American Revolution; a politically minded Smith named Samuel, who was active in the provincial politics of his colony; the Reverend

---

[1] Representative Benjamin E. Russell of Georgia, *Congressional Record*, 53 Cong., 2 Sess., 2690.

[2] *Ibid.*, 64 Cong., 1 Sess., 9756; 65 Cong., 1 Sess., 541.

Henry Smith, who came to Massachusetts Bay during the early
years of that colony and later migrated to Connecticut, where,
according to Edward Johnson's *Wonder-Working Providence*,
" he laboured in the Word and Doctrine with a people." [3] And
even further back was an English gentleman, a resident of Somer-
set, to whom family tradition gave the title "Sir" Hugh Smith.[4]

For a time Hildreth Smith attended Foxcroft Academy in
Maine, subsequently enrolling at Bowdoin College. He was
graduated near the head of his class in 1842. After teaching school
for a year or two, he returned to Bowdoin to study for the
Master's degree, which he received in 1845. Eventually he turned
to the study of law in Washington, D. C., was admitted to practice, but soon found it necessary to give up the profession because
of failing eyesight. He made the long trip by water to San
Francisco, evidently as a part of the California gold rush. Returning empty-handed to the East, Smith taught school for a
year at Lancaster, Pennsylvania; then, in the fall of 1851, he
went south with Professor Charles H. Albert to teach in a school
at Newton, North Carolina, soon to be known as Catawba
College. Here in Catawba County in western North Carolina
he served as assistant to Professor Albert and as Professor of
Mathematics, Natural Science, and Modern Languages. When
Albert returned to the North after two years, Hildreth Smith
became head of the new college. He saw the first permanent
building constructed at the institution and successfully directed
it during the following few years.[5]

Hildreth Smith was proficient in both ancient and modern

[3] J. Franklin Jameson (ed.), *Johnson's Wonder-Working Providence,
1628-1651* (New York, 1910), 194. Except where otherwise indicated the
sources for this chapter are the biographical memoranda in the Hoke Smith
Collection, University of Georgia Library.

[4] Hildreth was the first cousin, on his mother's side, of Mary Baker,
later famous as Mrs. Mary Baker Eddy, founder of Christian Science. Sibyl
Wilbur, *The Life of Mary Baker Eddy* (New York, 1907), 7-8.

[5] Jacob Calvin Leonard, *History of Catawba College* (Columbia, Mo.,
1927), 36, 63-66; Kemp P. Battle, *History of the University of North
Carolina* (Raleigh, 1907-12), I, 660; *General Catalogue of Bowdoin College
and the Medical School of Maine: A Biographical Record of Alumni and
Officers, 1794-1950* (Brunswick, Me., 1950), 81-82.

languages and in later years offered courses in French, German, Spanish, and Italian at the University of North Carolina.[6] He was described as a fine mathematician and was interested in astronomical research. According to Kemp P. Battle, "Professor Smith was a good teacher, has fine talents, and was accomplished in his department." Various accounts tell of his broad learning, of his gentleness and courtesy, and of his public spirit.[7] Like most teachers of his day, Hildreth Smith was a strict disciplinarian who required his students to follow a rigid program of study. But Smith realized that education was more than a matter of books. He himself was fond of athletic contests and while at Catawba College "taught the boys boxing and fencing." He enjoyed music and liked to get the young people of Newton together for song sessions. Huge and impressive in appearance, he was a man of such great physical strength that his students dubbed him "Old Tige." One of his students, however, recalled that there "Never was a more glowing misnomer, for while he had proved his courage . . . by a daring rescue of persons trapped in a fire, yet a milder mannered man never lived. It was Old Tige who was blown up in the gunpowder plot and that episode bears the indelible print of his gentleness, for he was the first to forgive the unforgivable scamps who perpetrated the outrage."[8]

It was during his years at Newton that Hildreth Smith met Mary Brent Hoke, the daughter of a prominent deceased lawyer and political leader of Lincolnton, the county seat of Lincoln County, which lay just south of Catawba. Tall, attractive, and intelligent, Mary Brent Hoke was a talented girl quite positive

[6] He was the author of a 110-page textbook entitled *The Robertsonian System of Teaching French, with Rules of Pronunciation, and a Full Vocabulary* (Chapel Hill, 1858).

[7] Leonard, *Catawba College*, 68-70; Battle, *University of North Carolina*, I, 660, 662-63.

[8] The "gunpowder plot" occurred in 1861, after the war mania had seized the University of North Carolina. On this occasion a charge of gunpowder was set off under Hildreth's chair. Peter M. Wilson, *Southern Exposure* (Chapel Hill, 1927), 46-47. Also Robert Watson Winston, *Horace Williams, Gadfly of Chapel Hill* (Chapel Hill, 1942), 50; Leonard, *Catawba College*, 64-67.

in her views. Although there was considerable disparity in their
ages, the schoolteacher and the young North Carolinian were
attracted to each other, and their friendship developed into a
courtship. They were married at Lincolnton, May 19, 1853.

Nineteen-year-old Mary Brent was a descendant of English,
German, and Swiss ancestors, and many of her North Carolina
kinsmen achieved prominent stations in the economic and political
life of the state. Her great-grandfather, a Swiss Presbyterian
named John Fulenwider, was one of the first manufacturers of
pig iron in western North Carolina. Her father, Michael Hoke,
was the unsuccessful Democratic candidate for governor of North
Carolina in 1844. Her mother was Frances Burton, daughter of
Judge Robert Burton, who, with his two brothers, was among
the first students to enter the University of North Carolina in
1795, and who was the grandson of Colonel Robert Burton,
delegate to the Continental Congress from North Carolina in
the 1780's. Her brother, Robert, became one of the youngest
major generals in the Confederate Army.

Hildreth and Mary Brent Smith spent the first years of their
married life in a spacious seven-room house on the Catawba
College campus. It was in this house, adorned with crape myrtles
in front and a pleasant cedar grove in the rear, that the second
of their children was born, on September 2, 1855. They named
him Michael Hoke, after his maternal grandfather. But Hoke
Smith's stay in the little town of Newton was brief, for Hildreth
Smith was soon elected by the trustees of the University of North
Carolina to fill the newly created Professorship of Modern Languages in the University,[9] and early in 1857 the Smiths moved
to the village of Chapel Hill.

It was in this university town, deep in the piedmont of the
Old North State, that Hoke spent his boyhood. Chapel Hill
was pre-eminently a college community. It was a small village
and a small college—the faculty of the university numbered only
fourteen in 1860—and there was a delightful, though sometimes

[9] The Modern Language Professorship superseded that of the Instructor-
ship in French, which was held until December, 1856, by Henri Herrisse,
the French scholar, who was unhappy at the University because of his
difficulties with students. Battle, *University of North Carolina*, I, 657-59.

gossip-provoking, intimacy among those who resided there. The Smith home had belonged to Professor Benjamin S. Hedrick, who precipitated a storm in Chapel Hill by supporting John C. Fremont and the free-soil doctrine in the campaign of 1856. Upon being forced out of the University as a result of his politics, Hedrick sold his home to Hildreth Smith. Located in a "grove of much beauty," the one-story stuccoed house was a rambling, inconvenient affair on the side of a steep incline. At the bottom of the hill was the "famous Roaring Fountain" and from this spring "and up that long incline water for the home must be toted." [10]

Hoke Smith came to know the rigors of "toting" water up that long hill soon enough, but his earliest impressions about the Chapel Hill home were of his "large fine looking Father and Mother" and of his older sister Fanny.[11] Descended from "Puritan ancestry" on his father's side, Hoke was taught the values of "sturdy self-reliance, an earnest acquisition of knowledge, advancement in various departments of industry, and an intense love of country." Hildreth Smith's requirement of systematic obedience to rules, particularly those having to do with things of the mind, was fortunate for the younger Smith's education, for the children who lived in Chapel Hill during those years were privately taught, if taught at all.[12]

The Smiths taught their children that family tradition and ancestral ties were, like the Christian virtues, to be valued highly, and to be perpetuated by precept and example. Throughout his life Hoke Smith made much of family background and illustrious kinsmen; and he accepted cheerfully the innumerable calls upon

[10] Winston, *Horace Williams*, 50. The Chapel Hill *Weekly*, April 15, 1949, contains a description of the old Smith home.

[11] Fanny (Frances) was the oldest of the Smith children, having been born in 1854. In addition to Hoke, there were two other children: Lizzie, born in 1861, and Burton, born in 1864.

[12] Hope Summerell Chamberlain, *Old Days in Chapel Hill: Being the Life and Letters of Cornelia Phillips Spencer* (Chapel Hill, 1926), 28; *Lamb's Biographical Dictionary of the United States* (Boston, 1903), VII, 120; Wallace Putnam Reed (ed.), *History of Atlanta, Georgia, with Illustrations and Biographical Sketches of Some of Its Prominent Men and Pioneers* (Syracuse, 1899), Pt. II, 137.

his time and money made by less fortunate members of the family. To him the family circle possessed an infinite strength and richness of meaning.

There was added reason, of course, to prize one's family during Hoke's boyhood, for the Civil War began when he was in his sixth year.[13] As the war progressed, the lad must have experienced the gloom and despair felt by the older people of the village in the wake of Southern reverses and in the face of impending defeat. Those who remained in Chapel Hill during the war were keenly interested in the military engagements, and although the town was undisturbed by actual fighting, its seclusion and lack of communications served only to increase the villagers' concern for the events at the front. The numerous casualties suffered by University students on the battlefields were constant reminders of the tragedy of the holocaust. The number of students in residence declined drastically, and it was a struggle for those at the University to make ends meet. From the pen of Cornelia Phillips Spencer came the poignant lament that "The suffering and want and grief around me is enough to shroud the stoutest soul in gloom." [14]

But even during the dark days of the war there were some things to cheer a boy's life. There were romps with playmates on the wide green meadow, and fishing and swimming expeditions to nearby streams. Mrs. Spencer was a favorite of the children in the community, and no doubt Hoke was with her on some of their outings, such as the time she "went with all the children to Mallett's mill pond." [15]

The war had so obsessed the villagers, and yet had provided such a paucity of marching men and dashing cavalry, that nine-year-old Hoke must have felt a tingling thrill that April day

[13] Hildreth Smith did not join the Confederate Army, possibly because of his dependents and because he seems to have been inclined toward pacificism. Perhaps his loyalties were divided between the North, from which he had migrated only a decade before, and the South, where strong ties bound him. A later writer declared that Hildreth had "allied himself with the Southern people." Reed (ed.), *History of Atlanta*, Pt. II, 137.

[14] Chamberlain, *Old Days in Chapel Hill*, 76; Battle, *University of North Carolina*, I, 745.

[15] Chamberlain, *Old Days in Chapel Hill*, 75-76.

in 1865 when Wheeler's cavalry rode into Chapel Hill. Pickets were stationed on every road, and the General appeared ready to fortify the hill against the pursuing Yankees. The entire town busied itself day and night in providing for the near-starved Confederates. After two days, the pickets were called in and Wheeler's men rode away, to be followed in a few hours by a dozen Yanks who dashed in from the Raleigh road and captured Chapel Hill. On the following day the villagers got their first glimpse of the enemy in large numbers when a brigade of Kilpatrick's cavalry occupied the town. These and other military movements touched the University town in the weeks prior to the fall of the Confederacy, and Cornelia Spencer wrote in her diary, " What sights have we not seen in this quiet and remote village." [16]

The vicissitudes of the war were followed by equally great privations for those connected with the University. The end of the struggle found Chapel Hill people "very poor" and so dependent on the University that "its decline carries the whole village down." [17] When the fall term began in 1865, there were but twenty-two students, and in two years this number increased only to fifty. The rigors of the war and the early years of Reconstruction staggered the University; its endowment was lost and its property mortgaged. It faced collapse. Under these circumstances and with the coming of military Reconstruction, Hildreth Smith and his fellow faculty members resigned in the fall of 1867, but agreed to continue in their positions until the commencement of 1868. In January, 1868, Hildreth Smith wrote a friend that there were only forty-two students; "our prospects," he continued, "look gloomy." [18] Within a few months the new state government closed the institution's doors.

Residence in the University had no appeal for Hildreth Smith after the Radicals secured power, even had he been able to keep his place. A letter from Cornelia Spencer in August, 1868,

[16] *Ibid.*, 84-87; Battle, *University of North Carolina*, I, 742-43.

[17] Cornelia Spencer to Ellen Trammell, undated (1866), in Cornelia Spencer Papers (Southern Historical Collection, University of North Carolina Library).

[18] Hildreth Smith to Sylvester Hassell, January 21, 1868, in Sylvester Hassell Papers (Duke University Library).

tells of the unsettled conditions in the lives of the Smith family:
"They all will be gone in a few weeks—Mrs. S. going back to
Linc[olnton]—to take care of her mother while Mr. S. takes
Fanny to Brooklyn. They have advertised their house & furni-
ture . . . . Mr. S. will have a school in Linc[olnton]." [19] Some-
time in the fall of 1868 thirteen-year-old Hoke moved with his
parents to Lincolnton, where Hildreth Smith and a Professor
Wetmore established a private school.

Little is known of the years Hoke Smith and his family spent
in Lincolnton. They were doubtless in close contact with the
members of Mary Brent Smith's family, the Hokes. As Hoke
recalled later, "My mind often goes back to Lincolnton with
affectionate recollection of those with whom my boyhood was
spent." He came to love the hills and mountains of western
North Carolina, and as an old man he was quite overcome by
visits to the region; in his mind's eye he became once more
"the boy who long ago, merrily traversed the woodland paths,
and without care, played on every hill of this beautiful country-
side." But there was also work to be done. His father cultivated
some land and Hoke did his part of the farm work. As a boy
in western North Carolina, he once declared, he had driven "a
good many loads of wheat to the mill, had it ground, left my
toll, and brought my flour home." Then there was his father's
school. In later years he asserted, somewhat immodestly, that
"it was here that he gained the academic foundation which has
been of vital assistance in his wide range of attainments." [20]

In the spring of 1872, Mary Brent Smith took her children
by train to Atlanta, Georgia, where Hildreth Smith had gone
some time before to accept a position in the recently organized
public school system of that city.[21] Located among the rolling

[19] Cornelia Spencer to "Fanny" (not Frances Smith), August 19, 1868,
in Spencer Papers. Hildreth Smith's sister, Elizabeth Smith, later a prominent educator, lived in Brooklyn, and apparently it was to her home that
Fanny Smith was taken in 1868.

[20] Smith to Nannie C. Hoke, February 12, 1891, in Smith Collection,
Legal Letterbook; Smith to Summey Alexander, August 31, 1929, in Smith
Collection; *Cong. Record*, 63 Cong., 2 Sess., 16640; 66 Cong., 2 Sess., 1664.

[21] Hildreth Smith served as principal of the Luckie Street Grammar
School.

red clay hills at the foot of the Appalachian mountains, Atlanta was a bustling town of twenty-five thousand people when Hoke Smith first saw it in 1872. It was rapidly overtaking Savannah, long supreme in size among Georgia towns. Already the promise of the city was clearly discernible, and its natural geographical position as a transportation center was swiftly making it a dominant distributing point.

A few years before the Smiths arrived in Atlanta, a sharp-eyed young correspondent named Sidney Andrews had written a description that caught much of the spirit of the city that was to be Hoke Smith's home. From all the "ruin and devastation" a new city was springing up, reported Andrews: "The narrow and irregular and numerous streets are alive from morning till night . . . with a never-ending throng of pushing and crowding and scrambling and eager and excited and enterprising men, all bent on building and trading and swift fortune-making. Chicago in her busiest days could scarcely show such a sight as clamors for observation here. . . . Men rush about the streets with little regard for comfort or pleasure, and yet find the days all too short and too few for the work in hand. The sound of the saw and plane and hammer rings out from daylight till dark. . . ." [22]

The hurrying, money-conscious, almost ruthless life of this city found an ardent exponent in Hoke Smith. In many ways the career of the young newcomer was to parallel the rapid growth of the Georgia city. Within Hoke there glowed an inordinate ambition to succeed, and this will to get ahead was constantly stimulated by the vigorous life of the city. He was often away from Atlanta in later years but his thoughts were never long removed from his home city. "Coming to this city twenty years ago, a boy," he recalled in 1893, the treatment he had received had not only "endeared all the people of this city to me, but absolutely every house and every street. . . ." [23]

In May, 1872, not yet seventeen, Hoke entered the law offices of Collier, Mynatt and Collier as a reader. But by the end of the year the pinch of economic necessity had forced the boy

[22] *The South Since the War: As Shown by Fourteen Weeks of Travel and Observation in Georgia and the Carolinas* (Boston, 1866), 340.
[23] Atlanta *Journal*, February 17, 1893.

who preferred law to accept a position as a schoolteacher. At the beginning of 1873 he became the village schoolmaster in Waynesboro, the county seat of Burke County, far to the east of Atlanta and just south of Augusta, in the cotton-growing section along the South Carolina border.[24] Waynesboro could claim some nine hundred people, three fourths of whom were Negroes. In this small community the brief career of Hoke Smith the schoolteacher began and ended; it lasted from January to July, 1873. In later years when he campaigned in Burke County, many inhabitants of that area recalled Smith's schoolmaster days, but no evidence has come to light concerning the quality of the young man's work.

But one may well believe that "school keeping" was irksome work for Hoke, and that his heart was not in it. He continued to "read law," and having saved enough money "to purchase two old worn volumes of Blackstone and the Georgia code," he devoted his energies during odd moments and at night to preparing for the bar examination. From boyhood Smith had planned to become a lawyer, and even during those early years he often persuaded his parents to allow him to attend sessions of the local court. As an old man he liked to recall, perhaps with some exaggeration, that "After teaching all day I found it a fascination to go to my room and in the light of a kerosene lamp read law far into the morning." [25]

Early in May, 1873, Hoke came to Atlanta to attend a teachers' convention, and while in the city took the bar examination. On the morning of May 4, 1873, a brief note in the Atlanta *Constitution* informed the community that two new lawyers had been admitted to the local bar, following an examination on the previous day. The two new members—James T. Wills and

[24] Smith to J. L. McNair, May 11, 1901, in Smith Collection, Legal Letterbook; Joe Mitchell Chapple, "Face to Face with Hoke Smith, the Man from Georgia," No. 216 in a series of printed articles called *Flashlights of Famous People* (n. p., 1924), in Smith Collection. Also Warren P. Hunnicutt, "Penniless at Seventeen—Cabinet Officer at Thirty-seven . . . ," clipping from *National Magazine* (Boston), undated, in Smith Collection.
[25] Chapple, "Face to Face with Hoke Smith," *loc. cit.*; article by "E. I. W.," in Smith Collection.

"Michael H. Smith"[26]—had been examined on their knowledge of the law and had "acquitted themselves creditably." It was in this way that Hoke Smith, whose legal knowledge could not have been very extensive and who had not yet reached his eighteenth birthday, entered into a new world in a strange, mushrooming city.

[26] Smith soon dropped the name "Michael" altogether.

CHAPTER

◆§ II §◆

Atlanta Lawyer

Hoke Smith became famous as a lawyer and a politician. His larger recognition came in the political realm, but his earliest achievements were in the legal profession and he spent most of his adult years as a lawyer. After his retirement from political life, after the glamor and excitement of politics had for the most part ended for him, he expressed the hope that people would speak of him first as "a good lawyer." There was an element of truth in the statement of one of his employees that "Everything in his life has really been subordinate to his love for and devotion to the practice of law." [1] His active political years divided his law career into three main phases: the early period, from 1873 to 1893, when he was primarily a damage-suit lawyer; the post-Cabinet years, 1896–1906, when his practice became more varied; and the years after 1921, during the first several of which he represented the interests of clients who were pressing claims against the Federal government. But it was during the first period that he laid the basis for his reputation as a lawyer and prepared the way for subsequent legal and political triumphs.

The circumstances under which the young lawyer began his practice were not auspicious.[2] His family had moved to Tennessee, leaving him in Atlanta entirely dependent upon his own resources.[3] His capital consisted of fifty dollars, which he had

[1] Hunnicutt, "Penniless at Seventeen—Cabinet Officer at Thirty-seven," *loc. cit.*

[2] The sources for this chapter are the biographical memoranda and the legal letterbooks in the Smith Collection unless otherwise noted.

[3] Hildreth Smith left Atlanta sometime in 1873 to organize the public schools of Shelbyville, Tennessee, at the request of Barnas Sears, director

14

saved while teaching, but this was soon depleted by the purchase
of law books, and his little office in the James Bank Building
was pressed into domestic service as kitchen, dining room, and
bedroom. A folding lounge served as his bed and as a seat for
the clients he hoped would engage his services. Times were hard
and for a long time the boyish lawyer's only business was an
occasional small case and a group of exceptionally poor accounts
turned his way by another lawyer. But Hoke was persistent;
no case was too small for him to accept and he did his work
well. Slowly, painfully so at times, he began to increase his
business and to make a niche for himself among the members
of the Atlanta bar.

Smith's first successful case of any size was a suit against a
large carpet manufacturing concern, but his earliest recognition
in the profession resulted from appearances as special assistant
attorney to the prosecution in two widely publicized murder
cases. In one of these, the so-called Stafford case of 1876, a
contemporary declared that the successful verdict was " largely
due " to Smith's " masterful handling of the law and facts " in
the case.[4] As early as 1875 he began to appear before the Georgia
supreme court, and Chief Justice Logan Edwin Bleckley remembered many years later that he had been " forcibly " impressed
by the young man from the beginning. The judge noticed that
Smith's arguments " were vigorous, accute [*sic*] and exhaustive,
without being lengthy or tedious," and that they blended " Common with legal sense." [5]

of the Peabody Fund. His success was marked, and in 1877 he performed
the same task for the schools of Houston, Texas. Two years later this
"gentleman of immense energy and perseverance" was elected principal
of the Sam Houston Normal College at Huntsville, Texas. About 1882
Smith and his family returned to Atlanta, where he served as principal
of Girl's High School. In recognition of his work as an educator, he
was awarded the LL.D. degree by Baylor University in 1880. *Proceedings
of the Trustees of the Peabody Education Fund from Their Original
Organization on the 8th of February, 1867* (Boston, 1875-1916), I, 304,
431, II, 166, 229-30, 262, 357.

    [4] Atlanta *Constitution*, February 5, 1876; Reed (ed.), *History of Atlanta*,
Pt. II, 138; Chapple, "Face to Face With Hoke Smith," *loc. cit.*

    [5] Logan E. Bleckley to John B. Gordon, February 10, 1893, in Smith
Collection, Manuscript Scrapbook.

Although he gained some early successes, the hard times that pervaded the country during much of the 1870's and the early 1880's were clearly reflected in the young barrister's practice. By busying himself with such small jobs as reclaiming property and collecting debts, he managed to keep his head above water. But it was touch and go, at best, as his note to a client in November, 1879, shows. "I am overdrawn in bank," he wrote, "and am much in need of money." Nevertheless, by 1880 the twenty-five-year-old attorney was sufficiently well known and respected to be chosen by Governor Alfred H. Colquitt to make some investigations into the operation of the convict leasing system, and in 1883 he was invited to assist General Lucius J. Gartrell and Judge Henry B. Tompkins in the notorious Banks County "White Cappers case" in the Federal district court of North Georgia.[6]

Hoke Smith was determined to succeed. He wrote a prospective client in 1881, for instance, to report that he had declined to accept a damage suit against him because "I do not wish to accept one of the cases if I am to represent you, and [yet] I do not wish to decline to represent them, and be left out all together." According to Woodrow Wilson, who attempted unsuccessfully to practice law in Atlanta for a brief period in 1882-83, Smith made "an eager, astute, unremitting, successful effort to get business."[7] To such a one there was work enough. Smith's legal records disclose that by late 1880 he was handling an ever-increasing amount of business, and a few months later he was so busy that he could not accept all of the cases offered to him.

As his practice increased, Smith fairly reveled in the daily routine of his work—in the excitement of new cases, in the satisfaction of concluding old ones with success, and in the opportunities he had to know all kinds of people. Much of his time

---

[6] The habeas corpus case growing out of this conviction resulted in the famous ex parte Yarbrough decision. 110 U. S. 652. See also Warren Grice, *The Georgia Bench and Bar. The Development of Georgia's Judicial System* (Macon, Ga., 1931), I, 373-74.

[7] Woodrow Wilson, "Mr. Cleveland's Cabinet," in *Review of Reviews*, VII (April, 1893), 292.

was spent in his office, into which drifted all the sounds of the city's life, particularly the street traffic—the "horse-drawn drays, sanitary carts, with their noisome loads, and horse-drawn carriages"—moving over the "rough cobblestone and Belgian blocks."

For all the hustle and bustle, the lawyers, whose offices were located mainly on Whitehall and Marietta streets, had time to enjoy their lives.[8] Hoke was not slow in taking advantage of his opportunities to become acquainted with such men as Linton Stephens, whom he considered one of the state's best lawyers, and Benjamin Harvey Hill, whom he remembered as "the ablest debater I ever heard." On a few occasions the young lawyer worked with the great Hill on legal matters.[9]

During the first ten years of his practice Hoke Smith was alone in his work, except for occasional collaboration with other lawyers in specific cases. But in 1882, his brother Burton, a handsome and strapping youth nine years his junior, entered his office at 6½ Whitehall Street to read law, having just graduated from the University of Georgia. After he was admitted to the bar in 1883, this "young gentleman of bright promise" entered into a partnership with his brother, their firm being known as Hoke and Burton Smith. The partnership lasted until 1893. Burton was a definite asset to the firm, especially because of his eloquence before juries. In June, 1888, he was married to Frances Gordon, daughter of the illustrious General John B. Gordon, to whom his brother gave political support in the 1880's.[10]

Although Hoke Smith was eager to accept whatever type of case was offered, it was soon apparent that he was most successful, at least from a financial point of view, as a personal damage suit lawyer. As Woodrow Wilson put it, he began to devote himself to anticorporation work, "representing anybody, and presently everybody, that had a grievance against any railroad

[8] Walter McElreath, "When Atlanta Was Just a Big Town and Some of Its Characters," in *Atlanta Historical Bulletin,* VIII (October, 1948), 82-83.

[9] Atlanta *Journal*, May 24, 1886, May 16, 1887; *Cong. Record*, 64 Cong., 2 Sess., 4248; Haywood J. Pearce, *Benjamin H. Hill, Secession and Reconstruction* (Chicago, 1928), 309.

[10] Atlanta *Journal*, June 30, 1883; unpublished sketches of alumni, University of Georgia, VII, 83 (University of Georgia Library).

especially. . . ." [11]. This was a severe judgment, but it was essentially correct. The rapid and often unsound railroad construction during the seventies and eighties led to innumerable railroad accidents, which a smart lawyer could turn to good advantage, especially when aided by the rising feeling of resentment on the part of the public toward the carriers because of their tendency to ignore the rights of the public. Finding this kind of practice remunerative, Smith did not hesitate to accept all such cases that came his way. It was this type of practice that brought him to the forefront of the legal profession in Georgia and yielded him by 1893 an annual income estimated as high as thirty-five thousand dollars. Smith was, declared the *American Law Review* in that year, " the damage lawyer of Georgia par excellence." [12]

Hoke Smith's talents were ideally suited to the rough-and-tumble civil cases in which he specialized. He was able to impress juries, which admired his " direct and forcible manner of speech," with the apparent righteousness of his cause. His physical attributes gave him a distinct advantage with juries. He was a tall man—broad, solid, and well-proportioned. His head was large, his features mobile; his voice was sonorous, far-reaching, flexible, and appealing. His reputation as a fighting young lawyer who could deal with railroad attorneys on even terms began to spread throughout the state. [13]

Fully three fourths of the cases that came to the Smiths during this period were of the personal-damage variety. [14] The most effective technique in securing a personal-damage award was a full documentation of the injuries sustained—and in the case of railroad employees, successful proof that the worker was not negligent—as many supporting witnesses as possible, a bold and

[11] Wilson, " Mr. Cleveland's Cabinet," *loc. cit.,* 292.

[12] " The New Secretary of the Interior," in *American Law Review,* XXVII (March-April, 1893), 264.

[13] Arthur G. Powell, " Memorial of Hoke Smith," in *Report of the Forty-Ninth Session of the Georgia Bar Association* (Macon, Ga., 1932), XLIX, 214-18.

[14] An examination of the Smith legal records for the years 1889-92 reveals that of approximately 196 petitions filed to bring suit, about 155 were for personal damages on behalf of individuals against railroad and express companies, while only 6 were on behalf of corporations.

aggressive stand against the railroad lawyers, and a ringing appeal to the jury, with great emphasis on the dire results of the injuries. In a typical case Hoke Smith requested this kind of information from his clients: "Please give me your age & the amount of your yearly income at the time of the accident. Detail a description of the injuries which you recd. and also let me know their probable effect upon your future work. Give me the effect of your injuries on your fall business. Let me know fully what your business was." Time after time this statement appears in the Smith records of the distant eighties: "Your petitioner has suffered, still suffers, and will always suffer great pain by reason of his injuries." The *American Law Review* stated admirably the factors in Smith's success in personal injury cases:

> His success lies in the fact that he is not merely an *advocate* before juries, but that he is also a *lawyer*. He attends with skill to the three great points in a damage suit: Getting the judge to submit his case to the jury in the first instance; getting the jury to render a verdict in his favor; and getting an appellate court to sustain the verdict. Most of the damage lawyers stumble at the first point, succeed at the second, and fail at the third.[15]

The strategy of the attorney was to demand large damages in an effort to bring about a favorable settlement out of court. The Smiths seldom initiated a suit for less than five thousand dollars, and they usually demanded amounts of ten to twenty-five thousand dollars and even more. But they were willing to compromise for as little as one fifth of their original demands, depending upon their client's attitude and their own work in the case. Their fees in damage suits appear to have been largely of a contingent nature, ranging from as low as 15 to as high as 50 per cent of the damages awarded. They brought most of their suits in the Atlanta city court and the superior court of Fulton County. Less frequently, and usually in appellate actions, they practiced in the Georgia supreme court and in the Federal courts, with an occasional suit in the United States Supreme Court.

[15] "The New Secretary of the Interior," *loc. cit.*, 264.

Burton Smith observed in 1891 that the firm's engagements "are
so close that we rarely leave the city to practice in other courts."
"When we do leave," he continued, "it is only for cases of
large size."

The Smith combination almost always represented the offensive
position. If Hoke Smith could find even a hint of negligence on
the part of the defense—usually a railroad—rotten crossties, inadequate rolling stock, excessive speeds, failure to stop at stations
or to sound warnings, he exploited it to the fullest. Perhaps
it is an exaggeration to say, as John Temple Graves said in 1912,
that the first fifteen years of Smith's professional life were years
of "a martial epic of continuous battle and achievement" against
the corporations of the state.[16] But it is true that the aggressive
young lawyer was almost constantly on the side of individuals
who had suffered at the hands of corporations, particularly railroads. Cast in such a role and confronted by the skillful and
disingenuous lawyers who so often represented the carriers, it
was not unnatural that he should come to be one of the critics
of the corporations. He discovered early in his career that the
judicial system operated strongly in favor of corporate interests.
He was particularly disturbed at the slow routine followed by
judges sympathetic with the corporations and at the ease with
which railroad lawyers won continuance after continuance in
the trial of their cases.

All accounts agree that Hoke Smith was one of the most
successful lawyers in Georgia by 1893. The historian Isaac
Wheeler Avery described him as "original, learned and inde-
fatigable," a "skillful pleader and a strong speaker," while
Wallace P. Reed wrote in 1889 that he was "unsurpassed as an
all round lawyer." His briefs were "masterpieces," declared
Judge Arthur G. Powell. "It is probable that he won a larger
percentage of his cases than any other lawyer of his time."[17]
In 1888 the Atlanta *Constitution* polled sixty-five or seventy
Atlanta lawyers as to whom they considered the city's ablest

[16] John Temple Graves, "Hoke Smith of Ga." in *Hearst's Magazine*, XXII
(November, 1912), 48.
[17] Powell, "Memorial of Hoke Smith," *loc. cit.*; Reed (ed.), *History of
Atlanta*, Pt. II, 140; Atlanta *Constitution*, February 12, 1893.

lawyer. Hoke Smith, then less than thirty-three years of age, was the choice of ten or twelve men. Some of those questioned observed that he was especially strong before juries, was "the best lawyer to win a case," and was the best "if success is the measure"; said one, "According to his age, Hoke Smith is the best lawyer in Atlanta." [18] His business was a prosperous one, as this letter written in 1891 indicates: "I expect it, when devoted exclusively to the law, to average me $200 a day. . . . I have never left the city for several years at a less charge than $250 a day, and from that to $500 a day." That he enjoyed his work is apparent from the personal records which remain from this early period. "I really think ours is a pretty case to try," he wrote a collaborating lawyer in 1891, "one for substantial service for our client and a good deal of fun for those engaged in it."

Although the Atlanta attorney devoted himself primarily to his law career during the first fifteen years of his practice, he was intensely interested in politics. He began to take an interest in Fulton County politics almost as soon as he arrived in Atlanta. Half a century later he recalled that as a boy he had worked all day at the polls on behalf of a candidate for the city council, and long afterward Judge George Hillyer asserted that "No man fought better, or did more for liberty and success in the crisis of reconstruction following the War Between the States, and for the delivery of our people from carpet-bag rule." That there was some truth to this is evident from the fact that Smith became chairman of the Fulton County Democratic Committee in 1876, while still less than twenty-one years of age. During the same year his name was mentioned as a possible candidate for solicitor of the city court, but the young man was not interested in the position. [19]

When the question of the location of the state capital absorbed the state in 1877, Hoke Smith became an enthusiastic champion of Atlanta. He campaigned in northwestern Georgia against Farish Furman, who spoke for Milledgeville. This hotly fought contest gave Smith some local reputation as a clear and forceful

[18] Atlanta *Constitution*, April 7, 1888.
[19] *Ibid.*, February 23, 24, April 16, 23, 1876; Atlanta *Journal*, September 7, 1920; pamphlet address, October 28, 1926, in Smith Collection.

speaker.[20] But he was reluctant to enter active politics unless he could be certain of success. In December, 1879, he thought he saw the possibility of obtaining a Federal appointment, but he noted discreetly that he "would not enter the contest openly as a candidate." [21] In 1880, he declined membership on the Democratic Executive Committee of the thirty-fifth senatorial district because he wanted "but little part in politics for the present." [22]

Two years later he was a delegate to the state Democratic convention that nominated Alexander H. Stephens for governor. He aligned himself with those who succeeded in repealing the "two-thirds rule," which had caused considerable difficulty in the convention of 1880. "I am much more in favor of the majority rule than I am of Mr. Stephens," he declared during the convention debate. "A strong man must have strong enemies —always enough to make one-third of a large body. Thus the rule cuts such men out. In comes a dark horse of whom nobody knows anything, whose only recommendation is that he never had will enough of his own to antagonize that of another." As one of the Stephens leaders in the convention, Smith was appointed to the committee to wait upon the candidate to inform him of his nomination.[23] During the election of 1884, Smith emerged as one of Atlanta's strong Cleveland men, but he was not yet ready to take time from his growing law practice for the uncertainties of active politics.

Meanwhile the lawyer was demonstrating an interest in the city's civic affairs. He served from 1881 to 1883 as president of the Young Men's Library of Atlanta—later to become the Carnegie Library—and inaugurated what was termed the "unique and successful Art Loan of 1882." He was also an ardent member of the Atlanta Manufacturers' Association, which was organized in 1883 to encourage the location of new manufacturing plants

[20] This question was submitted to the voters in December, 1877, at the same time the new constitution was voted upon. Atlanta received 99,147 votes to Milledgeville's 55,201.

[21] Smith to James Banks, December 5, 1879, in Smith Collection, Legal Letterbook (1879-82).

[22] Smith to Democratic Executive Committee of Thirty-fifth Senatorial District, September 3, 1880, *ibid.*

[23] Atlanta *Constitution*, July 20, 21, 1882.

in Atlanta. In 1885 he was appointed a member of the Atlanta Board of Education, and his appointment prompted the Atlanta *Journal* to compliment him as "a gentleman of force of character . . . [who] will prove a valuable member." [24]

The ambitious young man was not always concerned with law suits, business deals, and civic undertakings. He had his lighter side. The genial Hoke entered easily into the town's social life. He was a frequent visitor in the home of that rising young newspaperman and orator Henry Woodfin Grady, and it was probably in the Grady home or through the Grady family that he met Marion McHenry Cobb, the slender attractive girl with whom he fell in love.

Marion Cobb, or "Birdie," as her friends called her, was the daughter of Thomas R. R. Cobb, the lawyer and Confederate general; she was a niece of Howell Cobb and a member of one of the outstanding families of the state. Marion's mother was the daughter of Joseph Henry Lumpkin, the venerated first chief justice of the Georgia supreme court. She grew up in one of the white-columned homes in Athens, where her father had been professor of law in the University of Georgia before riding away to the war to meet a gallant death at Fredericksburg. Five years younger than Hoke, Birdie was a girl of intelligence and refinement, and she soon completely captivated Hoke Smith. "Her charm of manner and her bright intelligence have given her a warm place in the hearts of all who know her," wrote a contemporary. Just when Birdie and Hoke first met is not certain, but their courtship lasted for several years. In the meantime, the young Athens girl attended the famous Lucy Cobb Institute in her home town. [25]

They were married at a fashionable wedding in Athens on December 19, 1883, and immediately began housekeeping in Atlanta. [26] In November, 1884, their first child, a boy, was born. They named him Marion. A second child, Hildreth, was born

[24] Atlanta *Journal*, December 8, 1885.

[25] Lucy Cobb Institute, named for one of Birdie's sisters, was founded in 1858 with the support of Thomas R. R. Cobb.

[26] Athens *Banner*, December 19, 1883; Atlanta *Journal*, December 19, 20, 1883.

in 1886, but he died almost overnight on January 1, 1887. The Smiths' first daughter, whom they named Mary Brent, was born in May, 1888.

Hoke Smith's professional distinction and financial prosperity also ensured social prominence, and he and his wife moved among Atlanta's most affluent people. It soon became their custom, along with other well-to-do Atlantans, to spend summer vacations at Florida or Virginia resorts and to make seasonal trips to the North Carolina mountains. Smith also purchased a farm near Atlanta where for a time he indulged his fancy for thoroughbred horses. In the spring of 1884, the Smiths occupied their newly built home—an "unostentatious and modern dwelling"—on fashionable West Peachtree Street.

The Atlanta 'Journal' and Georgia Politics

The professional success that came to Hoke Smith in the 1880's caused him to undertake new financial ventures and encouraged him to give more attention to the political scene. Acquiring his own newspaper, the Atlanta *Journal*, he proceeded with his customary vigor to build it into one of the state's leading papers. As his newspaper became more important and as his reputation as a successful lawyer spread, his role in Georgia politics became larger, and by the late 1880's he was in position to exert great influence in the state's political affairs.

Georgia politics had long fascinated the lawyer. He had witnessed the exciting battles of the early 1870's between Democrats and Republicans and the state's "Redemption" by the Democrats; he had seen the threat to the Democracy posed by various independents in the late seventies; and he had followed with growing interest the factional struggles that prevailed within the "Bourbon Democracy" in control of Georgia throughout the eighties. Having resolutely put aside thoughts of more active participation in politics during the first years of his law practice, it was only natural that, with financial independence and professional prominence, he should turn to the political arena.

The swift ascent of his friend Henry W. Grady in the political world was both an inspiration and a challenge to Smith. The two men had been friends for years and had undertaken real estate ventures together in the early eighties;[1] both were pro-

[1] Smith and Grady were joint owners, for instance, of about $5,500

gressive champions of the "Atlanta Spirit." In 1882 Smith was one of those who had urged Grady to run for Congress. The journalist had refused to seek office himself, but during the next few years he became a dominant figure in the election of the state's governors and in speaking for the Georgia Democracy. By 1887 he was being mentioned in the South as a possible selection for the Vice Presidency. Perhaps it was because of his own increasing recognition, perhaps it was because he and Grady had begun to disagree on important issues, but for whatever reason their relations began to grow strained following the election of 1886, and Smith was no longer enthusiastic about Grady's political promise. He soon decided to contest Grady's powerful political hegemony.

Although Georgia was a one-party state in the 1880's, there was a good deal of maneuvering among the would-be managers— all of course within the confines of the party of Redemption. Factions inevitably developed—often of an ephemeral nature but not always so—to weld together for a time the supporters of leading aspirants and to push certain positions on real or fancied issues. Georgia politics, as a contemporary aptly declared, were "like clay in the hands of the potter."[2] Hoke Smith was aware— acutely so—that Henry W. Grady had used the Atlanta *Constitution* in this situation to make himself "the Warwick of Georgia politics." If he were to achieve a position comparable in power to that of Grady, there was but one thing to do: secure control of another newspaper. It would make all the difference between success and failure for an aspiring political leader.

Thus it was that Smith turned to the Atlanta *Evening Journal*, a small afternoon paper that emphasized local news. After an investigation in the spring of 1887, the lawyer found that the paper's publisher, John Paul Jones, was willing to sell. Smith formed a company of associates and purchased the newspaper on June 1, 1887, for about ten thousand dollars.[3]

worth of Atlanta real estate and railroad stock in 1881. Henry W. Grady Collection (Emory University Library), Financial Record Book; Smith Collection, Legal Letterbook (1879-82).

[2] William H. Felton, in Mrs. William H. Felton, "*My Memoirs of Georgia Politics*" (Atlanta, 1911), 634.

[3] In addition to Smith, the original stockholders were Henry H. Cabaniss,

The *Evening Journal* had first been published in early 1883, having been organized by Colonel E. F. Hoge, Confederate veteran and prominent lawyer, close on the heels of a series of short-lived Atlanta dailies in the 1870's. Following Colonel Hoge's death, the paper was controlled by Jones, the man from whom the Smith syndicate bought it.[4] In the beginning the *Journal* was not an important rival of the *Constitution*, and there was little difference in their editorial policies. The morning paper monopolized the United Press news service in the city and its infant contemporary was forced to obtain its national and international news from printed stories in other papers and from a few lines of telegraph each day. But the *Journal* did give a comprehensive coverage of local news. Its news items were lively and breezy and all had a personal touch.

Hoke Smith provided most of the money for the purchase of the paper, and as president of the newly organized Journal Publishing Company, he became the dominating personality in the enterprise. To his side he brought two notable men, Henry H. Cabaniss and Josiah Carter. Cabaniss was an experienced country journalist who had been business manager of the *Christian Index* and, at the time he joined the *Journal*, was the editor of a farm journal called the *Southern Ruralist*. He became the business manager and in Smith's absence the director. Carter, who had been city editor of the *Constitution*, became managing editor. According to a fellow journalist, he was a good executive and had a "graphic, attractive style of writing."[5] As professional newspapermen, Cabaniss and Carter devoted all of their time to the *Journal*, while Smith continued his heavy legal work and served only as the policy-maker and political strategist. He located his law offices at 32 South Broad Street in the same building as his paper, in order to be immediately available for conferences with the editors.

Josiah Carter, Charles A. Collier, Jacob Haas, "Captain" Harry Jackson, W. H. Parsons, R. M. Pulsifer, and Frank P. Rice. Randolph L. Fort, "History of the Atlanta Journal" (M. A. thesis, Emory University, 1930), 14-15; Atlanta *Journal*, June 21, 1928.

[4] Atlanta *Evening Journal*, June 1, 1887.

[5] Atlanta *Journal*, June 5, 1887, May 1, 1889, August 19, 1923; Reed, *History of Atlanta*, 412.

The new management took over after the issue of June 1, 1887, came off the press. "Our only purpose," declared Hoke Smith, "is to give the city a first-class afternoon paper backed by sufficient capital to let the people understand that it will be a permanent feature in Atlanta journalism. We believe that such a paper will prove beneficial to the best interests of our city, and will give handsome dividends to the holders of stock." [6] The Macon *Daily Telegraph* referred to "political designs" in discussing the *Journal*'s reorganization, and in after years Josiah Carter mentioned Smith's interest in "public affairs" as a motivating factor.[7] Nevertheless, Smith's desire to make the *Journal* a profitable enterprise should not be minimized.

During the years that Smith controlled the Atlanta *Journal*—from 1887 to 1900—the paper underwent an amazing expansion in its physical plant, circulation, and influence. When he first began to publish the paper it possessed very little equipment—Henry Cabaniss described it as "a flat bed press, hand type and one reporter." It had an extremely unstable and inadequate news service and a circulation of only three thousand. It gave the uniform and headlineless appearance of the nineteenth-century local news sheet. Thirteen years later it was a ten-page daily, very much like the *Journal* of today, with two hundred employees and a circulation of over thirty thousand. While the first few months of the undertaking proved difficult, the Journal Publishing Company had the financial resources and the efficient direction necessary to weather the storm of that early trying period. The paper grew steadily in circulation, boasting by early 1890 that it was the "Largest Daily in Georgia." Advertising contracts increased prodigiously. The staff was enlarged and new equipment was purchased, including after a few years a "fine engraving plant" and a second new press, which led the *Journal* to taunt its city rival, "We observe that it is still not necessary to run both presses on the daily Constitution." [8]

[6] Atlanta *Journal*, June 2, 1887.

[7] Raymond B. Nixon, *Henry W. Grady, Spokesman of the New South* (New York, 1943), 256; William J. Northen (ed.), *Men of Mark in Georgia* . . . (Atlanta, 1907-12), IV, 3.

[8] Atlanta *Journal*, January 21, 1891, June 21, 1928.

Various devices were used to make the *Journal* more attractive to the public: papers were given away, subscription contests were sponsored, trade editions were printed, Georgia towns were publicized, a woman's department was instituted, and in 1888 Hoke Smith's father was made literary editor. Features by Bill Nye, the wit of the day, Lillian Russell, and Sam Jones, the well-known Georgia evangelist, were introduced. Until the coming of the Spanish-American War, when the *Journal* filled its columns with war news under heavy black streamers, local news continued to dominate the pages of the newspaper, and the *Journal* prided itself on this emphasis.

For a time in 1888-89, the *Journal* encountered serious competition in the newly established Atlanta *Evening Capitol*. But like the ably edited Atlanta *Evening Herald*, started by Josiah Carter when he resigned from the *Journal* late in 1890, it failed for lack of solid financial support.[9] Meanwhile, the *Journal* had become a serious challenge to the *Constitution*'s leadership.

But the afternoon paper continued to face a perplexing problem for several years because of its inadequate news coverage on the national and foreign fronts. The morning papers in the South virtually monopolized the United Press service, making it impossible for the afternoon papers to secure news reports from this agency, except on the terms accorded by the morning papers. For a time the *Journal* did buy the full UP dispatches but soon found the rates prohibitive. After using makeshift arrangements involving small amounts of news contained in the "pony" UP and AP reports, the *Journal*, led by Henry Cabaniss, finally headed an organization of Southern afternoon papers which secured a satisfactory Associated Press news service beginning late in 1894.[10]

The *Journal* was a well-edited newspaper. The editorial page, where Hoke Smith's influence was often discernible, received careful attention. Under Smith's leadership the *Journal* became a tariff-reform paper and an opponent of corporation domination

[9] After working a year or two for the New York *Advertiser*, Carter returned to the *Journal*.

[10] Atlanta *Journal*, March 4, 1893, December 7, 1894, June 21, 1928, February 24, 1937; Fort, "History of the Atlanta Journal," 30.

of the state's politics. It advocated a good roads program and various city improvements, while urging the abolition of the "fee system" and campaigning against lynching, Atlanta's notorious "Bucket Shops," and the convict-leasing system.

In 1887 Smith and George Hillyer, a leading Atlanta attorney, were retained by Governor John B. Gordon to assist the attorney general in his investigation of charges that certain persons had violated the regulations governing leased convicts. Hearings before Governor Gordon were held for several days, beginning in September, 1887. In their arguments, Smith and Hillyer produced documentary evidence that the lessees had violated the law by cruel treatment of the prisoners, by failing to provide adequate housing for them, by subleasing, and by working the convicts without regard to the type of work for which they were competent. Smith took a leading part in the hearings and in his examination of witnesses brought out the ill treatment of the convicts. But despite the evidence produced by the investigation, the governor rendered innocuous judgments.[11]

Smith continued energetically to champion a greater Atlanta. Like Henry W. Grady, he wanted to encourage new industries to locate in the city, and when the *Constitution* editor revived the moribund Atlanta Manufacturers' Association in 1888, Smith became one of its directors. He took a prominent part in the Piedmont Exposition sponsored by Atlanta in 1887, serving as an officer in the exposition organization. At a state convention of Georgians that met in May, 1891, to consider the state's participation in the Chicago World's Fair, Smith represented the Fifth Congressional District. His resolution recommending that the state's rental money from the Western and Atlantic Railroad be used for this purpose was adopted by the convention.[12]

The most important of Smith's civic undertakings during this period, however, was his work as a member of the Atlanta school board. First chosen in 1885, he served on the board for the next seven years, and for the last two years of this period he was president. He was keenly interested in the improvement of

[11] Smith Collection, Legal Letterbook (1890-91); Atlanta *Constitution*, September 2, 9-11, 21-26, 1887.

[12] Atlanta *Journal*, October 15, 1890, May 6, 7, 1891.

the city's school system, revealing a genuine concern for such aspects of the school program as curriculum, textbooks, school facilities, and quality of teachers. He won the endorsement of local Negro leaders by strongly supporting their plea for the employment of Negro teachers in all positions in the city's Negro schools.[13] Smith felt that "Every child in Georgia is entitled to receive a thorough education, suited to the station in life to which he can reasonably aspire. This much should be demanded."[14]

Meanwhile, Smith had become increasingly active in politics. In the local election of 1886, in which the question of prohibition was an issue, he co-operated with Grady in supporting a special committee which recommended a compromise slate of municipal officers. Smith was a local optionist and Grady a prohibitionist, but the two men apparently resolved their major differences on local questions. Two years later, after the wets had won in a November referendum of 1887, Smith and Grady agreed upon a ticket for city positions. Reuben Arnold, a young lawyer, declared in 1888 that the "S. A. G. ticket" (Smith and Grady) represented a conservative movement on the part of "a few people to take charge of Atlanta." "Two years ago," he asserted, "they arranged a compromise, and they got a hold on your body and britches."[15]

Smith and Grady—and the *Journal* and the *Constitution*—might reach some common ground temporarily on local issues but they found it more and more difficult to arrive at any such agreement in the broader fields of state and national politics. The election of 1888 made this clear. Hoke Smith was one of the leaders of the Cleveland campaign in Georgia in that election year. Elected permanent chairman of the state Democratic convention

[13] *Ibid.*, December 8, 1885, June 11, 1887, January 25, April 26, 1889, September 24, 1890, February 14, 1891, June 1, 2, 1892; *Eighteenth Annual Report of the Board of Education, Atlanta, Georgia, for the Year Ending December 31, 1889* (Atlanta, 1890), 2.

[14] Hoke Smith, "The State of Georgia," in Alex L. Peterman, *Elements of Civil Government: A Text-Book for Use in Public Schools, High Schools and Normal Schools and a Manual of Reference for Teachers* (New York, rev. ed., 1914), 252-53.

[15] Atlanta *Constitution*, October 30, 1888.

when it met in Atlanta, Smith denounced the existing tariff
system; he declared that Georgians were thoroughly aroused
against it. He praised President Cleveland as a Jeffersonian and
Jacksonian Democrat.[16]

Grady, on the other hand, was never very enthusiastic about
Cleveland and, following the President's defeat in 1888, indicated
that he felt it had been brought on by the latter's position on
the tariff question. The *Constitution* called for a "judicious
revision" of the tariff and argued that "no reduction should be
made below the difference that exists between the prices paid
to labor in the United States and those paid to labor in foreign
countries." [17] Speaking in Athens immediately after the election,
Smith warned his audience that it would be told that Cleveland's
defeat had resulted from his advocacy of tariff reform, but the
lawyer announced his own "growing devotion to the fight" for
a reduction of the tariff.[18] During the following years the *Journal*
criticized the "self-complacent" attitude of the *Constitution* on
this issue.[19]

When Grady's friends began a movement in 1888 to send him
to the Senate, Hoke Smith and Governor John B. Gordon
expressed opposition. Smith and the Atlanta *Journal* were strong
supporters of Gordon's administration,[20] but by this time the
governor had broken with Grady, the man who had done more
than anyone else to elect him to the governorship two years before.
Smith declared that Grady had "no support whatever" for the
Senate, and the *Journal* referred to the rival editor derisively as

[16] *Ibid.*, May 10, 1888.

[17] Nixon, *Henry W. Grady*, 290-91; Atlanta *Constitution*, January 1,
February 17, March 8, 15, 31, November 7-9, 11, 12, 1888.

[18] *The Tariff and the Georgia Farmer, Address of Mr. Hoke Smith,
Delivered at the Northeast Georgia Fair, Athens, Ga., Nov. 9, 1888, To-
gether with Comparison of Tariff Bills Item by Item* (n. p., n. d.); Savannah
Morning News, November 9, 1888.

[19] Atlanta *Constitution*, March 31, 1888, March 10, 1889; Atlanta *Journal*,
February 5, March 11, 1889.

[20] The Smith brothers also represented Gordon in 1888 in a legal action
(John R. Dos Passos *v.* John B. Gordon & Hugh Gordon) involving the
International Railroad and Steamship Company of Florida, one of the
general's numerous railroad ventures. Smith Collection, Legal Letterbook
(1885-88).

a "protectionist" who was really standing on the Republican platform. Grady was hurt and disappointed and referred to "the studied attempt of one newspaper to decry the number and sincerity of my friends." [21]

The rivalry that developed between Smith's *Journal* and Grady's *Constitution* involved more than the exigencies of personal politics. A series of troublesome disputes between the two newspapers in 1888 and 1889 intensified the ill will that each had for the other. One factor in the worsening situation was the *Constitution*'s criticism of Hoke Smith's professional ethics, or lack of ethics. In April, 1888, a *Constitution* editorial spoke of "a lot of shysters, who make money by hunting up cases," and observed that a "newspaper reputation is a very poor reliance for a lawyer, if that is all he has." [22] This evidently was aimed at Smith because of the publicity given his legal activities by the Atlanta *Journal*. Another accusation appeared in a letter by "Lex" published in the *Constitution* on May 19, 1889. "Lex" charged that the recent attitude of the *Journal* toward the Western and Atlantic Railroad was the result of some pending suits of Smith against that company. "Captain" Harry Jackson, prominent railroad attorney, had declared on several occasions, according to "Lex," that he had noticed that the *Journal* often arraigned certain railroads severely just prior to the opening of Smith's cases against those roads.

A sharp exchange of letters resulted, participated in by Smith, Jackson, and the editors of the *Constitution* and *Journal*.[23] Hoke Smith and Josiah Carter vigorously denied that Smith had ever used the paper as "Lex" charged, and Smith demanded that Evan P. Howell, publisher of the *Constitution*, reveal the author of the damaging epistle, "for legal redress or personal satisfac-

---

[21] Atlanta *Constitution*, November 2, 1888; Atlanta *Journal*, November 12, 1888; Nixon, *Henry W. Grady*, 290, 292, 295. Grady and Smith had been so close in the early eighties that Grady prepared instructions directing his wife, in the event of his death, to go to "my friend, Hoke Smith" for guidance. After the two men broke, Grady carefully destroyed these directions. Nixon, *Henry W. Grady*, 295.

[22] Atlanta *Constitution*, April 8, 1888.

[23] The full correspondence was published in the Atlanta *Constitution*, May 22, 1889.

tion." After additional letters were exchanged by personal
bearer, Jackson repudiated some of the statements attributed to
him, and Howell, who had assumed responsibility for the "Lex"
letter on the basis of Jackson's alleged position, apologized to
Smith. The identity of "Lex" was not revealed, but the letter
doubtless was inspired by Jackson and the *Constitution*.[24] While
"Captain" Jackson exonerated Smith in one breath, he insisted
in the next that the Atlanta *Journal* had printed material calculated to prejudice juries and that there was a "sickening perjury"
every week in the Fulton County courts in personal-injury trials
and a successful "plundering" of the railroads.[25] Jackson would
have been more accurate had he accused the *Journal* of following
a general antirailroad policy, stemming in part from its publisher's
consistent opposition to railroads in the courts, and had he only
contended that Smith benefited by the acquisition of business
from the publicity he obtained in the columns of his newspaper.
Obviously, however, Smith the damage-suit attorney was also
Smith the newspaper publisher.

If "Captain" Jackson's exasperation is an indication of Hoke
Smith's success in personal-injury cases, the Atlanta *Constitution*'s
eagerness to publish what it believed to be damaging material
against Smith is evidence that the *Journal* was successfully chal-

[24] Jackson, strangely enough, was Smith's brother-in-law, having married
Mrs. Smith's sister. He had been one of the men who purchased stock
in the Atlanta *Journal* when Smith reorganized it in 1887, but he had sold
his holdings in the newspaper when its position in a railroad case embarrassed
him. In 1888 Jackson attacked George Martin, of the Atlanta *Avalanche*,
and Martin would have fired a pistol at Jackson had not Smith, who
happened to be with Jackson, knocked the weapon out of his hand.
Savannah *Morning News*, September 12, 1888; Atlanta *Constitution*, May
22, 1889.

[25] In 1892, when a grand jury recommended the repeal of contingent
fees in damage-suit cases, the *Constitution* endorsed the proposal, while
declaring that certain "respectable" lawyers in the city hired "bailiffs"
to solicit such cases for them. The morning paper also criticized the
Journal for opposing the abolition of contingent fees. The *Journal* replied
heatedly that it condemned such conduct by lawyers as described by the
Constitution and asked that paper to name lawyers who were guilty—
whereupon the *Constitution*, obviously aiming at Hoke Smith, exclaimed,
"What gall!" Atlanta *Journal*, July 16, 1892.

lenging the *Constitution*'s circulation leadership and commercial pre-eminence. As the rivalry between the Atlanta papers became more spirited, each journal seized every opportunity to cast a critical remark at the other—to boast of its greater circulation and to identify the other with such obnoxious terms as "Wall Street," "railroad monopoly," "Republicanism," and "protectionism." In time there coalesced around the two newspapers the elements that later became the two major factions of the Democratic party in Georgia. But when Henry W. Grady died unexpectedly in 1889, the *Journal* paid tribute to his leadership, and in after years Smith supported a movement to erect a monument to the journalist.

The agrarian uprising in the late eighties and early nineties found Hoke Smith and the Atlanta *Journal* giving vigorous expression to many of the demands put forward by the Georgia farmers. The *Journal* continued its crusade against the "Republican tariff" and attacked the railroad monopolies and trusts.[26] The Atlanta newspaper also inveighed against the "jute trust," demanded ballot reform and civil service laws, and urged the use of primary elections, which were becoming an important issue by the late 1880's. On the last point Smith early became a champion, recommending a "carefully guarded primary" that would "furnish the opportunity for all democrats to express their preference."[27] Early in 1889 one of the prominent agrarian leaders was quoted as saying that "Hoke Smith would be as acceptable a man [for governor] as I know. The position of The Atlanta Journal, his tariff speech at Athens, his well known integrity, and his anti-monopoly views are all greatly in his favor."[28]

The agrarian storm over the South gathered steadily in 1889. "There is an agrarian tendency among our people," wrote Joseph E. Brown in 1888. "There is a growing feeling among our people of opposition to all accumulations of capital, and it is becoming a crime for a man to have anything. . . ."[29] By 1890 the farmer

[26] See, for example, *ibid.*, April 4, 1889.

[27] Smith to L. S. Mitchell, August 7, 1888, in Smith Collection, Legal Letterbook (1888); Atlanta *Journal*, June 8, 1889.

[28] L. F. Livingston, in Atlanta *Journal*, February 27, 1889.

[29] Brown to L. M. Trammell, May 23, 1888, quoted in Judson C. Ward,

politicians of the state, although unwilling as yet to leave the
Democratic party, had formulated a series of demands for
stricter regulation of corporations (especially railroads), abolition
of the convict-leasing system, a more equitable tax structure,
an extended public school system, and laws to guarantee fair
primaries and elections. These demands plus the "yard-stick"
program adopted at St. Louis in December, 1889, were to be
used to measure candidates in 1890.[30]

As the election of 1890 approached, Georgia politics were a
bewildering river of crosscurrents in which uncertain personal
positions and confused issues all felt the steady undertow of the
growing agrarian radicalism. The Atlanta *Constitution*, which
had taken the lead in supporting the Farmers' Alliance in Georgia,
endorsed William J. Northen for governor rather than the somewhat more "radical" Lon F. Livingston. Both men were members of the Alliance, but some observers suspected that since the
Constitution, published by Evan P. Howell, a railroad promoter
and stout opponent of thorough railroad regulation, and other
"corporation organs" were supporting Northen, a plan was afoot
to sabotage the Alliance program. It was a fact that the more
radical sentiment in the state had endorsed Livingston, the president of the Georgia Alliance, who urged that the "yard-stick"
be strictly applied.[31]

The *Journal* reflected Hoke Smith's concern for a strong railroad regulatory program on the part of the state government.
The railroads, Smith had warned two years before, "will endeavor to parcel out our State, and to crush out all new railroad
enterprises; they will simply have us by the throat and we will
be helpless, except at their will, unless we hurl them to the
ground." [32] He charged that railroad rates were excessive and

"Bourbon Democracy in Georgia, 1872-1890" (Ph. D. dissertation, University of North Carolina, 1947), 192.

[30] Atlanta *Constitution*, August 8, 1890; Alex Mathews Arnett, *The Populist Movement in Georgia, a View of the "Agrarian Crusade" in the Light
of Solid-South Politics* (New York, 1922), 83-84, 105-106.

[31] Arnett, *Populist Movement in Georgia*, 103-109; James C. Bonner, "The
Alliance Legislature of 1890," in James C. Bonner and Lucien E. Roberts
(eds.), *Studies in Georgia History and Government* (Athens, 1940), 162.

[32] [Smith], *The Tariff and the Georgia Farmer*, 12.

launched a campaign in 1889 in support of the Olive bill, a measure designed to bring more stringent regulation of the carriers. Northen's position on the question of railroad regulation was thus a matter of considerable importance to Smith—and the fact that he had received the *Constitution*'s blessing was not to be disregarded.

Despite Northen's questionable position on the railroad problem, Hoke Smith decided to give him his support after Livingston retired from the contest to run for Congress. Perhaps Northen reassured the *Journal* men about his views on the railroad issue. But more important, probably, was Northen's endorsement of Governor Gordon for the Senate seat being vacated by Joseph E. Brown. Also, Smith found Northen's more moderate position on other Alliance demands to his liking, particularly his suspicion of the subtreasury plan, which Smith opposed. At any rate, the lawyer took a prominent part in the state convention that nominated Northen in August, 1890. He served as chairman of the Committee on Resolutions and in this capacity helped secure the convention's approval of the national Democratic platform of 1888 and of Gordon's administration. He made a strong plea for harmony within the party.[33]

Following the state convention, Smith's attention turned to the Senate contest, which would be decided when the legislature convened in the fall. He was especially concerned lest the agrarian reformism within the party get out of hand and prevent the election of Gordon, who appeared vulnerable to attack because of his attitude toward some of the Alliance proposals.

The Atlanta *Constitution* eventually decided to support Patrick Calhoun, a railroad attorney and businessman. Strangely enough, the wily Calhoun secured the backing of Lon Livingston and Charles W. Macune, the Texas leader of the Southern Alliance, and the *Constitution* endeavored skillfully to show that Calhoun could meet the Alliance " yard-stick," including the subtreasury plan. Gordon was shrewd enough to become a member of the Alliance and to court the farmers in other ways, but he refused

[33] Atlanta *Journal*, June 27, August 7, 8, 1890; Atlanta *Constitution*, August 8, 1890.

to endorse the subtreasury plan, urging instead free silver and tariff reduction.[34]

Smith had attempted to head off the threat to Gordon's election before Calhoun's candidacy was unveiled. In September, 1890, he conferred with Livingston, whose influence with the more radical members of the Alliance was great. Pointing out the "importance of perfect harmony" among Georgia Democrats, he called Livingston's attention to the rumor that the Alliance nominees for Congress would not abide by the action of the Democratic caucus. While approving many of the Alliance proposals, Smith vigorously opposed the idea of independent political action, and a *Journal* editorial declared that nothing could turn Southern farmers from their "fealty to the party."[35] It would be unwise, the *Journal* publisher told Livingston, for the Alliance leaders to make an endorsement of the subtreasury a "prerequisite to their support of democrats." As he said a short time later: "I called his attention to the fact that there were many democrats inside and outside the alliance who were heartily in favor of relief from the present financial system, and who were thoroughly in accord with the effort to increase the circulating medium, but who could not approve the subtreasury bill." Smith went on to express his fear that the provision in the plan requiring "products to be sold by the government, and the money received for the same canceled at the end of twelve months unless redemption had earlier taken place at the instance of the depositors," would necessitate a yearly contraction of the currency without regard for the public's monetary needs.[36]

Smith then proceeded to outline a number of reform measures which he felt the party could support, including the free coinage of silver, a graduated income tax, tariff reduction, and the issuance of legal tender notes to redeem government bonds. He also suggested a modified subtreasury scheme, which the Augusta *Chronicle* later ridiculed as a "pea-nut and corn-cobb treasury"

[34] Atlanta *Constitution*, March 28, October 3, 17, 1890; Atlanta *Journal*, May 27, 1890.

[35] Atlanta *Journal*, October 3, 1890.

[36] Smith to W. L. Peek, September 15, 1890, in Atlanta *Journal*, September 16, 1890.

bill.[37] After the conference, Smith reported that Livingston seemed "very favorable"; he had informed Smith that if Gordon endorsed this program all talk against him in the Alliance would cease. "I replied," said Smith, "that I had no doubt General Gordon was upon the line suggested." [38]

Livingston was not enlisted, however, and Calhoun's candidacy was soon apparent. But when the legislature met, Gordon was elected by a substantial majority. The legislators did not agree on the subtreasury plan, as Hoke Smith had predicted, and Tom Watson and others like him, who could not stomach "the paid attorney of a great railroad monopoly," supported Gordon as the lesser of two evils. Smith's "masterful championship" in the previous months had doubtless had some effect, although the general's stately bearing, his persuasive talk, and his familiar role as the "Chevalier of the Old South" and the living embodiment of the Lost Cause were probably more important in the outcome.[39] But it was fortunate for the general that the oncoming agricultural revolt had not yet reached floodtide.

It is clear that 1890 represented an important juncture for Hoke Smith, a crossroad in his political career. He was certainly no radical, but his professional work, his zeal for tariff reform, and his belief in railroad regulation inclined him toward the agrarian element of the Democracy. But his urban ties, his faith in the industrialization of the South, and his close association with such men as John B. Gordon disposed him to favor the Bourbons and a philosophy akin to that of Henry W. Grady. Perhaps there was no doubt in his mind as to the road he would take, but for a time at least he paused and, like many another, sought to avoid or postpone the day when he must announce his decision and move on.

[37] Augusta *Chronicle*, April 21, 1896.

[38] Atlanta *Journal*, September 16, 1890.

[39] Arnett, *Populist Movement in Georgia*, 120; C. Vann Woodward, *Tom Watson: Agrarian Rebel* (New York, 1938), 163; Atlanta *Journal*, November 14, 15, 1890, December 1, 1931, February 24, 1937.

"For Grover Cleveland and Tariff Reform"

The election of 1892 brought Hoke Smith an opportunity to prove his growing influence in Georgia's political life. With the force of his own personality and the increasing strength of the Atlanta *Journal*, he appropriated a leader and an issue and emerged triumphant, to find his victory at home part of the national success of Grover Cleveland and the demand for tariff reform. The election also brought its tangible rewards. Smith had long disclaimed any interest in holding office himself. As he declared in a printed " card " in 1888, " it is my fixed desire to follow the legal profession, taking no part in politics as an office-holder, but discussing, from time to time, questions of interest to Georgia and the masses of our people, free from the trammel of office-seeking." [1] But what was true in 1888 was not necessarily true in 1892, particularly if a national office was involved.

Following the election of John B. Gordon to the Senate in 1890, the Atlanta *Journal* called for a strengthening of the Farmers' Alliance and sought to allay agrarian discontent within the Democratic party. Smith would not even accept employment in legal action proposed against the *Southern Alliance Farmer*, feeling that his course might be misunderstood.[2] In an exchange of several letters in 1891 and 1892 with Thomas E. Watson, radical

[1] Atlanta *Constitution*, July 30, 1888.

[2] Smith to " Messrs. Lawson, Callaway & Scales," February 12, 1891, in Smith Collection, Legal Letterbook (1891).

young Alliance Congressman from the Tenth Congressional District, the Atlanta lawyer expressed sympathy for Watson's ideas. Like Watson, he believed that the people and the corporations were locked in a struggle to determine "which of the two shall rule the state." Smith felt that nothing could be "more fraught with evil to the State than the control of our politics by a Wall street corporation." In the summer of 1891, he wrote Watson, "I am reading your speeches with a great deal of interest, and while I regret to see an inclination on your part not to stand by the organized democracy, as to the great fight which you are making in behalf of the masses, and as to many of the positions which you take, I give the heartiest endorsement." [3]

The Atlanta *Journal* continued in 1891 to agitate for the enactment of stronger state railroad controls, urging the passage of a measure in the legislature known as the "Berner Bill." But at about the same time, *Journal* editorials criticized the "Alliance Legislature" of 1891 for extravagance and vigorously opposed the establishment of a third party.[4] The good will evidenced for the Alliancemen was steadily dissipated, and by October the *Journal* was declaring that the Ocala platform "contains some things which are as far from Democratic doctrine as the north pole is from the south." [5]

While the *Journal* was denouncing agrarian radicalism in its editorials, its publisher was speaking out along the same line in public addresses. In September, for instance, one report asserted that he gave Lon Livingston "the worst scoring ever received by a politician in Georgia." The same article predicted that Smith's voice would be "the clarion note that will lead the Democratic hosts to victory." [6] Meanwhile, Smith's work for the party began to attract some attention beyond the borders of the state, and he was invited to participate in the Ohio campaign in 1891.

Never had Hoke Smith been so busy. In addition to the heavy

[3] Smith to Watson, January 18, July 7, August 29, 1891, *ibid*.

[4] Atlanta *Journal*, December 23, 1890, May 2, 1891; Bonner, "The Alliance Legislature of 1890," *loc. cit.*, 168.

[5] Atlanta *Journal*, October 9, 14, 16, November 11, 1891.

[6] Clipping from *Southern Life*, September 19, 1891, in Smith scrapbooks.

professional work that he and Burton handled, to the political demands made upon him, to the necessity of shaping policies for the *Journal*, and to his duties as president of the Atlanta Board of Education, he interested himself early in 1891 in the railroad operations of his uncle, General Robert F. Hoke. General Hoke was attempting to extend the Georgia, Carolina, and Northern Railroad, and he turned to his nephew for legal advice and assistance in such matters as the acquisition of terminal rights. For a time Smith hobnobbed with the important railroad magnates of the South.[7]

Smith was simply trying to do too much. Even a man of his robust constitution could not maintain such a pace, and by early 1891 he found himself ill, completely worn out. He decided to spend a few weeks in Florida, where, he wrote Tom Watson, he was trying "to recruit a little my health, broken down by overwork." The trip and the rest "greatly improved" him, but a short time later he was again exhausted, "just run down."[8] Somehow he got through the heavy work of the spring and during the following summer spent a long vacation with his family at Martha's Vineyard.

During the first part of 1891, Hoke Smith toyed with the idea of selling his stock in the Atlanta *Journal* to Josiah Carter, who wished either to purchase a larger holding or.to sell his interest in the newspaper.[9] In February, 1891, Smith noted to a correspondent, "My professional work confines me so entirely that I am giving no attention to the Journal at present."[10] Nevertheless, the lawyer was reluctant to dispose of the paper. For one thing, he hesitated to sell unless Henry Cabaniss would also sell, since he felt responsible for having brought Cabaniss into the enterprise in the first place. In July, Smith definitely decided against disposing of his stock. Josiah Carter had by this time proposed a rival evening paper, and Smith said that "it would look as if I was afraid of competition." He would "never retire

[7] He was also one of the directors of the G. C. & N.

[8] Smith to Watson, February 12, 1891, and to Robert F. Hoke, February 12, 1891, in Smith Collection, Legal Letterbook (1891).

[9] Smith to Carter, February 25, 27, 1891, *ibid.*

[10] Smith to James T. Dixon, about February 12, 1891, *ibid.*

with a fight in front." Furthermore, "The Journal is doing a splendid business," wrote its publisher; "its circulation has increased very rapidly this year, and I wish to obtain full value when I let it go." [11]

Although he failed to mention it to Carter, one factor that probably influenced Smith in his decision to retain control of the *Journal* was the approach of the election of 1892. With the agrarian revolution gathering force daily, with the Democratic party in the state caught in the throes of a struggle and trying desperately to weather the storm, with the Atlanta *Constitution* trimming its sails in an effort to adjust to the agrarian winds, Hoke Smith found Georgia politics too tempting to resist. As the threat of a third party became more obvious, he reaffirmed his party regularity and tried to find a vital issue that would keep most Democrats true to the traditional party. He made use of two such issues: one, invoked by most Democrats in the South who opposed the agrarian reforms, included the whole complex of arguments used to justify the Solid South and the one-party system; the other was the demand for tariff reform, which, although an old party principle, was given renewed vigor in Georgia under his leadership.

Smith's advocacy of tariff reform was identified with his admiration for Grover Cleveland and the latter's famous tariff message of 1887. From that time the Atlanta *Journal* began to give vigorous support to the campaign for tariff reduction and within a short time its publisher had become known as the leader of the tariff reformers in Georgia. His comprehensive address on this issue at the Northeast Georgia Fair in 1888 brought him wide publicity throughout the state, and even attention from other parts of the country.[12] He soon became a visitor at the meetings of the New York Reform Club, whose position on the tariff question elicited his enthusiastic approval.

Although there was little original in his tariff views, Smith's arguments on the subject were aggressively delivered and abundantly buttressed with statistics, and were brought home to his

[11] Smith to Josiah Carter, July 14, 1891, *ibid.*
[12] Atlanta *Constitution*, November 6, 8, 1888; Savannah *Morning News*, November 9, 1888; Atlanta *Journal*, February 16, 1893.

Georgia audiences by vivid illustrative material. He made his position clear in his Athens address of 1888:

> I am here to-day to urge that you stand squarely by the principle of tariff reform. It is the greatest of all issues dividing the Democratic and Republican parties. It is a fight against the legalized but unjust concentration of the products of the many into the pockets of the few. If it be true that tariff reform caused our defeat, it is also true that organized monopoly has for years taught, without full contradiction, the false doctrine that a high tariff increases the wages of the laborer, while it also blesses the farmer with a home market.[13]

The Georgian was convinced that one of the great wrongs of American life was rooted in the protective tariff. It amounted, he felt, to an unjust and immoral tribute exacted from the mass of the people for the benefit of men like Andrew Carnegie and their "monopolies." In other words, the tariff permitted "one class of people to feed upon another class." "It does not rest upon property," Smith told the state Democratic convention in 1888; "it does not rest upon incomes; it does not rest upon luxuries of life, but it finds its way into every home, however humble, and places its burden upon the necessaries of life." Look at the position of the industrial worker: "while the laborer is prevented from buying the necessaries of life at European prices, nothing prevents European pauper labor from coming over to this country to turn him out of his work or reduce the amount of his pay." [14]

Smith warned Georgia farmers that their pockets were "being emptied to fill those of somebody else." Using steel rails as an example, he claimed that their cost in Georgia was increased by the tariff nearly $1,445,000 during the period 1886-88, and that most of this "tribute" went to the monopolies. Since the railroads were allowed to charge a "fair price"—taking into consideration the cost of construction—"the man who rides on the railroads and sends his property over them really pays the increased cost of the rails." Another example Smith used was that of the notorious

[13] [Smith], *The Tariff and the Georgia Farmer.*
[14] *Ibid.*; Atlanta *Constitution*, May 10, 1888.

cotton bagging-and-ties or "jute" combination, which worked a special hardship on the cotton farmers of the region.

Although asserting that well-established manufacturing enterprises profited from the protective tariff, Smith contended that they benefited only at the expense of new concerns. "They are rich and powerful and monopolize home trade," he declared; they "can put down the prices which they pay for labor" and "put up the prices of the commodities which they sell, for the markets of the world are not open to their customers." As for Georgia manufactures, so valiantly boosted by men like Grady in the eighties, Smith felt "no doubt that the tariff checks their growth," forcing them "to locations where they do not properly belong." Furthermore, he argued, the tariff "tribute" withdrew each year large sums which became lost as far as building up the state's industries was concerned.[15]

The Republican party, the party identified in the public mind with the protective tariff, was only a remnant in Georgia by this time, but as the third party proposal became more certain late in 1891, there was talk of fusion between the new party and the Republicans. But before Georgia Democrats could face an external menace in the election of 1892, they had to deal with a bitter factional struggle within their own ranks. The party was split into factions favoring the nomination of ex-President Cleveland on one hand and David B. Hill on the other.

The Atlanta *Constitution* and the Atlanta *Journal* spearheaded the two Democratic elements in the state. The *Constitution* was suspicious of Cleveland's tariff views and preferred Hill's emphasis of free silver. The editors of the morning paper believed that if Hill could capture Georgia's delegates to the Democratic national convention, he would be in a good position to win other Southern delegations and to secure the party's nomination. John S. Cohen, crack young *Journal* reporter, later recalled that "There was a clatter, a din, a clash, a scent of brilliant political coup, and pell-mell the professional editors and the professional politicians took seats in the Hill bandwagon."[16] But the *Journal* had given Cleveland favorable notices for years and had stated

[15] [Smith,] *The Tariff and the Georgia Farmer.*
[16] Atlanta *Journal*, June 5, 1897.

as early as the spring of 1890 that he was "the ablest and fore-most leader of the Democracy, and the next standard-bearer of our party." The paper assumed a sort of proprietary interest in the ex-President, and his success seemed all the more necessary in view of the *Constitution*'s opposition to him.[17]

Nevertheless, it was not easy for Smith and the *Journal* to make the decision to give full support to Cleveland, primarily because of the latter's position against free silver. Smith and his paper had endorsed free silver in 1890, and the proposal was becoming every day a more precious string in the harp being played by the farmer-politicians. Throughout 1891 the *Journal* gave evidence of being anxious to reconcile Cleveland's views on the money question with the free-silver demand, and for a time it grasped at the hope that the former President would modify his views.[18] When Cleveland indicated his firm oppo-sition to free silver, the *Journal* expressed regret but con-demned the "base attacks" made upon him by some Democratic newspapers. As the 1892 contest approached in Georgia, the two Atlanta newspapers presented an interesting study in contrasts on the two issues; the *Constitution* seemed as reluctant to face the tariff issue as the *Journal* was to meet free silver.

But the *Constitution-Journal* editorial struggle was vociferous and vituperative. There was much talk of "party loyalty," of the ability or inability of the two leading candidates to win, and of which of the two questions—tariff or money—was the real issue. The *Constitution* declared that some Democratic news-papers—meaning particularly the *Journal*, which it contemptu-ously referred to as "our featherhead contemporary"—had bor-rowed from "the vilest republican organs" terms of reproach to apply to David B. Hill.[19] In an editorial entitled "The Party and the Farmers," the *Constitution* struck one of its most familiar notes:

How can the Cleveland organs meet the exigencies of the

[17] *Ibid.*, May 22, 1890, January 13, 1891.

[18] See, for example, Smith to W. A. Candler, January 16, 1891, in Smith Collection, Legal Letterbook (1891).

[19] Atlanta *Constitution*, January 1, 2, 4, 8, February 11, March 1, 7, April 29, 1892.

situation? What influence can they hope to have on the farmers? They are responsible for the uncalled-for abuse of the alliance movement, and they are likewise responsible for the situation as it exists . . . but look at the causes that led to it—Cleveland independentism, Cleveland mugwumpism, and Cleveland goldbugism, and Wall street Clevelandism. For twenty years the democratic farmers have been the mainstay of the party, yet when they formulate their demands, they are hooted at and traduced. . . .[20]

The *Journal*, for its part, criticized David B. Hill just as strongly. It had no confidence in his tariff views and warned the people that he was not really a free-silverite. The afternoon paper devoted page after page to Cleveland's "hold" on Georgia, to his endorsement by other newspapers and by prominent people, and to the poll of the state which it was conducting. The "Hillstitution," as the *Journal* labeled the *Constitution*, had "winked" at the work of James B. Weaver and "Sockless Jerry" Simpson, had applauded Livingston as he "pranced" over the state, and was guilty of being soft toward the Populists.[21] By late April the two newspapers had long since cast all caution to the winds. The *Journal* referred to the "contemptible work" of its rival, which it accused of "fits of ungovernable jealousy." As for Hill, Smith's paper declared him to be "practically out of the race" and asserted that the tariff was rapidly becoming "the absorbing issue." Georgians were laughingly saying that Georgia was for Hill in the morning and Cleveland in the afternoon.[22]

Hoke Smith had begun to work diligently for Cleveland early in 1892. He was one of the organizers of the strong Cleveland Club formed in Atlanta at about that time. "It is a great privilege to be right," he confidently boasted at the organizational meeting of the club, "but it is a greater privilege to be right when you know you are going to win." The tariff received first consideration in his speeches, but he also spoke eloquently of Grover Cleveland. He denounced the Republicans for contracting the currency and launched a sharp attack against the Populists. "Who

[20] *Ibid.*, April 1, 1892.
[21] Atlanta *Journal*, January 1, 2, 5, 9, February 13, March 25, 1892.
[22] *Ibid.*, March 25, April 30, 1892, June 5, 1897.

are the people who are raising this trouble among you? " he
asked a Democratic rally in Douglasville. " Are they people who
have lived and suffered with you, or are they women from Ireland
and men from Kansas? [laughter and applause]." With Smith
it was always the party: " God silence the tongue and paralyze
the arm that would separate the people of Georgia in the very
hour of their deliverance." [23]

The central event in the Democratic intraparty battle in
Georgia was the state convention scheduled for May 18, 1892.
Strong efforts were made by both the Cleveland and the Hill
groups to have the counties instruct their delegates to vote
" right." During April and May, when the county delegates
were being elected, the struggle between the Smith faction and
its opposition was especially bitter in Fulton County.[24] The
remainder of the state witnessed a similar if somewhat less violent
battle.[25] The Fulton County fight was particularly significant,
for it was here that the important leadership of the two wings
of the party was centered. In April the Fulton County Executive
Committee adopted a resolution providing for the election of
the county's delegates to the state convention by primary, which
pleased the Hill faction. But on May 9, it was announced that the
executive committee had agreed to a compromise suggested by
" ten prominent citizens " for " the purpose of harmonizing the
party in this county "; the compromise called for an evenly
divided delegation, elected at a mass meeting, to represent the
county in the state convention.[26]

Despite this agreement the mass meeting, in the " most sensational political development Fulton county has had in a long
time," elected a solid Cleveland delegation. Subsequently, a
" bobtail contingent " of Hill men and supporters of the divided-

[23] *Ibid.*, February 9, 11, 1892; Atlanta *Constitution*, February 11, 1892.

[24] For example, see Atlanta *Journal*, April 20, 21, 23, 1892.

[25] The state's newspapers were divided, the prominent Savannah *Morning
News*, for example, endorsing Cleveland and the Augusta *Chronicle* supporting Hill.

[26] The " ten prominent citizens " included five from the Hill Club and
five from the Cleveland Club. Hoke Smith was one of the Cleveland men.
Savannah *Morning News*, April 14, May 10, 16, 1892; Atlanta *Journal*,
April 13, May 5, 6, 13, 16, 1892.

ticket plan chose the slate of delegates previously agreed upon, to contest those elected by the mass meeting. Hoke Smith, who had been elected to both delegations, had urged the election of the proposed compromise ticket, to which he was committed as a result of the compromise plan, but after the "straightouts" carried the day, the Atlanta *Journal* declared that the only thing to do was abide by the result of the mass meeting. In answer to what was evidently a rumor of trickery, Smith vehemently asserted, "Any insinuation that I did not in good faith support the compromise is maliciously false." "I agreed to the compromise, and did my part to carry it through," he said. "It was overwhelmingly defeated, and I shall support now the action of the regular democratic meeting." Another Cleveland man said of Smith's actions at the mass meeting, "He is a hard fighter, and amid the guying of a crowd and in the heat of debate he may have said things unpalatable to some of the crowd, but his zeal for the compromise was real and earnest." [27]

Just before the state convention assembled on May 18, Cleveland leaders warned that the anti-Cleveland Democrats would seek to win in the convention under the guise of an uninstructed delegation to the national convention. The newspapers reported that "Each faction is aggressive and argumentative, and both have begun the proselyting of delegates . . . by opening headquarters at the Kimball house and displaying banners bearing the watchword of the faction." According to the Associated Press, "Every prominent Democratic politician of Georgia is in the city to-night, and the breach between the two divisions of the Democratic party in the state is growing wider and wider." Caucuses were held by both sides, delegates agreed upon, and slogans adopted. While some conciliatory moves were initiated, Hoke Smith, speaking for the more aggressive Cleveland element, stated with determination: "We propose to fight for a pronounced Cleveland delegation. . . . We will elect such emphatic Cleveland men that they will not need instruction." [28]

[27] Atlanta *Journal*, May 14, 16, 17, 1892; Savannah *Morning News*, May 15, 1892.

[28] Atlanta *Journal*, May 14, 18, 1892; Savannah *Morning News*, May 15, 17, 18, 1892.

On the floor of the convention every step provoked a bitter dispute. The Cleveland men proved to be in a majority and succeeded in electing Pope Barrow, a former state senator, permanent chairman,[29] but the Hill leaders fought long and well for national delegates favorable to their man and for an uninstructed delegation. The hottest fight of the convention grew out of the struggle for recognition between the contesting Fulton County delegations. On an exciting roll call the Cleveland group was seated by a vote of 171 to 157. In the end, the Cleveland supporters were largely successful in electing the delegates they had agreed upon in caucus, including Hoke Smith.[30]

As chairman of the Cleveland faction's steering committee, Smith assumed a leading part in the work of the convention. Just before the convention adjourned, he endeavored to make the Cleveland victory complete by introducing resolutions endorsing Cleveland's first administration in an unqualified manner and instructing the Georgia delegation to vote as a unit at Chicago. The first point was adopted, but Smith withdrew the second when it became apparent that an acrimonious fight would ensue. The Cleveland men were now in a mood to heed Chairman William Y. Atkinson's plea, "for God's sake not to rub it into the Hill men too hard." The platform, which Smith helped to draft, declared for tariff reform, free silver, an income tax, the repeal of the 10 per cent Federal tax on state bank notes, economy in government, and increased powers for the state railroad commission.[31]

The Hill movement, crushed in Georgia, had been dealt a heavy blow in the South. Smith and the *Journal*, according to one of the Hill men in the state, had "stemmed the tide and turned the current for Cleveland" at a time when "all of the

[29] Smith delivered one of the speeches seconding the nomination of Barrow, "a forcible speech, declaring him to be the leader of tariff reform in Georgia." Atlanta *Journal*, May 18, 1892; Savannah *Morning News*, May 19, 1892.

[30] The Atlanta *Journal*, May 19, 1892, claimed that seventeen delegates chosen to the national convention were openly for Cleveland, while nine were listed as uncommitted.

[31] Atlanta *Journal*, May 18, 19, 1892.

old politicians of Georgia" were for Hill and it appeared that he would carry the state.[32]

Soon after the convention Hoke Smith dispatched John S. Cohen, news editor of the *Journal*, to confer with William C. Whitney of New York, leader of the Cleveland forces, " to learn if there is anything that you feel inclined to say to the people of the South " before the national convention.[33] Shortly before the convention assembled, Smith was invited to Chicago by Whitney and Don M. Dickinson to participate in the preconvention strategy being mapped by the Cleveland leaders. Among other things, the Georgian was delegated to confer with certain doubtful delegations in an effort to line them up for Cleveland.

During the convention, Smith co-operated with Don Dickinson, the Cleveland floor leader, and on the first ballot, which resulted in Cleveland's nomination, Georgia gave seventeen votes to the ex-President. A rumor was started during the convention, apparently by the Atlanta *Constitution*, that Smith desired to be appointed Democratic national committeeman from Georgia, and that he would oppose Clark Howell for the position. Very likely Smith did want the position—it would have been a fitting reward for his triumph in the state convention—but it was soon evident that Howell was too popular to be overthrown. Smith denied having any such ambition, labeling the report a " silly story." [34]

Following Cleveland's nomination, at least a superficial harmony was restored to the Democratic party in Georgia and the party leaders could concentrate against the People's party. Hoke Smith remained in close contact with William C. Whitney, making a number of suggestions about the conduct of the campaign.[35] The Atlanta *Journal* waged a vigorous campaign for the Democratic cause, and its publisher played a prominent role in the various Democratic ratifying ceremonies and rallies that accom-

[32] Julius L. Brown to Smith, February 11, 1893, in Smith Collection, MS. Scrapbook; Savannah *Morning News*, May 19, 1892.

[33] John B. Gordon to William C. Whitney, May 28, 1892, and Smith to Whitney, May 28, 1892, in Whitney Papers (Division of Manuscripts, Library of Congress).

[34] Atlanta *Constitution*, June 21, 1892; Atlanta *Journal*, June 22, 25, 1892; " The New Secretary of the Interior," *loc. cit.*, 264.

[35] Smith to Whitney, June 25, July 8, 1892, in Whitney Papers.

panied the formal opening of the national campaign. Smith made a number of speeches during the late summer and early fall in various Georgia towns, and in October he delivered several campaign addresses in Alabama and North Carolina.

Wherever he spoke, the Georgia lawyer invoked party loyalty and attacked the protective tariff. He missed no opportunity to identify the Republicans with the Force Bill, which he asserted would bring to his "beloved Georgia" six thousand Federal supervisors! He did not forget the Populists. At Jefferson early in August, he engaged in a joint debate with Colonel J. A. Mahaffey, a Populist speaker. While he astutely pointed out the similarity between the Democratic and Ocala platforms, he claimed that General James B. Weaver, the Populist candidate for President, hated the South, and he saw the handwriting of Terence V. Powderly in the Populist demand for government ownership of the railroads.[36]

When victory came to the Democrats within the state in October and on the national front in November, it was as sweet as nectar to Hoke Smith and his *Journal* lieutenants. De Give's opera house had been engaged by the *Journal* managers, and the Presidential election returns were announced from the stage and a balcony over Marietta Street as the reports came from the wires. On November 9, the day following the election, the *Journal* proclaimed a victory "For Grover Cleveland and Tariff Reform" and ran "Old Grover's" picture between two American flags. To climax its first national success in the political arena, the newspaper staged a "jubilee," with its publisher as one of the speakers.[37] "Somehow," wrote a young Atlanta schoolteacher, "it has seemed almost impossible for me to think or talk of anything else besides the election. This election certainly meant much for the South and probably marks an era in the political life of this country. . . ."[38]

[36] Atlanta *Journal*, August 4, 13, September 12, October 15, 19, 20, 22, 1892, February 16, 1893.

[37] *Ibid.*, November 5-9, 19, 1892.

[38] Vassar L. Allen to Miss B. A. Allen, November 12, 1892, in George and Alexander Allen Papers (Southern Historical Collection, University of North Carolina Library).

Hoke Smith was the man of the hour in Atlanta. He found that he had acquired something of a national reputation and that his newspaper would now be counted on as an administration organ. Almost immediately his name began to be mentioned as a Cabinet possibility, especially by Southern newspapers. The Macon *Telegraph*, for example, declared soon after the election that "all things considered we cannot but think that Mr. Hoke Smith, of Atlanta, combines the element of ability coupled with congeniality to Mr. Cleveland as much as any man in our state." [39]

Smith undoubtedly was flattered by the mention of his name for the Cabinet; indeed, it appears that he worked hard to secure the appointment. He managed to see Whitney soon after the election and in December he and Birdie gave a round of entertainments for such leading Democrats as Vice President-elect Adlai E. Stevenson, the Lucius Q. C. Lamars, and John B. Gordon. Smith had the support of Lamar, Secretary of the Interior in Cleveland's first Cabinet and at that time Associate Justice of the Supreme Court, and of Senator Gordon, both of whom were reported to have influence with Cleveland. [40]

By the end of the year a strong movement was under way in Georgia favoring Smith's selection to the Cabinet. A great many letters from prominent Georgians were addressed to Senator Gordon and to Cleveland urging that Smith be appointed. [41] ". . . Hoke Smith was at once the guiding spirit, the heart and the soul of the Cleveland sentiment in Georgia" was the recurring theme in these letters. "As a lawyer of learning and ability," wrote Augustus O. Bacon, "he ranks among the first in this State. As a public man he has been for several years past

---

[39] For a number of such quotations from Southern newspapers, see Atlanta *Journal*, November 12, 19, 1892.

[40] Lamar was a "family connection" of Birdie Smith. When he suffered a severe heart attack on a trip south in December, 1892, he was taken to Hoke Smith's home, "where he was kindly entertained for two days." He died in Macon, Georgia, within a few weeks. Smith delivered a eulogy of the Mississippian a few days later in the Federal District Court in Atlanta, on the occasion of the passage of resolutions memorializing Lamar. Atlanta *Journal*, January 30, 1893; Wirt Armistead Cate, *Lucius Q. C. Lamar: Secession and Reunion* (Chapel Hill, 1935), 521.

[41] See the scrapbook of these letters in the Smith Collection.

a leader in the advocacy of the personal claims of Mr. Cleveland.
. . ." According to James K. Hines, Smith, "by his pen, and
speech, and popularity, rallied the State to the support of the
President"; Governor William J. Northen wrote that no man in
the state had "more constantly & effectually" presented Cleveland's policies. One of the most interesting of these letters was
that of Negro Bishop Henry M. Turner, who wrote Cleveland
that both races would approve the choice of Hoke Smith, for
"we know him to be generous in disposition, liberal in every
thing involving human rights, regardless of race, color, or previous
condition," and "too great to be mean about anything."

Smith's enemies in Georgia, led by the managers of the Atlanta
Constitution, were not at all pleased by his triumph. Early in
1893, an acute observer in Atlanta reported: "All of Atlanta
is talking just now about the probable appointment of Mr. Hoke
Smith to the Secretaryship of the Interior. It is a very pronounced
slap in the face for the Howell-Constitution faction, and tells
them in unmistakable terms that they need expect nothing at the
hands of the Administration." [42] According to John T. Boifeuillet,
a young politician from Macon, Smith's enemies sent a special
envoy to Macon with the urgent request that James H. Blount,
prominent Georgia Congressman, allow the use of his name for
the Cabinet. But Blount refused and the anti-Smith men had no
other outstanding man around whom they could rally. [43]

At his home in Lakewood, New Jersey, meanwhile, Grover
Cleveland worried over the appointments to his Cabinet. One
of those consulted by the President-elect was his former secretary, George F. Parker, in whom he had much confidence.
Among those recommended by Parker was Hoke Smith, who
had impressed him during the campaign as "perhaps the most
effective helper that came to us in our nomination campaign,
from the South." Parker knew that Cleveland wanted someone
from the South to represent the new ideas of that region, and
Senator Gordon and others had already forwarded numerous
recommendations from the South. On February 9, 1893, Cleveland wrote Walter Q. Gresham: "I have settled, I think, on

---

[42] Vassar L. Allen to Willie M. Allen, February 12, 1893, in Allen Papers.
[43] Atlanta *Journal*, December 21, 24, 1892, December 1, 1931.

five members of the Cabinet. I mean to have Carlisle for the Treasury—Lamont for War—Bissell (of Buffalo, one of my oldest friends and former partner) for Postmaster-General, and Hoke Smith of Georgia (a very able representative of the new and progressive South) for Interior." After a conference with the Georgian, Cleveland announced on February 15 that Smith would be Secretary of the Interior in the new Cabinet.[44]

The coveted goal was a reality, and for the moment the future appeared bright indeed for Hoke Smith. During the past two or three years he had emerged rapidly as one of the most promising Democratic leaders in Georgia; his appointment to the Cabinet was evidence of the work he had done and an indication of greater distinction that he might achieve in the future. After a hurried round of preparations for removing his family to Washington and getting his professional and business affairs in order, Smith boarded a train in Atlanta that would carry him to new and more important duties.

[44] Allan Nevins (ed.), *Letters of Grover Cleveland, 1850-1908* (Boston, 1933), 315, 317; George F. Parker, *Recollections of Grover Cleveland* (New York, 1909), 175; Parker, "Cleveland's Second Administration as President," in *Saturday Evening Post*, CXCV (June 9, 1923), 42; Atlanta *Journal*, February 15, 16, 1893.

The Initiation of a

Cabinet Member

In Washington March 4, 1893, dawned gray and blustery with a swirl of snow, as if it were an evil omen for the Democratic administration soon to be inaugurated. But the harsh wind and freezing snow failed to dampen the enthusiasm of the triumphant Democrats, whose chant of "Grover, Grover, four more years of Grover," was borne across the city amid the inaugural parade, the evening receptions, and the hotel parties. One of the celebrating Democrats was Hoke Smith, who reveled in the festivities. He was the toast of all Georgians in the capital, and his good nature and youthful appearance were commented on at every hand.[1]

Few Democrats from the South had served in the Cabinet since the war—only David M. Key of Tennessee, Augustus H. Garland of Arkansas, and Mississippi's Lamar. Cleveland's appointment of three Southerners to his second Cabinet was hailed with delight in the South; Smith himself was deluged with messages of congratulations and expressions of confidence. There were letters from clients, North Carolina schoolmates, his father's friends, and people from all over the South whom the Georgian did not know.[2]

There were many references to Smith's "ardor and enthusi-

[1] Atlanta *Journal*, March 4, 1893.
[2] See the large number of letters to Smith and John B. Gordon, in Smith Collection, MS. Scrapbook.

asm " during the recent campaign, to his adherence to "those great principles of true Democracy "—tariff reform, honest money, and civil service reform—and to the recognition his appointment had brought to the "young progressive element of the South." The region would be in safe hands, wrote one young Southerner, "if the young men of the South would only follow the grand example your life thus far has given them." Another hoped "to live to see the day when I may grasp your hand as the *head* of the nation." It was "a singular coincidence," observed one correspondent, "that the mantle of that great Georgian, Howell Cobb, should have fallen on the shoulders of the man who married his niece." [3] Old Zebulon B. Vance of North Carolina said that he was glad to know that at least one man—"my good friend Hoke Smith "—was satisfactory to Southern Democrats. "How dear Nannie [Hoke] would have rejoiced to see her young Kinsman honored! " [4] Even the Atlanta *Constitution*, while pointing out that it had taken no part in promoting the *Journal* publisher—a disclaimer that was hardly necessary—added to the acclaim by predicting that Cleveland would find Smith "an active, energetic assistant " with a "conscientious desire " to do well. [5]

Favorable notices also came from other regions. The New York *Nation* observed that Smith's selection was "a sign of the times only second to the selection of Judge Gresham " and equally full of promise for the future. Indeed, declared the *Nation*, "a better representative of the New South could not be found." *Harper's Weekly* described Smith as "a young man who has won a high place at the Georgia bar," while the *Forum* had characterized him during the campaign as "one of the most vigorous of the post-bellum generation of Southern men." He represented the new era, declared the New York *World*—"the South of the mill, the mine, the railroad, of diversified industries, bustling cities and advancing commonwealths." [6]

[3] Cobb had served as Secretary of the Treasury in Buchanan's Cabinet, 1857-60.

[4] Vance to William A. Hoke, February 16, 1893, in Hoke Papers (Southern Historical Collection, University of North Carolina Library).

[5] Atlanta *Constitution*, February 12, 1893.

[6] *Forum*, XIII (August, 1892), 795; *Nation*, LVI (February 23, 1893),

Other references to the new Secretary of Interior were less complimentary. The *Review of Reviews* described him as Cleveland's "most dubious appointment," while pointing out that he would have to deal with "a great range of delicate questions with which it would be hard to find a public man less familiar than Mr. Smith." Writing in the same magazine, Professor Woodrow Wilson referred to the Georgian as a very successful trial lawyer but suspected that his training and experience had been the sort that "disposes a man habitually" to resort to expediency.[7]

The appointment of such a relatively unknown man to the Cabinet—and his arresting, one-syllable first name—led many to ask, "Who is Hoke Smith?" The following is one of the more interesting newspaper descriptions of Smith that appeared at the time: "Tall? Six feet two. Heavy? Two hundred and sixty-five, at least. Built like a pugilist, set as squarely on his feet as a wrestler. . . . No paunch to speak of, as is mostly the case with heavy men, and a movement of limb so free as to suggest that he took and loved much outdoor exercise, and yet with a whiteness of skin not at all in keeping with the general air of high spirits and perfect health that he wears."[8]

Grover Cleveland and the eight men who joined him around the White House conference table on Cabinet days made up an interesting group. Cleveland looked the part of the leader— elephantine in size and ponderous in movement, plodding, unimaginative, and independent. The Secretary of State, Walter Q. Gresham of Illinois, had served in Arthur's Cabinet but had recently quit the Republican party because of his reform views on the tariff. John G. Carlisle, tall and dignified Kentuckian, three times Speaker of the House of Representatives, was the new Secretary of the Treasury. "Colonel" Daniel S. Lamont of New York, the President's private secretary during the first

---

134; *Harper's Weekly*, XXXVII (March 4, 1893), 199; New York *World*, quoted in Atlanta *Journal*, February 22, 1893.

[7] *Review of Reviews*, VII (April, 1893), 262; Wilson, "Mr. Cleveland's Cabinet," *loc. cit.*, 287, 291-93.

[8] "The New Secretary of the Interior," *loc. cit.*, 264-65; Atlanta *Journal*, April 11, July 31, 1893, February 1, 1894.

Cleveland administration, became Secretary of War. The Post-master General was Wilson S. Bissell, Cleveland's law partner of earlier years in Buffalo. The Navy Department was headed by Hilary A. Herbert, a Confederate veteran and long-time Congress-man from Alabama who had served as chairman of the House Committee on Naval Affairs. J. Sterling Morton, pioneer Demo-crat from Nebraska, became Secretary of Agriculture. Richard Olney of Massachusetts, the Attorney General, was a man of " forceful personality," as his Cabinet career was soon to demon-strate; Hoke Smith considered him " a great lawyer." [9]

At the time of his appointment Smith knew almost nothing about the work of the Interior Department. He soon discovered that since its creation in 1849, it had become a vast, unwieldy, and decentralized part of the executive branch. Its functions had grown steadily until it had become, in the words of a con-temporary newspaper, " the most complex of departments, an omnium gatherum of matters left over after the other departments had taken charge of everything properly belonging to them." [10] A mere listing of the items under its jurisdiction in 1893 indicates how large and diverse was its work. Under its direction were matters relating to the public lands, Indian affairs, pensions, patents, the census, the geological survey, Federal education, land-grant railroads, territories, national parks and forests, public docu-ments, the Nicaraguan Canal, and certain eleemosynary institu-tions near Washington.[11]

Most of the department's affairs were administered directly by bureaus or offices, such as the Bureau of Public Lands, which were supervised by commissioners subordinate to the Secretary. These bureaus had offices separate from each other and from the offices of the Secretary. This arrangement made it necessary to maintain within the Secretary's office eleven divisions somewhat analogous to the bureaus to act upon the various items of business

---

[9] Smith Collection, " Memorandum for Mr. Parker," undated.

[10] Baltimore *News*, quoted in Atlanta *Journal*, November 28, 1893.

[11] *Report of the Secretary of the Interior; Being Part of the Message and Documents Communicated to the Two Houses of Congress at the Beginning of the Second Session of the Fifty-Third Congress* (Washington, 1893), I, iii. Hereinafter the reports of the Department of the Interior are cited as *Interior Report*, followed by the appropriate year.

coming to the central office.[12] A generation later Hoke Smith
still remembered his shock upon discovering that it took seven
to ten days for a communication to reach his offices from the
various bureaus and be returned after receiving action. One day
he asked the chief clerk to explain a document he had initialed,
and found that "he knew nothing about it." He then asked the
chief of division, "and he knew nothing about it." Thoroughly
alarmed, Smith directed that in the future each bureau must send
its business directly to the appropriate division in his office and,
to the astonishment of the division chiefs, that the matter must
reach his office from the divisions by 9 o'clock on the following
morning. No initials were to be placed on communications by
anyone who "could not discuss the subject without looking at
the papers." [13]

The first few weeks in his new position were hectic ones for
Smith. Despite importunings of eager office seekers, he applied
himself diligently to the affairs of the department. A Georgia
journalist noted his "courteous, vigilant and effective" handling
of the large crowds that pressed in to see him. He often reached
his offices, located in the big "patent building" on F Street, by
8 o'clock in the morning and many times lingered in the evenings
until after 6 o'clock.[14] Smith expected his subordinates to match
his own pace. One of them wrote a little wryly in September,
1893, that "the Secretary has mapped out enough work for me
to do Monday to keep me busy until late at night. . . ." [15] Sometimes Smith did ask department employees to work overtime.
He also promulgated an order directing that "official hours must
be devoted exclusively to official business, and all conversations
of a merely personal character, loitering in the halls and the like,
are forbidden." [16]

[12] Emmett Womack, *History and Business Methods of the Department
of the Interior, Its Bureaus and Offices* (Washington, 1896), 4-5.

[13] *Cong. Record,* 65 Cong., 2 Sess., 4949.

[14] Savannah *Press,* quoted in Atlanta *Journal,* August 15, 1893; Allan
Nevins, *Grover Cleveland, A Study in Courage* (New York, 1932), 521.

[15] Josephus Daniels to Mrs. Daniels, September 23, 1893, October 24, 1894,
in Daniels Papers (Division of Manuscripts, Library of Congress).

[16] "Chief Clerk's Orders," January 29, 1894, December 28, 1895, in Pension
Bureau Papers (National Archives); *Cong. Record,* 64 Cong., 2 Sess., 1815.

Generally, Smith's principal assistants in the department were adequate if not outstanding. The First Assistant Secretary was William H. Sims, a one-legged Confederate veteran who had served as lieutenant governor of Mississippi, his native state. The Assistant Secretary was John M. Reynolds, a lawyer from Pennsylvania. Silas W. Lamoreaux, a Wisconsin judge highly recommended by Senator William F. Vilas, became Commissioner of the General Land Office.[17] Other important subordinates included Edward A. Bowers, formerly counsel to the National Forestry Association, as Assistant Commissioner of the General Land Office; William Lochren of Minnesota, a Union veteran, as Commissioner of Pensions; John B. Seymour, a Connecticut politician, as Commissioner of Patents; and Daniel M. Browning of Illinois, as Commissioner of Indian Affairs.

Hoke Smith had little voice in the selection of these men. As he confided to a friend, "the President had determined to make the appointments himself" to the major positions, leaving the Secretary "no patronage at his disposal above $2,000 a year."[18] Smith was responsible, it appears, for the selection of John I. Hall, a fellow Georgian, as Assistant Attorney General for the Department of Interior. He was also instrumental in persuading Cleveland to appoint the celebrated South Carolinian and Confederate general Wade Hampton as Commissioner of Railroads. One of Smith's happiest appointments was that of Josephus Daniels, a newspaperman from North Carolina, who served first as chief of the appointment division in the Secretary's office, and later as chief clerk. In the latter position he had general supervision of the clerks and employees in Smith's office, and his own office served as a kind of clearinghouse for the department's business. The young Carolinian was flattered to find that Smith treated him as a sympathetic confidant. "It is very pleasant & agreeable to be with a man who appreciates you as Smith appears to do," Daniels wrote.[19]

[17] Vilas to Smith, March 6, 1893, in Department of Interior Papers (National Archives), Appointment Division, File 521.

[18] Daniels to Mrs. Daniels, March 8, 1893, in Daniels Papers.

[19] Daniels to Mrs. Daniels, March 9, 17, 1893, *ibid.*; Josephus Daniels, *Editor in Politics* (Chapel Hill, 1941), 11.

Except for the brief interlude represented by Cleveland's first administration, Democrats had had few opportunities to control Federal patronage in the postwar era. Members of the victorious party now demanded political rewards, and even the President's zeal for civil service reform could not withstand the irresistible insistence for political jobs. As the head of one of the largest departments, Smith had to face heavy demands. As a Southerner, he was under constant pressure from office seekers and their friends who felt that he would understand why good Southern Democrats should not be turned away. He was literally besieged by those demanding and begging for places, and their Congressmen and friends cluttered up his offices. "I have met up with many North Carolina people," wrote Josephus Daniels in March, 1893, "and every one of them is here after an office." Smith's receptions during this early period consumed "most of every day." When he returned to his office after a brief illness in April, the army of demanding Democrats was there to greet him, and in May the "state of siege" continued.[20]

Influenced no doubt by President Cleveland's well-known endorsement of the merit system, Hoke Smith issued a statement a few weeks after taking office in which he declared that "Public offices should be created and conducted exclusively for the benefit of those who do not fill them."[21] Democratic claims were not to be denied, however, and Republican removals were more or less accepted as the order of the day. The administration's policy of economy and the completion of the census work for 1890 also forced the Interior Department to release many employees. Department officials denied charges of discrimination against Republicans,[22] but there were many letters such as this: "You are removed from the office of Superintendent of the Hot Springs in Arkansas, to take effect upon the appointment and qualification of your successor." Furthermore, there were reports of extensive

[20] Daniels to Mrs. Daniels, March 7, 21, 1893, in Daniels Papers; Atlanta *Journal*, March 8, 9, 16, April 18, 20, 24, 1893; *Harper's Weekly*, XXXVII (May 6, 1893), 414-15.

[21] Atlanta *Journal*, May 2, 1893.

[22] For instance, see Henry C. Bell to Smith, January 11, 1894, in Department of Interior Papers, Appointment Division, File 521.

"grading up and down of clerks in the classified service" in the Interior and Treasury departments, "not according to merit, but according to party affiliation, locality, and political influence." [23] Smith entered upon the task of dispensing the Interior Department's patronage with his usual zest. He sympathized with the feeling among Democrats that Republicans had monopolized the Federal offices so long that it was only fair for Democrats to replace them. He could understand the admonition of one man, who wrote to urge "that all hell possible be visited upon our dear friends, the enemy," and he was soon earning the plaudits of Southerners for "turning the rascals out." [24] When Cleveland decided to use political offices in an effort to strengthen the administration in its fight for sound money, Smith did his part.

The Secretary did not hesitate to use his patronage powers to strengthen his own faction in Georgia. It was difficult for him to turn down the recommendations of such close political allies as Pope Barrow and John B. Gordon. So attentive was Smith to Georgia that one Republican wag was moved to write, "We once marched through Georgia under General Sherman, but now Georgia—under the leadership of Mr. Secretary Smith— is marching through us." [25] Eventually the President cautioned Smith about his Georgia appointments. As the Secretary said later, "I told him I had finished taking care of his active friends in the state." Earlier a friend of the administration had been moved to write of his fear that Smith and Commissioner Lamoreaux, "in their effort to obtain men whom they personally knew to be honest, have appointed too many men from Georgia and Wisconsin." [26]

[23] Smith to Frank M. Thompson, April 12, 1893, *ibid.*, Outgoing Letterbook, XIII, 440; A. Bower Sageser, *The First Two Decades of the Pendleton Act: A Study of Civil Service Reform*, Vols. XXXIV-XXXV in the University Studies of the University of Nebraska (Lincoln, 1935), 188; *Harper's Weekly*, XXXVII (December 23, 1893), 1218.

[24] Atlanta *Journal*, July 12, September 16, October 18, 1893; Harvey Johnson to Smith, undated (February, 1893), in Smith Collection, MS. Scrapbook.

[25] Quoted by Champ Clark, in *My Quarter Century of American Politics* (New York, 1920), I, 250.

[26] Milton McDonald to Richard Olney, December 15, 1893, in Olney

The anti-Smith element in Georgia soon declared that Smith was trying to control all of the Federal patronage in the state " to satisfy old personal grudges," especially in the Atlanta district, and the Atlanta *Constitution* sought without success to create a break between the Secretary and Senator Gordon over the patronage. At the very beginning of the administration the *Constitution* did succeed in embarrassing Smith by stating, no doubt with tongue in cheek, that Georgia was entitled to 2,487 Federal positions, and by suggesting that those interested apply to the Interior Department.[27]

Meanwhile, the Republicans were taking advantage of the display of partisanship by such Cabinet members as Smith and Carlisle. Republican newspapers furiously attacked leading Democrats, while recounting the " clean sweep " of Republican officeholders. As Champ Clark said of the attack on Hoke Smith, they "smote him hip and thigh, treated him with contumely and scorn, and metaphorically danced war jigs upon him." [28] When, for instance, a minor clerk in the Pension Bureau was dismissed because of inefficiency, the Republican press denounced Smith for days and challenged his patriotism because the clerk claimed to be the granddaughter of Francis Scott Key. " The dominant element in the Southern Democracy cares nothing for the Stars and Stripes," asserted a New York newspaper.[29]

Smith also came under fire in Congress. Representative John

Papers (Division of Manuscripts, Library of Congress); Smith Collection, " Memorandum for Mr. Parker," undated.

[27] Atlanta *Constitution*, March 14, 16, 17, April 1, 2, 1893; Atlanta *Journal*, March 18, 23, 25, 27, 1893.

Smith received much praise for his decision to appoint a number of Georgia boys to minor positions in order that they could attend night school in Washington. "I have the gratification of knowing," he declared long afterward, " that there are several good lawyers, a number of excellent doctors, and a number of high-class engineers who utilized the opportunity during my service here to attend night school, doing efficient work during the day as messengers. . . ." *Cong. Record*, 64 Cong., 2 Sess., 1815-16.

[28] Clark, *My Quarter Century of American Politics*, II, 291.

[29] Clippings from Hartford (Conn.) *Post*, July 10, 1893; New Orleans *Times-Democrat*, July 13, 1895; New York *Mail and Express*, July 18, 22, 25, August 13, 1895; New York *Advertiser*, July 25, 1895, in Smith scrapbooks.

L. Wilson of Washington, for example, appeared to take special delight in casting ridicule at the Secretary, and other Congressional opponents made exaggerated charges against his appointment policy. Much of the criticism leveled at Smith in Congress stemmed from the Representatives' opposition to the appointment of any outsider to a Federal position in their state, regardless of his home state or section.[30]

Demands by party members and friends, and his own willingness to reward the faithful, made it difficult for Smith to reconcile his liberality in giving out offices and his professed belief in civil service reform. Theodore Roosevelt, a zealous member of the Civil Service Commission during this period, soon expressed his doubts about Smith's sincerity in the application of the civil service rules. Roosevelt, who sometimes engaged "in a rough and tumble argument" with Smith, was certain, in his own inimitable way, that the Interior Secretary was a spoilsman. He felt that the Interior Department, along with the State and Treasury departments, had "gone back" in civil service reform during the early months of the new administration.[31] In August, 1893, Roosevelt asserted that in several of the Interior Department bureaus there had been "sweeping reductions of Republicans who were in the classified service, and a very considerable number of dismissals of them and corresponding promotions of Democrats."[32] The New York *Tribune* claimed that the "ingenious Democrats," including Hoke Smith, were getting around the civil service regulations by reducing the salaries of men they could not dismiss, thus humiliating them to such an extent that they often resigned. "Civil Service Reform is thus flouted and spit upon by the party which is never tired of proclaiming that 'public office is a public trust.'"[33]

[30] *Register of the Interior Department* (1897), 15-16, 30-31, 50-57; *Cong. Record,* 53 Cong., 2 Sess., 6067-70; *Harper's Weekly,* XXXVIII (March 3, 1894), 203.

[31] Theodore Roosevelt to Carl Schurz, August 23, 1893, to Anna Roosevelt, January 7, May 27, 1894, to William Dudley Foulke, February 10, 1894, to Smith, April 7, 1894, and to Lucius Burrie Swift, August 14, 1894, in Elting E. Morison (ed.), *The Letters of Theodore Roosevelt* (Cambridge, Mass., 1951-54), I, 328, 334-35, 345, 362, 371, 393-94.

[32] Roosevelt to Schurz, August 23, 1893, *ibid.,* 336.

[33] New York *Tribune,* July 10, 1893.

This testimony was not altogether free from partisanship, but there was a large amount of truth in it. Nevertheless, it does not provide the whole story of Hoke Smith's activities in this field, for he made some effort to abide by the civil service rules. Following the criticism of some appointments in Indian schools, he co-operated with the Civil Service Commission in conducting a thorough investigation of the status of teachers in such schools. He wrote Commissioner John R. Proctor, "It is my earnest desire to aid in establishing a permanent, nonpartisan, and efficient Indian-school service, and the rules governing the classified service should certainly be applied wherever practicable." Early in 1894 Smith initiated action to effect this reform, and for this step the Civil Service Commission declared that he was "greatly to be commended." [34]

Smith also co-operated with President Cleveland in later extensions of the classified service in his department. In July, 1895, the classified list was extended to all Pension Bureau employees; during the same year the Census Division and the Government Printing Office forces were classified, and in March, 1896, employees of Indian agencies and schools not before classified were covered by the rules. This scarcely qualified Smith as a civil service reformer, since it was a common practice for the party in power to add to the classified list. Late in 1895, *Harper's Weekly* noted that while the Georgian "was by no means an ardent civil service reformer when he entered upon his office, [he] is . . . zealously exerting himself to rescue the different branches of the service under his control from what grasp the spoils system still has upon them." A modern student of the civil service movement has given what is perhaps a fair evaluation of his position: "At the beginning of the administration . . . Smith abused the merit system, but he was a good secretary. When he left office he was pronounced a far better friend of reform than he had been in 1893." [35]

[34] *Eleventh Report of the United States Civil Service Commission, July 1, 1893, to June 30, 1894* (Washington, 1895), 11, 291-95; Roosevelt to Swift, February 1, 1894, in Morison (ed.), *Letters of Theodore Roosevelt*, I, 358.

[35] *Harper's Weekly*, XXXIX (December 28, 1895), 1232; Sageser, *First Two Decades of the Pendleton Act*, 177, 188.

If his new position brought control of large amounts of Federal patronage, a good deal of which could be distributed in his native section, it also brought him an opportunity to speak from the national stage as a propagandist of the New South. Many Southerners were optimistic about the role that he might play in this respect. Jabez L. M. Curry, who belonged to the new order no less than to the old, expressed his hopes for Hoke Smith by exclaiming: " What a magnificient opportunity for a young, capable, ambitious man to do good and make a lasting and honorable reputation! " [36] To understand Smith's own hopes along this line, it is necessary to examine his ideas about the South.

While Smith looked forward to a New South built on industrial and agricultural progress, and underpinned by a better educated citizenry, while he urged Southerners to be undeviating in their loyalty to the Union, he held firmly to many shibboleths of an older South. His analysis of the social structure of the Old South, for example, followed the well-known stereotype for the most part, although there were significant exceptions. Slavery, he insisted, had divided the South's population into three classes: the wealthy slaveowners, " cultivated, generous, and brave "; the poor whites, who competed with the slaves and had little opportunity to improve their condition; and the slaves, who were compelled to work for a bare existence. " Had it not been for the institution of slavery," which checked white immigration, destroyed the land, and hindered development in general, declared Smith, " the South, with natural resources in its favor in 1860, would have been the greatest manufacturing and mining, as well as agricultural, section in the Union." [37]

There were also other factors, argued Smith, that explained why the South had fallen behind the North and the West in economic development. Among these he emphasized Reconstruction. Like most Southerners of his day, he considered Radical Reconstruction " criminally stupid," and he deplored the use of Negroes by " designing men who moved South," although he conceded that " in time some of the men who came South for

[36] Curry to Smith, February 19, 1893, in Smith Collection, MS. Scrapbook.
[37] Hoke Smith, " The Resources and Development of the South," in *North American Review*, CLIX (August, 1894), 130-31.

political control turned their attention to business, and developed
into good citizens." Following Reconstruction, and especially
after 1880, said Smith, Southern economic progress had been
marked.[38]

To Hoke Smith the South of the nineties was a wonderful
panorama of economic opportunities—awaiting the magic power
of capital investment and Southern enthusiasm to spin the factory
wheels, elevate the economy, and bring a thousand good things
to the region. The South itself had much to offer, declared
Smith: abundant resources, good climate, and the " conservatism "
of its people. What it needed was outside capital, industrial
development, and immigration.

The Georgian continually sought to advertise Southern resources and to induce capital to flow southward.[39] He applauded
any scheme " to bring men from the South and men from the
North East, and West who have interests in the South, into closer
fraternal and business relations with each other." He urged the
advantages of establishing manufacturing plants in the localities
where raw materials were produced, and in addresses delivered
at the Augusta Exposition in 1893, at the Southern Industrial
Congress in 1894, and before various business groups in the
Northeast this was a favorite theme. Smith gave countless interviews in which he painted roseate pictures of Southern conditions
and possibilities. He was one of the moving spirits in the work
of the Georgia Immigration Bureau, an organization with
grandiose plans during the 1890's, one of which was to encourage
Northern veterans to settle in the South. He suggested the establishment of a Georgia development and information agency to
publicize the state's resources and offered the use of " facilities
growing out of my being a member of the cabinet " to accomplish
its end.[40] The Atlanta *Journal* had become a constant advocate of

[38] *Ibid.*; " The Possibilities and Responsibilities of North Carolina," commencement address by Smith at the University of North Carolina, 1894,
in Smith scrapbooks; New York *Times*, June 7, 1894.

[39] See, for example, his effort to persuade the Treasury Department to
purchase Georgia granite for some of its buildings. Atlanta *Journal*,
February 2, 1895.

[40] Smith to Patrick Walsh, December 28, 1893, in William J. Northen
Collection (Georgia State Department of Archives and History); Atlanta

Northern investment and Southern industrialization, and all kinds of articles calculated to demonstrate the logic of Southern industrial development found their way into its columns.

Smith was deeply interested in the Cotton States and Industrial Exposition held in Atlanta during the last months of 1895. Conceived by Atlanta businessmen, its goal was to promote Southern industry, especially cotton manufacturing, to exhibit the agricultural and manufacturing resources of the South, and to foster commerce between the South and other sections and countries. "It will broaden the views of the southern people themselves," declared Hoke Smith, "and will attract the attention of the world to the splendid resources of the southern states." He lent his assistance to the Georgia delegation that went to Washington to request an appropriation from Congress, and he arranged for the President and several Cabinet members and their wives to attend.[41]

Smith was particularly optimistic over the Southern economic outlook after several tours of the region in 1895. "I have never seen the South look so prosperous," he reported. He talked about a Southland of diversified economy, prosperous farmers, booming mills, and eager capital. Many Southern journals were highly pleased by these observations. Some observers, however, asserted that Smith's favorable reports were designed as propaganda to quiet unrest and criticism within the South aimed at the administration of which he was a spokesman.[42] Some Northern newspapers expressed the opinion that Smith was being "used by Southern industrial boomers who wish to induce Northern capital to flow toward and into the South."[43]

There were two other subjects that Hoke Smith emphasized in discussing progress in the New South. One was his attitude toward Negroes, the other was his interest in education. Like

Journal, December 13, 1893, August 7, 1894; Smith, "The Atlanta Exposition," in clipping from New York *Independent,* undated, and numerous newspaper clippings, Smith scrapbooks.

[41] Atlanta *Journal,* August 15-18, 25, September 5, December 5, 1894, September 23, October 22-24, 1895.

[42] See, for example, clippings from Augusta *Chronicle,* June 7, 1894, and New York *Tribune,* August 7, 1895, in Smith scrapbooks.

[43] See various editorial comments, in Smith scrapbooks.

Thomas Nelson Page and Basil Gildersleeve, who lovingly depicted the harmonies of race relations in the Old South, Smith eulogized the paternalistic approach toward Negroes in his day. "It is by the influence of the more intelligent whites," he declared, "that the best legislation and the best help can be given." He was emphatic in his opposition to social equality, but there was no doubt in his mind that Negroes, a "kind and hardy race," were in the South to stay. "Perhaps the negro is intended as the laborer to manufacture cotton as well as to hoe it," he observed on one occasion. He reminded Negroes of the "broken promises and disappointed hopes" of Reconstruction and referred to the sectional utterances of the North as an irritating factor in the relations between the two races in the South. In an article which appeared in the *Forum* during the campaign of 1892, the Georgian denounced the Force Bill as a scheme "to destroy home rule and local control." If the Southern people were appealed to "as a matter of justice in behalf of a weaker race, they are kind and generous, forbearing and sympathetic." But he warned that if the mass of white people had their "prejudices reinflamed," they "would not follow the conservative men of their own race." [44]

In some ways Smith's position was a moderate one. He regarded the Negro with genuine favor as a free laborer, conceded to him the ballot, and urged that he be educated. "What advances the mental and moral strength of your race adds to the power and security of our State and Nation," he wrote the trustees of Atlanta's Morris Brown College. "Passing by the higher obligation of every man who can to help those who need it, the interests of our entire section require that your people make the greatest possible progress, and I will be ready to contribute my part to such an end whenever the opportunity is presented." [45]

Although Hoke Smith placed strong faith in material advancement as a panacea for the South's difficulties, he believed that the foundation of material growth must rest upon the intellectual

[44] Smith, "The Disastrous Effects of a Force Bill," in *Forum*, XIII (August, 1892), 687-88, 690; Smith, "The Resources and Development of the South," *loc. cit.*, 132, 136.

[45] William H. Taylor to Smith, February 16, 1893, in Smith Collection, MS. Scrapbook; New York *Times*, June 7, 1895.

vigor and creative faculty of the people. A stanch individualist who undoubtedly was influenced by his own aggressive struggle to succeed, he thought the people of his region should be taught "what energy, industry, and opportunity can accomplish." Education was the touchstone. "My hearty sympathy goes out to those in our state who are giving their time to an earnest effort towards building up the educational interests of the state," he declared. "To strengthen the minds of our boys and girls is to bestow upon them wealth which in turn will develop the limitless resources of our state. . . ."[46]

In Washington, meanwhile, the Smiths had settled in an imposing house at 1623 K Street. Furnished with all the appurtenances of the Gilded Age—fireplaces of colorful tile, ornamented ceilings, brocaded curtains, rich carpets, and stuffed chairs—it was a "roomy, comfortable old dwelling." The Smiths participated in the social life of the administration, though they were hardly social leaders. Birdie Smith was unmistakably a Southern hostess, and at one gala dinner party in honor of the Clevelands, she served a menu composed of famous Southern dishes, adeptly prepared by the old family cook, to notables who dined under a canopy of Southern-grown camellias.

There were frequent comments on the society pages of the capital's newspapers about the "handsome and cordial" Secretary of Interior. Now and then a reference to the more reserved Mrs. Smith would appear. She "is a beauty and a lady of fine presence and equally fine accomplishments," reported the New York *Herald*. Birdie had a sharp mind and a keen wit. While shy, she met people with "warm cordiality" and in an "easy, naturally graceful way." There was nothing of the "new woman" about her; she was exceedingly domestic, and her life was bound up with her home and family.[47]

In the midst of his busy schedule, Hoke Smith found some time for his children. He enjoyed a bearish romp with Marion, a boy of nine in 1893, and with five-year-old Mary Brent, who

[46] Smith to S. B. Morris and others, May 13, 1891, in Smith Collection, Legal Letterbook (1891).
[47] Atlanta *Journal*, November 9, 1895; Richfield (N. Y.) *Mercury*, quoted in Atlanta *Journal*, December 2, 1893.

was "plump and blond and merry." By this time there was a third child, Lucy, who was born in 1892, and another daughter was born in 1895. Sometimes Marion accompanied his father on the older man's horseback rides over the city, the lad astride a "little dapple-gray pony." Riding, in fact, was one of Smith's chief diversions, and he often rode his horse to his office or to Cabinet meetings.

Within a few months after entering the Cabinet, Hoke Smith had settled down to the routine of his work with considerable poise. Much remained to be learned, but he had come to know the magnitude of his work and the difficulty of the decisions that daily confronted him. A year after he became Secretary, a fellow Democrat defended him against attack in Congress by declaring that the Georgian had exhibited "as much aptness for details, combined with as much comprehension of the larger concerns belonging to his Department, as any other member of the Cabinet." [48] Perhaps this was too flattering an estimate. But even his enemies had to admit that Smith approached his responsibilities with enthusiasm and industry.

[48] Benjamin E. Russell, in *Cong. Record*, 53 Cong., 2 Sess., 2690.

Secretary of the Interior at Work

The numerous responsibilities of the Interior Department in the 1890's are nowhere better illustrated than in Hoke Smith's annual reports. The Secretary's summary reports, sometimes running to more than one hundred pages, were part of the multivolumed report prepared by the various bureaus and offices every year. The information in these volumes related to such diverse functions of the Interior Department as the preparation of the census reports and the granting of patents. One subject that always received major consideration was the department's administration of the Federal pension system.

By 1893 there were almost a million pensioners, receiving over $156,000,000 annually, or almost one third of the entire expense of operating the government. President Cleveland had demonstrated his hostility toward the ever-increasing pension list during his first administration. That inveterate reformer Carl Schurz called the pension system "a biting satire on democratic government. Never has there been anything like it in point of extravagance and barefaced dishonesty. Everybody knows this; but the number of men in public life who have courage enough to admit that they know it is ludicrously small."[1] Schurz was not far wrong. The pressure exerted by the Grand Army of the Republic and the political dynamite in the pension question had continually

[1] *Harper's Weekly*, XXXVIII (May 5, 1894), 410.

precipitated more generous pension legislation. Furthermore, the lax administration of the pension laws allowed applicants with the weakest possible claims, as well as some who were guilty of "wholesale and gigantic frauds," to be admitted to the rolls.[2]

Hoke Smith was aware of the opportunity to effect important reforms in the handling of the Federal pensions. "With your magnificent energy and the aid of some honest Northern Democrat as the head of the Pension bureau," declared a fellow Georgian early in 1893, "many millions ought to be saved annually by the elimination of frauds now upon the pension rolls."[3] In May, 1893, Smith made his first important pension decision; he revoked the notorious " Order No. 164," which had been promulgated in October, 1890, by Commissioner of Pensions Green B. Raum. Commissioner Raum had given the act of 1890 an interpretation which proved highly advantageous to persons with minor disabilities not of service origin. Later investigations threw additional light on the low moral tone prevailing in the Raum administration.

Under Smith and Commissioner Lochren a board of revision was established in the Pension Bureau, "with instructions to examine the cases allowed under the act of June 27, 1890, and to cull out such as had no legal basis to rest upon." Within a few months thousands were suspended or given reduced pensions, but, possibly because of the vociferous protests raised against the new policy, a majority of those suspended were readmitted to the pension rolls after re-examination.[4] In August, 1893, Smith approved certain changes in the bureau's procedure for re-examining the cases allowed under the law of 1890, apparently to provide somewhat more liberal regulations than he and Lochren had at first laid down. Smith reported late in 1895 that the

[2] Two important measures that contributed to the increased pension burden were the Arrears of Pension Act of 1879 and the Disability Pension Act of 1890. William H. Glasson, *Federal Military Pensions in the United States* (New York, 1918), 163-64, 234-35.

[3] J. A. Anderson to Smith, February 11, 1893, in Smith Collection, MS. Scrapbook.

[4] *Interior Report* (1893), I, xxxii; *Cong. Record*, 53 Cong., 2 Sess., 364; Glasson, *Federal Military Pensions*, 228, 239-40.

board of revision's work was almost completed, and that 4,149 persons had been dropped and 20,359 reduced to lower ratings.[5]

The Pension Bureau's special examination division was expanded during Smith's administration of the department, and Lochren stated late in 1893 that 2,753 cases were pending in which fraud was alleged or suspected. Assistant Secretary Reynolds pushed through a reorganization of the board of pension appeals in the Secretary's office. More equitable rules of practice governing the recognition and fees of pension attorneys were promulgated.[6] Following Smith's suggestion, Congress passed a bill designed to clarify the rules for paying accrued pensions. Smith was also responsible for the creation early in 1896 of a division of pension affairs in his office which brought all matters relating to pensions into one division under the Assistant Secretary's supervision. "The result has been to harmonize and systematize this work," wrote Smith's successor, David R. Francis, "and has led to its greater expedition in the hands of a competent force."[7]

During the second Cleveland administration the spiraling cost of the Federal pensions was checked, but despite the vigilance displayed by the administration, the President sorrowfully reported in his annual message of 1896 that "the diminution of our enormous pension roll and the decrease of pension expenditure, which have been so often confidently foretold, still fail in material realization."[8] That Hoke Smith wavered before the reaction which some of his orders precipitated cannot be doubted. But basically the hope that Cleveland voiced could not be realized without Congressional direction, for it was in Congress that fundamental pension policy was determined and the Congressmen were in a liberal mood as far as the veterans were concerned.

For the reforms they attempted, Smith and Lochren were denounced from one end of the land to the other. Democratic

[5] *Cong. Record*, 53 Cong., 2 Sess., 407; *Interior Report* (1895), I, xxvii.

[6] *Interior Report* (1893), I, xxxi, III, 50-60; *ibid.* (1894), I, xxi; *ibid.* (1896), I, xxxi; *Cong. Record*, 53 Cong., 2 Sess., 372-73.

[7] *Interior Report* (1896), I, xxxi. See also Smith to John M. Palmer, March 29, 1894, in Department of Interior Papers, Patents and Miscellaneous Letterbook, XLIII (hereinafter cited as Patents letterbooks).

[8] James D. Richardson (comp.), *A Compilation of the Messages and Papers of the Presidents, 1789-1897* (Washington, 1896-1899), IX, 736.

Congressmen and newspapers defended them, but most Republicans acted as if Smith had taken the advice of a South Carolina Democrat who had urged him early in the administration to give the Pension Bureau "a shaking up," to rid it of the influence of the "Grand old humbug *Robber* Tariff, Force Bill and negro domination Republican Party." [9] Republicans criticized Smith's "cowardly reduction of pensions" and his "Bourbon" policy of withholding from the Grand Old Men in Blue the subsistence necessary to keep body and soul together. The Toledo *Blade* declared that the tomb of an old soldier in that city should be inscribed with the words: "Alexander Cavashere . . . Killed by Hoke Smith, September 3, 1893." The editorials of many Southern editors who thought they correctly interpreted Smith's policy as one of completely reversing earlier pension orders added fuel to the flames of the Northern hostility toward Smith and Lochren. [10] The onslaught had its political overtones, for the members of the G. A. R. were urged to "vote as you shot." Numerous bills and resolutions were introduced in Congress designed to nullify pension orders or to investigate the work of the Pension Bureau. Representatives Jacob Gallinger and Joseph G. Cannon were particularly outspoken in their denunciation of a policy "akin to crime"—one applied with a "niggardly and technical exactness." [11]

Another responsibility of the Interior Department was its supervision of the country's 250,000 Indians. They were concentrated on 161 reservations comprising some 86,000,000 acres of land, much of which was coveted by white men. Gradually, in the wake of a generation of Indian wars and such work as the annual Lake Mohonk conferences on Indian affairs, a growing concern for the plight of the Indians emerged. Most reformers felt that the best solution to the Indian problem lay in the dissolution of the tribes, the admission of Indians to citizenship, and the distribution of land to them in severalty. Grover Cleveland and L. Q. C. Lamar had endorsed this approach during the first Cleveland

[9] James A. Shuler to Smith, May 21, 1893, in Department of Interior Papers, Appointment Division, File 538.
[10] See numerous clippings in Smith scrapbooks.
[11] *Cong. Record*, 53 Cong., 1 Sess., 1185, 2127; 2 Sess., 279, 307, 2689.

administration, and Hoke Smith soon became an advocate of the same policy.

As he came to know more about Indian affairs, Smith assumed an optimistic attitude. In his first report, for example, he declared that "slowly, but steadily, these wards of the nation are being advanced to a condition suited for citizenship." The problem, Smith thought, was ". . . first, to distribute the Indians upon well-selected pieces of land, and then to require them to do such skillful work upon their farms as will put an end in the shortest possible time to the heavy charge which now rests upon the Government for their support. In addition to this, of course, the schools upon the reservation should advance the children mentally and morally as rapidly as possible." [12]

Much depended upon the Indian agent, "the most important instrumentality for the development of the Indian," in the Secretary's opinion. He felt that something of the missionary spirit "should be in the heart of every employe at an Indian agency or Indian school." In time, Smith recommended the application of the civil service rules to all workers in the Indian service.[13] Yet the Georgian was criticized for some of the appointments he made to these positions, and he conceded that during the first few months "we made changes too fast." [14]

The Boston *Congregationalist* described Hoke Smith as "a Christian man" who "takes a Christian view of the Indian problem." But if he looked kindly upon the Indians, there was nothing sentimental in his proposals for their advancement. When the Indians proved shiftless and lazy, he urged the agents to "put them to work, and . . . teach them that they will obtain nothing from the Government or in any way except as the result of their own efforts." [15] He believed that the Indians should demonstrate

[12] *Interior Report* (1895), I, iv. See also *ibid.* (1893), I, xvi, and *Cong. Record*, 64 Cong., 2 Sess., 2110.

[13] *Interior Report* (1895), I, vi; *ibid.* (1896), I, xxxvii; Atlanta *Journal*, January 25, 1895; Smith to all Indian agents, November 22, 1894, in Department of Interior Papers, Indian Division, Letterbook, XCIV (hereinafter cited as Indian letterbooks).

[14] Clippings from Washington *Star*, May 23, 1893, and Lincoln (Neb.) *Journal*, May 2, 1895, in Smith scrapbooks.

[15] *Interior Report* (1893), I, xvii; *ibid.* (1894), I, iii, v; *ibid.* (1895), I, v;

their capacity to own land before receiving citizenship. When the Indian became a citizen, Smith wanted the government " to let him alone and leave him to take his place, surrounding him then with no more restraint and giving him no more than is accorded to other citizens." [16]

Smith's belief in " hard and useful work " found expression in his proposals for Indian education. He realized that some Indians would leave the reservations, but he confessed that he could " not help believing that by far the greater number of Indian children are to work out their future in connection with the resources upon the reservations of their respective tribes, and that that education, for the most part, is wisest which trains them in this direction." [17] Under the direction of Dr. W. N. Hailmann, superintendent of Indian schools, the school system was reorganized " with the view of making it purely and simply an educational department." Secretary Smith skillfully guided the department through a controversy involving government contributions to a number of sectarian schools that were maintained for Indians. " The schools have grown up," he pointed out. " Money has been invested in their construction. . . . I do not think it proper to allow the intense feeling of opposition to sectarian education . . . to induce the Department to disregard existing conditions." He suggested a compromise that proved acceptable.[18]

Hoke Smith spoke out against those who sought to invade the reservations with whisky and evil plans to take advantage of the red men. When some white men attacked a group of innocent Indian hunters at Jackson's Hole, Wyoming, he expressed indig-

Smith to chairman of Senate Appropriations Committee, July 9, 1894, in Indian Letterbook, XCIII; clippings from Boston *Congregationalist*, August 1, 1895, and other papers, in Smith scrapbooks.

[16] *Interior Report* (1894), I, iii-iv; *ibid.* (1895), I, v, ix.

[17] *Ibid.* (1893), I, xvi; *ibid.* (1894), I, v-vi; *ibid.* (1895), I, iii, vii.

[18] *Ibid.* (1893), I, xix; *ibid.* (1894), I, vi; *ibid.* (1895), I, vii; Smith to John W. Cadman, March 27, 1894, and to Commissioner of Indian Affairs, April 24, 1894, in Indian Letterbook, XCII; Herbert Welsh, " The Secretary of the Interior and the Indian Educational Problem—A Rift in the Cloud," report of the Indian Rights Association, January 10, 1894, in Smith Collection.

nation at such treatment of the Indians and requested the War Department to send troops to the area. " My desire," Smith wrote while investigating the charges of immoral conduct against one agent, " is that the facts be fully obtained, but in as quiet a manner as possible, so as not to affect the good name of the agent or the Indians if the charges made cannot be sustained." [19] He wanted the government to act as a " faithful trustee " in disposing of Indian lands, and he instructed the agents of his department " to act as the friend of the Indians in all their disputes with white men." They must not act as " representatives of white men who desire possession of these lands." [20]

The Georgian saw the dangers in too rapid a reduction of the reservations and opposed such a course. But at the same time, believing that the best hope for Indian progress lay in his imitation of the white man's culture, and understanding the " insatiable desire " of the white men for land, he was sympathetic with the general policy of reduction. He and Commissioner Browning managed to obtain the dissolution of several reservations, and they made a sustained effort through the Dawes Commission to persuade the Five Nations to give up their lands and tribal governments. According to Smith, mixed bloods and adopted citizens had secured control of their government, and they had everything to gain by coming " under an Administration favorable to their rights." Nevertheless, he agreed with Cleveland that the confidence of the Indians must be won, and that they themselves must " see the wisdom and advantage " of making the change.[21]

Although he favored the reduction of reservations, Smith would not be stampeded into indiscriminate openings. " There are ample public lands in the United States for home seekers," he wrote in 1894; " can we not be satisfied to allow to be administered in behalf of the Indians the little we have left them? " A few months later Dennis T. Flynn, delegate to Congress from the

[19] Smith to Paul Faison, February 3, 1894, to William M. Moss, March 28, 1894, and to George C. Pendleton, April 11, 1894, in Indian Letterbook, XCII.

[20] *Interior Report* (1894), I, iii-iv; *ibid*. (1895), I, x.

[21] *Ibid*. (1895), I, xx-xxi, lxxx.

Oklahoma Territory, made a "fierce and vehement" attack upon the Secretary for not opening the Wichita Indian reservation. Smith also incurred the hostility of Congressmen who opposed his system of reserving from entry mineral lands in the Uncompaghre reservation.[22]

The West had a real attraction for Smith, and it irritated him to have the Western press refer to him as a greenhorn who had never crossed the Mississippi River. In July, 1893, he and his family began a tour of the Indian agencies and reservations. Impressed with the wisdom of teaching the Indians practical things that would help them achieve economic independence, he was shocked to discover that "on one reservation there was not an Indian who could milk a cow." This word from the Secretary gave the anti-Smith newspapers a field day. A "capital remedy"—this milking solution—boomed the Atlanta *Constitution*. Imagine the "inspiring spectacle when the Honorable Hocus shall trip gaily to the corral, and surrounded by a bevy of fascinating and fascinated squaws, give them instruction in the bucolic art of milking a wild-eyed cow fresh from the range." [23]

Several Indian reformers felt that Smith was a genuine friend of the red man. George Bird Grinnell wrote early in 1896 that "there is substantial agreement among persons interested in such matters that Indian affairs have never been so well conducted as during the last two or three years. The Secretary of the Interior and his office and the Indian Bureau and its office seem to have made an honest effort toward a better treatment of the Indians and a more businesslike conduct of Indian affairs." In its reports of 1895 and 1896, the Indian Rights Association praised Smith for his work.[24]

The Indian problem was closely associated with the Interior Department's guardianship of the public domain. The depart-

[22] *Ibid.* (1894), I, iv; Atlanta *Journal*, December 16, 26, 1895; clippings from Birmingham *News*, December 17, 1895, and New York *Morning Advertiser*, December 26, 1895, in Smith scrapbooks.

[23] Atlanta *Constitution*, August 2, 1893; clipping from Salem (Ore.) *Statesman*, August 11, 1893, in Smith scrapbooks.

[24] New York *Tribune*, February 24, 1896; clippings from New York *Evangelist*, April 4, 1894; New York *Sun*, December 12, 1894; and Boston *Congregationalist*, August 1, 1895, in Smith scrapbooks.

ment was responsible for administering numerous land laws, and
for settling claims and contests involving settlers, railroads, and
states. It was under constant pressure from persons and corporations who wanted to exploit the grasslands, the timber, and the
minerals on the public lands.

In September, 1893, the spectacular opening of the " Cherokee
Outlet," a desolate sixty-mile stretch of 6,500,000 acres north of
the Oklahoma Territory, resulted in the disposition of one of
the last large tracts of the public domain to be claimed in the
old fashion. The land rush that attended the opening revealed
in microcosm all the restless adventure, the cupidity, and the
drama of the westward movement. The attention of the Secretary and the General Land Office had been focused on the
opening for weeks before the event took place. Smith exhibited
a keen interest in the matter and personally considered many of
the questions involved in the preparations. His first inclination
was to use some type of lottery in order to avoid a mad scramble,
but the legality of such a system was doubtful; in any case, as
the Lawrence (Kansas) *Journal* shrewdly observed, to deprive
a man of rushing to just the piece of land he wanted would " take
away all the fun of being a boomer." [25]

In this situation, plans were made for opening a number of
booths along the borders of the " Outlet," and beginning on
September 11, 1893, they were kept open ten hours a day. Certifi-
cates of claim were issued to those who could qualify for home-
stead or town sites. One newspaper reported that a multitude
" of restless, homeless people had been swarming upon the border
for weeks. . . . They suffered terrible hardships from the heat,
the dust, and from weariness." At exactly noon on September 16,
the " Cherokee Outlet " was opened with the firing of cannon
and carbines along the border. Over a hundred thousand certifi-
cates had been issued, and a hectic race by all kinds of men began.
What followed can be described best by one of the witnesses:
" The shouting of the men, the screaming of the women, the

[25] Clipping from Lawrence (Kans.) *Journal*, undated, in Smith scrapbooks;
Smith to Robert Oder, March 14, 1893, and to Abram J. Seay, March 18,
1893, in Indian Letterbook, XC; *Interior Report* (1893), I, xii; *Cong. Record*,
53 Cong., 1 Sess., 1894.

neighing of the frightened horses, the cracking of whips, the
creaking of prairie schooners, the rattling of wheels, the clatter of
hoofs and the explosion of fire-arms combined to make a confusion of sounds in keeping with the general confusion of the
start and to render the spectacle utterly indescribable." [26] It was
a wild and unforgettable scene.

Disillusionment followed hard on the heels of exaltation.
Thousands found themselves empty-handed when the race was
over; other thousands were dissatisfied with the land they did get.
Reports of speculation and of unfair methods used by cattle
barons and others soon began to reach Washington. Hoke Smith
himself stated that while the opening " was relieved of many
difficulties by the regulations legally made, yet it must be confessed that the manner of entry was not satisfactory." [27] A vigorous debate followed in the nation's press. Republicans and Populists made political capital out of the department's mistakes and
in the process Smith became a convenient victim. His registration
plan was denounced as red-tape folly and a " diabolical scheme ";
some newspapers even accused him of having populated the
" Outlet " with Southern colonels. The delegate from Oklahoma
inserted numerous letters and newspaper accounts in the *Congressional Record* purporting to show the existence of bribery,
inefficiency, and brutality on the part of Federal officials in the
" Cherokee Outlet." [28]

Administration supporters in Congress forced Dennis T. Flynn
to admit that the Interior Department officials were " doubtless
honest and sincere " in establishing the registration system. The
real difficulty, declared " Fightin' Joe " Wheeler of Alabama,
was that " there was very little land and a great many persons
who desired to enter. . . ." According to Representative William

[26] Clippings from Manchester (N.Y.) *Union*, September 18, 1893, Philadelphia *Methodist*, October 7, 1893, and numerous other newspapers, in
Smith scrapbooks.

[27] *Harper's Weekly*, XXXVII (September 30, 1893), 926; *Interior Report*
(1893), I, xiii.

[28] *Cong. Record*, 53 Cong., 1 Sess., 1824-27.

Following the rush, it was reported that Hoke Smith was so unpopular
in Oklahoma that settlers were naming their dogs, spavined horses, and
mules " Hoke! " See newspaper clippings in Smith scrapbooks.

K. Springer of Illinois, the Secretary had tried "to do justice to all the people in the Outlet" and had taken "the responsibility of locating the land offices at other places than the railroad stations, so that the new towns should be elsewhere than at the points where . . . speculators had made their locations. . . ." Smith's motives were good, asserted one Western newspaper, but they "have been impugned and what he intended to be for the good of genuine home-seekers has been turned into a weapon of attack upon him." [29]

Smith did indeed profess a determination to deal sympathetically with Western problems, and in after years he proudly recalled those occasions on which he had settled a contest in favor of small farmers. He discovered almost at once that the department's decisions with respect to such matters as land claims and the allocation of timber and mineral rights were likely to be interpreted as either favorable or hostile to the railroads and other corporations. Coming to Washington with an anticorporation reputation, Smith found that many people expected him to decide against the corporations in all cases. After all, the New York *Sun* declared, "He has fought the grasping blood-sucking corporation in all its forms." [30]

Nevertheless, Smith was accused from the first of being sympathetic with the railroads in the contests before his department. There were rumors, for instance, that he had been the choice of Henry Villard of the Northern Pacific Railroad to head the Interior Department, and that his selection had been supported by conservatives like Senator William F. Vilas, some of whom were closely associated with Western corporations. To the delight of his enemies, Smith was accused of collusion with large land rings, of rendering decisions against homesteaders and in favor of railroads, and of mismanaging the nation's resources. [31]

[29] *Cong. Record*, 53 Cong., 1 Sess., 1826, 1893-94; *Interior Report* (1893), III, 460; clipping from Kansas City *Star*, October 6, 1893, in Smith scrapbooks.

[30] Clipping from Spokane *Chronicle*, quoting New York *Sun*, undated, in Smith scrapbooks.

[31] Clippings from Palouse (Wash.) *News*, March 10, October 6, 1893, and other newspapers, in Smith scrapbooks.

In a much-publicized case involving the Michigan Land and Iron Company, in which Smith held that the corporation had legal title to a contested tract of land, the Secretary incurred the wrath of many homesteaders who felt that hundreds of thousands of acres of the public domain had been stolen by this powerful company. Smith concluded, however, that while the land had been wrongly certified to the corporation, nevertheless, under an act of 1887, it had legal title to the area in dispute.[32] Acting under a law passed in 1896, the Secretary also endorsed Commissioner Lamoreaux's recommendation that several suits against railroads be withdrawn, following the submission of evidence indicating that railroad lands had been disposed of to bona fide purchasers.[33] Apparently Smith and other department officials were sometimes guilty of favoritism. A Wisconsin Democratic leader named Edward C. Wall, an associate of William F. Vilas, had a profitable arrangement with the Northern Pacific Railroad receivers that allowed him a fee for every acre of government-confiscated land he recovered for the company. According to Wall, his success was the result in large part of his friendship with Vilas, Lamoreaux, and Smith.[34]

During Theodore Roosevelt's administration, Secretary of the Interior Ethan A. Hitchcock aroused nationwide attention when he described a lease of the oil rights on the Osage Indian reservation, negotiated by the Interior Department in 1896, as " nothing short of a public scandal." Smith immediately went to Washington, checked the records, and issued a statement defending the lease and calling Hitchcock's charges " misleading and deceptive." He argued that at the time the lease was signed there seemed " scant hope " of discovering oil in the Osage country; he also asserted that the lease was " carefully guarded with provisions and forfeitures unless the work of prospecting and mining was

[32] Clippings from Chicago *Herald*, September 27, 1894, and Detroit *News*, September 15, 1895, in Smith scrapbooks.

[33] Smith to Lamoreaux, June 9, 1893, and to the Attorney General, April 2, 25, 1896, in Department of Interior Papers, Land and Railroad Division, Letterbooks No. 267, No. 327 (hereinafter cited as Land and Railroad letterbooks).

[34] Horace Samuel Merrill, *William Freeman Vilas, Doctrinaire Democrat* (Madison, Wis., 1954), 214.

prosecuted with diligence." Smith was indignant at Hitchcock's statement, but as a South Carolina paper remarked, "Admit everything Mr. Smith claims, and still there is room for legitimate inquiry as to whether the Government should have granted concessions under which a 'gigantic monopoly' was possible." [35]

Many of Hoke Smith's decisions were against the railroads. In his first important land decision, the Georgian ruled that the Southern Pacific Railroad had not acquired title to valuable lands along its route in California, and that the land must be thrown open to settlement. The decision "vindicates his reputation as a terror to railroads," declared a Maine newspaper, while a New York journal asserted that it would set "a precedent in similar cases for the restoration of the lands so lavishly and recklessly squandered on railroad speculators." [36] Early in the administration Smith directed Lamoreaux to call on the railroads to revise their lists of indemnity selections within six months, so that all land not properly held might be disposed of under the rules for restoring indemnity land. He urged the Attorney General to

[35] Atlanta *Journal*, February 17-19, 22, 23, 1905; clipping from Charleston *News & Courier*, February 20, 1905, in Smith scrapbooks.

Another case threatened to embarrass Smith during the Wilson administration. In January, 1896, the Interior Department had issued a patent to the Southern Pacific Railroad, despite a protest filed with the department by the California Miners' Association which contended that the land being patented possessed valuable minerals and should therefore be excepted under Federal laws. Attorney General Thomas W. Gregory informed Smith in 1914 that his department faced the difficult task of "explaining and excusing the Government for the issuance of the patent." Smith conferred several times with Justice officials and appears to have claimed that Southern Railroad representatives deceived the Interior Department as to the true character of the land in question. A special assistant in the Justice Department was startled in 1914 to find how much land the Southern Pacific obtained in the 1890's to which it was not entitled. "It seems to me," he declared, "to be very strange that so many things favorable to the Railroad Company should 'just happen' without design during this period." See Ernest Knaebel to Smith, March 26, 1913; E. J. Justice to the Attorney General, August 21, 1914, and to Clay Tallman, January 5, 1915; Thomas W. Gregory to Smith, December 5, 1914, in Department of Justice Papers (National Archives).

[36] Clippings from Portland (Me.) *Advertiser*, March 25, 1893, and New York *World*, March 25, 1893, in Smith scrapbooks.

take steps to protect certain settlers holding patents for land
within the indemnity limits of some of the railroads, and he
restored to entry land claimed by various roads, including the
Atlantic and Pacific, and the Northern Pacific.[37]

Smith and Lamoreaux endeavored to recover land erroneously
or illegally patented to railroads, but the roads held tenaciously
to their claims, often resorting to the courts. In a comprehensive
statement to the President, in December, 1895, the Secretary
pointed out the exasperating legal difficulties that confronted
the department in this work.[38] He also complained that the
department was unable under existing laws to determine satisfactorily which of the lands claimed by land grant railroads
were "mineral lands," and thus not patentable to the roads; and
in an effort to avoid previous mistakes he promulgated a more
definite procedure for the land commissioner to follow. Smith
objected to legislation designed to permit corporations that leased
public lands to sublease without obtaining the department's prior
consent.[39] In later years a Republican Senator from the West
praised the Georgian's effort to be fair in these matters: "I
appeared before [him] . . . when he was Secretary of the Interior
many times on important business connected with . . . western
irrigation and public-land matters, and I am frank to say that . . .
he had surrounded himself with men who had placed him in a
position so that he could render an honest, fair decision, and in
every case it was. . . ."[40]

When the bond-aided railroads began to falter in carrying out
their obligations to the government, some of them on the brink
of foreclosure, Smith warned that it was "impossible for Congress
longer to postpone action with regard to these bonds and the
property upon which they constitute a lien." By early 1895,

[37] Smith to Commissioner of General Land Office, May 13, 1893, in Land
and Railroad Letterbook, No. 267; *Interior Report* (1893), I, xiv, 48.

[38] Smith to Thomas C. McRae, January 7, 1895, and to Grover Cleveland,
December 27, 1895, in Land and Railroad letterbooks, No. 298, No. 320;
Interior Report (1893), I, xiv-xv; *ibid.* (1896), I, 57.

[39] Smith to James H. Berry, September 14, 1893, and to Silas W. Lamoreaux, July 9, 1894, in Land and Railroad letterbooks, No. 270, No. 290;
Smith to Grover Cleveland, August 17, 1894, in Patents Letterbook, XLIV.

[40] James H. Brady, in *Cong. Record*, 65 Cong., 1 Sess., 1791.

the Georgian had decided that it was "unquestionably advisable" for the department to patent no additional land to the delinquent railroads until an adjustment of their indebtedness could be made. In November, 1895, he ordered Lamoreaux to cease issuing patents to the bond-aided railroads.[41] Smith thought the government might have to assume the first-mortgage bonds the roads had sold, so that it could "secure its own claim." It could then foreclose and negotiate for the sale of the railroads. But foreclosure, Smith told a House committee, "does not imply Government ownership and operation of the railroads." The Secretary pointed out other violations by the roads of their original agreements and produced statistics to show that some of the companies had been operated more profitably than they would admit.[42]

Hoke Smith's firm stand evoked a chorus of approval from newspapers, many of which endorsed his proposal to move against the carriers. The Secretary was showing a "refreshing bluntness" about the whole thing, observed a California paper early in 1896. Yet no solution to the problem was reached during Smith's tenure, and his policy of withholding patents from unco-operative railroads was overthrown by a Congressional resolution in June, 1896.[43]

Smith's administration of the Interior Department brought about some real reforms in the machinery created to settle land contests and claims. Of the thousands of contest cases involving the disposal of public lands, many were appealed from the General Land Office to the Secretary's office, where they were first examined by the Assistant Attorney General for the department and ultimately decided by the Secretary. In order to facilitate this work in his office, Smith created a three-man board of review composed of the most experienced assistant attorneys to inspect the work of the seventeen assistant attorneys before it passed

[41] Smith to James H. Berry, February 20, 1895, and to Commissioner of General Land Office, December 11, 1895, in Land and Railroad letterbooks, No. 301, No. 320; *Interior Report* (1895), I, xliv-xlviii; *ibid.* (1896), I, lxiv.

[42] Atlanta *Journal*, September 22, 1894, November 15, 1895; *Interior Report* (1895), I, xlviii.

[43] *Interior Report* (1896), I, lxiv. For the public reaction to Smith's position, see various newspaper clippings in Smith scrapbooks.

to the immediate attention of the Assistant Attorney General.[44] In an effort to "curtail the opportunities for prolonged and vexatious litigation" Smith directed the General Land Office not to receive motions for "re-review" and second consideration, although a defeated party might still invite the attention of the Secretary's office to important points of law or fact not previously presented in the case. Seeking to correct faults on the local level, Smith "earnestly" recommended the passage of legislation to compel the attendance of witnesses and submission of written evidence at local hearings. He insisted that attorneys practicing before the department abide by the rules. As he wrote Lamoreaux, "There are many . . . whose pretentions to legal skill, erudition and honesty deceive and entrap the unwary but honest litigants, and it is the province of this Department, under the general powers conferred by statute, to protect as far as possible the public from such persons."[45]

Yet Smith was inclined to adopt a legalistic attitude in many cases, all the more perhaps because the system had so often been abused and pulled out of shape in the past. In a letter to a lawyer who had written a stirring appeal on behalf of a litigant in an appealed case, the Secretary admitted that the claimant's poverty commended him to the kindest consideration. Nevertheless, wrote Smith, "personal considerations can no more be allowed to enter into the judgment of a contest case before the Department than before the courts, and this must commend itself to all fair minded men as the only true course, for otherwise there would be no guarantee that one would receive justice in appeals to the Departments."[46]

In the field of conservation, Smith talked a great deal but accomplished relatively little. In his report of 1895, he described the need for a "comprehensive and practical" plan for reclaiming and disposing of the arid land, calling this one of the "most

---

[44] *Interior Report* (1894), I, xviii-xix; *ibid.* (1895), I, xvi, xcvii; Womack, *History of the Interior Department*, 5-6.

[45] Smith to Lamoreaux, June 11, 1896, in Patents Letterbook, XLVIII; *Interior Report* (1893), I, 30; *ibid.* (1894), I, xix.

[46] Smith to James Hamilton Lewis, July 11, 1894, in Land and Railroad Letterbook, No. 290.

important and pressing duties" facing Congress. Earlier Smith and Secretary of Agriculture Morton had established a joint board of irrigation to correlate the several lines of irrigation research and investigation being carried on by the two departments, but little had come from its report. Smith was inclined to believe that the best solution was to give the states "direct control" of the arid areas, and he suggested that if the Carey Act of 1894 were retained all desert lands as defined in the act of 1877 should be given outright to the states.[47]

The protection of the four national parks—the Yellowstone in Montana and Wyoming, and the Yosemite, Sequoia, and General Grant in California—presented the Interior Department with another problem of conservation, particularly in preventing "poachers" from taking the fish and game and destroying the timber. Smith took a personal interest in the Yellowstone and corresponded with its superintendent. A Congressional measure proposing to reduce this park by over a thousand square miles drew vigorous opposition from the Secretary, who contended that if the bill were enacted it would "only be the commencement of the turning of the entire reservation over to private interests, for if Congress diminishes these reservations . . . it cannot consistently refuse to take off other portions for restoration to the public domain." Theodore Roosevelt wrote to express his appreciation for "the stand you have taken in forestry matters and in the preservation of these parks."[48]

More important than the parks were the national forests and the timber on millions of acres of public land. "Information comes almost daily," declared an official of the General Land Office in 1893, "showing continued trespassing and depredating within the reserves, committed by lumbermen, prospectors, sheep herders, and others, and forest fires caused by the careless and vicious, resulting in irreparable damage. . . ."[49] Congress passed an act in 1891 authorizing the Secretary of Interior to permit

[47] *Interior Report* (1895), I, xvii-xix, 76; *ibid.* (1896), I, xvii, xix-xxii.

[48] Smith to Thomas C. McRae, March 30, 1894, in Patents Letterbook, XLIII; Roosevelt to Smith, April 7, 1894, in Morison (ed.), *Letters of Theodore Roosevelt*, I, 371.

[49] Clipping from New York *Sun*, October 29, 1893, in Smith scrapbooks.

the cutting of timber on the public domain; but as one newspaper commented, " The unscrupulous rapacity of some men in taking advantage of the opportunity afforded by the issuing of such permits, to steal timber for commercial purposes, has defeated the sole purpose for which the law was ever intended." Every Secretary of the Interior who tried to enforce the land laws, observed the New York *Journal of Commerce*, " finds himself working against an irresistible force." [50]

In the absence of remedial legislation, Smith and Lamoreaux did their best to conserve the public timber. The Secretary urged the Attorney General to take legal action against persons suspected of timber frauds, and many times he decided against granting permits to cut timber in cases passed on to him by Lamoreaux. After two and a half years in office, however, Smith conceded that his department was waging a losing battle, that the force in the General Land Office was inadequate to protect the timber, and that unless Congress devised some plan of protection the timber permit law would " utterly fail." [51] Lamoreaux's close association with Senator Vilas and his earlier involvement in Wisconsin timber deals made it difficult to convince the public that the department was really reform-minded about the public timber.[52]

During Hoke Smith's Cabinet service a significant step was taken in the evolution of a comprehensive forest policy. " The fact that timber is still plentiful," declared Smith in 1893, " should not blind our eyes to its present rapid removal, and to the condition which will confront the country a few years hence." [53]

[50] Clippings from Omaha *Bee*, May 4, 1893, and New York *Journal of Commerce*, September 11, 1895, *ibid.*

[51] Smith to Commissioner of General Land Office, April 8, May 13, September 27, October 17, 1893, April 26, 1894, and to the Attorney General, November 27, 1894, April 11, October 3, 1895, April 22, 1896, in Land and Railroad letterbooks, No. 263, No. 267, No. 274, No. 283, No. 297, No. 304, No. 315, No. 331; *Interior Report* (1894), I, xvii-xviii; *ibid.* (1895), I, xxii-xxiii.

[52] Merrill, *William Freeman Vilas*, 216-17; clippings from Racine (Wis.) *Journal*, March 5, 1894, and Chicago *Times*, November 18, 1894, in Smith scrapbooks.

[53] *Interior Report* (1893), I, ix.

For some years advocates of forestry reform had urged a comprehensive investigation of forest administration in the United States. In 1895, Professor Wolcott Gibbs, president of the National Academy of Sciences, Charles S. Sargent, Gifford Pinchot, and a few others set out to persuade the Interior Department to call on the National Academy of Sciences to undertake such an investigation. President Cleveland and Secretary Smith were approached, and agreed to the plan; Smith then wrote to Gibbs to request that the investigation be undertaken.[54] The Secretary pointed out the need for a "radical change" in existing policy and asked for an early report. Gibbs appointed six outstanding forestry and scientific leaders to carry out the investigation. Following Smith's recommendation Congress appropriated twenty-five thousand dollars to defray the expenses of the commission, which began work in July, 1896.[55] Smith's measure of praise for his part in the establishment of the commission was large. The *Nation* stated, for example, that "Secretary Smith has performed a genuine public service which will be remembered in his favor long after he has passed out of office."[56]

In dealing with Federal pensioners and the Indians Smith and his assistants introduced few drastic changes of policy. Handicapped from the beginning by patronage difficulties and partisan activities, only slowly did they achieve any real improvements. But administrative procedures were improved, civil service rules were applied, and some capable appointments were made to responsible positions. Aside from administrative ability, Hoke Smith demonstrated integrity and an infectious enthusiasm in his approach to these problems. This scarcely added up to successful reform, but it was a creditable record.

His work as a guardian of the public domain was not without mistakes, but as in other divisions of the department, he infused vigor and life into a lethargic establishment, and he demonstrated

---

[54] Gifford Pinchot, *Breaking New Ground* (New York, 1947), 86-89.

[55] Pinchot, *Breaking New Ground*, 89-90, 119; *Cong. Record*, 65 Cong., 2 Sess., 4949; *Interior Report* (1896), I, xiii-xv.

The commission prepared an extensive report which was not finally transmitted to the Interior Department until May, 1897.

[56] *Nation*, LXII (March 12, 1896), 208; clippings in Smith scrapbooks.

considerable administrative ability in handling such matters as
land case appeals. In dealing with problems involving land,
minerals, and timber, the Georgian had little knowledge; he had
to depend on others, and his policies were not always carried out
wisely by his far-flung subordinates, many of whom were appointed because of political considerations. If at times his judgments seemed to favor the big railroad companies, at other times
they went against those corporations. Fundamentally, Smith was
the victim of a system that had long encouraged the exploitation
of the public domain. He saw the need for greater efficiency and
honesty in the administration of the system—and he worked in
that direction—but in the main he himself accepted the rationale
that underlay the system.

The Fight For Sound Money

In the Cabinet Hoke Smith supported Grover Cleveland on almost every question. To him Cleveland was the essence of common sense, industry, and Christian gentleness; he admired the President's rugged courage in public life and his devotion to the principles of conservative Democracy. He never ceased to treasure his years of association with Cleveland and to pride himself upon his loyal support of the administration. The Southerner gave unstinted approval to the President's handling of the Hawaiian situation, the repeal of the Sherman Silver Purchase Act, the tariff-reform battle, and the aggressive diplomacy in the case of Venezuela. But the administration's struggle against free silver was the issue, running throughout the period of his Cabinet service, that proved to be the major test of the Georgian's loyalty to Cleveland and of his own position in Georgia politics.

Smith turned with a will to the role of chief administration spokesman in Georgia. With the control of a good deal of Federal patronage in the state and with the administration's backing, he doubtless anticipated a precious opportunity to deliver a blow to the local opposition within the party led by men like the Howells of the Atlanta *Constitution*. He handed out Federal appointments, he sent out Federal documents, he signed all Interior Department correspondence with people in Georgia, he tried to be a friendly source of help to Georgians who came to Washington, and he worked enthusiastically for the economic betterment of his state and section.

Smith's Cabinet position was a constant reminder to the Howells of their sharp defeat in 1892. They repeatedly condemned

Cleveland and the administration for departing from the Democratic platform and pursuing Republican policies. According to the *Constitution*, Hoke Smith was Cleveland's cuckoo, and the Atlanta *Journal* was Smith's parrot.[1] The *Constitution* editors used every opportunity to attack the Secretary, whether by criticizing his patronage policies, by reprinting attacks on his official decisions, or by giving publicity to the humorous columns from the New York *Sun*. The *Sun* had conceived the idea of printing Smith's name as "Hoax Myth" and it began a special column of "Hokeiana," treating the Georgian as a sort of myth and a hoax on the American people. The New York paper linked him with lugubrious Georgia characters it created, called "Dink Botts," "Pod Dismuke," and "Potsdam Sams," and had no end of fun. Other newspapers soon began to treat Smith in the same fashion. This amused him at first but when the *Constitution* and other Georgia papers began to reprint the *Sun's* witticisms, he ceased to enjoy them. The references to his Southern speech, to his huge figure, and to "Hoax Myth" began to irritate him. He stubbornly refused to engage in repartee with these partisan funsters, yet he was hurt and discomfited by his increasing notoriety.[2]

The petulant criticism of the administration by newspapers like the *Constitution* would not have been so serious had it not been for the growing agricultural depression in the South and the rising insurgency of the farmers in the region. When Cleveland made it clear that he was unalterably opposed to the free coinage of silver, a proposal that most Georgia farmers considered a sure means of economic relief, it was not difficult for his enemies to convince the farmers that he was in close touch with the Eastern money power, and that he was incapable of comprehending the suffering and poverty of the masses. The truth was that mounting debts, high interest rates, a deficiency of circulating money, and the discrimination by railroads had undermined the conservatism

[1] Atlanta *Constitution*, March 1, 12, 14, 22, April 30, August 29, 1893, April 5, 1894; Atlanta *Journal*, March 13, 14, 1893, May 23, 1894.

[2] Atlanta *Journal*, March 20, June 8, 12, 1893; New York *Sun*, April 3, 4, 1893, April 22, 1895; Nashville *American*, July 19, 1895; Daniels, *Editor in Politics*, 183.

of the farmer, leading him to espouse new and radical causes. The new political doctrines were strongest perhaps in the West, yet cheap cotton, increasing mortgages, and other grievances inspired revolt in the South, and as early as 1890 the Bourbon Democrats had been overwhelmed in Georgia, South Carolina, and Tennessee, and were on the run in other Southern states.

Sound-money men, who blamed the dwindling gold supply in the Treasury and the panic of 1893 on the government's silver-purchase policy, feared that the continued coinage of silver would lead to the substitution of the intrinsically inferior silver dollar for the gold one and increase the severity of the depression. Cleveland was determined to maintain the gold standard, however, and in June, 1893, called a special session of Congress to repeal the Sherman Silver Act. The Democrats were divided over the administration demand, and although Cleveland won this first battle, it was at the expense of losing the West, focusing the eyes of the discontented on William Jennings Bryan, and hurrying the South along the road to revolt. When the Treasury Department was compelled to float three bond issues within the next two years to maintain the gold reserve, the silver men were convinced that the "bloated aristocracy" of Wall Street was in control of the government.[3]

Hoke Smith urged the repeal of the Sherman Act, but he called himself a "strong bimetallist" rather than a single-standard man. He was inclined to favor the Bland bill for coining the silver seigniorage and other loose bullion in the Treasury, which Cleveland vetoed in 1894, and as late as July, 1895, he stated that under certain conditions it might be a good idea to coin the silver bullion in order to expand the currency.[4] But as for the demand for free and unlimited coinage, the Georgian joined with administration leaders in steadfastly opposing it.

During the months following the repeal of the silver act, it became apparent that the silver forces were gaining ground,

[3] James A. Barnes, "The Gold-Standard Democrats and the Party Conflict," in *Mississippi Valley Historical Review*, XVII (December, 1930), 425-27; Nevins, *Grover Cleveland*, 525-26.

[4] Daniels, *Editor in Politics*, 54. See also Atlanta *Journal*, May 3, June 23, July 22, August 10, 16, 18, 1893.

that the Democratic party itself was in danger of being captured by the silver leaders, and that free silver would be an important issue in the elections of 1894. Party conventions throughout the South and West soon proved that this was no idle threat, and more than twenty state platforms urged free coinage. In Georgia both candidates for the Democratic nomination for governor attacked the administration's currency policies and endorsed free silver. The Smith forces were unable to obtain an unqualified endorsement of the administration in the Fulton County Democratic convention in June, and they were dealt another blow when the state convention wrote a free-silver platform early in August.[5]

It was rumored in the Georgia press during the spring of 1894 that Smith would use his influence in the Georgia Congressional contests in an effort to bolster the administration. In July the Secretary issued a statement denying these reports.[6] But as fall approached the heat of the battle lured him to Georgia. He was unwilling to allow antiadministration Democrats to interpret the party doctrine and cast aspersions upon the Cleveland program. On a hot September evening in Atlanta, Smith began a three-week tour of Georgia in which he delivered ten addresses. In opening his campaign, he " divided time " with Charles Frederick Crisp, Speaker of the United States House of Representatives, a free-silver Democrat, and a member of the Howell wing of the party.

The popular Crisp spoke first. There was a note of moderation in his address, but his references to free silver drew great applause. When Smith arose, the closely packed crowd had been seated in the warm auditorium for two hours, and most of them apparently disagreed with the administration on the currency issue. But the Secretary received " as hearty applause as had Crisp." He reviewed the financial troubles of the past eighteen months and spoke of Georgia's marked recovery and of his faith in its future

---

[5] The state convention did endorse the state and national platforms of 1892, which was perhaps a moral victory for the Smith faction. Atlanta *Journal*, May 29, June 9, August 2, 3, 6, 1894.

[6] Smith to William J. Northen, April 13, 1894, in Smith Collection; Atlanta *Journal*, July 7, 1894; Atlanta *Constitution*, July 9, 1894.

prosperity. He compared the Republican "misrule" of the Harrison administration with the accomplishments of Cleveland's first term. On the currency question he spoke "from a straight administration point of view," although he did advocate as an inflationary step the removal of the Federal tax on state bank issues. Crisp had declared that legislation to coin silver would "afford great relief to the people," but Smith asserted that free silver would drive all the gold out of circulation, and he predicted dire results if the "wild vagaries of the Populists" were enacted.[7]

Smiling and confident, the stalwart young Cabinet officer left Atlanta to invade the deeper recesses of the state. He spoke to large audiences at Thomasville, Waycross, Macon, Gainesville, and other towns. Few Georgians had seen him, but almost all who heard him were attracted by his aggressive and direct manner of speech, and by his ability to make himself understood. What he had to say followed the same line as his Atlanta address, with more emphasis on the money issue. The editor of the Thomasville *Sun* reported that the universal opinion in his town was that "Hoke Smith is the smartest man in Georgia."[8] But it is doubtful that he converted many to sound money.

The Democrats won the governorship and all of the Congressional seats in the fall elections, but the Populists elected over fifty members of the state legislature and polled 45 per cent of all the votes cast in Georgia. The campaign appeared to have widened the breach between the administration and antiadministration elements in the state, and each faction was quick to blame the other's financial position for the Democratic decline. The Atlanta *Constitution* referred to "John Sherman's Apostles in Georgia" and deplored the fact that "goldbug bushwhackers" had opposed the free-silver plank. Hoke Smith, however, contended that "no reduction of majorities took place in districts where the fight was conducted in line with a platform demanding

[7] Atlanta *Journal*, September 8, 1894; clippings from Columbus *Enquirer-Sun*, September 8, 1894; Augusta *Chronicle*, September 9, 1894; Macon *Telegraph*, September 9, 1894; Savannah *Press*, September 13, 1894; and Washington *Post*, October 9, 1894, in Smith scrapbooks.

[8] Atlanta *Journal*, September 15, 24, 26, 28, 29, October 2, 1894; clipping from Thomasville *Sunday Sun*, September 23, 1894, in Smith scrapbooks.

a sound currency." As a Nebraska newspaper observed from afar, "The democratic war is on in Georgia." [9]

Smith's 1894 campaign in his home state had attracted a good deal of national attention. The New York *Herald* asserted that he had made the most vigorous campaign of any of the Cabinet members, and the Chicago *Inter-Ocean* declared in a humorous vein that the Secretary had been "gallivanting" through Georgia, "here stiffening the joints of a weak-kneed Democrat, and there cajoling a dubious Populist." Some Eastern newspapers even suggested that the Georgian would make a good candidate for the Presidential nomination in 1896. Other national journals called this a ridiculous suggestion, and the New York *Sun* contributed its usual doggerel, this time declaring, "Not Hoke, but Dink for '96." [10] There were some reports in 1895 that the Secretary would be appointed to a Supreme Court vacancy. Smith himself stated that his fixed purpose on leaving the Cabinet was "to return to Georgia and enter upon more active work than that of a supreme court justice." Meanwhile, he was being mentioned as the administration candidate for John B. Gordon's Senate post, since the general planned to retire at the end of his term.[11]

The administration had lost ground almost everywhere in 1894 and by early 1895 it was clear that the silver wing of the party had won the West and was taking steps to make sure that the South would support its cause. In the spring of 1895 John G. Carlisle addressed a sound money convention in Nashville, Tennessee, and a systematic campaign by administration leaders was soon under way in the South. In Georgia during the campaign of 1894 the silver plank, like the "old darky's fishnet, caught 'em a-coming an' a gwine." [12] But Hoke Smith was not

[9] Arnett, *Populist Movement in Georgia*, 184; Atlanta *Journal*, October 5, 6, 9, 11, 15, 1894; Atlanta *Constitution*, October 7, 8, 10, 1894; clipping from Lincoln (Neb.) *Journal*, October 21, 1894, in Smith scrapbooks.

[10] Clippings from Chicago *Inter-Ocean*, October 4, 1894; New York *Herald*, undated; Baltimore *News* (quoting the New York *Sun*), April 27, 1895; and other papers, in Smith scrapbooks.

[11] Atlanta *Journal*, February 9, 1895; clippings from Washington *News*, April 16, 1895, New York *Daily Mercury*, June 11, August 13, 1895, and Raleigh *News and Observer*, November 15, 1895, in Smith scrapbooks.

[12] Clippings from Milwaukee *Sentinel*, September 11, 1894, and New York *Times*, October 2, 1894, in Smith scrapbooks.

one to give up easily, and he now joined the administration campaign, cherishing the hope that he could revolutionize party sentiment in his state.

Near the end of April, 1895, the Secretary journeyed to Georgia to survey the political scene and to encourage administration supporters. While in Macon, on April 30, Smith gave an interview to the *Telegraph*, a sound-money newspaper, in which he declared that the financial question divided men into three classes: gold monometallists, silver monometallists, and bimetallists. The issue, he shrewdly suggested, would be for or against silver monometallism, and he reiterated his belief that free silver would not bring a bimetallic standard but instead would drive gold out of circulation, making the silver dollar worth little more than half that of gold.[13] Administration newspapers acclaimed Smith's interview, and even the Augusta *Chronicle*, a free-silver organ, declared that he stated the case against silver "pleasingly and plausibly," observing also that that interview represented an "audacious attempt" to shift the onus of monometallism to the silverites.[14]

The Atlanta *Constitution* grew ever sharper in its criticisms of the administration's financial policies. Its cartoonist, Ernest W. Wilkinson, belittled Cleveland and his Cabinet for working with the Eastern money barons and for truckling to John Bull and "Heidelback, Ickenheimer & Company." No goldbug had any business outside of the Republican party, declared the Atlanta morning paper. Turning to Smith, the *Constitution* averred that the Cabinet knew better than to defy Cleveland; they were like a bunch of boys, for "whenever there is the slightest breach of discipline, the old man will invite them out to the woodshed and apply a No. 2 shingle to the gable end of their pantaloons." The *Journal* replied by quoting Uncle Remus: "Marse Evin and Marse Clarke [Howell] dey ain needer wunner dem had a good nite ress sence Marse Grober went in de white 'ouse twill dess

---

[13] Atlanta *Constitution*, April 8, 1895; clippings from Philadelphia *Bulletin*, April 20, 1895, Macon *Telegraph*, May 1, 1895, and New York *Times*, May 1, 1895, in Smith scrapbooks.

[14] Atlanta *Journal*, May 2, 3, 1895; Augusta *Chronicle*, May 2, 1895.

de yudder nite wen de leckshun news come, and dat mean dey say, dat Marse Grober dess bleeged fer ter go." [15]

The editors of the *Constitution* had been charging Hoke Smith with inconsistency, pointing out that he had advocated free silver in earlier years, and the focal point of their attack became the "Peek letter," which they resurrected as Smith prepared to renew his campaign in Georgia. He had written the agrarian leader William L. Peek on September 15, 1890, in the interest of "perfect harmony" among Georgia Democrats, proposing a reform program that included the free coinage of silver. Copies of Smith's letter to Peek were now circulated widely over the state and unquestionably minimized the impact of his sound-money speeches. The *Constitution* had written the Secretary's "political obituary," declared the Washington *Times*.[16] Smith admitted having endorsed free silver in 1890, but asserted that professional work had claimed most of his attention at that time and he had not thoroughly understood the intricacies of the matter. Since then, he stated, "I have given to the subject much more study, and being thoroughly satisfied that the free, unlimited and independent coinage of silver at the ratio of 16 to 1 would result in silver monometallism, I have for years openly opposed it." While the silver newspapers scored him for being inconsistent, the gold papers seemed to feel that he had been honestly converted. As the New Haven *Register* put it, "We congratulate Secretary Smith upon the fact that he has seen a new light and is willing to acknowledge that he now knows more than he did five years ago." [17]

On July 23, 1895, at about the same time the silver Democrats assembled in a state bimetallic league at Griffin, Georgia, Smith began the administration's campaign in the state by addressing a large audience at Gainesville. The Secretary then moved on to make speeches at Columbus and Cordele. He returned to Georgia

[15] Atlanta *Constitution*, February 1, 8, 14, 23, March 1, 27, April 4, 26, 27, May 5, 1895; Atlanta *Journal*, September 15, November 7, 9, 1894, February 25, April 4, 8, 10, 1895.

[16] Atlanta *Constitution*, May 5, July 14, 1895; clipping from Washington (D.C.) *Times*, July 14, 1895, in Smith scrapbooks.

[17] Clippings from Dallas (Texas) *Herald*, July 16, 1895, and New Haven *Register*, July 16, 1895, in Smith scrapbooks.

in August and September to make a number of speeches on the money question, and early in December, he delivered a long address to the Georgia General Assembly, which had invited him and Crisp to address its members.

Wherever Smith appeared, he had "a bright smile, a hearty handshake and a pleasant word for every comer, numbers of whom he had met before." Harry Litchfield West, a Washington *Post* correspondent who accompanied the Secretary on one of his tours of Georgia, pictured him as a "sound money mission-ary" to his people. "To tell the whole story of Mr. Smith's trip through Georgia," wrote West, "would be simply to emphasize this earnest, ever-present desire to allow no opportunity to pass without dropping the seed of a sound money idea." Smith urged his audiences to pledge their support to the next Democratic platform, and he gave his word that he would do likewise. "There was no effort to flatter the audience," declared the Columbus *Ledger*, following one of his addresses, "no resort to oratorical climax for effect, no appeals to prejudice. . . ." In simple terms Smith explained what money was, how it could be used, its common forms, and what the terms "free," "unlimited," and "independent" meant when applied to the coinage of silver.[18]

The production of silver had increased so rapidly during recent years, explained Smith, that the intrinsic value of the silver in a minted dollar was worth only fifty cents in terms of gold. He had "no hostility to silver money," he declared, "not a particle; I am not anxious to see the volume of silver money lessened in Georgia or lessened in the United States; but I am in favor of [keeping] every single dollar . . . as good as every other dollar. . . ." If free silver were adopted, argued Smith, gold would be driven from circulation in accordance with Gresham's law, pre-cipitating "the most serious consequences." Free silver would only benefit the "silver mine kings" of the West. He denied the silverites' claim that the demonetization act of 1873—the "crime of 1873"—represented a conspiracy. The fall in the price of silver was simply the result of increased production. As for

[18] Clippings from Atlanta *People's Party Paper*, July 26, 1895, Macon *Telegraph*, July 29, 1895, and Washington *Post*, August 2, 1895, in Smith scrapbooks; Atlanta *Journal*, July 29, 1895.

the prevailing low commodity prices, he attributed them to the panic. If currency inflation were needed, said Smith, the wisest step would be to repeal the 10 per cent tax on state bank notes. Like many other sound-money exponents, he urged an international conference to deal with the money problem. He recalled that the great Benjamin Harvey Hill and L. Q. C. Lamar had stood for sound money, and he missed no opportunity to emphasize to his Southern audiences the connection between a stable currency and the economic development of the South. "Shall we involve our land in financial convulsion . . . at the very hour that we seem at last about to receive the benefits from immigration and investment that we have so long desired?" he asked.[19]

A local bard in the *Georgia Cracker* found time to describe the reaction to one of "Hoke's speeches":

> Well, as I was jest a-sayin', they jes'
>   flowed to town in streams,
> Some a-foot, an' some a-mule-back,
>   some a-drivin' of the teams.
>
> Some come up aboard the locals, some
>   come down aboard the Belle,
> An' exactly what the number was is
>   mighty hard to tell.
> . . . .
> Well, they came an' listened to it, an'
>   it's set 'em thinkin' clost,
> Some still differ with the speaker, some
>   he nigh converted—most.

Meanwhile, the Populist press lent a hand: "Go it Hoke. We want to see how many of these brave Democratic Free-silverites will 'clear the track.'"[20]

The anti-Cleveland Democrats in the state reacted much more violently to the Secretary's campaign. The Atlanta *Constitu-*

[19] Atlanta *Constitution*, July 28, 1895; Atlanta *Journal*, July 29, August 10, December 12, 1895. See also J. Chal Vinson, "Hoke Smith and the 'Battle of the Standards' in Georgia, 1895-1896," in *Georgia Historical Quarterly*, XXXVI (September, 1952), 201-19.

[20] Clippings from *Georgia Cracker*, undated, and Atlanta *People's Party Paper*, July 26, 1895, in Smith scrapbooks.

tion, which described his addresses as "scattering, illogical, inaccurate," and other antiadministration newspapers discovered that Smith had sent some of Carlisle's speeches to various postmasters in Georgia with the request that they be distributed to interested persons. Such "pernicious activity" brought forth a loud chorus of denunciation from the silver journals.[21] The Eastern press was generally favorable to Smith's fight against silver, although there were some critical notes. A Massachusetts newspaper announced that the Secretary was starring in a new administration comedy in Georgia, entitled "The Changed Man." Within the state Smith received considerable praise. Even the Augusta *Chronicle* described him as a "bold and vigorous combatant," who "knows how to state his case strongly and how to constantly force the burden of proof on the other side."[22]

Smith made a vigorous effort to have his speeches publicized. The Atlanta *Journal* not only provided a full coverage of its publisher's work for sound money but also waged a continuous campaign against such a "Populist nostrum" as free silver. Following his address to the legislature in December, 1895, Smith wrote the proprietor of the Macon *Telegraph*: "I am quite anxious to have my Atlanta speech appear in full in the Macon TELEGRAPH. I wish you would print it Sunday morning and send me the bill for doing so. . . . I would appreciate editorial comment calling attention to the fact that while free silver was exceedingly popular in Georgia I took the stump against it and fought it all over the State, and that I did this at a time when unquestionably the overwhelming majority of the people in the State were against Sound Money."[23]

Although administration leaders worked sturdily to hold back the tide of free silver, it was evident as 1896 began that only by a miracle in the coming months could the sound-money position triumph in the national convention. But Hoke Smith continued

[21] Smith to Cader H. Thomas, undated, in Smith scrapbooks; Atlanta *Constitution*, May 5, July 23, 24, 28, 1895; New York *Tribune*, July 19, 22, 1895.

[22] Clippings from Augusta *Chronicle*, July 24, 1895, Springfield (Mass.) *Union*, July 25, 1895, and other papers, in Smith scrapbooks.

[23] Smith to A. A. Allen, December 12, 1895, in Allen Papers; Atlanta *Journal*, July 4, 8, 13, 15, 26, 30, 1895.

to devote himself to the campaign. In the main he spent his
energies in his own state, but occasionally—as in his Jackson Day
remarks in Philadelphia and his address to the New York Reform
Club—he spoke to more cosmopolitan audiences. His most spectacular role in the "battle of the standards" was his series of
joint debates in early spring with ex-Speaker Charles F. Crisp.
If the Secretary was the sound-money leader in Georgia, Crisp
was easily the most prominent exponent of free silver in the state.
An accomplished parliamentarian and a skillful performer on the
hustings, he was a formidable opponent.

Smith took advantage of the campaign Crisp was conducting
for the Senate by writing the Congressman on March 17, 1896,
disclosing his plan "to spend a portion of the next two months
in Georgia speaking upon the financial question," and "cheerfully" offering to "divide time" with him. Crisp asked the
Secretary if he desired to be regarded as a candidate for the
Senate. This was a shrewd move, for numerous reports had been
circulated during the past year intimating that Smith would be
the administration candidate for Gordon's seat. For a time in
1895 it appeared that Smith actually planned to enter the Senate
contest, but he had no popular following in Georgia to compare
with that of Crisp. As the Savannah *Morning News* astutely
pointed out, "In order to get a following that would give him
hope of success he would have to be the recognized leader of
one side or other of an issue in which the people are profoundly
interested." [24] That Smith had his own political aspirations in mind
when he began to take an interest in the administration's money
battle is clear enough.

Many observers predicted that the debates between the Congressman and the Cabinet official would be a part of the Senate
contest. But Hoke Smith was cautious and when prodded by
Crisp would only say: "It is seven months until the Senatorial
election will take place in Georgia. I am not *now* a candidate,
and do not wish to become one." His purpose, he wrote, was
to do all in his power to prevent the Democrats of Georgia from
committing themselves to free silver. Crisp felt that it was "quite

[24] Savannah *Morning News*, June 18, 1895; Atlanta *Journal*, February 29,
March 10, 17, 1896.

unusual" for a candidate to debate with a person not running for office, but after some additional correspondence the two men agreed to a series of six to eight joint appearances, with the first engagement to be in Augusta on March 31.[25]

The debates began with great fanfare, but almost at once Crisp's illness imperiled the scheduled tour. His voice failed and he was weakened by a heart ailment. One engagement had to be postponed, and finally, after completing debates in Augusta, Atlanta, Newnan, and Albany, Crisp was forced to withdraw. But during the two weeks that the four meetings spanned, rapt attention was focused on the clash of the two representatives of the contesting factions.

The standard arguments were invoked. Crisp was conversational, urbane, skillful, and at times witty; Smith was direct, aggressive, and earnest. Smith argued the case for sound money well. When Crisp would ensnare him he usually managed to avoid the trap, and he refuted many of the Congressman's arguments. The two Democrats disagreed mainly on the money question. As Smith pointed out in opening one address, " Judge Crisp and I address you today as democrats; both of us are loyal, both of us will later on stand by the nominees of the democratic convention, whatever our present views." [26] Some of the debates occurred in an atmosphere of intense hostility and personal criticisms on the part of the participants, with the audiences plainly favoring Crisp. In closing his speech at Newnan, Smith referred to his opponent's use of ridicule: " Judge Crisp is a very funny man, as you will soon discover. He has 20 minutes to answer my arguments, but he will exercise his undoubted talent by amusing [you] at my expense. Now he must not think I am going to get mad. I promise him that I shall laugh as much as you will." [27]

Supporters of the administration declared that Crisp's with-

[25] Atlanta *Journal*, March 17, 21, 1896; clipping from Washington *Star*, March 20, 1896, in Smith scrapbooks.

[26] Atlanta *Journal*, March 21, 28, 31, April 1, 2, 1896; Atlanta *Constitution*, April 1-5, 1896.

[27] Atlanta *Journal*, April 3, 6-8, 11, 13, 14, 1896; Atlanta *Constitution*, April 2, 4, 6-10, 19, 27, May 20-30, 1896; and numerous clippings in Smith scrapbooks.

drawal from the joint debates indicated a victory for Hoke Smith, but the issue was never in doubt. As Smith's secretary, John S. Cohen, later recalled, "All hell couldn't stop" the silver forces in Georgia.[28] Smith found it difficult to believe that Georgians would "wander away from sound Democratic principles," but he acknowledged his defeat. And he withdrew from the Senate race he had never formally entered. "I am a candidate for no office," he declared. "I do not expect to be one. . . ."[29]

Smith continued to work for the administration cause, however, and the Atlanta *Journal* bravely beat the drums for sound money. But Cleveland men everywhere were being defeated: Carlisle in Kentucky, Morton in Nebraska, and William L. Wilson in West Virginia. When the state convention in Georgia came, the silver men won a resounding victory. "The Jig's Up," chortled the *Constitution*. A strong silver newspaper from South Georgia was at least more sympathetic: "Mr. Smith came into the state as the champion of President Cleveland and his financial policy, and he came in the attitude of a man who was conscious of the righteousness of his cause. He was open to all comers, and met the ablest champions of free coinage in joint debate."[30]

Smith seems to have realized only late in the currency fight that the Bryan men would capture the convention of 1896, although he undoubtedly knew long before the end of his campaign that Georgia was lost. He was staking a great deal on the outcome of the national convention. Perhaps he had studied his clippings from the Eastern newspapers too long. Perhaps he allowed his fondness for the spotlight of national publicity to dull his appreciation of practical considerations. While the contest over silver involved a political struggle between the major factions of the state's Democratic party, it also represented a substratum of economic reality, and this fact made the triumph of the silver element in Georgia almost inevitable. Smith learned too late the depth of the demand for economic relief through radical

[28] Nevins, *Grover Cleveland*, 693; Atlanta *Journal*, April 14, 15, 25, May 28, 30, June 2, 1896.

[29] Atlanta *Journal*, April 16, May 5, 9, 16, 1896.

[30] Atlanta *Constitution*, June 6, 1896; Atlanta *Journal*, June 8, 9, 25, 26, 1896; clipping from Albany (Ga.) *Herald*, undated, in Smith scrapbooks.

measures, and his connection with a conservative administration tended to immobilize him in his original position. Even so, by the end of the campaign he was beginning to change his views. As he wrote a friend, "We cannot expect the people . . . to be satisfied with what financiers call sound money, until a part of the scheme is prepared with a view of meeting the just needs of those living away from . . . [the banking centers]."[31]

By mid-May Hoke Smith was privately conceding the defeat of sound money at the national convention, though administration men continued to hope for a miracle at Chicago. But July came and this last hope proved futile when Bryan and the silverites swept the convention. What were the administration men to do? Cleveland himself was befuddled, and he wrote Smith from Gray Gables on July 15 that in his opinion "it is best for the present to think much and *talk none*."[32] On the same day it was announced that Secretaries Herbert and Olney would not support Bryan, and many Democratic newspapers in the East repudiated the Nebraskan as their candidate.

Hoke Smith was in a dilemma; he had debated his course for two months and there was no way to escape unscathed. Should he bolt the party? Months earlier the Atlanta *Constitution* had suggested that Smith might leave the party rather than support a silver ticket, and it was now calling for a recantation by all wayward Democrats: ". . . no man can say that he is a democrat, and at the same time refuse to support the democratic candidates."[33] Smith's own views inclined him to oppose the work at Chicago, but he had promised loyalty to the party's nominees, and he believed in party regularity. If he struck down the Chicago ticket he would be condemned as a traitor in Democratic Georgia; if he endorsed the Chicago ticket he would face a break with Cleveland and his friends, while in effect repudiating his work of the past two years. There was also the future of his newspaper and his profession in Georgia to consider. For a

[31] Atlanta *Journal*, September 2, 1896; clipping from Philadelphia *Enquirer*, June 27, 1896, in Smith scrapbooks.
[32] Nevins (ed.), *Letters of Grover Cleveland*, 447; Nevins, *Grover Cleveland*, 705.
[33] Atlanta *Constitution*, April 19, July 12, 15, 1896.

time he delayed his decision, hoping perhaps that Cleveland would
bow to the will of the party majority. Then, on July 20, he
wrote the President of his trouble:

> I am deeply distressed by the action of the Chicago Conven-
> tion, and by the situation it has produced. Just indignation at
> first led me to feel that I should openly oppose the nominees,
> and this seems to be the course that will be pursued by the
> other members of the Cabinet. But an earnest desire to reach
> a conclusion which will be in the line of my real duty, has
> satisfied me that I can not pursue such a course.
>
> All through the campaign, in a number of speeches, I urged
> my hearers to pledge themselves in advance to support the
> nominees of the national convention, and I frequently pledged
> myself to do so.[34]

He could not refrain from supporting his party in its contest
with the Republicans, Smith continued, and because of the "local
situation" he felt it necessary for "the protection of person and
property" to maintain the local Democratic organization. "I
would strike my own people a severe blow if I repudiated a
nominee of a regular convention thereby setting a precedent for
disorganization," he said. He assumed the anomalous position of
accepting the Democratic nominees but not the platform. Finally,
the Georgian spoke of the pain this decision had cost him and
of his "deep appreciation" for the opportunity of associating
with "one so wise, brave and patriotic."[35]

On the following day the Atlanta *Journal* announced its support of Bryan. "We have made this fight inside the party and
not by threats to go outside of party lines," asserted the Atlanta
paper.[36] Eastern newspapers were especially severe in their criticism of Smith and the *Journal* for endorsing the Chicago ticket.
Some administration men suggested that he was anxious to make
known his loyalty to the party before the new sound-money
ticket made its appearance. Postmaster General Wilson noted in
his diary that Smith and some other administration leaders had
hastened "to commit themselves before there is such a ticket,

[34] Smith to Cleveland, July 20, 1896, in Cleveland Papers.
[35] *Ibid.*
[36] Atlanta *Journal*, July 21, 1896.

so as to be relieved from the embarrassment of doing an unpopular duty when brought face to face with it." [37]

When Cleveland finally answered Smith, he expressed astonishment and disappointment at the Secretary's course; he rebuked him but he also remonstrated with him. When Smith addressed the people of his state " so nobly & patriotically," wrote Cleveland, he " surely could not have intended to promise support to a platform directly opposed not only to sound money but to every other safe & conservative doctrine or policy, and framed in every line & word in condemnation of all the acts & policies of an administration of which you have from the first, been a loyal, useful & honorable member." The President found Smith's attempt to separate the platform and the nominees " like straining at a gnat & swallowing a camel." He wrote cuttingly of the local situation referred to by Smith: " I suppose much was said about the ' local situation ' in 1860." While Cleveland could not understand his Secretary's reasoning, he did not doubt his sincerity. " I am perfectly satisfied," he declared, " that you have been influenced in the position you have taken, by the same desire to do exactly right, that has guided you in all your acts as a member of the Cabinet." [38]

The press was soon filled with speculation as to Smith's course. Many commentators predicted that he would resign, and there were reports that Cleveland had snubbed him in making a recent appointment.[39] In fact, the President had turned to his Cabinet for advice. Secretary Carlisle, with whom Smith had often conferred, recommended that the Georgian be retained in the Cabinet. Secretary Wilson, who described Smith as " an able Secretary " and " an able and aggressive champion of sound money," also urged that he be kept in his position. The administration " has but a few months to continue," Wilson pointed out. More-

[37] Festus P. Summers (ed.), *The Cabinet Diary of William L. Wilson, 1896-1897* (Chapel Hill, 1957), 127; *Harper's Weekly*, XL (August 22, 1896), 819; clippings from New York *Morning Advertiser*, July 23, 1896; Washington *Star*, July 23, 25, 1896; New York *Sun*, July 29, 31, 1896; and Boston *Globe*, August 2, 1896, in Smith scrapbooks.

[38] Cleveland to Smith, August 4, 1896, in Cleveland Papers.

[39] Nashville *Banner*, July 28, 1896; New York *Times*, July 30, 1896; New York *Sun*, July 31, 1896.

over, Smith's retirement "would make some stir in the country, and give him somewhat the position of a 'persecuted' man, for party's sake. . . ."[40]

Meanwhile, Smith had already decided to resign. On August 5, even before he received the President's letter, he sent in his resignation. "I have every thing in good order here," he wrote. "My successor can take charge without trouble." When Cleveland's reply to his first letter arrived, Smith received the President's rebuke in good humor, although he admitted being "a little hurt" by Cleveland's long silence. Referring to Cleveland's chiding remark about 1860 he replied, "I hope I am sufficiently devoted to the Nation, but in 1860 I should have gone with my state, and now I must stand by it." That night he left Washington to spend ten days with his family in western North Carolina.[41]

There was nothing left for Cleveland but to accede to Smith's request. This he did, accepting the Secretary's offer to stay on until September 1. "I hope I need not say how deeply I regret your retirement," wrote the President, "and how much I appreciate the devotion, industry and ability which have characterized your discharge of duty as a member of my official family."[42]

In time Hoke Smith magnified the importance of his course in supporting the party in 1896. "I had received many letters," he recalled many years afterward, "urging me to bolt the nomination and lead a break among the white people of the state, and this I believed would result in conditions disastrous almost to our civilization."[43] Smith would certainly have agreed with the observation of the Gainesville *Eagle* following the Democratic National Convention in 1896, with respect to the division among Democrats: "With us there is only one way. It is a road that never forks. It is the pathway of duty. We are a Democrat first, and then a gold bug."[44]

[40] Carlisle to Cleveland, August 7, 1896, and Wilson to Cleveland, August 9, 1896, in Cleveland Papers.

[41] Smith to Cleveland, August 5, 6, 1896, *ibid.*

[42] Cleveland to Smith, August 16, 1896, and Smith to Cleveland, August 19, 1896, *ibid.*

[43] Smith to Thomas J. Hamilton, June 27, 1920, in Smith Collection; Atlanta *Journal*, August 10, 1896; *Cong. Record*, 66 Cong., 2 Sess., 4592.

[44] Clipping from Gainesville *Eagle*, July 16, 1896, in Smith scrapbooks.

During the campaign Smith offered his services to the party leaders in Georgia, where he made two addresses, but he refused to speak outside of the state. He adhered to his sound-money position and in his speeches spent a good deal of time on the tariff and the need for an income tax. He made a special plea to the sound-money men to remain loyal, but he did not fail to pay tribute to his fallen leader, Grover Cleveland.[45] All in all, Smith and the *Journal* presented a strange spectacle as they sought to support the Democratic ticket but not all of the platform, and to promote the cause of the very elements within the party whose triumph they had shortly before predicted would bring disaster. But such were the exigencies of Southern politics in 1896. Following Bryan's defeat in November, the *Journal* could not forbear declaring that "The Democratic Party Still Lives," and referring to the "inevitable disaster."[46]

A few days before Smith left Washington, a newspaper reporter noted that the Secretary's "riding boots and English saddle, his favorite bicycle, his books, his bric-a-brac and his household goods have been shipped to his Georgia home. His law books are already in place in his office there and he expects at once to resume his legal practice in Atlanta."[47] By early September the Smiths were once more in the spacious Atlanta home on West Peachtree and Smith was soon immersed in his legal work. There was no ill feeling between him and Cleveland. In December Smith wrote Cleveland to express his "great pleasure" over the President's annual message, and in same month the Clevelands invited him and Mrs. Smith to attend the annual Cabinet party in January.[48]

Surprisingly, in view of all the attacks he had undergone, the press was almost unanimous in praising Smith's work in the Cabinet. The Washington *Post* declared that he had a "brilliant official record," and the New York *Journal* asserted that the

---

[45] Atlanta *Journal*, August 17, 1896; Savannah *Morning News*, August 16, 20, 1896.

[46] Atlanta *Journal*, November 4, 1896.

[47] Brooklyn *Daily Eagle*, August 23, 1896.

[48] Smith to Cleveland, August 19, December 19, 1896, in Cleveland Papers; Cleveland to Smith, December 21, 1896, in Nevins (ed.), *Letters of Grover Cleveland*, 464.

Interior Department was losing "the best head it ever had."
David R. Francis of Missouri, the succeeding Secretary of the
Interior, paid high tribute to the Georgian's efficient and faithful
service. "He introduced discipline and business methods," observed one newspaper, "that not only enabled and forced . . .
the Interior Department to clear up the work that had accumulated for years, but made it possible for them to keep that work
current." [49]

In many ways Smith had been a successful Cabinet member.
Under happier circumstances he might well have achieved a better
record and a less tarnished reputation. The disruption of the
party and the fight for sound money proved unfortunate for the
Georgian, forcing him into a political situation out of which
there was no escape congenial to him. It would take new avenues
of service to his fellow citizens and ten years of political exile
for him to emerge once more as a powerful leader in Georgia
politics.

[49] Clippings in Smith scrapbooks.

Political Exile, 1896-1905

"I never played poker," Hoke Smith once declared, "but if I had I would not have been one of those who mourned over losses."[1] Neither did he indulge in remorse over the political setback he had suffered in 1896; instead he plunged into his law practice with all of his characteristic energy. As the years passed, the even tenor of his life in Atlanta was seldom ruffled, but his ambition, his varied interests, and his recognized ability led him to take an increasingly active part in civic enterprises and reform movements. His success in these endeavors brought him, when the passage of time had dimmed his defeat of the nineties, to the threshold of a great political opportunity.

Upon his return to Atlanta Smith formed a partnership with Henry C. Peeples, with offices located at 10½ South Broad Street. The new firm attracted a great many damage suits, and eventually a younger lawyer in the organization, Jack J. Hastings, was given supervision of these cases. But Smith himself continued to handle many of the damage suits, particularly those involving large sums of money. His practice became more varied than in former years, and his firm numbered among its clients the Brotherhood of Locomotive Engineers, the Atlanta Freight Bureau, and such business corporations as the Consolidated Rubber Tire Company. Amazingly resourceful and seldom discouraged, Smith won a surprisingly large number of his cases, probably, recalled a fellow lawyer, a larger percentage " than any other lawyer of his time." [2] By the early years of the new century, he was earning twenty-five

[1] Smith to S. H. Venable, March 22, 1898, in Smith letterbooks.
[2] Powell, "Memorial of Hoke Smith," *loc. cit.*

thousand dollars or more a year from his legal work. And after 1903 there was another reason for him to be pleased with his profession: his son Marion entered his office to study for the bar and soon became a member of his father's organization.

Smith remained in control of the Atlanta *Journal* for several years after leaving the Cabinet. The competition between the *Journal* and the *Constitution* continued to be as intense as ever, and for a brief period in 1897 the morning paper challenged Smith's paper by publishing an *Evening Constitution*. When the Spanish-American War came, the *Journal* enthusiastically endorsed an aggressive policy and adopted a sensational approach in describing the events of the war, thereby increasing its circulation. But the *Journal*'s old zeal for national politics seemed to be lacking in the late years of the decade, and its editorials were less vituperative and more restrained.[3] It was the better part of wisdom, no doubt, to adopt a cautious attitude in politics until the repudiation of 1896 could be forgotten. Even in state and local politics the afternoon paper seldom announced itself in favor of particular candidates, although its editors opposed prohibition and urged politicians not to make an issue of the currency question.

Smith found it increasingly difficult to give much time to the newspaper. As he wrote early in 1898, " I give scarcely any time to its management." But he hesitated to dispose of his holdings in the *Journal*; the paper was profitable and he had created an organization that he did not want to disrupt. The *Journal* had paved the way for his entrance into Cleveland's Cabinet and for a time had made him a power in state politics. Still, Smith disliked being a nominal director, and the compelling urgency of a great cause was no longer present.[4] Furthermore, he could use his investment for larger ventures.

In this situation Smith decided in April, 1900, to sell his stock.

[3] The fact that Smith acquired fifty shares of *Constitution* stock during these years possibly influenced the quiescent attitude of the *Journal* toward politics, but more fundamentally the paper's course was directed by its sharp defeat of the mid-nineties.

[4] Smith to George F. Parker, February 2, 1898, to W. K. Staley, February 2, 1898, to Henry H. Cabaniss, February 28, 1898, and to W. B. Roberts, March 22, 1898, in Smith letterbooks.

He and the other stockholders, with the exception of Henry H. Cabaniss, sold their holdings to James Richard Gray, Morris Brandon, and H. M. Atkinson for $276,500. Smith received $159,000 for his stock. In the last issue under the old management he explained his reasons for selling. To the public he expressed the thanks of the retiring management for " so cordial a support," and declared that he left the *Journal* with " great regret." But compelled " to choose between two lines of business, I could not abandon the profession, the pursuit of which I anticipated as a child, and to which I was admitted as a member before reaching manhood." [5]

It was some time after he returned to Atlanta before Hoke Smith considered himself in a prosperous condition. The depression of the 1890's and the expenses of living in Washington had cost him heavily. As he wrote a relative in November, 1897, " Lately I have been very far from flush. Losses which I incurred during my absence amounted to nearly $25,000, which I was compelled to pay off and this has put me in debt and it will take me several years to pay out." [6] At that time the *Journal* was paying a steady profit and the returns from his legal work seldom slackened, but he was thinking in large financial terms.

One project that received much of Smith's attention in the late nineties was the Venable Construction Company, a concern he represented and in which he invested about thirty-five thousand dollars. Organized in the fall of 1897, the company was engaged in constructing Federal fortifications at Key West, Florida, and Savannah, Georgia. Unfortunately, the Venable Company experienced difficulty in securing adequate capital, fell behind in its schedule, and had to plead with Federal authorities for additional time to carry out its contract. Smith assisted in raising money to keep the enterprise going, spent a good deal of time in the East attending to the company's affairs, and called on such friends as Senator Augustus O. Bacon from his own state to help obtain generous terms from the government. When the work

---

[5] Atlanta *Journal*, April 16, 1900; Fort, "History of the Atlanta Journal," 38–39.

[6] Smith to Mrs. T. S. Brice, November 18, 1897, in Smith letterbooks.

was finally completed, Smith observed that "instead of making a profit, I have made a loss."[7]

Numerous other schemes also interested Smith, and some of them proved as disastrous as the Venable Construction Company. He prepared a plan for the organization of a company to handle foreign investments in the South, but nothing came of the project. He considered purchasing farm lands in South Georgia and was briefly associated with a group of promoters interested in the construction of a railroad between Atlanta and Pensacola, Florida. He bought an undeveloped Idaho mine which he held for twenty years, and he made modest investments in some textile mills.

The lawyer's investments in Atlanta were more successful. He continued his early practice of buying centrally located property in the city, and in the long run these purchases paid off handsomely. He bought a number of business properties during this period, including a five-story department store on Peachtree Street. With George and Sam F. Parrott, Smith constructed the Piedmont Hotel, a ten-story building which the Atlanta *Journal* described on completion, in 1903, as "an architectural dream in marble, steel and mahogany." Smith owned about one third of the stock in this large undertaking, and while it taxed his resources to the utmost to raise his share of the money required to construct and furnish the hotel, he never regretted his decision to make the investment.

When Hoke Smith paused sometime near the end of this decade of political retirement to set down his investments, he found that they added up to an impressive total. In addition to his stock in the Piedmont Hotel, he owned two or three stores; numerous houses and city lots; stock in two banks, a large land company, a textile mill, a furnace company, and a baggage concern; and a farm and several hundred acres of suburban land, including 250 acres on the Howell Mill Road. All of this was worth at least three hundred thousand dollars. Although some of Smith's property was mortgaged, he estimated that after all

[7] Smith to Alexander S. Clay, February 22, 1898, to S. H. Venable, March 22, 1898, to Augustus O. Bacon, March 12, April 23, May 8, 28, June 3, 11, 1898, and to Fitzhugh Lee, May 19, 1898, *ibid*.

of his obligations had been met, his estate would provide an annual net income of about fifteen thousand dollars.[8]

Smith was active in a large number of organizations. In addition to his membership in such professional groups as the American and Georgia bar associations, he belonged to numerous fraternal bodies and to such social clubs as the Piedmont Driving Club. He was often called on to participate in special celebrations in the city, and when famous men like Admiral George Dewey and President McKinley visited Atlanta he was usually involved in the receptions accorded them.

The Atlanta attorney was a faithful member of the Presbyterian church, and a strong and orthodox believer. As he said on one occasion in the mid-nineties, "Every step of progress given to one of us here on earth brings with it a duty to our fellow men, to be performed under the eyes of our Heavenly Father."[9] In 1897 the Smiths joined with a number of other Atlantans in organizing the North Avenue Presbyterian Church, which remained the family church for the remainder of Smith's life. In earlier years Smith had taught a Sunday school class and he served for many years as superintendent of the Sunday school of the new church. He was often invited to give Sunday school talks in other churches, but he confined his efforts to his own "Sabbath School" and to the county conventions held throughout the state. In 1899 he was elected president of the Ninth Triennial International Sunday School Convention, which met that year in Atlanta.[10]

The center of Smith's life was his home on West Peachtree. In the evenings he liked to watch the ebb and flow of life in the city as he sat on the veranda, or occasionally to drive with Birdie in an open buggy, "drawn by a pair of handsome roadsters." Numerous relatives and friends were in and out of the house almost every day, and the children were a delight to their father. By the end of the century Marion was a tall lad getting ready to

[8] Undated financial statement, in Smith Collection.
[9] *Thirty-Seventh Annual Report of the Columbian Institution for Deaf and Dumb* (Washington, 1894), in Smith Collection.
[10] Atlanta *Journal*, April 27, 1899, March 27, 1902; Smith to J. S. Palmer, March 29, 1901, in Smith letterbooks.

enter the University of Georgia, and pretty Mary Brent was reaching adolescence; but Lucy and Callie were still under ten. One thing about his domestic life caused Hoke Smith much concern: his wife's health had become so impaired that she was chronically nervous and, for long periods of time, practically an invalid. Many times her husband had to report that "Mrs. Smith has been quite unwell for some time, and is not able to leave home." Smith himself was not always well. Yet as he noted in 1901, "It is almost impossible for me to get away any distance from home, except during the period of the summer which I take for complete rest with my wife and children in the mountains of North Georgia." [11]

If any one thing stands out in the record of Hoke Smith's work during these years, it is his contribution to public education. An important factor in his growing interest in education was his re-election to the Atlanta Board of Education in 1897 and his selection as president a short time later.

As a member of the board for almost a decade after 1897, Smith urged numerous reforms in the city schools. When a distinguished educator like J. L. M. Curry came to Atlanta, Smith sought to have the teachers meet him. He devoted himself enthusiastically to the successful effort to have the National Educational Association meet in Atlanta. From the first he worked to secure larger appropriations for the city schools, pointing out that almost every year there were several hundred more applicants for admission than the schools could handle. Yet he did not think the board should beg for money; instead it should lay the facts before the people. "If they want the children accommodated," declared Smith, "they should take an interest in the question, and should know how candidates stand at the time they are elected." [12]

Hoke Smith's most cherished reform in the Atlanta school system was the introduction of vocational training. "The spirit

[11] Smith to J. S. Palmer, March 29, 1901, and to W. A. Hemphill, April 23, 1901, in Smith letterbooks; Atlanta *Journal*, June 30, July 8, 1898, April 4, 1902.

[12] Atlanta *Journal*, August 6, 1897, September 7, 1899, January 1, September 15, 1900, September 6, 1901, September 11, 1902, October 6, 1903; Martin, *Atlanta and Its Builders*, II, 195-96, 234, 239.

of the education in the south until very recent years," he observed in 1901, "has lacked a practical side." Yet each year the New South was taking "a more definite shape and children must be trained to meet new conditions." Early in 1898 he proposed "a series of practical lectures" for the students at Boy's High, and during the next year he made "a notable address in favor of the introduction of manual training in all the schools." Smith suggested that the board initiate instruction in drawing and modeling in the elementary grades, domestic science for girls in some grammar grades and high school, and shop for boys beginning at the seventh- or eighth-grade levels. In June, 1899, the board introduced a modest program of vocational training, and in his report of 1901 the president observed that it was working better than he had expected. In 1903 the board began, as a result of Smith's "urgent advocacy, a distinct technological course in the boys' high school."[13]

This was all a part of Smith's dream of Southern diversification and industrialization. If the children of Atlanta "are inspired with the desire to create through their hands," he said, "and are trained as to their hands as well as their minds this city will become a perfect bee hive, inhabited by thrifty, prosperous, producing people." Education must include moral training as well, Smith believed. He also felt "a deep interest in the proper recognition of the South in all the histories published and in all collections of literature."[14]

Smith's leadership in the school affairs of Atlanta was widely praised, but it was not without criticism. The new vocational education was criticized and in 1903 was subjected to review by the board and the city council, although it was allowed to continue. There were complaints from some local book dealers at the board's policy of selling textbooks directly to the students. There were also disagreements among the members of the board, and on one occasion Smith and another member became so angry

[13] Smith to G. Gunby Jordan, March 17, 1898, and to George J. Baldwin, March 15, 1904, in Smith letterbooks; Atlanta *Journal*, August 26, 1898, June 10, 1899, September 15, 1900, November 15, 1901, January 6, 1902.

[14] Atlanta *Journal*, January 16, 1899, January 6, 1902; Smith to W. A. Courtenay, November 4, 1903, and to E. P. Gamble, November 4, 1903, in Smith letterbooks.

at each other that "it seemed as though a personal encounter might result." Smith wrote a correspondent in 1901 that he had heard of an "active effort" to defeat him for re-election,[15] but if such an effort was made it was unsuccessful.

During this period Smith began to make generous contributions of money to various educational institutions, including Lucy Cobb Institute, and to needy students who desired to continue their education. More important were the libraries and encyclopedia sets that he donated. Impressed by the appalling lack of library resources in most of the state's schools, the lawyer decided in 1900 to give to each of sixteen needy counties a circulating library of sixty volumes. He selected the books himself, mostly classics ranging from *Plutarch's Lives* to *Alice in Wonderland*, and had constructed for each set a special bookcase designed to stand up under constant travel. He urged the local superintendents to see that the library in each county was moved around so that each school in the county might use it. In some counties Smith's library became the first real collection of free books in the locality. Other counties soon requested sets of the books and by 1905 about seventy sets were circulating in the state.[16]

In the late nineties interest in public education in Georgia, as in many other Southern states, noticeably increased, and during the following few years an education movement, sponsored to a considerable extent by outside interest and money, swept across the region. Hoke Smith took a conspicuous part in the educational revival in Georgia. During the early years of the twentieth century he made hundreds of speeches on education at Chatauquas, education rallies, and commencement exercises. As he said in 1901, "There is no work in which I feel a deeper interest than in the development of the educational facilities for the children of Georgia."[17] He was a member of a special educational campaign committee for Georgia organized in 1903. The secretary of the committee wrote that "the man who was asked for as

---

[15] Smith to W. R. Hammond, May 11, 1901, in Smith letterbooks.

[16] Smith to the principal, Buena Vista City Schools, November 20, 1903, and to Homer Upchurch, December 7, 1903, *ibid.*; Atlanta *Journal*, May 11, 1901, September 13, 1904, August 20, 1905.

[17] Smith to R. B. Daniel, March 29, 1901, in Smith letterbooks.

speaker at the educational rallies more frequently than any one else was the Hon. Hoke Smith." [18] A local newspaper described the effect of one of Smith's educational addresses: "No public man in one single address ever won his audience so completely as did Mr. Smith in his address at Chattoogo. His earnestness, his sincerity, his plain common sense at once gained him a warm spot in the hearts of all who heard him." [19]

Wherever he appeared Smith pleaded for the development of the common schools and for the establishment of agricultural high schools. He urged longer terms for rural schools, declaring that it was "impossible to have a thorough system of schools in the country until we run them eight months during the year." He helped to draft the McMichael amendment to the state constitution, allowing school districts to call local elections for levying school taxes, and asked the people to ratify it.[20]

Education in the South, Smith often asserted, had failed "to inspire the minds of the young with an ambition to investigate and develop the resources of the state and section." He took pains to demonstrate that a state's wealth increased in direct proportion to its increase in educational expenditures, and to link education with industrial expansion and agricultural diversification. To this theme, so often expounded to Georgia audiences, he also turned when he delivered addresses in other regions. There was no doubt, Smith declared on one occasion, that "if 50 years ago we had established all over the South a thorough system of education, and . . . technical schools that ours today would be the most prosperous manufacturing section of the world." [21]

The Atlanta lawyer was an enthusiastic advocate of the Southern Education Conferences sponsored annually in the South during this period. He made one of the principal addresses at the fifth conference, held in Athens in 1902. Here he spoke with

[18] Atlanta *Journal*, August 20, 1905.

[19] Clipping from Walker County *Messenger*, September 25, 1903, in Smith scrapbooks.

[20] Augusta *Chronicle*, December 1, 1901; Atlanta *Journal*, July 21, September 13, 1904; Atlanta *Constitution*, July 22, 26, 1904.

[21] Atlanta *Journal*, June 12, 1901; Philadelphia *Public-Ledger*, June 12, 1901.

such educational reformers as Charles B. Aycock and Charles
D. McIver. Speaking on "Popular Education as the Primary
Policy of the South," Smith welcomed the educators and the
"big-hearted, patriotic philanthropists" from the Northeast who
had come "to confer upon what to us is the most important of
subjects—Education." "The work to which I call you today,"
he went on, "is an earnest, devoted, consecrated work. It is
our work, work for us of the South. . . . And we mean to carry
it on until every child within the borders of the South, white and
black, shall have a thorough education." Smith sought to impress
his audience with the need for rural education, pointing out the
handicaps presented by a sparse population and the tenant system.
He emphasized the necessity of persuading the people to tax
themselves for education. Negroes also must share in the educational awakening if the region was to move ahead. "The Negroes
are free, independent men and women," he declared, "and unless
their minds and characters are lifted upwards, the danger is that
they may rapidly go backwards."[22]

Hoke Smith's work in education led to his selection in November, 1901, as a trustee of the Peabody Education Fund, which had
promoted the development of education in the South for a
generation.[23] The Georgian, who was appointed to the executive
committee, was soon in the center of the Fund's activities. Within
a short time he became involved in the controversy over the
proposal to concentrate the Peabody money in support of the
Peabody Normal College in Nashville, rather than dividing it
among many schools. At the fall meeting of the trustees in 1903,
he presented a resolution which stated that the "policy of this
Board for the next few years shall be to aid Normal Schools, and
furthermore to stimulate the development of rural schools." The
resolution was adopted, and a year later Smith secured the

[22] *Proceedings of the Fifth Conference For Education in the South, Held
at Athens, Georgia April 24, 25 and 26, 1902* (Knoxville, 1902), 43-51;
Atlanta *Journal*, April 23-26, 28, 1902.

[23] Smith was unanimously chosen, on the motion of Richard Olney, to
replace William Wirt Henry of Virginia, who had died. Theodore Roosevelt and Seth Low were also elected trustees at the same time. *Proceedings
of the Peabody Education Fund*, VI, 95.

approval of a proposal to allot ten thousand dollars to the promotion of rural schools in the South.[24]

When the Southern Education Conference met in Atlanta, in December, 1903, Smith urged the Peabody trustees to attend the meeting in order to learn at first hand what conditions in the South were like and how Peabody money should be distributed. He desired to distribute the funds "more evenly . . . to the different states, giving particular attention to rural schools." In addressing the Atlanta meeting of the conference, he made it a point to stress the "conviction that the rural schools presented our great problem" and to point to the resolutions of the Peabody trustees approving such an approach.[25] Smith had already begun to receive pleas for help from various schools in Georgia and to promise his aid in securing Peabody funds. Such a school as that being developed at Bremen, in Carrol County, appealed to him; there "the people have raised $5000 towards equipping a school, which with wagons is to reach for four miles in every direction, and bring in the children."[26]

It was soon apparent, however, that those who were interested in maintaining and expanding the work of Peabody College were opposed to Smith's proposals for the distribution of the Peabody money among numerous normal colleges and rural schools. This led Smith to make some scathing remarks about the Nashville institution and such of its supporters as ex-Governor James D. Porter of Tennessee. It irked him to think of postponing the work he considered most vital: "The time is so ripe for this work and this delay will mean such a loss in the school progress of the south."[27]

In June, 1904, the lawyer vigorously stated his position in two letters to Richard Olney, a member of the special committee

[24] *Ibid.*, 159-61, 209-10, 249; Atlanta *Journal*, January 31, 1903.

[25] Smith to Samuel A. Green, October 16, 1903, to T. P. Venable, October 16, 31, 1903, and to Daniel C. Gilman, January 4, 1904, in Smith letterbooks.

[26] Smith to William C. Adamson, November 17, 1903, and to A. J. Ritchie, December 9, 1903, *ibid.*; E. C. Branson to Smith, February 9, 1904, W. B. Merritt to Green, February 9, March 10, 1904, and Smith to Green, February 10, 1904, in Peabody Papers (George Peabody College for Teachers Library).

[27] Smith to Gilman, January 4, 11, 1904, in Smith letterbooks.

studying the proposed grant of a million dollars to Peabody
College. Smith sought to delay action, pointing out at length
what he considered to be weaknesses in the plans submitted by
the college in its request for the money. He described the good
results already evident from small grants recently made in Georgia
for summer school institutes and rural schools. "Here is a field
more inviting than the work which opened to Dr. Sears in
1869-70," he declared.[28]

How seriously Smith really considered his objections to the
type of college proposed in Nashville is not clear, but his sincerity
in sponsoring rural education and his determination to obtain
funds for his own state are obvious. Richard Olney noted that
Smith approached the question "not theoretically, as I have to
do, but practically." [29] The Peabody report, as it came to be
called, occupied the attention of the trustees for several years;
in the end it was approved and the grant was awarded to Peabody
College. But the Fund also made generous grants in many other
Southern states, including Georgia.

Meanwhile, following several years of political inactivity, Hoke
Smith was beginning to show greater interest in politics. For
some time after leaving the Cabinet, the Georgian was distrusted
by both elements in the Democratic party. He remained on good
terms with Cleveland, whom he visited a few times at Princeton,
and he was grateful for the ex-President's continued confidence
in him. He also maintained some contact with fellow Cabinet
members. Although his name was mentioned occasionally in
connection with public office, Smith did not delude himself into
thinking that his return to active political life could be imminent.
When several people wrote him in the autumn of 1896, urging
him, in view of Charles F. Crisp's death, to become a candidate
for the Senate, he firmly refused to allow his name to be used.
As he wrote one man in 1898, "I am not taking any part in
politics as my time is entirely consumed with my professional
work." [30] Yet he retained his keen interest in the results of
political action. He gave his support to a proposal to reform the

[28] Smith to Richard Olney, June 6, 27, 1904, in Peabody Papers.
[29] Olney to Gilman, June 14, 1904, ibid.
[30] Smith to J. Allen, April 23, 1898, in Smith letterbooks.

nation's banking system, and he urged the Georgia Senators to help obtain an additional Federal circuit court judge for the South. "If you can put it through the Senate," he wrote Senator Clay, "I will come on to Washington, and I think I can get [Republican Congressman John] Dalzell to help put it through the House." [31]

Smith supported the Democratic ticket in 1900, but without much enthusiasm. In March, 1897, he was quoted as saying that "if Mr. Bryan should be nominated again on the same platform, my obligations will be different; I will not vote for him." But just before the Democratic National Convention of 1900, the Georgian pledged himself to support the party nominees, "no matter whom they nominate or what platform they adopt at Kansas City." [32] During the campaign he declared that the major issue was the trusts, and like Bryan, he also tried to make an issue of the McKinley administration's imperialism. Smith himself favored some expansion, including the domination of Cuba by the United States, but according to the Atlanta *Journal*, while the lawyer was still its publisher, the annexation of the Philippines would add to the country several "mongrel and semi-savage millions of people who would never be . . . anything but a burden and an expense." [33]

Soon after the Republican triumph in 1900, Smith openly expressed his opposition to his party's continued adherence to Bryanism. He stated his position this way:

> I disapproved the suggested reorganization for the party by certain persons in the east, and I think Colonel Bryan is making a mistake equal to that which would have resulted from any serious movement toward eastern reorganization.
>
> The Democratic party should stand between the plutocrat and the socialist as the party of the Constitution and of the people. . . .

[31] Smith to J. O. C. Black, December 16, 1897, to Augustus O. Bacon, February 2, March 30, 1898, and to Alexander S. Clay, April 2, May 16, 1898, *ibid.*

[32] Chattanooga *Times*, quoted in New York *Tribune*, March 12, 1897; New York *Tribune*, July 8, 1900.

[33] Atlanta *Journal*, November 5, 19, 23, 1898, January 19, February 24, October 5, 1900.

The party must regain the confidence of the voters in New York, Connecticut, New Jersey, Maryland, Indiana and other states by convincing them that its policies will be wise and conservative, protecting not only personal rights but also property rights. There are no people in the Union today more conservative than the rank and file of Democratic voters in the south. They are not willing to submit to illegal trusts, but they do not favor useless agitation or attacks upon property.[34]

Smith, then, remained a Cleveland Democrat. He observed in 1901 that "the almost unanimous desire of Southern Democrats is against any further agitation of the silver question." He insisted that the party could not afford "to follow defeated candidates who harp on dead issues." It must shun anarchy on the one hand and attack the illegal trusts on the other.[35]

While Smith took little part in state politics, he became more and more active in working for certain local and state reforms. As a member of a committee representing the Atlanta Bar Association, he appeared before a committee of the state legislature in 1898, to urge the election of local judges and solicitors for Atlanta. In 1899 the Atlanta *Journal*, with its publisher's support, conducted a long campaign against the reckless distribution of city franchises, and two years later Smith and George Hillyer were appointed by the mayor to represent Atlanta in discussions with the city's street-railroad and electric companies, involving a proposal to consolidate these companies. Smith and Hillyer engaged in a bitter argument with the railroad and electric companies; they urged more adequate regulation of public utilities and contended that these companies paid ad valorem taxes on a mere 20 per cent of the value of their holdings. Smith appeared before the city council to oppose the consolidation scheme and he and Hillyer issued a "card" explaining their position. The consolidation proposal was defeated.[36]

[34] Atlanta *Journal*, November 24, 1900; New York *Tribune*, November 25, 1900.

[35] Smith to R. B. Daniel, April 6, 1901, to F. M. Tuley, April 11, 1901, and to Jeremiah W. Jenks, May 9, 1901, in Smith letterbooks; Atlanta *Journal*, November 24, December 14, 18, 1900.

[36] Atlanta *Journal*, November 16, 1898, June 29, 1899, November 27, December 4, 10, 13, 16, 18, 20, 1901, January 7, 1902.

In the late nineties the Atlanta *Journal* began to urge the passage of a state child-labor law, and when an organized movement began in 1901, Hoke Smith gave it strong support. Smith felt that millowners in the South generally were "kind and helpful," but "in spite of that fact you will find ignorant and pallid faces, dejected countenances," and an "appearance which indicates sickness and the lowest vitality." Besides, if a child worked all day in a textile mill, he could not be in the classroom. While men like Clark Howell were reluctant to join in the child-labor movement, Smith gave it his help, joining the National Child Labor Committee and playing an important role in the enactment of the Georgia child-labor act of 1906.[37]

All of these interests, and especially the increasing attention he gave to education after 1900, eventually brought Smith's name once more into political speculation, but he denied that he wanted to return to politics in the near future. "I am very much interested in my professional work," he wrote one man, "and I feel that the intelligent thing for me to do is to stick to it a few years longer." He expressed the belief that he could do more good "as a private citizen than as a public office holder."[38] But the speculation would not cease, and in 1902 Smith was forced to issue a statement making his position clear. "My engagements are such," he stated, "that it is impossible for me to entertain the suggestion of entering the race for governor."[39] The Atlantan did serve as a delegate to the state Democratic convention in 1902, where he joined other conservatives in a successful effort to prevent the endorsement of the Kansas City platform of 1900.

As the national election of 1904 approached, Cleveland men in the South, supporting the candidacy of Alton B. Parker, were optimistic. Early in 1904 Smith wrote a friend, "I would like to see the friends of Mr. Cleveland, Senator [Arthur Pue] Gor-

[37] Smith to Edgar Gardner Murphy, April 6, 1904, in Smith letterbooks; Atlanta *Constitution*, November 25, 27, 1901, July 4, 6, 1903; Elizabeth H. Davidson, *Child Labor Legislation in the Southern Textile States* (Chapel Hill, 1939), 81-82, 124, 199-203.

[38] Smith to Hooper Alexander, March 25, 1901, to C. C. Duncan, April 5, 1901, and to J. W. Lowrey, June 4, 1901, in Smith letterbooks.

[39] Atlanta *Journal*, January 9, 10, 1902, and numerous clippings in Smith scrapbooks.

man and Mr. Bryan get together and present the one man upon
whom, in my opinion, they may all unite, and that is Judge
Parker." [40] In a widely quoted interview of early March, the
lawyer predicted that the national convention would be a contest
between "Bryan—Tom Johnson—Hearst Democrats and Parker-
Gorman-Olney men." The Georgian preferred an "old-time platform" that would inspire confidence. [41] A few weeks earlier
he had outlined the situation in Georgia:

> We are at present in a state of great uncertainty as to just
> what will be done. There is still a strong element in favor of
> the re-nomination of Mr. Cleveland. There is a strong Gorman
> following. There is an active Hearst organization in the state.
> ... I believe the conservative democrats, next to Mr. Cleveland,
> will come nearer uniting on Judge Parker than any one else
> against Hearst.
> I am primarily in favor of bringing the Georgia Democracy
> squarely up to an endorsement of those views which were
> represented by the last democratic administration. . . . [42]

Late in March, Smith invited a number of prominent political
friends from all over the state to confer with him in Atlanta
about national politics. He took a leading part in the organization
of the Parker Democratic Club of Georgia, and when the state
convention met in June, he was probably the most effective
strategist for the Parker cause, although he was not a delegate.
In the convention the Parker men won an easy victory and the
Georgia delegation was instructed for the New Yorker. Hoke
Smith was "the colossal figure in the Parker campaign," declared
the Atlanta *Journal*; he "organized the campaign and directed
all its movements that required attention from the Atlanta end." [43]
Although Smith was not a delegate, he attended the national
convention, conferring with the platform committee and a number of state committeemen. He wrote Cleveland for an outline
of his ideas some time before the convention, and in St. Louis

---

[40] Smith to Charles L. Bartlett, January 9, 1904, in Smith letterbooks.

[41] Augusta *Chronicle*, March 6, 1904.

[42] Smith to Charles S. Hamlin, January 30, 1904, in Smith letterbooks.

[43] Atlanta *Journal*, June 2, 4, 1904; Smith to J. E. Mercer and others,
March 22, 1904, in Smith letterbooks.

he joined in the strategy of using the ex-President as a rallying point for the party's conservatives. He was delighted over Parker's nomination, and on his return to Atlanta described him as an "ideal supporter of law and order." Roosevelt, on the other hand, was "a threatening Cromwell." [44]

During the campaign Smith delivered a number of addresses for the Democratic ticket. He spoke in New York in August, in an appearance advertised as a reply to Secretary of the Treasury Leslie M. Shaw, and in September and October he made speeches in North Carolina, New York, Connecticut, and other states. The Georgian lauded Grover Cleveland as the greatest living American; he exulted in the new Democratic harmony and contended that conservative Democrats throughout the country had rejoined "the councils of their party." According to Smith, the party was once more the defender of sound money and a low tariff. He scored Theodore Roosevelt for his "restless egotism," for sowing the "seed of sectional hatred," and for what he called an "audacious usurpation of executive authority." [45]

One of Smith's most publicized speeches was delivered in Augusta just before the election. The Young Men's Democratic Club there arranged for him to answer the strictures of Tom Watson, the Populist candidate for President. When the lawyer arrived in Augusta he was given an enthusiastic reception, and when he began his speech there were great shouts of applause. "Time after time the outburst was renewed," reported the Augusta *Chronicle*. Watson had denounced both of the major parties and had scathingly criticized August Belmont and other financiers favorable to the Democratic party. In answer to these attacks, Hoke Smith not only appropriated Thomas Jefferson as the Democracy's own but strongly defended Belmont himself! He did not believe the rumors that the Republicans had paid Watson to make the race for President, asserted Smith, but there was as much truth in such accusations "as there is in the statement that eastern money bought Parker's nomination (Cheers)." While Alton B. Parker was fighting Republican imperialism and

[44] Smith to Cleveland, June 13, 1904, in Cleveland Papers; Atlanta *Journal*, July 13, 1904.

[45] Atlanta *Journal*, August 9, 12, 22, October 22, November 5, 1904.

sectionalism, declared Smith with fine sarcasm, "a Georgian is traveling throughout the land comparing him with Roosevelt, to the disparity of the Democratic candidate." [46]

The Democrats were overwhelmed by the tidal wave of Roosevelt's popular vote, and Hoke Smith returned to his law practice. Later in the year, his name was again in the state's political news when it was rumored that he planned to contest Senator Clay's bid for re-election. In a public statement Smith denied these reports, pointing out that he and Clay had been "close friends for many years." [47]

During the final stages of the recent campaign, the New York *Tribune* had printed a sarcastic editorial entitled "The Revival of Hoke," in which the editors had criticized the Georgian for his part in the Parker campaign. The New York paper spoke sharply of Smith's failure to stand by sound money in 1896, describing him as a man of "india rubber convictions conformable to any shape required by his political interests." [48]

Looked at from the local point of view, this was not a fair appraisal, for in spite of Smith's efforts to compromise in 1896, he had not abandoned his essential position. Furthermore, it had taken hard work in other fields and the better part of a decade to place him once more in a favorable position in Georgia. However the *Tribune* might have intended its comments on the "Revival of Hoke," it proved to be an accurate prophecy. The old issues were passing out of currency, and new ones, less prejudicial to Smith's political ambitions, were coming to the fore. Within a few months Hoke Smith's political exile came to an end.

[46] Augusta *Chronicle*, November 8, 1904.
[47] Atlanta *Journal*, December 25, 1904.
[48] New York *Tribune*, November 2, 1904.

Political Ferment in Georgia

During the years since Reconstruction the conservatives who controlled political affairs in Georgia had introduced few reforms in the operation of the state government. The agrarian revolution had unseated the Bourbons, but with the passing of the Populist threat and the return of better times the more conservative Democrats appeared to have secured impregnable control. The calm proved deceptive, however, and by 1905 the state's politics were in an uproar.

The political storm that broke over Georgia was in part merely the upheaval occasioned by the clash of the two major factions in the Democratic party, but the very existence of this struggle revealed underlying grievances and social disorders that demanded attention. Early in the new century reform-minded people had urged with increasing vigor the enactment of child-labor legislation, the abolition of the convict-leasing system, more adequate support of public education, and control of corporations. The favored position of the railroads drew their heaviest fire. One reformer declared in 1905, for example, that the carriers "had so completely subjugated the state government, and were so thoroughly masters of the people, that there was not a public man in this state who would dare raise his voice against this power. . . ."[1] A liberal Democrat named Dupont Guerry had campaigned for governor in 1902 on an anticorporation platform, and during the next few years there were signs in the legislature that some of the demands Guerry had made were growing more

---

[1] Joseph Hill Hall, in Macon *Telegraph*, June 7, 1905.

popular. But until 1905-1906 reform sentiment in Georgia remained inchoate and largely leaderless.

One of the most important factors in giving direction to the
reform movement in Georgia was the Atlanta *Journal*, whose
managers were friends of Hoke Smith. Like the lawyer, the
Journal was an advocate of what might be called the Cleveland-
Parker Democracy on the national level, but in local politics it
became a genuine reform paper some time before Smith announced
his own conversion. It was a leader in the campaign for a franchise tax, it agitated against free passes and lobbying, it promoted
child-labor legislation, it opposed the convict-leasing system, and
it spoke favorably of woman suffrage. After 1904 the focus of
the *Journal*'s reform agitation became the corporations, particularly the railroads. By March, 1905, the *Journal* had decided that
"Affairs have reached that place where the idea of electing a
governor whose political record shows him to have owed any of
his past preferment or present position to corporation support is
not to be tolerated." [2]

James R. Gray and his associates on the Atlanta *Journal* had
reached this conclusion largely as a result of their disappointment
over the failure of the state railroad commission to order substantial freight-rate reductions. When the Atlanta Freight Bureau
and the Atlanta Chamber of Commerce began a fight early in
1904 to reduce rates, the *Journal* ardently supported the effort,
describing it as "the most vital question that confronts Atlanta
today." During the following year a fierce struggle occurred
between the Atlanta shippers and the railroads. One of the
leaders in the freight-rate fight was Hoke Smith, who represented
the Atlanta Freight Bureau. He talked "forcibly of the freight
rate discriminations" before the chamber of commerce and other
groups, and he acted for the freight bureau in some of the
negotiations with the railroads. [3]

Ultimately the railroad companies granted a number of rate
reductions, but the Atlanta merchants continued to urge favorable
action on the so-called port rates, that is, the rates on articles

[2] Atlanta *Journal*, January 12, 21, March 8, 26, 1905.
[3] *Ibid.*, April 24-29, July 13, 21, October 7, 11, 28, November 28-30, 1904,
March 12, April 23, 25, 1905.

shipped to and from interior cities and the Georgia ports. A petition for the reduction of these rates had been pending before the railroad commission since 1902. Finally, in May, 1905, the commission acted unfavorably on the Atlanta petition. " The railroads know what they want, and they are going out to get it," declared the Atlanta *News*. ". . . The ass knoweth his owner and the ox his master's crib." The Atlanta *Journal* called for the resignation of the railroad commissioners and printed an editorial under the heading, " Wanted—A Trust-Buster in Georgia." The state could never achieve its potential development as long as the railroads dominated politics, asserted the editor. Georgia needed " a big, conservative man, who is resolved on seeing that justice is done to the railroad interests as well as to the public; one who will have force enough to give the proper direction to the present public sentiment, but who will have poise enough not to let himself be carried into any wild-eyed position by the inevitable coming reaction against long years of railroad domination. . . ." [4]

The Atlanta newspaper mentioned no names but it was apparent that none of those who had announced an intention to enter the Democratic gubernatorial primary of 1906 could qualify as the *Journal*'s man. Even before Governor Joseph M. Terrell's un-opposed renomination in 1904, there were widespread reports that Clark Howell of the Atlanta *Constitution* would receive the support of the Terrell administration in the campaign of 1906, and in November, 1904, Howell had indicated that he would be a candidate. A number of other prominent Georgians had also been mentioned as possible candidates, including James Pope Brown, chairman of the railroad commission. In April, 1905, Brown formally announced his decision to enter the contest.

An important element in Brown's plans was the Populist leader Tom Watson, who had almost decided that his only hope of political success was to lead his followers into the Democratic primary. Numerous appeals for such a course came from old Populists and sympathetic Democrats. The following from a progressive Democrat is typical: " The old populist party of Georgia can to-day almost turn the wavering balance. Their present incorporation into the democratic party, coupled with

[4] *Ibid.*, May 3, 4, 11, 1905; Atlanta *News*, May 30, 1905.

that great body of democrats who always sympathised [sic] in many of your populist views, and the ever growing increment of those who are disciples of the new ideas,— these things seem to me to give assurance that such a leader as yourself, acting within the democratic, or rather the white party of Georgia, can accomplish uncountable good for this state. . . ." [5]

Of all the incidents and circumstances that had combined to defeat the youthful hopes of the Populists, it seemed to Tom Watson that the "nigger" was the key. "For more than a generation," he wrote in 1905, "'the nigger' has been the stock-in-trade of the Democratic Party in the South," and "nothing can be done as long as the South is forever frightened into political paralysis by the cry of 'negro domination.'" By whatever process of rationalization, Watson became a vigorous advocate of Negro disfranchisement. In an address in Atlanta during the campaign of 1904, he offered his support to any "anti-machine" Democrat for the governorship—if his platform included Negro disfranchisement. [6]

Watson's most direct connection with the Democratic party in Georgia was his friendship with young Thomas William Hardwick, Representative in Congress from Watson's district and outspoken advocate of disfranchisement. Early in 1905 Watson and Hardwick agreed to support Pope Brown for governor, on a platform that included disfranchisement and a demand for stringent railroad regulation. Hardwick did not believe Clark Howell could win "in a hot fight, if the opposition *can get to the people.*" Unfortunately, Brown's easygoing campaign seemed unlikely to accomplish this result, and the Congressman was soon urging "a more aggressive and definite policy" for their candidate. [7]

Meanwhile, the Atlanta *Journal's* plea for a "trust-busting" governor had created considerable discussion. Was it just another example of the old-time newspaper rivalry in the Georgia capital? Since the *Constitution* had its candidate, must the *Journal* have

[5] Hooper Alexander to Watson, August 1, 1904, in Watson Papers.

[6] *Tom Watson's Magazine,* II (October, 1905), 398; Woodward, *Tom Watson,* 370-72.

[7] Hardwick to Watson, February 1, March 2, May 4, 1905, in Watson Papers.

one of its own? When one newspaper expressed the suspicion that the *Journal* had "a boat in the slips to launch," Gray's paper declared that it cared "nothing for the man—that is to say, for individuals." At the same time the Atlanta paper virtually admitted that it did have a candidate in mind.[8] His identity was not long in coming.

On May 21, 1905, the *Journal* ran three-column headlines announcing that "HOKE SMITH IS URGED TO RUN FOR GOVERNOR." According to its article, "Politicians and public men generally are discussing with avidity a rumor which has been widely circulated, within the past week or ten days, to the effect that the strongest kind of pressure was being brought upon Hon. Hoke Smith . . . to enter the approaching Democratic primary as a candidate for governor." The *Journal* was enthusiastic about the possibility, pointing out that Smith's life and career typified opposition to "corporate aggression, and domination," and asserting that his candidacy would enlist the support of farmers, shippers, small manufacturers, and "educational people."

Just when the Atlanta *Journal* managers first thought of sponsoring Smith for the governorship is not apparent, but that he had emerged steadily during the past few months as a political possibility is plain enough from a survey of his activities and the responses to them. His name had been mentioned at recent meetings of the Georgia Child Labor Committee when "the talk inevitably turned toward the necessity of a political revolution in Georgia, before anything could be accomplished. . . ." Then Gray published his editorial describing the kind of governor Georgia needed and, according to Alexander Jeffrey McKelway, secretary of the Georgia Child Labor Committee, "the description happened to fit Hoke Smith like the paper on the wall." On the day following the appearance of Gray's editorial a committee of Atlanta businessmen called upon the *Journal* editor to discuss Smith as a possible candidate. Gray reminded his callers that he had made no reference to Smith in his editorial. "But you described him," was the reply of the committee spokesman.[9]

[8] Atlanta *Journal*, May 14, 18, 21, 1905.

[9] Davidson, *Child Labor Legislation in the South*, 199; Herbert Quick, "Hoke Smith and the Revolution in Georgia," in *Reader*, X (August, 1907), 244.

About the time the *Journal* began its campaign for Hoke Smith, the lawyer was quoted in another newspaper as saying that the suggestion of his name for the governorship was "entirely unauthorized." Earlier in the spring Smith had taken no public notice of the recurrent rumors that he planned to run for the Senate. Yet he had begun to act suspiciously like a candidate. In mid-May he began to cover the "commencement circuit" in a manner that caused some observers to suspect that more was involved than his usual willingness to support education. As one journal put it, "The eloquence of . . . Hoke Smith is being heard in different parts of the state . . . [and it] may or may not be of political significance." [10]

During the last week in May Smith's possible candidacy absorbed the state. A ground swell of tremendous proportions was set off by the mention of his name. His ability was universally conceded, and much was said about his service in the Cabinet, about his long interest in public education and other "uplift" endeavors, and about his hostility to the "soulless corporations." An editorial in the Augusta *Herald* reflected the spirit of many newspaper comments:

> There can be little argument as to the standing or strength of Mr. Smith in Georgia. He is a brave, intellectual man, whose honesty has never been questioned. There has never been a public matter in Georgia on which Mr. Smith did not have an opinion and he always expressed it with the greatest force at his command. In the practice of his profession he has always been opposed to the great corporations and the railroads in particular. . . . If Mr. Smith should consent to become a candidate for governor the people would be assured of a splendid campaign.[11]

Numerous petitions, the first one signed by 150 people in Morgan County, began to arrive at Smith's office and to find their way into the columns of the Atlanta *Journal*. Smith's office force was virtually inundated by the mail that suddenly began to

---

[10] Clippings from Fitzgerald *Enterprise*, May 16, 1905, and Brunswick *Journal*, May 22, 1905, in Smith scrapbooks.

[11] Augusta *Herald*, May 22, 1905. See also numerous other newspaper clippings in Smith scrapbooks.

come in. "Hoke Smith as governor of Georgia," ran a characteristic appeal, "would give us a pride and lend us a distinction from a national viewpoint that would do us untold good." One correspondent recalled her profound impression of Smith as an educational crusader when, three years before, she had heard him address a rural audience that had come over rough country roads from miles around to drink in his eloquent words. Many of the petitions and letters alluded to the need for a man to lead the fight against the corporations.[12]

Not all Georgians were enthusiastic about the prospect of Smith's candidacy. The Augusta *Chronicle*, which was especially critical of Smith, referred to the *Journal*'s " double-column generalities " of the past few weeks and asserted that the " one thing upon which all observers here agree is that this launching of a Hoke Smith boom means the abandonment of Pope Brown's candidacy by those most responsible for the Pulaski man's entering the race." Smith's hostility toward Clark Howell, declared the Augusta paper, had " permeated the Journal during his ownership of the property, and seems to have been one of the inheritances of the present ownership." [13]

The Atlanta *Journal* contended that these caustic remarks had been " inspired " by Clark Howell in an effort to create enmity " between the friends of Mr. Smith and those of Mr. Brown and Senator Clay." Smith, who had hitherto been a " veritable political sphinx," issued a long public statement: " I am a private citizen. I have not announced for governor. I have not announced for the senate. I have been deeply gratified by the many expressions of confidence in . . . asking me to run for the office of governor. I have done nothing to encourage it. I have never said that I would run; I have never said that I would not. I believe next year will see the people of the state fighting for freedom from corporation and ring rule. I will do what I can to help in the fight." The Atlantan denounced what he called " misrepresentation and carefully concocted stories " in some Georgia newspapers. " I am a very busy man," he concluded, " and this

---

[12] Atlanta *Journal*, May 23-26, 29, June 3, 1905; Atlanta *News*, May 30, 1905.

[13] Augusta *Chronicle*, May 23, 26, 1905.

question of running for governor has been brought up to me only within the past two or three weeks. When I make up my mind about it I shall promptly inform the public." [14]

On May 25 Clark Howell issued a statement which seemed to be " a direct challenge " to Smith. If the lawyer entered the race, proclaimed Howell, " we will see [who] . . . really has the best anti-corporation record." This angered Smith, who told newspapermen that Howell's suggestion that they compare records " inclines me strongly to make the race." In a second statement, the *Constitution* editor announced that if Smith entered the contest, " I will prove that for twenty years he has, time and again, been engaged at enormous retainers as special attorney for the railroads, and that his corporation record is as vulnerable as his record as an attorney." [15] If Howell's object was to bluff Smith out of the race, as some people suspected, he probably overplayed his hand.

Two days after Howell's first statement an important conference was held in James R. Gray's office. Gray, Thomas W. Hardwick, Pope Brown, and Hoke Smith had assembled to discuss the advisability of Brown's withdrawing from the campaign. Brown promised that after further thought he would give the other men an answer. Later in the day Smith wrote him, commenting on their agreement that the state must be rescued from " railroad emissaries and machine politicians," and calling attention to the pressure being brought to bear upon him to enter the race. He declared that he would not run for governor if Brown remained in the contest. On the last day of May Brown wrote Smith, manfully withdrawing from the race. His letter declared:

> We are in thorough accord on the issues that confront the people. For each of us to make the race would bring defeat. The question is, which one of us will more surely lead to victory the great mass of the people in their fight for the principles upon which our government was founded. . . . According to my custom, I have advised with my friends. . . . The majority advise that you are the man to make the race at this

---

[14] Atlanta *Journal*, May 24, 1905; Augusta *Chronicle*, May 26, 1905.
[15] Atlanta *Journal*, May 25, 26, 1905; Atlanta *News*, May 25, 27, 1905.

time. In that view I shall cheerfully acquiesce and give you my most hearty support.[16]

On June 3 Brown publicly withdrew from the race and Smith announced his candidacy.

Having made the decision to run for governor, Smith immediately sought Watson's support. Smith and Watson had belabored each other in the nineties, and as late as 1904 Smith had sharply criticized the Populist leader. But Hardwick and other friends of Smith began a campaign of persuasion, and ultimately, but with some reluctance, Watson agreed to support Smith. James K. Hines, a Populist leader in the 1890's, wrote Watson in June to say that Smith was " crazy " for his backing. He summed up the factors for and against the Atlanta lawyer: " He embraced & abandoned the Alliance. He was for Cleveland. He was for Parker. He is strongly against corruption in politics, for stringent control of railroads, against corporation domination, and for negro disfranchisement." Hardwick advised Watson that Smith was the only man in the state independent of the corporations, with the necessary strength " mentally, physically, and financially to beat Clark and ' the boys.' " [17] Smith himself wrote Watson on June 20: " It is true that we may differ on questions of national policy, but as to the issues of the present campaign in Georgia I feel sure that your views and mine will thoroughly coincide." He had not wanted to run for governor, continued the Atlantan. " It was only because I felt called upon to help free the people of the State from domination by railroad corporations and machine politicians. . . ." [18]

Watson took his time in replying to these overtures. An indispensable price of his support was a commitment to Negro disfranchisement. This Smith gave, although in earlier years he

[16] Smith to Brown, May 27, 1905, and Brown to Smith, May 31, 1905, in Atlanta *Journal*, June 4, 1905. Brown stated later that Smith had been so impatient for his friend's decision that he called him by telephone to ask what he had decided. Brown to Watson, February 22, 23, 1908, in Watson Papers.

[17] Hines to Watson, June 8, 14, 1905, and Hardwick to Watson, June 26, 1905, in Watson Papers.

[18] Smith to Watson, June 20, 1905, *ibid.*

had opposed such action. The Atlanta *Journal* had also opposed disfranchisement, but on the day after the Atlanta conference it came out in favor of the proposal. Finally, on September 12, Watson wrote Smith pledging his help, because, he said, they were both committed to disfranchisement and because Smith had promised to smash the corrupt "corporation ring." The "Sage of Hickory Hill" was soon appealing to Populists to help elect "Hoke," whom Watson referred to as "a strong, fearless, indomitable man." Most Populists were prepared, as always, to do Watson's bidding. Smith was grateful. "I cannot tell you how much I appreciate your cooperation," he wrote Watson. ". . . I well know how much your influence will mean, and I hope you may deem it proper to give public expression to your views at an early date." [19]

As soon as it became apparent that Smith was definitely in the race for governor, Clark Howell and the Atlanta *Constitution* launched a violent campaign of abuse and innuendo against the new candidate. At the same time Howell sought to show that he was really an anticorporation man, and his paper put itself on record as favoring the popular election of the members of the railroad commission and the enactment of antipass legislation. The *Constitution* was quick to encourage some of those who had been laboring in the vineyard of reform for many years—men like Joseph Hill Hall and Sidney Tapp—when they accused Hoke Smith of being a Johnny-come-lately. Hall, a veteran legislator from Macon, issued a sharp statement early in June, charging Smith with having helped defeat Dupont Guerry in the campaign of 1902, and pointing out that as a delegate to the state convention that year the lawyer had voted for Terrell. Tapp, an Atlanta lawyer who had also supported Guerry in 1902, was even more critical of Smith. He charged that Smith "only wishes to use this reform movement for his own selfish ends." Furthermore, declared Tapp, "he has surrendered, lock, stock and barrel, to the corporations, and he dares not deny it." [20]

[19] Smith to Watson, September 16, 1905, *ibid.*; Woodward, *Tom Watson*, 375.

[20] Atlanta *Constitution*, May 28, 30, June 11, 13, 1905, March 23, 1906; Macon *Telegraph*, June 7, 1905; Tapp to Watson, May 30, 1905, in Watson Papers.

Seizing on such allegations, the Atlanta *Constitution* sarcastically referred to "sham reformers," and asserted that Smith acted as if he had received a "Divine Call" to save Georgia from the corporations. Yet, declared Howell's paper, Smith had received large fees for defending business combinations and had borrowed $50,000 from New York financiers in 1896, on the endorsement of the Southern Railroad Company. After that time, continued the *Constitution*, the Atlanta *Journal* had been as quiet as "a clam on the subject" of corporation abuses. The Augusta *Chronicle* joined in; it had no confidence in a "reformer" who would "now play the demagogue in order to snatch the governorship from a hated rival."[21]

Smith issued several statements defending his record on the corporation question, and later in the campaign had a special pamphlet prepared in an effort to answer Howell's charges. He stated that he had represented railroads only twice during the past nine years, and that of $250,000 collected by his firm during that period, only $12,500 had come from railroads. He described an effort by Samuel Spencer of the Southern Railroad to retain him in 1896, and his refusal to represent the railroad because of his doubts concerning the legitimacy of certain of its holdings. The attorney also related how he had agreed to represent the Southern Railroad early in 1898, after he had become convinced that the Central of Georgia Railroad was not controlled by the Southern. He assisted in the preparation of the railroad's answer in this antitrust case, but he maintained, "I COULD NOT BE EMPLOYED BY THE SOUTHERN RAILWAY COMPANY IN ANY LITIGATION WHICH WAS IN CONFLICT WITH MY VIEWS OF THE CONSTITUTION . . . OR THE INTERESTS OF THE PUBLIC." As for the New York loan, Smith admitted having borrowed $40,000 in 1898, with the aid but not the formal endorsement of Samuel Spencer. He claimed that he had received no money from the Southern Railroad or any other railroad between the time he had borrowed the money and the time he paid it back in full, in 1900.[22]

[21] Atlanta *Constitution*, June 13, 15, July 1, 6-9, 14, August 27, 1905; Augusta *Chronicle*, July 5, 6, 1905.

[22] Smith to Samuel Spencer, January 16, 24, 1898, and to Francis Lynde

Before the discussion of the *Constitution*'s corporation charges had ceased, the state was rocked by the Guerry controversy. Guerry and some of those associated with him in the campaign of 1902 announced that Smith had encouraged the reformer to enter the primary for governor in 1902, only to support Terrell in the long run. Smith and the Atlanta *Journal*, which was also supposed to have encouraged Guerry at one point, emphatically denied these accusations, and Smith complained that Guerry had mistaken " ordinary courtesy and common politeness for implied assurance of political support." [23] Nevertheless, this was more grist for Clark Howell's mill.

Some charges made against Smith by " moral reformers " were not without a humorous side. A story soon spread over the state to the effect that as one of the owners of the Piedmont Hotel, Smith shared in the profits from the barroom operated in the hotel. Forced to take notice of this report, Smith declared that the bar had been opened over his protest and that his share of the profits was given to charity. This moved the *Constitution* to observe, " Gentle reader, you may pause here—to smile! " Smith was also arraigned for immorality because the "nude " statue of a woman was exhibited in " that palatial hell-gate," the Piedmont Hotel barroom. " The Gal in the Fountain " was discussed from one end of Georgia to the other. [24]

Although the primary would not be held until the summer of 1906, Smith began his campaign in June, 1905. For over a year he crisscrossed the state numerous times, making an estimated 300 addresses and speaking in all but two or three of Georgia's 145 counties. He spoke in cities, towns, crossroads, and " bridle-paths." He traveled by train, automobile, buggy, and wagon; he spoke in courthouses, opera houses, schoolhouses, and out in the open. Georgia had never witnessed a campaign quite like it.

Smith presented a comprehensive program from the beginning

Stetson, February 10, 1898, in Smith letterbooks; Atlanta *Journal*, July 3, 13, 24, 1905; *Mr. Hoke Smith Replies to the False Charges Made by the Atlanta Constitution*, undated pamphlet, in Smith Collection.

[23] Atlanta *Constitution*, August 16, 17, 20, 1905; Atlanta *Journal*, August 16-18, 20, 21, 25, 27, September 3, 1905.

[24] Atlanta *Journal*, July 17, 18, 1905; Atlanta *Constitution*, July 18, October 4, 1905, January 24, February 22, 1906.

of his long campaign. In his formal announcement of June 3, 1905, he dwelt upon the great influence exerted by "railroad corporations, aided by astute politicians," and demanded the passage of an antilobbying law, a strengthened railroad commission elected by the voters, the development of the educational system of the state, and a constitutional amendment to "insure a continuation of white supremacy." On June 29, 1905, Smith made the opening address of his campaign at Madison. There the Morgan County Hoke Smith Club had made elaborate preparations; there was a barbecue dinner, the inevitable brass band, special trains, and an audience of 3,500 people, many of whom had come by wagon and buggy from distant farms. The speech was a clear, direct, and earnest statement of the candidate's position. The emphasis was on the railroad issue. Smith discussed the evils associated with railroad political agents, free passes, and money in elections. He charged that the railroad politicians controlled legislation in Georgia, that foreign corporations operated the state's railroads, and that the carriers levied prohibitive rates by agreement among themselves to prevent Georgia produce from being shipped to the coast, where water transportation could be used. He criticized the railroad commission, especially Joseph M. Brown, for allowing this situation, and recommended stringent railroad regulation, including the domestication of all railroads in the state.[25]

Eventually five other men entered the campaign. One of the major candidates was John H. Estill, the affable publisher of the Savannah *Morning News*, who had made a creditable showing when he ran for governor in 1902. He hoped, no doubt, to capitalize on the frequent complaints in South Georgia about "the long continued practice . . . of parcelling out the offices among the people from the upper part of the state." [26] Another candidate was Richard B. Russell, an ex-judge of the superior court. He described himself as an "anti-ringer," and proposed a number of tax reforms. Two minor candidates were James M. Smith, a wealthy planter from Oglethorpe County, and Dr. G. A.

[25] Atlanta *Journal*, June 4, 10, 28, 30, 1905.

[26] Clippings from Brunswick *Journal*, May 16, 1905, and Savannah *Morning News*, January 19, 1906, in Smith scrapbooks.

Nunnally, a crusading minister from Newnan who withdrew before the end of the campaign. Nunnally seemed to delight in denouncing Smith for his part-ownership of the Piedmont Hotel bar.

Smith's leading opponent, apparently, was Clark Howell, who was widely regarded as the "machine candidate." Forty-two years of age, Howell was a dapper little man who had successfully edited the Atlanta *Constitution* for many years. He had served in the General Assembly for over a decade, having been chosen speaker of the house and, later, president of the senate. He had been Democratic national committeeman for Georgia since 1892. Howell was a "nice little man," declared a South Georgia newspaper. "He keeps his mustache waxed, wears clothes fit for a walking advertisement of a clothing store and keeps his beaver hat rubbed the right way always. He practices the art of rubbing things and people and corporations the right way. . . ." [27]

Howell issued his formal platform in November, 1905. He praised the Terrell administration, referred to the current prosperity, and pledged himself to work for an extension of the cotton trade, the reduction of taxes, liberal Confederate pensions, an elective railroad commission, and the abolition of free passes. He lamented the "traduction" of the state and promised to give capital a "square deal." He opposed disfranchisement as unnecessary and likely to bring discord and division. [28]

The center of the campaign was the fight between Smith and Howell, which found its most violent expression in the daily columns of the *Journal* and the *Constitution*. As the Atlanta *News* observed, "All the epithets that disfigure the calendar of current politics are applied and re-applied, freely, fiercely and frequently between two daily journals who have enjoyed for many years reputations of at least comparative respectability." [29] The *Constitution* condemned the Smith men as "Jeremiahs of calamity in the much-abused name of reform," and described the Smith campaign as an attempt to "pillory Georgia in the eyes of the nation as a state hopelessly in the clutches of corruptors.

[27] Waycross *Journal*, quoted in Atlanta *Journal*, June 13, 1905.
[28] Atlanta *Constitution*, November 9, 17, 1905.
[29] Atlanta *News*, October 28, 1905.

. . ." [30] Smith and the *Journal* charged that Howell had opposed the election of General John B. Gordon to the Senate in 1890, and scored Howell's record on the question of railroad regulation.[31]

While denouncing Howell the *Journal* was busily engaged, with the aid of most of the afternoon newspapers in the state, in acclaiming Smith as "the people's candidate." It filled its columns with testimonials of Smith's popularity and with lengthy reports of his speeches and of the numerous activities involved in his campaign. The *Journal* associated its candidate with a wave of reform that was sweeping the country: "The people of the United States are beginning to reassert themselves. They have awakened, and are showing the determination to take their power back into their own hands. Party slogans fool them no longer. . . . They have finally discovered that a ring or a boss exists only by public sufferance, that the people . . . can control, if they choose to control, in spite of the efforts of any clique, ring or conspiracy." [32]

Hoke Smith's campaign, asserted the Macon *Telegraph*, which was bitterly hostile to the Atlantan, was "anti-nigger and anti-railroad." At the outset Smith emphasized the railroad issue, because the sentiment for railroad regulation was strong and widespread in the state. The people believed, declared the Atlanta *News* immediately after the election, that the railroads had "been unfair to them in the matter of freight and passenger rates, and service, and payment of just and fair taxes, the reasonable fixing of franchise values, and that the general policy of the corporations is inimicable to the public welfare." According to a contemporary writer, the railroads fought Smith "at every turn and corner, by speeches, newspapers, circulars, affidavits, and reckless assertions." [33]

The railroads had reason to oppose Smith. His speeches were

[30] Atlanta *Constitution*, June 15, July 4, 5, 7, 9, 12, August 6, 14, 27, 28, September 10, October 26, 1905, May 1, 1906.

[31] Atlanta *Journal*, June 9, 13, 17, 26, 27, July 17, October 2, 1905, June 23, 1906.

[32] *Ibid.*, November 12, 1905.

[33] John C. Reed, "The Recent Primary Election in Georgia," in *South Atlantic Quarterly*, VI (January, 1907), 30; Atlanta *News*, August 23, 1906.

full of such terms as "railroad ring crowd," "eastern capitalists," and "the man with the railroad pass," and references to lobbyists, who made up a "third house" of the legislature. He denounced the railroads for watering their stock and for not paying adequate taxes. He demonstrated, for instance, that in 1904 the roads in Georgia returned their property for tax purposes at twenty million dollars, yet earned net profits during the same year of almost nine million. He spent a great deal of time discussing freight rates, pointing out that the rates had remained practically stationary during the past ten years, despite the fact that railroad earnings had doubled. He was especially critical of preferential rates and alleged discriminations in rate schedules.[34]

Clark Howell charged that Smith favored the confiscation of railroad property, but the lawyer denied this, contending that he advocated "no crusade against corporations." More effective than Howell in answering Smith's attack on railroad rates was Joseph M. Brown, who earned the epithet "card writing commissioner" as a result of his series of open letters to Smith and the Atlanta *Journal*. He challenged the arguments of the rate reformers and tended to give credit for some recent reductions to the railroad commission rather than to the Atlanta shippers. Brown was subtle while Smith was direct. He accused Smith of opposing railroad improvements because of his interest in damage suits, and he appealed to sectional and agrarian interests by attempting to show that Atlanta merchants sought favorable rates at the expense of other areas of the state.[35]

Smith partisans, meanwhile, accused Brown of having "danced attendance" on the railroads, and Smith declared that he would remove Brown if he won the governorship. Contrary to Brown's contention, argued the *Journal*, the freight rates in Georgia were 25 per cent higher than those in surrounding states; in answer to the commissioner's charge that the port rate reductions would help only Atlanta, it declared that such reductions would aid cities throughout the state.[36]

[34] Atlanta *Journal*, July 25, August 5, September 26, October 10, December 10, 1905, January 10, April 12, June 20, 23, July 9, 1906.
[35] Atlanta *Constitution*, August 8, September 10, 24, October 1, 8, November 5, 1905; Atlanta *Journal*, June 23, 1906.
[36] Atlanta *Journal*, June 19, 25, July 9, 11, August 6, 13, 27, September 3, December 10, 1905.

Late in the summer of 1905 the *Constitution* began to publicize a report that Hoke Smith had appointed Negroes to office while in the Cabinet. Names and salaries were published, including those of members of the family of Bishop Henry M. Turner, a prominent Negro leader who had written Cleveland recommending Smith in 1893. The most sensational aspect of the *Constitution*'s story, which was often repeated, was that Smith had given Negroes positions which could have been given to white men and women: "No amount of disclaimer can conceal that picture of the door of opportunity shut to southern white men and women by black hands. . . ."[37] Smith supporters cited errors in the list of Negroes published in the *Constitution*, and claimed that the only Negroes Smith appointed had been given menial positions. Claude N. Bennett wrote a series of articles describing the Secretary's liberality in awarding Federal positions to white Georgians. Bishop Turner declared that he believed Smith to be, at heart, "a broad humanitarian and a grand man generally," but he was sorry that as a candidate he should "descend to the lowly and ignoble plane of trifling his precious time away with so much of the negro question as to advocate the theoretical disfranchisement of my race, when we are practically disfranchised already."[38]

Whether as a result of Howell's attack, the influence of Watson and Hardwick, or the growing popularity of the issue, Smith began to give more emphasis to disfranchisement as the campaign proceeded. That Smith had not thought much about disfranchisement before he entered the campaign is evident in a letter Hardwick wrote to Watson in June, 1905: "I still think that there will be no trouble in getting Mr. Smith to do the right thing, and I will undertake to do my best in that direction."[39]

Until the campaign of 1905-1906, Smith seemed to be in agreement with those Southern leaders who around the turn of the century were beginning to be optimistic about race relations

[37] Atlanta *Constitution*, September 2, 5, 9, 10, 12, 17, October 2, 8, 1905; Atlanta *Journal*, September 7, 1905.

[38] Atlanta *Journal*, September 12, 16, 20, 22, 27, October 26, November 2, 9, 11, December 4, 1905; Atlanta *Constitution*, September 26, October 8, 1905.

[39] Hardwick to Watson, June 26, 1905, in Watson Papers.

in the South and the effect that the lessening of racial tensions might have on the region. Smith subscribed to the belief that a policy of tolerant white paternalism was the best hope for Negro progress. He advocated Negro education; he opposed disfranchisement when it became an issue in Georgia in 1899; and under his leadership the Atlanta *Journal* condemned lynching as " inconsistent with proper reverence for the law." He was an ardent supporter of Booker T. Washington's philosophy. " The race problem is no longer a menace," he asserted in 1901, and he was quoted as saying two years later that the only trouble " affecting the colored man is agitation." [40]

Under Thomas W. Hardwick's skillful direction, disfranchisement was added to the Smith platform in 1905. Suddenly it had become a matter of political expediency, and Smith was willing to embrace the proposal if it would mean Tom Watson's support. He realized Watson's power in the state; he perhaps realized too that if he failed to win Watson's endorsement Clark Howell would. Many people were surprised and disquieted by Smith's acceptance of disfranchisement. As an Athens businessman said in the summer of 1905: " Especially am I surprised at Mr. Hoke Smith who has given much thought and time to educational matters. . . . Smith is determined to be governor, cost what it may. His sole purpose now is to get there. When he gets there (if he does) he probably thinks he would make a good governor and make good for such let down's as he has announced in his plea for disfranchisement." [41]

Smith probably did not intend to emphasize disfranchisement when he first agreed to support the movement, but when Howell accused him of having discriminated against whites and in favor of Negroes as Secretary of Interior, when the *Constitution* editor told Georgians that disfranchisement would hurt whites more than Negroes, and when he ridiculed Smith's proposals for amending the constitution, the lawyer threw caution to the winds. Doubtless the railroads and other corporations in the state,

[40] Atlanta *Journal*, July 20-22, 29-31, 1897, November 5, 12, 23, 1898, December 9, 1899, June 12, 1901; New York *Tribune*, October 10, 1903.
[41] Harry Hodgson to " G. F. P.," July 30, 1905, copy in possession of Mrs. Anne Scott, Haverford, Pennsylvania.

so sharply attacked by Smith earlier in the campaign, were glad to have attention directed toward the race question. Whether or not they promoted this diversion is hard to determine, though Smith partisans later contended that they did. " Now it happened that in the progress of the campaign," asserted the Atlanta *Journal* a few months later, " the political managers, whose slogan was, ' let well enough alone,' found themselves most vulnerable on the railroad question. The facts and the arguments were all with the people's candidate. So the attempt was made to shift the issue from the main one to the minor one of negro disfranchise-ment." [42]

The position Smith assumed is evident from this selection from one of his campaign addresses:

No more important question can be presented to the people of Georgia than the disfranchisement of the ignorant, pur-chasable negro vote. . . .

This is a white man's country, and we are all agreed that not only in the state at large, BUT IN EVERY COUNTY AND IN EVERY COMMUNITY the white man must control by some means, or life could not be worth living.

No matter how secure we may feel at present from negro domination, if . . . there is danger to the state at large, or to any county or community in Georgia from this curse, it will be folly for us to neglect any means within our reach to remove the danger. . . .

I plant my case upon the intellectual superiority of the white man; the capacity of every white boy who has a fair show to fit himself for duties the negro can never discharge, no matter what his opportunities.[43]

Many of Smith's arguments were disingenuous. He contended, for example, that disfranchisement would improve the conditions of labor. " It is a fact which experience has shown in Georgia," he said, " that negroes are better laborers and citizens when out of politics." Time and again he stated that Negroes were in a majority in thirty-one Georgia towns and in at least fifty counties.

[42] Atlanta *Journal*, March 3, 1907; Reed, " The Recent Primary Election in Georgia," *loc. cit.*, 33-34.
[43] Atlanta *Journal*, December 10, 1905.

He cited the "humiliation" of McIntosh County, which had a
Negro in the legislature. "I have conferred with leading men
from those southern states which have adopted constitutional provisions establishing white supremacy," Smith assured Georgians.
"They bear testimony to the value of the legislation. . . ."[44] His
enemies attributed to him such assertions as this:

> Whenever and wherever a negro qualifies as a voter, by
> reason of his educational advancement, it would be an easy
> matter to handle him as they do in Mississippi, ask him what
> is the meaning of "ex post facto" law, or some other question
> couched in such language as you know he cannot answer. And
> when a poor, ignorant white man, who by reason of his poverty
> and conditions otherwise unfavorable to his opportunities to
> qualify as a voter comes ask him some simple question, such
> as: Can a man be imprisoned for debt? And should it ever
> become necessary we can handle them as they did in Wil-
> mington.[45]

Following the campaign Smith denied that he had advised dis-
honest administration of the laws, citing the "false construction"
put upon his speeches by his opponents.[46]

Smith newspapers like the *Journal* and the Augusta *Herald*
kept up a constant barrage of editorials and articles on the need
for disfranchisement. It was all very well for the *Constitution*
to talk of "letting well enough alone," argued the *Journal*, yet
"there is no legal barrier to prevent these dusky hordes from
holding primaries of their own and proceeding to the polls to
vote for their candidates." Watson lent his pen in his newspaper
and magazine, and Hardwick issued a widely circulated letter
to the "white voters" urging support for the plan.[47] Meanwhile,
Smith's opponents sought desperately to minimize the influence
of the disfranchisement appeal. Clark Howell, for instance, de-

---

[44] *Ibid.*, December 10, 1905, January 10, June 23, 1906; *White Supremacy
in Georgia and How to Protect the Rights of the People*, undated pamphlet,
in Smith Collection.

[45] Macon *Telegraph*, March 15, 1906. See also Atlanta *Journal*, May 28,
29, June 23, 1906.

[46] Macon *Telegraph*, October 12, 1906; Augusta *Herald*, October 14, 1906.

[47] Atlanta *Journal*, November 24, 1905, August 21, 1906; *Tom Watson's
Magazine*, III (January, 1906), 263-64.

clared that the educational clause would only serve as a magnet
to "draw the negroes of Georgia out of the cotton patch into
the negro colleges." Remember, warned the *Constitution* editor,
"whenever the nigger learns his [hic,] haec, hoc, he right away
forgets all about gee-whoa-buck! " [48]

Not since Populist days, observed one Atlanta newspaper, had
there been "a clear-cut fight before the wool-hat boys, with the
stump speeches, the torch light processions and all the accompani-
ments of such a campaign in Georgia politics." To add to the
excitement, Hoke Smith demanded that Clark Howell meet him
on the stump. When Howell showed no alacrity in accepting
this challenge, Smith began to open his addresses with the query,
"Is Mr. Clark Howell in the audience? I invited him to meet
me here face to face. . . . He does not seem to have had the
courage to come." [49] Later in the campaign Smith and Howell
did meet in two or three joint debates. [50]

Their contest at Columbus on January 10, 1906, was one of
the most spectacular events of the long campaign. All of the
old arguments were repeated, with a liberal addition of personalities, before a packed audience in the local opera house. The
moment of most dramatic interest was Howell's disclosure of the
"Sibley letter." This letter was allegedly written to the *Constitution* editor on July 14, 1905, by John A. Sibley of Marietta,
who claimed that Tom Watson had recently indicated his willingness to support Clark Howell for governor if the latter would
come out for disfranchisement. At Columbus Howell disdain-
fully informed his audience that he had declined to seek Watson's
support. On the day following the debate Watson sent a telegram
to the *Journal* in which he declared that he had given no one
"authority to offer my support to Howell on any terms." [51]

As the campaign progressed, Tom Watson provided strong
support to Smith's cause. His chief bête noire, of course, was

[48] Atlanta *Constitution*, September 15, 1905, January 10, 11, and files for
March-April, 1906.

[49] Atlanta *News*, June 3, 27, 1905; Atlanta *Journal*, July 2, 3, 10, September
26, 28, 1905, June 4, 20-24, 1906.

[50] Smith also met Richard B. Russell in two or three joint debates.

[51] Atlanta *Journal*, January 10-12, June 20-24, 1906; Atlanta *Constitution*,
January 10-12, 1906.

the Negro issue, but he also bitterly assailed Clark Howell, Governor Terrell, and others affiliated with the Howell element.[52] Howell and the *Constitution*, with strong assistance from the Augusta *Chronicle* and the Macon *Telegraph*, charged time after time that Smith was endeavoring to open the Democratic primary to all Populists and to wreck the party. Much was said about a deal between Smith and Watson.[53] The State Democratic Executive Committee, which was made up largely of anti-Smith men, caused this caption to be printed on the ballot prepared for the primary in 1906: "By voting this ticket, I hereby declare that I am an organized Democrat, and I hereby pledge myself to support the organized democracy, both state and national." Smith leaders denounced this as a ruse to keep Watson men out of the primary.[54]

Smith and his advisers constantly tried to please Watson. Smith himself referred to the Populist leader in many of his speeches and took occasion during the campaign to write him several times, in one instance saying hopefully, "How I wish you could come back to the democratic party!" Since Watson did not announce such an intention, Smith strategists tried to play down the Populist leader's part in the campaign, and thus to avoid criticism.[55]

Despite the frequent references in Smith newspapers to a "spontaneous uprising of the people," Smith's campaign was capably organized. Hundreds of Hoke Smith clubs were formed throughout the state, and men like Hooper Alexander, Pope Brown, and Congressman Charles L. Bartlett made speeches for the Smith cause. In June, 1906, the Smith managers invited a number of prominent Georgians to come to Atlanta in order to

[52] *Tom Watson's Magazine*, II (October, 1905), 398; *ibid.*, IV (March, 1906), 1-7; *ibid.*, V (July, 1906), 6-15.

[53] Atlanta *Constitution*, October 22, 24, 30, November 3, 1905, January 17, 18, 1906; Augusta *Chronicle*, December 10, 1905; Macon *Telegraph*, June 7, 28, 1906.

[54] Smith to Watson, December 19, 1905, in Watson Papers; Atlanta *Journal*, May 1, 3, 9, 1906.

[55] Smith to Watson, September 16, December 19, 1905, July 29, August 12, 1906, and James K. Hines to Watson, December 9, 11, 16, 1905, in Watson Papers.

represent Smith to the members of the legislature, which convened in late June for its annual session.[56]

As the end of the campaign approached, the hectic fight between the *Journal* and the *Constitution* continued without letup,
each newspaper seeking to win over the smaller state papers. One
of the most colorful aspects of this clash was the series of slashing,
satirical cartoons, often huge, front-page drawings depicting the
Howell-Smith contest. Picturing Hoke Smith as a rotund, blank-
faced politician wearing a halo and Tom Watson as a lean-
featured old pirate in full regalia, putting the ax to the "polluted,
corrupt vagabond, Democracy," Lewis C. Gregg of the *Constitution* gave his cartoons such titles as "The Cruise of the
Buccaneers." Beneath one of these drawings was the following
rhyme, supposedly chanted by "Tom" and "Hoke":

> There's peace and plenty in the old State now
> But before we're through with our orgy
> We'll make the "Vagabond Democrats" howl
> "Hell's broke loose in Georgia."

William F. Henderson's cartoons in the *Journal* were perhaps
more effective. He often showed the stout figure of the "Railroad Trust" playing a street organ, while Clark Howell danced
to the tune and "Little Albert," Clark's brother, was included.[57]

The campaign continued without slackening through the long,
hot days of the summer of 1906. "I would give my right arm,"
Smith wrote Tom Watson, "to see the principals [*sic*] for which
I am struggling win." [58] Smith leaders warned that the "machine"
had deliberately encouraged a number of candidates in order to
divide the reform vote, pointing out that the new rules announced
by the state committee would make it easy for the opposition
to Smith to consolidate on one of his opponents.[59] Smith himself

[56] Marion Smith to Gerard Glenn, April 30, 1906, and Smith's office to
Warren Grice, June 26, 1906, in Smith letterbooks; Atlanta *Journal*, June 6,
9, 12, 13, September 26, 1905.

[57] Atlanta *Constitution*, February 9, August 12, 19, 21, 22, 1906; Atlanta
Journal, July 6, August 24, September 17, 1906.

[58] Smith to Watson, June 29, 1906, in Watson Papers.

[59] The executive committee had directed the selection of delegates to the
state convention by the candidate who carried a particular county rather
than by the county committee as had been the custom.

was later quoted as saying, "If I don't get enough delegates to beat them all combined, I am beaten; for, after the first ballot, they will combine." Smith's friend Robert L. Berner wrote a few weeks before the election: "I confess that I have entertained up to this time but little hope of the people ever making a successful fight against the combination of forces arrayed by the corporations in this state against its welfare, but I am hopeful now in the present campaign, and I believe the dawn is breaking on corporation-ridden Georgia." [60]

As far as Smith's hopes were concerned, Berner was right. For in the primary of August 22, Hoke Smith rode into office on a great wave of popular support. He received 104,796 popular votes to 70,477 for all of his opponents and 312 county-unit votes to 52 for the opposition. Clark Howell had carried only six counties. [61]

The state Democratic convention, which assembled in Macon on September 4, 1906, to ratify the primary results, was a personal triumph for Smith. The delegates were in a triumphant mood, and the early September weather brought out a shirt-sleeved crowd, with many ladies in "white dresses and shirt waists" in the gallery. Smith was nominated by acclamation, amid tumultuous enthusiasm. There were eloquent addresses, excited talk of reform, and references to Hoke Smith as the greatest living Southerner. The nominee appeared before the delegates to make a spirited address, in which he alluded to the days of 1868 when white civilization was at stake and to Robert Toombs's warning against "corporation aggression." He cautioned his followers that the victory would not be complete until the platform was

[60] Berner to W. B. Crawford, August 13, 1906, in Watson Papers; Atlanta *Journal*, July 24, August 14, 19-22, 1906; Quick, "Hoke Smith and the Revolution in Georgia," *loc. cit.*, 247.

[61] One hundred and eighty-four county-unit votes were required to win. The popular and county-unit vote of the other candidates were: Russell— 25,290 and 24; Howell—23,006 and 12; Estill—22,958 and 10; and James M. Smith—8,223 and 6. Atlanta *Journal*, August 25, September 4, 1906.

In the general election that followed in the fall, Smith received 76,962 votes to 148 for a Populist named J. B. Osburn. *Journal of House of Representatives of the State of Georgia at the Regular Session of the General Assembly* (Atlanta, 1907), 86.

translated into legislation, and he pledged his own enlistment in the reform movement for life. "We have begun a contest for popular rights and higher ideals of civic righteousness in Georgia," he declared, "and our success will inspire hope and action beyond the borders of our state. It will help to swell the tide which is daily rising throughout our country. . . ." [62]

The platform was a reiteration of Smith's hundreds of campaign speeches. "The state Democratic convention was an aggregation of new men and new measures," asserted the Savannah *Press*. "The old crowd, which has been running things for the past twelve years, seems to have disappeared from view. Now and then one of the old guard would turn up in Macon on the outskirts of the crowd, but he was merely a spectator, and had no voice in the proceedings." [63] The curtain had come down on the prologue.

[62] Atlanta *Journal*, September 1-5, 1906; Macon *Telegraph*, September 6, 1906.

[63] Savannah *Press*, September 5, 1906.

Reaction and Reform

Hoke Smith's popularity during the months following his victory
in the primary of 1906 was reminiscent of his swift rise in the
political world in 1892-93. Suddenly he was the subject of
national attention and the object of considerable speculation concerning the Democratic national ticket for 1908. William Jennings
Bryan himself suggested that the Georgian would be "a good
southern Democrat for the presidency."[1] All of this was grati-
fying to Smith, but a little premature. The first order of business
was the governorship and the reforms he had promised to carry
out if elected.

In the long interval between his nomination in August, 1906,
and his inauguration in June, 1907, Smith had plenty of time to
perfect the details of his program and to give further expression
to his ideas. "I expect to spend the rest of my life in studying
the problems which concern the state and the South and in
writing and talking about them," he was quoted as saying. He
delivered several speeches in which he struck an aggressive attitude toward the corporations.[2] Early in 1907 he gave the major
address at the convention of the Southern Cotton Association in
Birmingham, Alabama, criticizing the efforts of outsiders to de-
press the market but calling on Southerners to effect their own
redemption.[3]

[1] *Commoner*, April 12, 1907. See also Atlanta *Georgian and News*,
January 21, June 8, 19, 20, 1907; Atlanta *Journal*, February 21, June 6, 1907.
[2] Atlanta *Journal*, October 10, 23, 1906, January 6, 27, February 16, 1907;
Atlanta *Constitution*, March 15, 1907.
[3] Atlanta *Journal*, January 18, 1907; Smith to Watson, December 20,
1906, January 24, 1907, in Watson Papers.

During this period Smith devoted a good deal of time to a plan to induce European immigrants to come to Georgia. Selected white immigrants would bring needed skills to the state and "relieve our dependence upon the negroes," he argued. In February, 1907, a large immigration convention assembled in Macon and made plans for encouraging immigration. Soon afterward Smith agreed to accompany W. W. Williamson of Savannah and G. Gunby Jordan, president of the Georgia Immigration Association, on an exploratory trip to Europe in the interest of the movement. The three men, with Mrs. Smith, embarked for Europe on the *Kaiser Wilhelm II* in April and returned a month later after visiting Bremen, Hamburg, Berlin, and Vienna. They conferred with officials of the North German Lloyd Company and attempted to persuade them to establish a direct emigrant line to Savannah and Charleston.[4]

Smith seemed to think some success had been achieved, but as governor he did not attempt to force any legislation through the General Assembly to give further encouragement to the movement. The reason was soon apparent: It had become politically inexpedient to push the proposal. Tom Watson discouraged the immigration talk at the Farmers' Union convention in 1907, and others opposed the idea in the Southern Cotton Association. Both the Farmers' Union and the Georgia State Federation of Labor adopted strong resolutions opposing immigration. Smith's enemies were getting ready to use the immigration proposal as a tool against him, and he was determined not " to permit at this time a fight which might jeopardize other measures of great importance." [5]

Following the European trip, the governor-elect began to make careful plans for the forthcoming legislative session. He conferred with his supporters in the General Assembly, corresponded with numerous people about the legislation to be introduced, and arranged to have his lieutenants draft several bills. " We are trying to have ready a bill covering every provision of the platform

[4] Atlanta *Journal*, April 6, 21, May 2, 8, 10, 1907.
The Smiths returned via Geneva, Paris, and London.
[5] Smith to Watson, June 17, 1907, in Watson Papers; Atlanta *Constitution*, May 1, July 20, 1907; Atlanta *Georgian and News*, July 10, 25, 1907.

adopted at Macon to meet our promises to the people," wrote Smith. "As I continue my study of the conditions of affairs in the state, I see more and more where the rights of the people have been disregarded and where work is to be done." [6]

The day of Hoke Smith's inauguration—June 29, 1907—was an occasion to remember. There had been nothing like it, asserted an Atlanta newspaper, since "colonial patriots gathered at Savannah to declare Georgia a sovereign state." Since early morning the streets had been lined with people eager to greet the marching soldiers, the brass bands, and the political clubs. Almost every building was decked with masses of bunting and flags, and festoons of flowers encircled portraits of the state's leading politician. At noon the center of attention became the improvised pavilion on the capitol grounds, where a tall, somewhat ponderous figure attired in a light silk coat and a plain straw hat was preparing to take the oath of office as governor of Georgia. A few minutes later the new governor began to read his inaugural address.

Smith said little that was new to his audience; his address was a comprehensive summary of the familiar reform proposals. "I accept office," he declared, "under solemn direction by the people to carry out the platform pledges." Foreseeing, perhaps, the temptations of reformers to follow the siren calls of other movements, he warned that "We must not be led away to other tasks until our specific pledges to the people have been performed." In a one-two-three fashion he outlined his plans to prohibit lobbying, outlaw free passes, ensure clean elections, regulate the primaries by state law, amend the constitution by adopting a literacy test and a "grandfather clause," extend the Western and Atlantic Railroad, and strengthen the railroad commission and regulate public-service companies. Georgia must move forward, declared Smith, and "constantly broaden opportunities for mental, moral and financial growth to [the] less fortunate." [7]

Smith seemed to see nothing incongruous in this plea for progress and his plan to disfranchise Georgia Negroes. He

---

[6] Smith to Watson, May 14, June 17, 1907, in Watson Papers.

[7] *Senate Journal* (1907), 90-92; Executive Minutes of Georgia (1907-1909), 3-14, in Georgia Department of Archives and History.

apparently paid no heed to those who had blamed him for the terrible Atlanta race riot that occurred soon after the primary of 1906; he was determined to push disfranchisement through the legislature. Smith provided the details of the administration's disfranchisement scheme in his inaugural address. His proposal was similar to the measure adopted by Alabama in 1901. To register under the new plan a man must have all the existing qualifications and meet at least one of these six conditions: (1) have served in any war of the United States, the Confederate States, or Georgia; (2) be a lawful descendant of a person who had fought in one of these wars; (3) be a person of " good character " who understands the duties and obligations of citizenship; (4) be able to read and write correctly any paragraph of the constitution of the United States or of Georgia; (5) own forty acres of land; or (6) own five hundred dollars' worth of tax-assessed property. "If it happens that the members of some particular race lack more than others these qualification," the governor explained, "their inability to become voters is not ' denied or abridged on account of ' race or color. . . ." [8]

Soon after the General Assembly convened in June, 1907, the administration's disfranchisement bill was introduced in both houses. The measure had been prepared by Senator Thomas S. Felder of the twenty-second district and Representative George W. Williams of Laurens County, with the assistance of Congressman Hardwick. In the senate the bill received a favorable committee report in mid-July. Debate on the floor was perfunctory, and the opposition was slight and scattered. A few amendments were offered, and two or three of the senators argued that the bill would disfranchise whites as well as Negroes. Senator Felder sought to reassure the men from the white counties. "Do you not see how white people can be allowed registration where few Negroes ever come? " he asked. If the scheme would " disfranchise one white man and yet take four hundred and ninety Negroes away from the polls, would not that community be better? " After two days of debate the amendments were voted down, and the bill was passed by a vote of 37 to 6. [9]

[8] Executive Minutes (1907-1909), 3-4, 6.
[9] *Senate Journal* (1907), 152, 178, 294-96; Atlanta *Georgian and News*, July 30, 31, 1907.

The disfranchisement bill provoked a sharp debate in the house. Hardwick wrote Watson from Atlanta that the representatives "seem to be afraid of it and while enough are at heart against it to defeat it, I do not believe they will muster up courage to do so." [10] During the debate Joseph Hill Hall pointed out that the proposal would give wide discretionary powers to the registrars, and that unscrupulous men serving in this capacity could disfranchise white men as well as Negroes and for partisan purposes. "I know they call it a negro disfranchisement bill," declared Hall, "but nowhere in this bill is the word 'nigger' written." Evidently this fear of white disfranchisement bothered a number of the representatives. There were also indications that some of their constituents were dubious about the plan.[11] Nevertheless, W. H. Rogers, a Negro from McIntosh County, was the only legislator who opposed the measure because it would disfranchise Negroes. There was little organized opposition outside of the Assembly, although Negro leaders had criticized the scheme during the campaign of 1906 and several Negroes appeared during the session to oppose it at a committee hearing.

The bill passed the house under Representative Williams' direction on August 14, by the decisive vote of 159 to 16. The only significant amendment added to the plan in the lower house was one which made the "good character and understanding clause" permanent instead of limiting its operation to January 1, 1910, as the original proposal provided.[12] The senate finally accepted this amendment on the last day of the session. The two houses agreed to extend the time limit for registering under the "grandfather clause" to January 1, 1915, instead of January 1, 1910, as had been provided in the original bill.[13] These were concessions to the white counties of North Georgia. Hoke Smith, who had worked closely with his friends in the legislature to secure the approval of disfranchisement, signed the bill on August 23.

[10] Hardwick to Watson, August 8, 1907, in Watson Papers.
[11] House Journal (1907), 926-27; Atlanta Journal, August 12, 1907; Watson's Magazine, V (July, 1906), 103.
[12] House Journal (1907), 922-23, 928-29; Atlanta Constitution, August 15, 16, 1907.
[13] Senate Journal (1907), 687, 695, 708, 1057; House Journal (1907), 1064; Georgia Acts (1907), 47-50; Atlanta Journal, August 18, 23, 1907.

Georgia newspapers generally rejoiced because the "incubus of the negro franchise" had been removed.

Before becoming effective the disfranchisement plan had to be ratified by the voters in the regular election of 1908. There was some concern among Smith leaders, following the primary of June, 1908, that the opposing faction would seek to defeat the amendment's ratification. Public interest in the issue also seemed to be flagging, despite reports that Negroes were trying to register in order to vote against the measure. The Atlanta *Journal* tried to rally support for the amendment, and the governor took pains to see that the proclamation informing the people of the approaching vote on the question was widely published in the state. Political differences would not always end in the primary, he declared. "This amendment is a matter of such over-shadowing influence upon our future that I cannot place it too strongly upon your minds and hearts." [14]

In the election of October 7, 1908, the balloting on the constitutional amendment was light, but the vote was two to one in favor of disfranchisement. There were 79,968 votes in favor of ratification and 40,260 against.[15] The remarkable thing was not that the amendment was ratified, but that more than 40,000 Georgians were willing to vote against it. This was perhaps additional evidence that there had been no real demand for disfranchisement in Georgia until the issue was injected into the fierce intraparty conflict that flared up in 1905.

Negroes in Georgia, as Tom Watson said, had already been "white primaried," but until the adoption of disfranchisement in 1907-1908 their votes had been important in a few counties and their chances of voting in general elections had been much greater than was the case in later years. Disfranchisement almost completely eliminated Negro voting in Georgia. Thomas W. Hardwick was probably correct when he predicted that the amendment would "disfranchise at least 95% of the negro vote— in fact about all of them." [16] Negro suffrage in the country and

[14] Executive Minutes (1907-1909), 121-23; Atlanta *Journal*, June 14, September 26, 28, 1908.

[15] Executive Minutes (1907-1909), 151-52; Atlanta *Journal*, October 8, 17, 1908.

[16] Hardwick to Watson, August 17, 1907, in Watson Papers.

small towns became a thing of the past, while the situation in
the larger towns and cities was little different. Total Negro
registration for 1910 was 11,285 as compared with 261,145 whites.
The Atlanta *Journal* reported that 400 Negroes were registered
in Elbert County (Augusta) in 1908, but that less than 20 had
registered by April, 1910, under the new requirements.[17]

Whatever motivated disfranchisement leaders, they took advantage of a general feeling among white Georgians that Negroes
should not have the ballot. Men like Hoke Smith and Tom
Watson contended—and many responsible whites accepted their
arguments—that the "ignorant and purchasable negro vote" was
both cause and effect of primary election abuses. Smith said in
1910, for instance: "With the negro gone from the politics of
Georgia, with no excuse under any circumstances for resort to
conduct other than that which is lawful or clean in elections,
we can reach a higher standard of purity on the part of our
citizens than would have been possible under prior conditions."
Such men as Benjamin B. Kendrick, the historian who lived in
Georgia during this period, believed that disfranchisement was
the price that must be paid for the disruption of the Solid South.[18]
But the illusory character of such hopes soon became apparent,
and the disfranchisement movement in Georgia, as in other states,
proved to be an important factor in the heightening of racism.

Smith had hoped to force his program rapidly through the
legislature of 1907. But no sooner had the General Assembly
met than an unexpected issue—prohibition—emerged to complicate
the situation. It had played no part in the campaign of 1906,
but after Smith's term began, it assumed an importance that made
it impossible to evade. Under the local-option law of 1883,
approximately 125 of Georgia's 145 counties had adopted prohibition by 1907, but most of the larger urban centers remained
wet. Prohibition advocates like Fred Loring Seely, editor of
the Atlanta *Georgian and News*, now saw in the new reform

[17] Paul Lewinson, *Race, Class, & Party, A History of Negro Suffrage and
White Politics in the South* (New York, 1932), 218; Atlanta *Journal*,
April 15, 1910.

[18] Benjamin B. Kendrick, "The Political Situation in Georgia," in *Outlook*,
LXXXIX (August 8, 1908), 817-18; Atlanta *Constitution*, July 30, 1910.

administration a golden opportunity to secure statewide prohibition. Smith was a long-time proponent of local option, but he was careful not to make an issue of the prohibition proposal.[19] To take a stand either way would divide his followers in the General Assembly and jeopardize the chances of enacting his reforms.

The prohibition bill encountered strong opposition and long filibustering tactics before its supporters managed to get it through the legislature early in August, making Georgia the first Southern state to adopt statewide prohibition during this era.[20] Despite Smith's efforts to effect a compromise and hasten the disposal of the issue by the embattled legislators, it largely consumed thirty of the fifty days of the annual session. On the evening of the bill's passage by the house, prohibition champions led 1,500 cheering people to the executive mansion, where the governor promised to sign the measure and pledged himself to do all he could to enforce it. A few weeks later he was quoted as saying, "We have driven liquor out of Georgia at last, and, please God, it shall stay out." [21]

Although Smith could count on such leaders as Hooper Alexander and William A. Covington, the General Assembly as a whole was not strongly in favor of his proposals. Joseph Hill Hall of Bibb County was the great obstructor. But there were others, including John M. Slaton, the popular speaker of the house. Smith wrote Watson during the session that he was "up against a legislature which was elected long before I was elected, and which really is not with us I fear. . . . The old crowd is fighting at every point; first secretly and now almost openly seeking to prevent legislation." [22] But the governor was determined to secure at least some of the reforms he had promised, and he threatened to call an extra session of the legislature unless it achieved results. He kept in touch with his lieutenants in the

[19] Atlanta *Constitution*, February 10, 1907; "Prohibition in Georgia," in *Outlook*, LXXXVI (August 10, 1907), 757-58; "Georgia's Example to the Nation," in *Independent*, LXIV (January 16, 1908), 162-63.

[20] *Georgia Acts* (1907), 81-83; Atlanta *Georgian and News*, July 1, 12-16, 22-31, August 1, 5, 6, 1907.

[21] Atlanta *Georgian and News*, August 6, September 14, 1907.

[22] Smith to Watson, July 30, 1907, in Watson Papers.

Assembly, sought to put pressure on individual legislators, and used patronage to good advantage. During the hectic days near the end of the session, Smith and his legislative leaders succeeded in passing a number of administration measures. The most important of these was the Candler-Overstreet Act, which completely reorganized the railroad commission and made it into a kind of public utilities commission.

During recent years the railroad commission, which had been created in 1879, appeared to have lost much of its zeal and had come under attack by reformers. A large part of the difficulty undoubtedly lay in the type of men appointed to the commission, but the agency also lacked something in the way of organization and authority. It had no power to supervise the issuance of securities, it had no control over certain corporations affiliated with the railroads, its staff and resources were limited, and until 1906 its members were appointed by the governor.[23]

The new railroad commission bill was drafted by Charles Murphy Candler, an able member of the lower house. It was based on the New York public utilities law and other state measures. "It is prepared upon the theory that the chairman is the real head of the commission," wrote Smith, ". . . and that the other four members will sit with him a large portion of the time to fix the policies."[24] The bill was introduced in the house by Candler and in the senate by E. K. Overstreet. It was quickly met by a powerful railroad lobby. In the senate Smith forces had a hard struggle before they managed to increase the commission's membership from three to five—thus allowing the governor to make two temporary appointments favorable to his ideas—and to defeat an amendment to limit the commission's jurisdiction over street railroads. When the bill finally came to a vote in the house, it passed easily, under the skillful guidance of Murphy Candler.[25]

This legislation gave the commission extensive authority over

[23] Jim David Cherry, "The Georgia Railroad Commission, 1879-1888" (M. A. thesis, University of North Carolina, 1941).

[24] Smith to Watson, May 14, June 17, July 30, 1907, in Watson Papers.

[25] *Senate Journal* (1907), 241-42, 694-95; *House Journal* (1907), 1003; Atlanta *Georgian and News*, July 25, 29, 30, August 15, 17, 1907.

all common carriers, express companies, street railroads, docks, wharves, terminals, cotton compress corporations, telegraph and telephone companies, and gas, electric light, and power companies operating in the state. The commission was given exclusive power to determine just and reasonable rates and charges; it could hear complaints, but also could take action on its own initiative and require all corporations under its jurisdiction to establish and maintain such public services and facilities as it considered "reasonable and just." The law went far beyond other Southern states in providing for the supervision of corporation securities. The commission was also empowered to hire rate experts, as Smith had urged, was given the services of a special prosecuting attorney, could resort to any state court to secure damages from companies guilty of violating its rules, and could use its printed reports as prima-facie evidence in court actions. Public utility companies had to obey the commission's orders pending the outcome of court decisions, and violations of the law or of the commission's rulings were subject to heavy penalties.[26]

Smith was less successful in his efforts to obtain the adoption of two other major proposals having to do with railroads. Bills to abolish free passes and to regulate lobbying at the state capitol failed to pass the General Assembly. Both measures were closely associated in the minds of reformers with plans to reduce the influence of corporations in Georgia politics, and Smith had often stressed their importance.

The administration's antipass bill, introduced in the senate by Henry E. Born and in the house by H. H. Perry, exempted only railroad employees and their families. In the senate a milder plan was substituted for the Born bill, and in the house the defiant Joe Hill Hall managed to get his own bill passed which applied only to public officers. The two houses failed to agree in conference, and a deadlock occurred throughout the remainder of the session.[27] The antilobbying bill, a thoroughgoing measure prepared by Seaborn Wright and patterned after the La Follette bill in Wisconsin, passed the house on July 11 by the impressive

[26] *Georgia Acts* (1907), 72-81.
[27] *Senate Journal* (1907), 226; *House Journal* (1907), 755-56, 764; Atlanta *Georgian and News*, July 23, August 7, 8, 15, 1907.

vote of 159 to 0. But in the senate the bill was severely mutilated, and when it was passed the registration of lobbyists was almost the only house provision left intact. Again the two houses failed to agree in conference, and the measure died with the session.[28]

A number of other anticorporation measures failed to receive the General Assembly's approval, including a bill to force all out-of-state corporations operating in Georgia to secure state charters and Hooper Alexander's bill providing for the extension of the Western and Atlantic Railroad. The legislature did enact a measure to require railroads in the state to furnish adequate shipping facilities for perishable products. But despite Smith's backing, a bill to prohibit corporations from contributing to campaign funds failed to pass, as did a measure designed to liberalize the Georgia code with respect to the collection of damages by railroad employees. The governor lent his support to a resolution demanding an investigation of the ownership of the Central of Georgia Railroad, but it was tabled during the confusion attending the final hours of the session.[29]

The Smith administration made some progress in dealing with another matter involving corporations—the question of corporation taxes. Smith hoped to realize from public utility corporations " not less than $250,000 more in the way of taxes than they have been paying in past years." Soon after he entered office he sent a special message to the legislature urging the passage of a bill to force such companies to pay more taxes. He pointed out major discrepancies between the tax returns of certain railroads and the value of their property as listed in Federal court suits to enjoin rate reductions.[30] Although the General Assembly failed to pass any substantial legislation in answer to his request, it did enact a measure prepared by the governor and Representative Alexander to improve the arbitration system. Smith also urged the legislature to levy a one per cent occupation tax on the gross

[28] House Journal (1907), 300; Senate Journal (1907), 395-401; Atlanta Georgian and News, August 7, 17, 1907.

[29] Executive Minutes (1907-1909), 4-7, 9-10; House Journal (1907), 122, 665, 992-94; Senate Journal (1907), 270, 319, 690; Georgia Acts (1907), 84-85.

[30] Executive Minutes (1907-1909), 17-19; Atlanta Journal, July 17, 18, 1907; Smith to Watson, June 17, 1907, in Watson Papers.

incomes of all utility companies in the state. The house passed the bill, but the senate voted it down.[31]

Several other bills with administration approval were enacted during the summer of 1907, including measures to effect closer state supervision of banks and trust companies and to restrict the sale of narcotic drugs in the state.[32] When the legislature adjourned, Smith's program was far from complete; but he adopted an optimistic attitude, predicting that many of the legislators could be converted before the General Assembly met in 1908. Hardwick voiced the feeling of the Smith leaders when he declared that "Rome was not built in a day, but we feel that we have made great progress."[33]

Many Georgia newspapers praised the accomplishments of the 1907 session, but antiadministration organs found much to criticize. According to the Atlanta *Constitution*, the legislature of 1907 was notable for the things it left undone. The Macon *Telegraph* also attacked the record of the administration, poking fun at the "Refawm" program and accusing its supporters of "lining up at the feed trough."[34]

Smith's campaign for railroad control and rate reductions in Georgia coincided with a popular movement of national proportions that came to a climax about 1907. The only way to get at the railroad problem, Smith often said, was to insist upon "a bold and vigorous enforcement of the rights of the public by national and state governments." Railroads were given special privileges by their charters, and they should assume special duties, he asserted: "A railroad is a public carrier, and the courts have held that it stands upon a different footing from an ordinary corporation; that it is charged with public duties, both as to the nature of its service and the charges which it makes for the service, and courts have furthermore held that the nation and the states have the right, through duly constituted authorities,

---

[31] *Georgia Acts* (1907), 96-97; *Senate Journal* (1907), 646-48; *House Journal* (1907), 749-50; Atlanta *Constitution*, August 9, 10, 16, 1907.

[32] *Georgia Acts* (1907), 85-95, 117-23; Atlanta *Constitution*, August 19, 1907.

[33] Hardwick to Watson, August 17, 1907, in Watson Papers.

[34] Macon *Telegraph*, August 14, 18, September 24, 1907; Atlanta *Constitution*, August 19, December 1, 1907.

to supervise and control the rates and the services of railroad companies." [35]

Hoke Smith had promised not merely to secure a stronger railroad commission law but also to reorganize the commission and see that its work was improved, and to obtain substantial freight- and passenger-rate reductions. He reorganized the commission soon after the enactment of the railroad commission law. During his term he appointed S. Guyton McLendon, George Hillyer, Fuller E. Callaway, and Murphy Candler, all reform leaders, to the commission. James K. Hines, a splendid choice, was selected for the new office of special attorney to the commission. In considering men for these positions, the governor declared, " I must have men who will represent the people and with ability sufficient to do so wisely and successfully." [36] They must be members of the Smith faction, of course, but it was Smith's good fortune to have some able men from whom to choose.

Under Governor Smith's watchful eye, the new commission proved to be diligent in disposing of all types of claims. In April, 1908, the chairman of the commission reported that since its reorganization the commission had " handled 914 subjects, hundreds of which were claims for loss or damage, for demurrage or for overcharge." The regulatory body also insisted upon improved physical equipment and more efficient service by the railroads.[37] In October, 1907, the commission promulgated an order prohibiting free intrastate passenger and freight transportation, except under the same conditions as specified in the Federal Hepburn Act. The Smith administration thus secured indirectly what it had not been able to get by legislative action. The commission also ordered the carriers to prepare a sworn statement of their physical valuation. The very fact that there was a commission with " some sympathy for the people's side

[35] Atlanta *Journal*, January 15, 1908.
[36] Smith to Watson, August 23, 27, 1907, in Watson Papers.
[37] S. Guyton McLendon to Smith, April 20, 1908, in Smith Collection; *Thirty-Fifth Annual Report of the Railroad Commission of Georgia, October 15, 1906—June 24, 1908* (Atlanta, 1908), 78-80; *Thirty-Sixth Report of the Railroad Commission of Georgia for 1908-1909* (Atlanta, 1909), 3-4.

in the contest with the railroads," declared Alexander J. McKelway, "has led to far more numerous and prompt adjustments
of differences than have been made by the Commission itself." [38]

Shortly before Smith's inauguration, the railroad commission
ordered a general reduction of passenger rates in the state. The
commission's action seemed to give substance to Smith's campaign of the previous year. But the railroads were not yet prepared to accept the new schedule of rates, and they petitioned
the commission to revoke the order on the ground that the new
rates were confiscatory. After an extended hearing, the commission refused to make changes in its revised schedule. The roads
then suggested to Smith that a compromise be worked out, but
he stood resolutely on the commission's decision. The railroads
thereupon sought an injunction to prevent the rates from going
into effect, but the administration aggressively met this attack
and prevented the issuance of such an order.[39]

In co-operation with Governors Braxton B. Comer of Alabama
and Robert B. Glenn of North Carolina, Smith was able to
obtain some reductions in passenger rates from the Southern and
the Atlantic Coast Line railroad companies. In November, 1907,
the Georgian acted as host to the other two governors at a
meeting to discuss common railroad problems. A few weeks
later they completed agreements with the two railroad companies
which provided special rates for families and businessmen, and
for long-distance tickets. The Atlanta *Journal* called this arrangement "the most signal victory which Governor Smith and the
new Railroad Commission have yet won for the people of
Georgia." [40]

Smith's campaign to secure lower freight rates in Georgia

[38] Alexander J. McKelway, "Hoke Smith: A Progressive Democrat,"
in *Outlook*, XCVI (October 1, 1910), 269; Executive Minutes (1907-1909),
227-28, 241-43; *Thirty-Fifth Annual Report of the Railroad Commission*,
78-80.

[39] *Thirty-Fifth Annual Report of the Railroad Commission*, 14, 78-80;
Atlanta *Journal*, June 7, 8, September 16, 26, October 11, November 9,
December 1, 1907.

[40] Smith to McLendon, January 11, 1908, in Smith Collection; Executive
Minutes (1907-1909), 98-100; Atlanta *Journal*, October 27, November 1, 2,
December 7, 8, 15, 1907, January 12, 1908.

was unsuccessful. He had hoped most of all to win reductions in the port rates, but although he appointed men he thought would vote for lower rates, he was never able to get a majority of the commission to approve the petitions for reductions. S. Guyton McLendon, for instance, came to feel that the port rates would upset the whole "rate fabric" throughout the Eastern territory, and that the interstate nature of most of the larger roads made it impossible for the commission to act in the matter.[41]

One of the main factors in frustrating Smith's hopes for freight-rate reductions was the panic of 1907 and the resulting accusations against the administration. As commerce lagged in the state and several industrial plants were forced to suspend operation, anti-Smith men pointed to the administration reforms as the cause of the trouble, and the railroads argued that they were in no position to allow rate reductions. Administration leaders were soon on the defensive. The governor endeavored to demonstrate to Georgians that the depression was the result of speculation and an overextension of credit, not of regulatory legislation. In a letter to the editor of the New York *World* he declared: "We are engaged here in the earnest effort to help work out the problem of State regulation in harmony with national regulation, having in view the protection of the . . . railroad companies . . . and of those who deal with the railroad companies."[42] Smith's problem was made more difficult by the efforts of Joseph M. Brown and other critics to make a sectional issue of the rate question; they asserted that the port rate agitation was aimed at helping only Atlanta and Atlanta politicians.

"There is no doubt but that Hoke Smith is in somewhat of a dilemma," Pope Brown wrote Tom Watson in February, 1908. "He is in a position to be assailed by friends from within and foes without."[43] The result was a noticeable softening of Smith's attitude toward the railroads. He persuaded himself that the place "where the people will at once get the benefit" was in the case of passenger rates, and he claimed that the new rates of 1907 would save Georgians almost one million dollars a year.

[41] McLendon to Smith, April 22, 23, 1909, in Smith Collection.
[42] New York *World*, November 11, 1907.
[43] Brown to Watson, February 22, 1908, in Watson Papers.

If capital were to be kept in the state, if the railroads and other public service companies were to provide good facilities, Smith decided, "We cannot reduce too greatly the railroads' revenues and yet carry on this work." [44]

As if to mock Smith's failure to secure lower intrastate freight rates, the railroads announced an increase of interstate rates for the southeastern territory, effective August 1, 1908. The governor urged the railroad commission to oppose the new rates in Georgia. "I know we can find a way to resist the increase," he wrote the chairman of the commission. "I do not intend to submit to an increase of rates if there is any way I, as Governor, can help the people of the State to resist them." [45] But since the rates involved interstate travel, he could do little except lend his support to the state commission in its appeal to the Interstate Commerce Commission.

As the end of his term approached, Hoke Smith seemed to grow more militant toward the railroads. He pressed for national legislation to make the findings of state railroad commissions prima-facie evidence in Federal courts. He made a vigorous attempt in 1909 to have freight rates on cotton shipped in the state reduced five cents per hundred pounds, but Chairman McLendon opposed the reduction and the governor was unsuccessful. When reports were circulated in 1909 that Edward H. Harriman had promised to spend ten million dollars improving the Central of Georgia Railroad, which he controlled, if the state would repeal some of its railroad legislation, Smith became sarcastic. What did Harriman want, he asked reporters, the emasculation of the railroad commission? [46]

Meanwhile, Smith had tried to accomplish certain other reforms. When the General Assembly convened in June, 1908, he had presented a series of proposals calling for closer regulation

[44] Smith to Watson, August 23, 1907, *ibid.*; Smith to railroad commission, August 25, 1908, in Smith Collection.

[45] Smith to McLendon, July 18, 1908, and to railroad commission, August 25, 1908, *ibid.*

[46] Smith to railroad commission, April 19, 1909, McLendon to Smith, April 22, 23, 1909, and Smith to McLendon, April 24, 1909, in Smith Collection; Atlanta *Journal*, January 13, February 13, April 22, 24, May 5, June 18, 23-25, 1909.

of primary elections and a " pure ballot." A major complaint
of Georgia progressives was the influence exerted by money,
liquor, free passes, and corporation contributions in elections,
particularly in the all-important primary elections. Numerous
testimonials of these years tell of the corruption and dishonesty
that characterized the election process. Most of the rules governing the primaries were party rather than state regulations. This
meant that the executive committee of the party possessed great
latitude in determining how the system would operate. Furthermore, state primaries used the county-unit system, which allowed
the candidate with a plurality of votes in each county to receive
the county's unit votes and gave the rural counties a dispropor-
tionately large voice in the outcome of statewide primaries.

The Smith movement had already effected some changes. The
state convention of 1906 went on record as favoring the election
of United States Senators and state officials by direct popular
vote, and the new state executive committee soon adopted rules
to carry this into effect, thus abolishing the county-unit system.
The committee liberalized the rules admitting white men to the
primaries, adopted a provision calling for a " run-off " primary in
cases where candidates for the Senate and the governorship failed
to receive a majority in the first primary, and promulgated rules
calling for each candidate to file with the state chairman for
publication an affidavit setting forth a detailed statement of the
amount of money expended in the campaign.[47]

In response to Smith's detailed recommendations in 1908, the
General Assembly enacted a primary regulatory act, a registration
law, a measure requiring candidates to submit a sworn statement
of their campaign expenses, and a corrupt-practices act designed
to prohibit corporation contributions to any political campaign
or through contributions to influence political action. The registration plan defined the duties of the registrars and tax collectors
and laid down detailed requirements for the payment of taxes
before registering, the taking of a special oath by every voter,
and the right of appeal from the action of the registrars. The
primary act stipulated that statewide primaries must be held on
the same day for candidates for governor, state house officers,

[47] Atlanta *Journal*, September 5, 1906.

Congressmen, members of the General Assembly, and state judicial officials, the date to be fixed by the state executive committee. Primaries could not be held earlier than sixty days before the regular elections, and electors must vote in the militia districts in which they resided.[48]

In addition to the election laws enacted by the legislature in 1908, several other measures of a reform nature were passed. A pure food and drug act extended the provisions of a law of 1906 by providing for a food inspector and a drug inspector. Another act limited the interest rate on loans made in the state, and other legislation provided for the regulation of telegraphic service and for the establishment of a tuberculosis sanitarium.[49]

By the time the legislature met in 1908, the Atlanta *Georgian and News* and such reformers as Dr. John E. White, an Atlanta minister, had launched a vigorous crusade against the convict-leasing system in Georgia. The leasing system had long been criticized. "Every one knows that the question of the convict lease system is so rotten that it smells to heaven," exclaimed Senator Thomas S. Felder. Yet many legislators, worried by the loss of revenue its abolition would entail, urged that it be continued when the current leases expired April 1, 1909.[50]

In his initial message to the General Assembly in 1908, Hoke Smith called the "whole [penal] system . . . unsound in that it too nearly stamps all criminals alike and provides no plan for their reformation." Yet he offered no solution to the leasing problem. The disclosures resulting from an investigation of the leasing practice by a joint legislative committee stimulated the demand for reform, and on July 30, 1908, the governor announced that he believed the leases could be ended without damage to the state's finances. He soon fell in line with lease reformers and let it be known late in the session that he would veto any bill to continue convict leasing. The question was "too important to the people of Georgia" and involved too greatly the future of

[48] Executive Minutes (1907-1909), 7, 101-102, 123-24, 225; Savannah *Morning News*, June 24, 1908; *Georgia Acts* (1908), 55-66.

[49] *Georgia Acts* (1908), 49-53, 80-83, 94-95, 101-103.

[50] A. Elizabeth Taylor, "The Convict Lease System in Georgia, 1866-1908" (M. A. thesis, University of North Carolina, 1940); Atlanta *Georgian and News*, July 7, 1908.

the state, he declared, "for us to hesitate about spending a few thousand dollars to handle it in the most intelligent and best manner possible." When it became apparent that the problem could not be dealt with in the regular session, he decided to call an extra session to end the leasing system.[51]

When the legislature convened in extra session near the end of August, 1908, Smith recommended a plan to abolish the leasing system by constitutional amendment and to use the convicts "to complete and perfect public highways and other internal improvements, using the farm as a basis of operation." He suggested that the convicts might also be used to extend the Western and Atlantic Railroad. "Good roads and common schools go together," he reminded the legislators. He also urged them to adopt the parole system, and to improve the prison farm and the reformatory.[52]

Given a committee report that fairly bristled with evidences of the leasing system's abuses and with charges of "grave neglect of duty," and faced by an increasingly indignant public, the General Assembly abolished the leasing system in September, 1908, after numerous disagreements between the two houses. The legislature provided for the use of the convicts on the public works and roads in the counties, created a parole system, established juvenile courts as branches of the superior courts, provided for improved treatment of women prisoners, and set up a commission to investigate the possibility of using the convicts to extend the Western and Atlantic Railroad.[53]

In later years Hoke Smith tended to magnify his own part in the abolition of the convict-lease system. Actually, his role was no more than a supporting one. Like prohibition, however, the ending of the leasing system and the improvements made in the state's prisons were inseparable parts of the widespread reform movement of which Smith was a principal leader.

Smith demonstrated considerable interest in certain other

[51] Executive Minutes (1907-1909), 105-106, 123-24, 129.
[52] Ibid., 134-41.
[53] House Journal (Extra Session, 1908), 114, 145, 195, 277, 298, 340, 343; Senate Journal (Extra Session, 1908), 108-109, 123, 142-43, 146, 150-54, 247; Georgia Acts (1908), 1059-92, 1107-33.

aspects of the penal system. He urged the prison commission to consider plans for improving the reformatories, and he advocated a generous use of the parole system. Early in 1908 he suggested that the prison commission turn its attention to the selection of a second prison farm, but when the commission chose a large farm near Macon he refused to approve the selection on the ground that the property was unsuitable. The resulting controversy was seized upon by Smith's enemies as another example of his "dictatorial" administration.[54]

No fundamental changes in the state's tax laws were made during Smith's tenure as governor, but his administration witnessed the largest appropriations that had been made in the state's history.[55] The public schools were among the chief beneficiaries of the increased appropriations, receiving about 30 per cent more money from the state in 1909 than in 1907. The state school superintendent, Jere M. Pound, praised Smith's "loyal support and cooperation in every effort to increase the efficiency of the Common School System. . . ."[56] Smith urged that the governor be authorized to borrow up to six hundred thousand dollars in order that school teachers could be paid more promptly. He recommended larger appropriations for the district agricultural and mechanical schools, whose establishment he had supported in earlier years, and he suggested the reorganization of the state colleges and experiment stations. He gave his support to the special education train sponsored by the state college of agriculture, accompanying the train on a number of occasions. "I want to see its work not simply limited to the students that attend the college," he declared, "but distributed to the whole people of Georgia through university extension work."[57]

[54] Smith to Joseph S. Turner, January 4, August 21, September 12, November 21, 1908, January 4, March 11, 15, 25, May 4, 1909, and Turner to Smith, September 16, 1908, March 11, 25, 1909, in Smith Collection; Atlanta *Journal*, September 20, 30, 1908, March 23, 24, 1909.

[55] Smith reported in 1909 that the railroads and the utility companies were paying $550,000 more each year than before 1907. Executive Minutes (1907-1909), 17-19, 100-105, 205.

[56] *Thirty-Seventh Annual Report of the Department of Education to the General Assembly of the State of Georgia for the School Year Ending Dec. 31st, 1908* (Atlanta, n. d.), 3, 5, 7-12, 16-19.

[57] Smith to Watson, January 14, 1907, in Watson Papers; Smith to

Near the end of his administration, Hoke Smith was confronted by another race problem. White firemen, supported by the Brotherhood of Locomotive Firemen and Enginemen, engaged in a strike against the management of the Georgia Railroad in an effort to prevent the use of Negro firemen. The head of the railroad, "crazed with fear," as Smith recalled, urged the governor to use his authority aggressively to make sure that the trains were run and the property of the road was protected. But Smith was cautious. He hesitated to issue a general order warning strikers and citizens, since "such a course might increase rather than lessen excitement." Furthermore, he did not want to appear sympathetic with the Negroes in the controversy.[58]

For a week in late May, 1909, the state tottered on the brink of violence. Public opinion seemed to indicate strong support for the strikers. "When the railroad undertook to fill the places of the strikers or to run any of their trains with negro firemen, crowds collected at the stations, stoned the cabs and cars, set the brakes and assaulted the firemen." Thomas K. Scott, general manager of the Georgia Railroad, reported on May 21 that the assaults and intimidations of the railroad's employees—evidently strikebreakers—made it virtually impossible to operate trains. He and others demanded that the governor take "speedy and very vigorous measures." [59]

Smith refused to become excited. He dispatched Attorney General John C. Hart on a tour of the railroad's line, and Hart secured the confidence of the railroad managers and of the strike leaders. He recommended that the governor refrain from calling out the state troops and suggested a plan of arbitration. Smith approved the proposal and formally requested its acceptance by both sides. Meanwhile, he kept in touch with local officials and

McLendon, December 31, 1907, in Smith Collection; Executive Minutes (1907-1909), 11-13, 108, 131-32.

[58] Smith to Thomas K. Scott, May 20, 1909, and to the sheriff of McDuffie County, May 21, 1909, in Smith Collection; Atlanta *Constitution*, July 30, 1910.

[59] Scott to Smith, May 21, 22, 23, 24, 1909, Jacob Phinizy to Smith, May 24, 1909, and Clement C. Cary to Smith, May 24, 1909, in Smith Collection; "The Great Strike Down South," in *Current Literature*, XLVII (July, 1909), 12.

used his office to assist towns running short of certain supplies. On May 25, he issued an executive proclamation, citing reports of disorder and pointing to his responsibility to keep the peace. He warned that violations of state laws would be prosecuted vigorously and called on local officials to see that all laws were obeyed.[60]

Near the end of May the strikers returned to their jobs, having agreed with management to await the results of Federal mediation. Smith found himself the center of much admiring attention from white men in Georgia for having refused to help crush the strike. An Augusta man reported, for example, that many people in that city were "recruits for you in the next race." There was some criticism of the governor's course. The Augusta *Chronicle* condemned what it called his "deliberate and wanton refusal to do his duty." Thomas K. Scott described the strike as "the first step of a movement which is planned to eventuate in the abolition of the negro as an industrial factor." The New York *Sun* declared that the Smith administration sympathized "with mob rule." Smith himself thought the strike had been handled well. "It is one of the things in connection with my administration which gives me the greatest gratification," he wrote a little later, "because I am sure I helped to allay racial hatred, to prevent the spilling of blood and the loss of life, and to prevent the destruction of property."[61]

During his governorship Smith spoke out against lynchings and used state troops on at least one occasion to protect Negroes accused of molesting white women. But for the most part his attitude toward Negroes had become harsh and unsympathetic. He now attributed bad agricultural methods in the South "solely to the presence of the negro" and claimed that the Negro was content "to occupy the natural status of his race, the position of inferiority." What most Negroes needed, asserted Smith, was to be "supervised and directed by the white man." If Negroes

[60] John C. Hart to Josiah Carter, May 22, 1909, Smith to T. K. Scott, May 23, 24, 1909, and E. A. Ball to Smith, May 24, 1909, in Smith Collection.

[61] Smith to C. C. Cary, June 5, 1909, and numerous letters to Smith, in Smith Collection; Executive Minutes (1907-1909), 237-39; "The Great Strike Down South," *loc. cit.*, 13-14; "The Georgia Strike Arbitration," in *Harper's Weekly*, LIII (July 3, 1909), 4.

would work hard, look to reliable whites for guidance, and
eschew politics, they would get along well.[62]

All of this sounded like Tom Watson and James K. Vardaman,
but there was one difference. Watson and Vardaman believed
sincerely and passionately in the white supremacy arguments they
advanced. Hoke Smith, on the other hand, was at heart a moderate, a Southerner of the Wade Hampton persuasion. Smith might
have chosen to follow a more conservative approach in dealing
with the thorny problems of race; he might have continued to
adhere to the moderate course he had followed during earlier
years. But the exigencies of politics and his own lack of resolution caused him to act the demagogue at a time when he might
have made a genuine contribution to the alleviation of racial
tensions.[63] Like other politicians of "the people" who sprang
up during this period, Smith thought he saw the advantage and
the necessity of appealing to the passions of the people, whether
to denounce the abuses of corporations or to urge the threat
of Negro domination. But the publicity given his anti-Negro
measures during the years 1905-1909 stamped him in the eyes of
the nation as a Southern demagogue. It was unfortunate for his
reputation as a progressive political leader that his work should
have been marred in this respect.

In his final message to the General Assembly, on June 23, 1909,
Smith reviewed the accomplishments of his administration. Proudly, he pointed to the constitutional amendment that disfranchised
Negroes in Georgia; the registration law, the primary regulatory
act, and the corrupt-practices legislation; the railroad commission
act, the reduction of passenger rates, and the abolition of free

[62] Atlanta *Journal*, October 10, 1906, June 29, 1907; Atlanta *Constitution*,
July 29, 30, 1910; New York *Times*, September 17, 1911.
[63] The evaluation of William E. B. Du Bois, who lived in Atlanta during
Smith's governorship, is interesting on this point. Du Bois described Smith
as a man of "brains, experience, and wide acquaintance . . . [who] was
absolutely without conscience when it came to his political career." According to the Negro scholar, Smith was offered "great inducements" to
moderate his attack on the corporations during his campaign of 1906, and
"he found that the easiest way to do this was to direct his attack upon
the Negro." Du Bois to the author, September 3, 1952.

passes; the destruction of the convict-lease system, the establishment of juvenile courts, and the adoption of other penal reforms; and the increased support given to public educational and eleemosynary institutions. Smith also cited the increased taxes paid by corporations and the work of the railroad commission in opposing freight-rate increases.[64] He admitted that the port rates had not been obtained. He might also have indicated that the antilobbying bill, the corporation tax, and a strong railroad employer's liability law had not been enacted. In reviewing Smith's accomplishments, one should not overlook the intimate connection between the reforms of the Terrell administration in 1905-1906—including the child-labor act, the establishment of a state reformatory, and several educational advances—and the campaign Smith began in 1905.

Hoke Smith proved to be one of the most successful of the Southern anti-machine governors of his day. His administration achieved a large number of its objectives, in spite of certain unfortunate circumstances and the bitter factionalism that rent the party. Smith was an excellent administrator, and much of the success of his administration was the result of some good appointments and his own vigorous supervision of the affairs of the state, including the work of such agencies as the railroad commission. Except in matters of race, Smith was a genuine reform governor.

[64] Executive Minutes (1907-1909), 225-36.

The Smith-Brown
Controversy

One of the bitterest and most colorful political feuds in Georgia history was the controversy between Hoke Smith and Joseph Mackey Brown. The two men opposed each other in four elections and for many years were aligned on opposite sides of the issues that divided their party. The personalities of these men and the fierce political campaigns they led obsessed the state for a decade, sometimes dividing father and son and brother and brother. The rivalry between Smith and Brown, linked with that between Smith and Clark Howell, did much to promote the dual factionalism of the Georgia Democracy during the progressive era.

Smith and Brown were a study in opposites. Smith was large and commanding in appearance, and Brown was small and meek, even mousy. On the platform the lawyer was powerful, whereas Brown was mediocre at best and seldom spoke in public. But if Smith was impressive on the hustings, Brown was superb with the pen. One man was a damage suit lawyer, the other a railroad official.

When Brown burst upon the political stage in 1907-1908, he was a political unknown. The son of Joseph E. Brown, the Civil War and Reconstruction leader, he had demonstrated little of his father's flair for politics. In 1907 he was fifty-six years of age and had never been elected to public office. For over twenty years he was an employee of the Western and Atlantic Railroad, rising from freight clerk to traffic manager and achieving a reputation as an expert in railroad problems. Governor Terrell appointed him to the railroad commission in 1904, and it was in that capacity that he and Smith first came to challenge each other.

The friction between the two men stemmed from the freight-rate issue. Brown and Warner Hill were the two commissioners who defeated the petition of Smith's clients in the port-rate decision of May, 1905. During the following primary Smith had threatened " deadly war " upon the two commissioners, and especially on Brown. If he were elected governor, Smith was quoted as saying, " it would take me just as long to suspend a commissioner with his views as it would to sign my name." [1] With a facile pen Brown defended his actions in a dozen or more widely circulated letters to the public during the campaign. He challenged the arguments of the rate reformers and contended that Smith and the Atlanta *Journal* had been friendly to him until his vote against the rate petition.[2]

Following his election in 1906, Smith made it clear that he had not forgotten the activities of the " card writing commissioner." In his inaugural address he declared: " A railroad commissioner who cannot unite with his associates in a vigorous resistance to any attacks made upon the commission's findings owes it to the state to retire from the position which he holds. . . . If the views of a commissioner are so hostile to the work of the majority that he is not in a position to help sustain the action of the commission, his presence . . . would be a hindrance to effective service and it would be the duty of the governor to suspend him." [3]

A few weeks earlier Brown had voted against the passenger-rate reductions, yet the new governor made no immediate move to unseat the commissioner, possibly because he was awaiting the passage of the Candler-Overstreet bill, which would allow him to enlarge the commission, and also because Brown's term had

[1] Atlanta *Constitution*, January 11, May 6, June 17, 24, 1906; Atlanta *Journal*, June 19, 20, 1906.
[2] Atlanta *Constitution*, June 23, July 25, 30, August 5, 6, 14, 17, October 1, 1905, April 8, June 28, July 30, 1906, July 5, August 22, 1907.
[3] Executive Minutes (1907-1909), 9-10.

only a few months to run. But three days after the General
Assembly adjourned, on August 21, 1907, Smith suspended Brown
from office and appointed S. Guyton McLendon as his successor.
The newspapers hinted that a big story would soon break, but
Smith's office gave out little information. Brown maintained that
his removal was illegal, that the governor was simply being loyal
to " his former clients, the manufacturers and jobbers," and that
he had waited until after the legislature adjourned to suspend him
because he knew it would not sustain his action.[4]

Smith did not officially disclose his reasons for suspending
the commissioner until July 20, 1908, when, in accordance with
the railroad commission law, he sent an explanation to the General
Assembly. First, the governor stated, he had decided before the
primary of 1906 that Brown was not carrying out his duties
properly, and he had promised to remove him. In the second
place, Commissioner Brown had opposed the reduction of passenger rates in June, 1907, and had prepared an eighty-page
pamphlet arguing against the reductions, which the railroads had
helped circulate. Smith conceded Brown's right to differ with
his fellow commissioners, but he denied his right " to remain
upon the Commission, and furnish arguments and evidence for
the railroad companies to attack the action of the Commission in
the courts." He had not suspended Brown immediately after
his inauguration, Smith explained, because he wanted to avoid any
threat to his reforms in the legislature.

Hoke Smith's third reason involved a strange account of veiled
threats and a secret letter. According to the governor, a letter
from Brown had been left in his reception room without explanation on August 20, 1907. Great care had been taken to bring
the letter to Smith's personal attention. In a large sealed envelope,
marked " personal and confidential," was this letter:

Dear Sir:—

During the past campaign for the Democratic nomination
for Governor you repeatedly referred to me as a " card writing
Commissioner." I did write several cards exposing the fallacy
of some of the charges against the railroad commission and

[4] *Ibid.*, 115-17; Atlanta *Journal*, June 7, August 21, 1907; Atlanta *Constitution*, August 23, 25, 1907.

against me individually, but there was one "card" which I refrained from writing. Its text could have been the enclosure in the sealed envelope which accompanies this note.

Respectfully, etc.

(Signed) Joseph M. Brown.

Smith had not broken the seal of the inner envelope, being unwilling, he said, for Brown to force upon his attention "offensive matter which he had refrained from publishing." He contended that Brown was trying to force him to retain him on the commission or, failing in that, to "affront" him. The day after the letter was left, the commissioner was suspended.[5]

Joseph M. Brown never denied Smith's version of this affair. A legislative committee to which the governor's explanation was referred recommended that no further action be taken in the matter.[6] After his suspension, Brown continued his card writing. He perhaps realized that he had made for himself a political opportunity that would bear fruit with proper cultivation.

An important thread in the tangled skein of events that contributed to the Smith-Brown controversy was the estrangement of Tom Watson and Hoke Smith. During the first few months of the administration Watson appeared to be enthusiastic over the new governor and his program. Smith and his advisers, meanwhile, did all they could to cement the alliance with the Populist leader. Smith complimented Watson on his work, invited him to accept certain state appointments, and demonstrated a considerate regard for his patronage wishes.

Some of the "Old Pops," remembering Smith's earlier hostility toward their cause, supported him reluctantly, if at all. "I never could bring myself to believe that Mr. Smith was any nearer being a reformer in 1906 than he was in 1892-94-96," wrote one of the doubters in 1907.[7] But the pressure from the anti-Smith faction to break the tenuous alliance between Smith and Watson was a more important consideration. Hardwick wrote Watson in June, 1907, for instance, that there were a "great many people

[5] Executive Minutes (1907-1909), 115-17; Atlanta *Constitution*, July 22, 23, 1908.

[6] *House Journal* (1908), 546-47; Atlanta *Constitution*, July 21, 29, 1908.

[7] J. E. Bodenhamer to Watson, November 22, 1907, in Watson Papers.

in Georgia who would be willing to give their ears to see a row
started up between us all and more especially between yourself
and Mr. Smith." [8] Clark Howell and other anti-Smith men encouraged the feeling Watson seemed to have against the Southern
Cotton Association, of which Hoke Smith was an ardent supporter, and they cheered on the leaders of the Farmers' Union
in their opposition to Smith's immigration scheme. Watson was
active in the affairs of the Farmers' Union, yet that organization
was a kind of center of opposition to the Smith administration.

A steady stream of little incidents played into the hands of
Smith's enemies. There were many stories calculated to arouse
Watson's suspicions: reports that Smith was giving credit to other
political leaders instead of Watson for having secured rural free
delivery legislation, that the governor was showing favoritism
toward the local machine in Augusta, with which the Populist
leader had long been at odds, and that Smith was not really
pushing his antirailroad reforms.[9] Smith could not always appoint
Watson men to office, and he resisted Watson's entreaties to call
a special session of the legislature in the fall of 1907. When the
governor declared in a speech at McRae that he had "no adverse
criticism to place upon the legislature" for its work in 1907,
the "Sage of Hickory Hill" was indignant. Furthermore, he
began to be impatient with the railroad commission for not
moving more rapidly. "GOVERNOR SMITH!" he warned in
October, "FOR GOD'S SAKE DO SOMETHING!"[10] An-
other cause of friction was Watson's rift with James R. Gray, the
leading Smith editor in the state. Gray opposed the talk of an
extra session and seemed to minimize the influence of the Populists
in Smith's victory of 1906.

Tom Watson was also irritated by the rumors that Smith
planned to run for the Senate in 1908. Watson later claimed that
Hardwick and Smith had offered to support him for the Senate.

[8] Hardwick to Watson, June 17, 1907, ibid.
[9] J. G. Wilson to Watson, July 5, 1907, and Clark Howell to Watson,
September 7, 1907, ibid.; Atlanta Constitution, October 6, November 3-17,
1907.
[10] Smith to Watson, August 23, 1907, and L. D. McGregor to Watson,
September 13, November 21, 1907, in Watson Papers; Watson's Weekly
Jeffersonian, October 10, 31, November 21, 1907.

As he facetiously put it, "Hoke and Hardwick and Watson formed a Mutual Admiration Society. We were the Big Three; and when it came to such trifling affairs as Governorships and Senatorial mantles, it was a case of 'after you, Alphonse!' 'No! After you, my dear Gaston!'"[11] Hoke Smith had indeed begun to consider the possibility of running for the Senate. Hardwick wrote Watson in mid-September, 1907: "I think it would be a serious political mistake for Hoke to run for the Senate *now*—one that might backset the cause of reform in Georgia for many years. . . . He is very anxious to run, in fact I am beginning to think that about the only thing that will *certainly* keep him from doing so is for either you or I to make the race—"[12]

The precipitating factor in the Smith-Watson break, however, was the Glover case. Arthur Price Glover was an uneducated factory worker in Augusta who was convicted and sentenced to hang for shooting a woman millworker with whom he had been having an illicit love affair. Glover had fearlessly supported Watson in the bitter struggle of 1892 in Augusta, and when the Populist leader received letters from Glover and his wife beseeching him to secure clemency for the prisoner, he was profoundly moved. His determination to help Glover was increased by his belief that Boykin Wright, the prosecuting attorney who secured the conviction, and an enemy of the Populists in the nineties, hated Glover intensely for having supported Watson. Rescuing Glover became a great crusade for Watson, and he warned the governor that he must not be influenced by Wright. "Governor Smith should weigh these matters well," he wrote Hardwick, "for it will make a world of difference in the relations between himself and me, if he should fail to measure up to the size of a full grown man in the emergency."[13]

In December, 1907, Watson stopped in at Smith's office, and as he later recalled, "With one leg thrown across the corner of his big working desk, I sat there for more than an hour looking down into the governor's eyes . . . and I pleaded for Glover's life with all the earnestness of my nature." Upon leaving Smith's

[11] Atlanta *Journal*, June 22, 1910.
[12] Hardwick to Watson, September 19, 1907, in Watson Papers.
[13] Woodward, *Tom Watson*, 386-87; Atlanta *Journal*, August 7, 1910.

office, he was confident that Glover's life would be spared. Smith
told friends that he would like to gratify Watson in this matter,
but he refused to commit himself before the prison commission
acted on Glover's petition.[14] When the commission reported
adversely, Smith wrote Watson that he was "deeply grieved to
see no other alternative in the discharge of my official duty than
to leave the sentence placed upon him to take its course." The
governor hoped that in time Watson would appreciate the fact
that he had done his duty in the case. A few days later he invited
Watson to accompany him to Roosevelt's White House Conference.[15]

Thomas R. Wright, a friend of Watson and a member of the
special committee appointed by Smith to investigate Glover's
case, reported that "no man was ever given a fairer, more pains-
taking and exhaustive examination than Mr. Glover received."
But Watson seemed to feel that by refusing clemency for Glover,
Smith was paying a political debt to Boykin Wright, and he
implied that the governor's decision was influenced by Watson's
opposition to his desire to run for the Senate. To Hardwick he
vented his spleen with these words: "The governor has chosen
and will take the natural consequences. No such cold-hearted
and selfish politician can ever be a friend of mine again." [16] A few
weeks later he sent a friend to see Joseph M. Brown to discuss
the possibility of Brown's opposing Smith for the governorship
in 1908.[17]

Meanwhile, after deliberating for months, Hoke Smith had
finally reached a definite decision not to run for the Senate. Late
in January, 1908, he issued a statement withdrawing his name
from the speculation about the Senate race and announcing his
determination to seek re-election as governor. The Glover case,

[14] Atlanta *Journal*, August 8, 1910; Hardwick to Watson, December 26,
1907, and A. L. Franklin to Watson, January 11, 15, 26, 27, 1908, in Watson
Papers.
[15] Smith to Watson, January 23, 25, 1908, and Hardwick to Watson,
January 30, 1908, in Watson Papers.
[16] Thomas R. Wright to Watson, January 13, 27, 1908, and James K.
Hines to Watson, January 28, 1908, *ibid.*; Atlanta *Journal*, August 7, 8, 1910.
[17] L. D. McGregor to Watson, February 25, 27, 1908, in Watson Papers;
Woodward, *Tom Watson*, 388-89.

which he undoubtedly realized would alienate Watson, the advice of such men as Hardwick and Gray, and the increasingly complicated political situation in Georgia certainly entered into his decision. Smith admitted that he had wanted to make the Senate race. "I have tried to see that it was no abandonment of obligations assumed by me to run for the senate at this time," he stated, "but have failed to do so." His reforms were not complete, he said. "I believe in them as intensely today as I did when a candidate." [18]

Joseph M. Brown may well have determined to run for governor, if an auspicious opportunity presented itself, even before his removal from the railroad commission. Immediately after he was suspended, he spoke of securing justice "at the proper time and before the proper tribunal," and some time later he wrote an elaborate criticism of "reformers." [19] Encouraged by the break between Smith and Watson, and reassured by anti-Smith politicians, Brown formally announced his candidacy on March 18, 1908.

His platform was a plea for conservatism. He favored reduced taxes, the repeal of much of the Candler-Overstreet Railroad Commission Act, the enforcement of prohibition, the establishment of a department of labor, antilobbying legislation, and the encouragement of out-of-state investments in Georgia. He opposed "undesirable immigration" and astutely declared his intention to raise cotton prices and "to restore employment . . . and good wages to those who are now the unmerited victims of an unnecessary panic." "I confess that I have none of the arts of the politician," wrote Brown, "and no great newspaper to urge my candidacy, but I have faith in the people." [20]

Brown and his campaign managers waged an unusual campaign. Not once did the candidate address the people. Obviously no match for Smith on the speaker's platform, he confined his campaign activities to some fifteen smoothly written, epigrammatic cards and to organizational work at his headquarters in the Kim-

[18] Atlanta *Journal*, January 28, 1908; Hardwick to Watson, January 30, 1908, in Watson Papers.

[19] Atlanta *Constitution*, August 23, December 8, 1907.

[20] *Ibid.*, March 19, 1908.

ball House in Atlanta. What the people needed, asserted Brown, was "PROSPERITY RATHER THAN ORATORY." He depicted himself, with splendid assistance from his friends, as a mistreated soul, and he pointed to Smith's campaign of "silent contempt" as further evidence. Yet Brown sharply attacked Smith. He condemned his "unbridled extravagance and maximum tax rate" and accused him of having driven capital out of Georgia. He contended that the governor had promised to secure an annual saving of five hundred thousand dollars for cotton farmers in rate reductions and an overall freight rate saving for Georgians of four million dollars a year. He charged that the passenger rates Smith had helped obtain would aid businessmen rather than farmers. As for the port rates, declared Brown, the mere threat of such rates "had brought disaster to our prosperity." [21]

Although Brown himself did not take the stump, there was no paucity of speakers for his cause. A large group of newspapers, led by the Atlanta *Constitution* and the Macon *Telegraph*, supported him, and Joe Brown clubs were organized throughout the state. Brown spokesmen described Smith as a selfish and ambitious man, a dangerous politician. They accused Smith partisans of attempting "to make out that the Brown men were 'niggerites.'" But the rallying cry of the Brown supporters was "Brown and Bread; Hoke and Hunger." The Smith movement, they charged, had caused the panic. They circulated a report that a large knitting mill in Barnesville had suspended operation, having posted a sign on its doors reading: "Closed for want of orders, owing to too much reform legislation." Late in the campaign one newspaper observed: "The thing that is helping Mr. Brown more than anything else . . . is the desire for good times and the belief that in some way a change in the office of Governor would contribute greatly to the restoration of prosperity." [22]

At the beginning of the campaign Smith's managers urged their local leaders to conduct a quiet campaign. They were reluctant to admit that Joseph M. Brown was a strong candidate, but as the opposition coalesced behind him and began to make effective use of the charge that the governor had caused the panic, they

[21] *Ibid.*, February 2, April 22, 23, May 3, 29, 1908.
[22] Savannah *Morning News*, May 15, 24, 1908.

became disturbed. The Dawson *News* tickled the fancy of Brown
followers with this rhyme:

> Little Joe—Big Joke,
> Silent Contempt—Holy Hoke,
> Trouble Brewing—Anxious Hoke,
> Governor Joe—Smaller Joke.[23]

Smith tried sarcasm, asking his audiences if anyone had ever
heard of Joe Brown making a speech. "All the engines on the
Central of Georgia Railway couldn't bring my opponent out of
his headquarters in the Kimball House," the governor declared.
But it was difficult to come to blows with an opponent who would
not talk back. In Savannah, an anti-Smith stronghold, he lost
his temper. "There is not a man here who will commend him
to you," he exclaimed. "You just want anybody to beat Hoke
Smith, and that's why you are going to vote for Brown." [24]

Smith conducted a vigorous canvass of the state in April and
May. Yet it was evident that he was on the defensive. He must
answer the charges that he had brought on the panic, he must
show that his reforms had not discouraged the investment of
capital in Georgia, and he must demonstrate that the achievements
of his first year in office had brought such benefits as rate reductions to the people. He sought to make these points as aggressively as possible and to prove that his administration had obtained
many of its objectives. He was sharply critical of the corporations: "They have seized upon this hour of hard times to
distribute their hirelings and to endeavor to break down what
has been done in your behalf." [25] He charged again and again
that Brown was supported by corporation and liquor interests,
and by the old "Terrell machine." He claimed that the Louisville and Nashville Railroad had flooded Georgia with literature
attacking his reforms.[26] The governor also tried to link prohibi-

[23] Quoted in Atlanta *Constitution*, May 7, 1908.

[24] Macon *Telegraph*, April 26, 1908; Atlanta *Journal*, May 3, 1908;
Savannah *Morning News*, May 13, 1908.

[25] Atlanta *Journal*, March 9, April 14-18, 20, 22-30, May 16, 29, 1908.

[26] Smith made a great point of the charge that Brown had furnished
prorailroad material for a pamphlet " 20,000 copies of which were published
in Louisville, Ky., the headquarters of the Louisville and Nashville Rail-

tion and disfranchisement. "The combination of the liquor
interests and the negro threatens white civilization in Georgia,"
he asserted.[27]

The Smith leaders tried desperately to minimize the effect
of the split between their candidate and Tom Watson, and Smith
himself stated that Watson was irrelevant to the contest. Watson
purported to be neutral, but it was obvious that Brown was his
choice. As one of Watson's friends wrote near the end of the
campaign, "your editorials are fine and doing Smith a lot of
damage." Despite the pleas of Hardwick, James K. Hines, and
other mutual friends of Smith and Watson, the latter stubbornly
held to his course. Hardwick warned Watson that the forces
behind Brown were "trying to turn over the State again to the
corporations, their allies, hirelings, and lobbyists." Hines wrote
Watson along the same lines, pointing out that "Brown stands
for the influence which you and I have been long fighting." He
reminded his friend of the constructive work of the Smith
administration and told how their mutual friends were "deeply
grieved" over his break with Smith. "They have come to me
time and time again and urged me to advocate a reconciliation."[28]
Many "Old Pops" wrote Watson that they disagreed with him
for the first time in their political careers. It seemed to one man
"that the crowd that has always fought you and cheated you out
of your rights is the crowd that is lined up with Joe Brown. . . ."[29]

The anti-Smith leaders naturally encouraged Watson. Such
men as Clark Howell and R. F. Duckworth, the Farmers' Union
official, constantly reminded Watson of Smith's perfidies. "If you
name the man who beats Hoke Smith this time," wrote Duckworth early in 1908, "no one will dare run for Governor of
Georgia without your consent."[30] Watson put the best face

road and the home of Milton Smith, the arch enemy of railroad control."
Atlanta *Constitution*, March 19, April 3, 12, 1908.

[27] Atlanta *Journal*, April 8-12, 19, May 6, 28, 1908.

[28] William Walden to Watson, May 25, 1908, Hardwick to Watson,
February 17, 24, April 13, 20, 25, 29, May 6, 1908, and Hines to Watson,
February 20, May 7, 1908, in Watson Papers.

[29] Roger D. Flynt to Watson, April 30, 1908, and John A. Boykin to
Watson, April 30, 1908, in Watson Papers.

[30] Duckworth to Watson, February 19, 28, 1908, *ibid*.

possible on his position. He insisted that he opposed Smith not because of the Glover affair, but because the governor was "back-sliding," had failed to carry out enough railroad reforms, and had appointed notorious politicians to office. The election of "Little Joe" would mean no defeat for reform principles, asserted Watson.[31]

The most effective complaint Watson made against Smith was that the governor had entered into a conspiracy to place the political control of the state in the hands of its largest cities. He charged that Smith was responsible for the abrogation by the State Democratic Executive Committee of the county-unit rule, previously used in state primaries, and for the substitution of a majority rule: "My deliberate opinion after the coolest reflection, is that Hoke Smith, being jealous of me politically, and attributing to me the ambition to go to the senate from Georgia, deliberately devised this scheme for the purpose of preventing the country counties from having the full weight of their influence in elections. He knew that my following was mainly composed of country people. . . ."[32]

Smith and his supporters pointed out that the new majority rule had been endorsed by the Democratic party in the state convention of 1906, and that a majority-vote plan had been good Populist doctrine in the nineties. A few of Watson's followers expressed uneasiness over their leader's position, but the anti-Smith men saw to it that Watson was frequently reminded of Smith's alleged duplicity. "If this rule is ever once established in Georgia," cautioned Clark Howell, "it means that every country county in this state becomes *a way station on the political road*." Meanwhile, reports came in that the rural areas were "on fire" over the issue; it had "awakened the people of Georgia as no other fight has in a generation."[33]

Joseph M. Brown proclaimed his own support of the "time-

[31] Atlanta *Constitution*, April 14, May 5, 9, 14, 18-22, 1908; *Watson's Jeffersonian Magazine*, II (July, 1908), 359-62.

[32] Atlanta *Constitution*, May 24, 1908; *Watson's Jeffersonian Magazine*, II (July, 1908), 429-30, IV (March, 1910), 260.

[33] Howell to Watson, May 14, 28, 29, 1908, Bodenhamer to Watson, May 22, 1908, and Benjamin M. Blackburn to Watson, May 24, 1908, in Watson Papers.

honored principle of home rule." He and his advisers shrewdly
anointed Watson with the oil of complimentary statements,
gently solicited the help of his journals, which they distributed
throughout the state, and boasted of his support. "I would be
quite untrue to my sense of propriety," Brown wrote his new
friend, "were I to fail to write and express to you my high
appreciation of the kind editorials you have been writing in the
Jeffersonian." [34]

The campaign ended with wild demonstrations and prophecies
of victory by both sides. Smith was worried, although he had
received many encouraging reports. In his final address he
accepted the fight as "a special crown of glory. I accept it as
a gage of battle between an equal chance and special privilege,
and I will win a glorious victory." [35]

Joseph M. Brown won, however, receiving an impressive total
of 109,806 popular votes to 98,949 for Smith. It was a "long
dream of delirium," declared the Atlanta *Journal*. "Little Joe's"
vindication was complete, and the Brown partisans immediately
staged a massive victory demonstration in Atlanta.[36] "The seed
of deception, of demagogy and of unrelenting hate have produced
their inevitable fruit," exulted the *Constitution*. "Sanity, Justice
and Conservatism Triumph! " [37]

What lay behind the swift reversal of public opinion that led
to Hoke Smith's defeat? Part of the answer lay in Smith's own
lack of political astuteness; part of it lay in a remarkable series
of developments over which he had little control. The panic of
1907, Watson's use of the county-unit issue, and the opposition
of Farmers' Union leaders because of low cotton prices all had
their effect. The "coterie of politicians" who had long dominated Georgia was quick to seize on these complaints, and
to make use of Watson's defection from the Smith administration.
The circumstances under which Brown was suspended, without
recourse to the legislature for a year and with only a few weeks
of his term left, also played into the anti-Smith strategy. This

[34] Brown to Watson, May 2, 5, 19, 27, 1908, *ibid.*; Atlanta *Constitution*,
March 25, April 10, May 23, 1908.

[35] Atlanta *Journal*, June 3, 1908.

[36] *Ibid.*, June 5, 11, 1908; Atlanta *Constitution*, June 5, 1908.

[37] Atlanta *Constitution*, June 5-7, 11, 1908.

gave Brown a moral advantage, a "halo of martyrdom," which was increased by his relative obscurity, his insignificant physical appearance, and the contemptuous manner in which Smith spoke of him.[38]

Smith took his defeat philosophically. "I am not discouraged," he wrote a North Carolina relative. "I believe the defeat of the principles which I advocated is only temporary; they still live and will yet be endorsed by the good citizens of the state." He also noted, significantly, "They, the railroad-liquor men—& old machine had over $250 000, and under our lax primary law were able to handle many men not entitled to vote. . . . We will perfect primary laws and be ready next time." Marion Smith wrote about the same time that "we certainly expect to make the fight over again, at the earliest opportunity."[39]

The triumphant Brown forces assembled in the state convention on June 23, 1908, to ratify the results of the primary. The platform favored the regulation of public utilities and the passage of an antilobbying measure, but opposed legislation unfriendly to capital invested in Georgia. It approved the county-unit system and endorsed prohibition and disfranchisement. Tom Watson had been led to believe by some Brown spokesmen that the convention would endorse him for the Vice-Presidency, but, to his keen disappointment, this was not done.[40]

The Atlanta *Constitution* spoke darkly of a rumor that Smith would not vote for Brown in the general election, but the governor professed his regularity to the party and cast his ballot for his recent opponent. Although defeated in his own state, Smith devoted considerable time to the national Democratic ticket in the fall of 1908, perhaps hoping to recoup his political standing. He made a speaking tour across the country and appeared with William Jennings Bryan in New York City.[41]

[38] Raleigh *News and Observer*, June 11, 1908; "Smith vs. Brown," in *Outlook*, LXXXIX (June 13, 1908), 312-13.

[39] Marion Smith to J. O. Procter, Jr., June 25, 1908, in Smith letterbooks; Smith to William A. Hoke, June 29, 1908, in Hoke Papers (Southern Historical Collection, University of North Carolina Library).

[40] Hewlette A. Hall to Watson, June 5, 16, 1908, in Watson Papers; Atlanta *Journal*, June 23, 1908.

[41] Atlanta *Constitution*, September 3, 13, 17-19, 22, 24, 27, October 2, 1908; Atlanta *Journal*, September 5, October 5, 13, 16, 21, 26, 28, 1908.

Although the achievements of the Smith administration during the regular and extra sessions of the General Assembly that followed the primary of 1908 were substantial, the final months of Smith's incumbency were not harmonious. The defeated governor fought with the prison commission over the location of the new prison farm, disagreed with the commission and with the state treasurer over the manner in which appropriations were to be expended, and engaged in a newspaper tilt with Clark Howell over the accomplishments of his administration.

Perhaps in part because of such criticisms as those of Howell, and also because after examining the profits made by Georgia railroads in 1908, he had decided that they were in position to reduce freight rates, Smith urged the railroad commission in 1909 to act on two pending port-rate petitions. Chairman McLendon, who in earlier years had given hearty support to Smith's position on the rate question, prepared a lengthy statement in which he argued that the reductions should not be granted. This angered Smith. "The summary you present is made as an argument," he wrote the commissioner, "and contains no definite information of fact, and might well carry an answer which would relieve the minds of the commissioners from any point that great losses have been incurred by the railroads in Georgia." Reports were soon being circulated by Smith's enemies that McLendon would vote against rate reductions and that a break between the two men was about to take place.[42]

In June the railroad commission turned down the rate petitions, with McLendon casting the deciding vote. Smith then suspended him from office, giving as his reasons McLendon's unwillingness to oppose certain rate increases before the Interstate Commerce Commission in 1908, his desire to increase passenger rates on the Georgia Railroad, his tendency to anticipate decisions of the commission by getting into press arguments, and his use of free transportation. "He unites abandonment of election obligations with policies hostile to the interests of the people of the State," the governor asserted.[43]

[42] Smith to McLendon, April 24, 1909, in Smith Collection; Atlanta *Constitution*, April 23, 29, 1909; Savannah *Morning News*, May 5, 1909.
[43] Executive Minutes (1907-1909), 241-43.

An acrimonious debate followed between Smith and McLendon, continuing after Smith left office. A joint committee of the General Assembly, appointed to investigate the removal, soon discovered that McLendon had been involved while on the commission in buying and selling municipal railroad securities. McLendon attempted to justify his behavior, and Smith's enemies tried to involve him in this aspect of the case by implying that he had known about McLendon's bond deals when he suspended the commissioner, yet had failed to mention them in his message to the legislature. Smith, no longer governor, wrote a long letter to the chairman of the committee, refuting these implications. He also issued a detailed reply to McLendon's charges. When the committee made its report, it recommended that McLendon's suspension be upheld, and the General Assembly approved its recommendations by a vote of 23 to 18 in the senate and 129 to 40 in the house.[44]

After surrendering the governorship to Joseph M. Brown in late June, 1909, Hoke Smith rejoined his old law firm, which now became known as Smith, Hastings, and Ransom. In addition to the two Smiths, the concern included Jack J. Hastings, who had been associated with Smith in earlier years, and Ronald Ransom, the husband of Mary Brent Smith, the oldest Smith daughter. The ex-governor was soon immersed once more in the exciting business of practicing law, but he expressed a wish to devote some time to other activities, such as his library and his farm. "It is not my desire personally to go into the court house," he wrote, "except in cases where large recoveries may be expected."[45] One of the lawyer's most important business steps during these years was his part in the organization of the Fulton National Bank in 1909. He provided the necessary legal services for the new venture, purchased stock in it, and became one of its directors.[46]

[44] *Senate Journal* (1909), 568, 653-56; *House Journal* (1909), 287-313, 1123-25; Atlanta *Journal*, June 25, July 1, 2, 5, 11-15, 19-24, 1909; Atlanta *Constitution*, July 31, August 7, 19, 1909.

[45] Smith to W. P. Varner, July 14, 1909, in Smith letterbooks.

[46] Smith to R. J. Atkinson, September 25, 1909, and to E. W. Kramer, September 28, 1909, *ibid.*

Politics, of course, refused to take a holiday. Almost as soon as the primary of 1908 was over, the Georgia press began to predict that Smith would run again in 1910. Governor Brown's inauguration meant that the roles of the two factions were reversed, and the Smith newspapers, led by the Atlanta *Journal*, immediately launched a vigorous attack on the new administration. The Smith papers criticized Brown's recommendations for the revision of the railroad commission law and attacked the governor for disregarding a legislative directive to purchase railroad terminals near Chattanooga for the Western and Atlantic Railroad. Smith followers also expressed alarm over Brown's proposals for changing the registration law and criticized his liberal use of the pardoning power.[47]

Another matter that led to angry charges and countercharges was the assertion by Brown spokesmen that the state was virtually bankrupt and unable to meet its obligations. In reality, this was a condition that Smith had complained about even before entering office himself. The trouble was that most state taxes were collected in the fall, too late to meet many obligations falling due earlier in the year. Governor Brown and Representative J. Randolph Anderson, a Brown leader from Chatham County, began to contend early in the Brown administration that Smith was responsible for a treasury deficit.[48]

During the last part of 1909 this became an important issue in the Smith-Brown controversy. Brown employed an expert public accountant to examine the condition of the treasury, and he submitted a report estimating a deficit of $728,566.50 on January 1, 1910. Meanwhile, Murphy Candler issued a detailed statement showing the losses in revenue resulting from the prohibition act and the abolition of the convict-leasing system, and pointing out that the Smith administration had nevertheless increased the public school fund and paid a larger share of the teachers' salaries than the previous administration. "The plain truth of the matter is that Georgia's treasury is empty every summer," he declared, "and has been for many, many summers."

[47] Atlanta *Journal*, July 4, 24, 28, August 12, September 27, October 5, 15, 17, 1909, March 2, 1910.
[48] *Ibid.*, June 7, July 8-10, August 4, 1909.

Smith emphasized the same points in a long statement following the release of the special auditor's report.[49] Eventually the state treasurer, J. Pope Brown, made a "most thorough" investigation that vindicated the Smith administration. When the year ended, the Atlanta *Journal* triumphantly observed, "The Treasury is all right; it has always been all right." [50]

The controversies of Brown's first year in office made it clear that Smithism was not dead. The legislature of 1909, which seemed to have more Smith than Brown supporters, provided further evidence of this fact. Smith's popular support had begun to increase soon after his defeat in 1908. The abolition of the leasing system, the enactment of primary and registration laws, the renewed effort to bring about rate reductions, and Smith's handling of the railroad strike in the spring of 1909 contributed to this public esteem.

The Atlanta attorney found it easy to remain in the news following his retirement from office. He received many invitations to address educational rallies, labor groups, and business conventions, and on such occasions he vigorously defended the principal legislation of his recent administration. As the deadline for registration approached in the spring of 1910, Smith issued an outspoken statement defending the new registration law and urging Georgians to register. Pointing out that the measure was a product of "the reform element," he took particular pains to reassure farmers that it was not designed to disfranchise them, as the Brownites had charged.[51]

As the spring advanced, Smith said nothing publicly about the forthcoming gubernatorial primary. Numerous men were mentioned as possible candidates, and some Brown newspapers hopefully suggested that their candidate might be unopposed. Meanwhile, the pressure built up for Smith to announce his candidacy. Late in April two delegations visited his home to

[49] *Ibid.*, August 28, September 1, 9, 13, October 12-14, 1909; Atlanta *Constitution*, October 10, 13, 14, 1909.

[50] Atlanta *Journal*, October 14, 15, 27, 28, December 20, 1909, January 3, 4, 18, 1910.

[51] *Ibid.*, March 27, 1910.

urge him to oppose "Little Joe." He refused to give them a
definite answer but promised "to determine that question in a
very short while." Two weeks later he gave his answer. He
announced that for "reasons of a personal nature" and because
most of the reforms he had advocated had been carried out, he
could not enter the race "at the present time." He observed,
somewhat cryptically, that he would enter the campaign "without hesitation" if his "individual preferences alone" were involved. This led some newspapers to surmise that the state of his
wife's health was the deciding factor in Smith's decision.[52]

Smith's statement referred to "an extended movement" to
force him into the race; during the following few days there
was abundant evidence of this. Letters and telegrams poured
into his office, and many people stopped by to talk to him
personally about the matter. But Hoke Smith stood firm. "I
cannot alter the decision. . . . If my friends fully understood those
reasons they would not criticize my action, and I sincerely hope
they will attach no blame to my course, as it distresses me very
much to know I cannot do as they wish."[53]

Early in June the State Democratic Executive Committee promulgated the rules for the approaching primary and fixed its date
for August 23. On the following day Governor Brown announced
that he would be a candidate for renomination. In the meantime,
appeals continued to reach Smith urging him to reconsider.
Whether purposely or not, Smith abetted this movement by
delivering a number of educational and Chautauqua addresses
early in the month.[54]

When Brown stoutly reaffirmed his hostility to the Smith
reforms in his annual message to the legislature on June 22, the
Kimball House, filled with newly arrived legislators, became a
hotbed of political talk. Everybody was speculating about Hoke
Smith's reaction to Brown's defiant message. Hooper Alexander
interpreted the governor's remarks as "a clear-cut unmistakable

[52] *Ibid.*, April 30, May 14, 1910; Atlanta *Georgian*, May 14, 1910; Atlanta
Constitution, May 15, 1910.

[53] Atlanta *Journal*, May 15, 18, 25, 1910.

[54] One of Smith's Chautauqua performances was "his famous lecture"
on "Dixie in the Sixties." Atlanta *Journal*, June 4, 6, 15, 19, 1910.

challenge to the progressives," and the Atlanta *Journal* declared that Smith simply had to run. Smith supporters staged a parade and other demonstrations to convince their leader that he must accept Brown's challenge. On the day after the governor delivered his message, Smith opened the door of his office in the Peters Building and announced to newspapermen, "You may say that I'll be in the race for governor this year." [55]

Perhaps Smith was angered by Brown's defiant statement, perhaps he felt that progressive measures were in danger, but whatever the motivating factors may have been, it is clear that he was too closely identified with one faction of the party and too susceptible to the challenge of a political fight to avoid being drawn into the campaign of 1910. Anti-Smith newspapers emphasized his desire for revenge and his ambition, but sympathetic papers stated that he was probably influenced by the facts that the campaign would be a short one and that Mrs. Smith's health had improved during the past few days.

The primary contest proved to be a two-man affair, as it had been in 1908. H. H. Perry, a Smith leader, withdrew from the race when the Atlantan made his announcement, and Richard B. Russell soon indicated that he would not enter the campaign, as had been predicted. A few days after Smith entered the race, Attorney General John C. Hart announced that he would be a candidate in the interest of peace between the two Democratic factions. He called on Brown and Smith to withdraw from the race, but when they paid no heed to his request, he himself left the contest. [56]

The campaign was brief. Smith's approach was in decided contrast to his vigorous campaigns of 1905-1906 and 1908. He made only twelve or fifteen speeches, and most of those were confined to the last few days before the election. Governor Brown made no speeches and wrote only a few short cards. But in spite of the languorous appearance of the campaign, both sides were well-organized and made effective use of supporting speakers and campaign literature.

[55] *Ibid.*, June 22-24, 1910; Atlanta *Constitution*, June 23, 24, 1910.
[56] Savannah *Morning News*, June 4, 26, 1910; Atlanta *Constitution*, July 10, 15, 1910.

Hoke Smith planned to open his campaign with a major address
in Waycross on July 31, but an acute attack of " kidney colic "
which kept him in bed for several days prevented him from
going. Instead, Reuben R. Arnold spoke for him, delivering a
comprehensive address which Smith had prepared. The ex-
governor reviewed the accomplishments of his administration and
declared that the work " in 1911 will be to perfect what has
been already done, not an effort to destroy it." Smith's first
appearance was in Atlanta on August 5, where an estimated ten
thousand enthusiastic people heard him speak. He described his
program as one of " progressive democracy " and compared it
with the work of the " reactionary democrats." The progressives
believed " in popular government and in the dignity of being a
citizen of Georgia," asserted the candidate, not in a " do nothing "
and " truckling " government.[57]

While the Smith forces emphasized the " progressive democracy," the Brown supporters described their policy as one of
" progressive prosperity," and pointed to good crops and high
cotton prices as evidence that their champion was a good governor. " Little Joe " contended that the state needed a rest after
the Smith upheaval and called Smith's " political ambition more
progressive than his democracy." The Brown spokesmen declared
that Smith had " inflamed the minds " of the people by " arraying
class against class " and " the poor against corporate interests." [58]

There were several issues in the campaign, in addition to the
personalities of the two contestants. The railroad commission
act and Brown's proposals for changing it, the Smith demand for
port rates, and the general question of corporation control attracted considerable attention. Smith contended that the " progressive democracy " was responsible for an annual saving of
a million dollars in passenger rates and an increase of half a
million dollars in taxes collected from public service companies;
yet, he claimed, Georgia railroads were prospering. He continued
to urge stringent regulation of public utility companies, but he
was more moderate in his recommendations than in the past two
campaigns. He was careful to place himself on record as favoring

[57] Atlanta *Journal*, July 24, 28-31, August 1, 5, 6, 1910.
[58] Atlanta *Constitution*, July 3, 29, August 1, 10, 13, 16, 21, 1910.

the investment of foreign capital in Georgia, although he insisted that "fair and just supervision of transportation companies is absolutely essential to the growth and prosperity of the commerce of the state. . . ." [59]

The registration law of 1908 also provoked debate. Brown proposed a thirty-day period between registration and elections, instead of six months, as the Smith measure specified, and anti-Smith leaders claimed that the act would disfranchise thousands of white men. It had been designed "to legislate Brown out of office," declared the Macon *Telegraph*. Smith argued that the registration lists should be closed early in order that they could be purged of illegal voters and so the sale of votes would be discouraged. Each faction accused the other of having defeated the antilobbying bill. The Smith adherents criticized the state committee's rules for the primary, particularly the plan for pro-rating the votes among the candidates in counties where no one received a majority. They scored Brown for his proposal to float a six hundred thousand dollar bond issue in order to pay school teachers promptly. Smith advocated, instead of the bond issue, a plan whereby public service companies could pay their taxes by September 1, and receive a one per cent tax reduction.[60]

Smith partisans were quick to seize on "Little Joe's" use of state troops to quell a small labor threat by some Italian miners in the Durham coal mines of Colonel James W. English, Jr., a strong Brown supporter. According to the Atlanta *Journal*, the governor "overstepped all civil authorities, all legal precedents and, pell mell upon a peaceful community, thrust military force to conquer the ill temper of eighteen Italian laborers." Brown leaders countered by asserting that Smith favored foreign immigration and by praising Brown for squelching "the Dago mob." [61] But it was difficult for them to overcome the contrast between

[59] *Ibid.*, July 21, 30, August 9, September 2, 1910; Atlanta *Journal*, July 31, August 12, 1910.

[60] Atlanta *Journal*, May 29, June 23, 29, July 8-14, 16, 20, 31, August 9, 13, September 1, 1910; Atlanta *Constitution*, July 6, 7, 14, 19, 20, 31, August 9, 10, 14, 1910; Macon *Telegraph*, July 8, 1910.

[61] Atlanta *Constitution*, May 27, July 6, 7, 20, 21, 26, 29-31, August 6, 1910; Atlanta *Journal*, May 27, 29, June 8-11, July 22, 26, 29, 1910.

the governor's actions and Smith's calm handling of the railroad strike of 1909.

The lineup of major newspapers and political leaders remained substantially the same as in 1908, with one exception. Tom Watson withdrew his support from the Brown administration, having made certain charges of graft against one of Brown's appointees. His attention during the campaign was concentrated on Thomas W. Hardwick, whose renomination to Congress he unsuccessfully tried to prevent. Following the bitter campaign of 1908, the two men had gradually drifted into open hostility, and by May, 1910, they had commenced such a campaign of abuse as the state had seldom witnessed. Early in August Smith received word from a friend that Watson would not oppose him, and he replied at once, declaring that he had never impugned the Populist leader's motives "in the slightest for the position that he took." A few days later James K. Hines sent out a circular letter to many of the subscribers of Watson's magazine, apparently without Watson's knowledge, urging Smith's election.[62]

The campaign ended with both sides confidently predicting victory. At a huge Brown rally in Atlanta, enthusiastic supporters of the governor paraded with thousands of torches. To the tune of "The Old Gray Bonnet" they sang:

Get your old Gray Bonnet with the Brown Button on it,
And we'll hitch Hoke Smith to the dray,
From the fields of clover,
We'll drive him to cover,
On this grand Brown Rally Day!

Meanwhile Smith had returned from a swift tour of the state. He was met at the station and given a rousing reception by his followers, who chanted "Hoke! Hoke! Hoke! " "I have visited every section of the state," declared Smith; "I have received more than 20,000 letters from different individuals. They manifest the deepest interest and concern everywhere."[63]

When the ballots had been tallied, it was apparent that Hoke

[62] Smith to James J. Green, August 2, 1910, and James K. Hines circular letter dated August 15, 1910, in Watson Papers.

[63] Atlanta *Journal*, August 17-23, 1910; Atlanta *Constitution*, August 23, 1910.

Smith had eked out a narrow victory. He received 96,638 popular votes to 92,469 for Brown; the county-unit vote was 233 to 78. Many counties had been won or lost by 25 votes or less, and in over fifty counties the margin of victory was less than 100 votes. It was significant that Governor Brown received over 17,000 fewer votes than in 1908. The loss of Watson's support was disastrous, and the labor vote cost him heavily. Smith carried every county, for instance, along the route of the railroad strike of 1909.[64]

Smith was formally nominated on September 1, when the state convention met in Atlanta. The platform, drafted under James R. Gray's direction, commended the accomplishments of the Smith administration, recommended the creation of a state labor bureau, demanded the port rates, expressed friendship for foreign capital if legitimately invested, advocated certain financial reforms, and urged party nominations by direct vote. In his address of acceptance, Smith urged a conciliatory approach toward the Brown faction. He praised the " progressive democracy "; it should protect property rights but always strive " for the betterment of the human race." [65]

One additional moment of excitement occurred in connection with the election of 1910. With Joseph M. Brown's tacit consent, Watson sponsored him as an independent candidate against Smith in the general election that followed in October. Watson was especially opposed to the registration act of 1908, which he claimed had disfranchised nearly a hundred thousand white men, thus making Negroes " the balance of power in Georgia." He condemned the " gag-rule " methods which he said the Smith men used in the September convention, and he accused Hardwick and Smith of having promoted the riotous reception he was given while attempting to deliver an address in Atlanta on the night of September 2. Furthermore, Watson made the sensational charge that Smith was guilty of immorality.[66]

[64] Atlanta *Journal*, August 17, 23, 24, 27, 28, September 1, 1910.

[65] *Ibid.*, August 30, September 1, 2, 1910.

[66] Watson to Smith, September 4, 1910, in Watson Papers; *Watson's Magazine*, V (November, 1910), 909; Atlanta *Journal*, September 3, October 1, 1910; Atlanta *Georgian*, November 12, 1910.

The Atlanta *Georgian* reported that Watson's charges "were almost beyond human belief." As the Atlanta newspaper described them, "Hoke Smith is accused of being a moral leper who has wrecked homes, deported unfortunate victims, and [taken] . . . advantage of the sister of a state prisoner while she was pleading for a pardon for her brother." Watson claimed that the ex-governor had been sexually intimate with several women in past years. He sent Smith the following telegram on September 27: "It is closing in on you. I give you one more chance to save your wife & son. Resign by two o clock today, or your crimes will be known to all the world." [67]

Smith paid no attention to Watson's charges. In mid-September he issued a brief statement thanking his supporters for their work in the recent campaign and, after Watson asserted that Smith owned and dominated the Atlanta *Journal*, exchanged public letters with Gray denying that this was true. The *Journal* was more outspoken, denouncing Watson as an "embittered and disappointed man." "Unable to dominate, he cried corrupt," declared the *Journal*, and exclaimed that "The world is plunging hellward." [68]

In the October election Smith was easily victorious. [69] But Watson continued his efforts to prove his sensational charges against Smith. Fred L. Seely of the Atlanta *Georgian* had agreed to help the Populist leader, but on November 12, he devoted the entire front page of the *Georgian* to photostatic evidence which disproved the charges. Seely had contacted every person Watson mentioned as a source and found that there were no affidavits or other concrete evidence: "The Georgian is compelled to say . . . that not the first suggestion of a foundation in fact has been obtainable, and that, after the employment of the best talent, detective, legal and otherwise, even giving his political enemies every opportunity to supply facts or evidence, we must say unequivocally, in the interest of a square deal, that Hoke Smith is as innocent of misconduct, moral or otherwise, as any man in Georgia—"

[67] See telegram in Watson Papers; Atlanta *Georgian*, November 12, 1910.
[68] Atlanta *Journal*, September 4, 10-12, 22, October 1-3, 1910.
[69] The popular vote was 75,163 to 15,896. *House Journal* (1911), 162.

For the moment, at least, Tom Watson's influence in Georgia politics was at a low ebb, while Hoke Smith's was in the ascendancy. The Smith-Brown controversy had not yet run its course, but Smith would soon have another opportunity to demonstrate what the "progressive democracy" could do.

"Progressive Democracy"

Most leaders of the Smith faction contended that the differences between their group and the Howell-Brown element were funda-mental and far-reaching. As Hooper Alexander put it in 1918: "In the South we vainly fancy that we have only a Democratic party. Both parties are in fact fully developed among us, all claiming the same name and fighting out their battles under the same party organization. Milton Smith and the Macon Telegraph are just as different from me and my Panthersville constituents as Prussian junkers are from the Social Democrats." [1] The fact that the state's political factions in the decade after 1905 became highly competitive and rather enduring gave considerable plausi-bility to such statements. Many Smith supporters looked upon the adherents of the opposing faction as the rankest conservatives, regarding themselves as "progressive democrats." Progressivism in Georgia, asserted that redoubtable champion of the Smith faction, the Atlanta *Journal*, had arrived "in the thick of a nation-wide movement toward Democratic principles." It was a move-ment to cut away "outworn customs" and to uproot "old abuses" in order "that industrial and social developments may proceed unhampered." [2]

The first Smith administration had sponsored a lengthy array of anticorporation measures and election reforms. But the more extreme anticorporation bills, as well as the demand for extensive rate reductions, had failed, and following the panic of 1907 and the vociferous accusations leveled at the Smith administration

[1] Alexander to Smith, November 16, 1918, in Smith Collection.
[2] Atlanta *Journal*, August 11, September 16, 1910.

by its critics, the whole approach toward corporations tended
to become less militant. Furthermore, Smith's attempt to institute
a primary system based on majority rule rather than the county-
unit arrangement provoked such a strong reaction, especially in
the rural districts, that it was abandoned.

This more moderate attitude toward business, this new orienta-
tion of Smith progressives, was reflected in Smith's inaugural
address on July 1, 1911. The new governor reviewed and defended the major work of his first administration, declaring that
it " marked an epoch in our history." He urged the passage of
an antilobbying law and the establishment of a bureau of labor
and a highway commission. He suggested that the railroad commission be given jurisdiction over water-power companies, which
were acquiring the state's best water-power sites. He renewed
his demand for port rates, advising the legislature to investigate
the entire problem, and expressed his unalterable opposition to
the sale of the Western and Atlantic Railroad. He presented a
series of proposals for improving the financial affairs of Georgia
and recommended several additional reforms in the state's election
machinery. Perhaps the most notable feature of Smith's address
was his comprehensive discussion of education and agriculture.[3]

Before the new administration could turn to these tasks, however, an important political question had to be settled. The
General Assembly had to elect a United States Senator to fill the
unexpired term of Alexander S. Clay, who had died in November
of the previous year after serving less than two years of his
current term. Governor Brown had appointed ex-Governor
Joseph M. Terrell, a popular leader of the anti-Smith faction,
to serve until the legislature could elect a successor at its next
annual session. Terrell was anxious to be chosen by the legislature.

Clay's death placed the Smithites in a dilemma. Smith's name
was immediately mentioned in connection with the election of
Clay's successor, despite the fact that the election was many
months in the future. The governor-elect was pledged to complete his state reforms, yet here perhaps was a golden opportunity
to obtain the office he had long wanted. The situation also

[3] *House Journal* (1911), 205a-228a.

presented its thorny side to the Howell-Brown leaders. They would have liked nothing better than to remove Hoke Smith from the governorship, but they were not eager to see him achieve a higher office.

During the months before his inauguration Smith said nothing publicly about the Senate seat. His enemies tried to embarrass him by demanding that the Smith-dominated State Democratic Executive Committee order a Senatorial primary, but the committee refused to take this step. The Atlanta *Journal* argued that the people were either thoroughly indifferent or emphatically against a primary. Other Smith partisans contended that a Senate primary would violate the Federal Constitution, that the custom in the state had been for the General Assembly to elect Senators to unexpired terms, and that farmers were too busy with their crops to go to the polls. The Atlanta *Constitution*, on the other hand, described the state committee as "canned" and declared that the other side "doesn't want the primary because they feel sure one of them can more easily win the toga before the legislature than before the people." [4]

Meanwhile, as the spring of 1911 advanced and the legislative session approached, some Smith leaders grew impatient with their chief's coyness. Murphy Candler of the railroad commission, Pleasant A. Stovall, publisher of the Savannah *Press*, and William A. Covington, a prominent legislator from Moultrie, expressed interest in the Senate position and discussed the matter with Smith. Stovall and Covington eventually announced themselves as candidates for the post. Tom Watson and ex-Congressman William G. Brantley were also mentioned as aspirants. On a trip to New York in May, Smith refused to let reporters draw him out about the approaching election. Instead, he spoke enthusiastically about his state program.[5]

The *Constitution* reported that Smith had promised Stovall and Covington that he would not enter the race, but legislators who conferred with the governor-elect a few days before the General Assembly convened were quoted as saying that he would

[4] Atlanta *Journal*, November 24, 1910, May 14, 21, 1911; Atlanta *Constitution*, May 11, 14, 19, June 14, 29, July 1, 1911.

[5] Atlanta *Journal*, March 3, May 12, 1911.

allow his name to be presented as a candidate. Tom Watson charged that Stovall and Covington were "dummy candidates," designed "to march votes" into Smith's camp.[6]

Hoke Smith finally showed his hand on June 26. In a letter to Covington he wrote: "The situation is such that it now seems inevitable that my name will be presented to the legislature for the senate, and, of course, in this event I shall hope to be elected." Smith seems to have deliberately allowed matters to drift until support built up for his own selection. By this time Covington and Stovall had declared their intention to remain in the contest.[7]

In the legislature Smith's enemies attempted to secure the passage of resolutions requesting the state committee to call a special primary, or to ascertain from each candidate whether or not he would agree to resign fifty days before the next Democratic primary and submit his candidacy to the voters. But they were unsuccessful in these maneuvers. Following a four-day recess of the General Assembly early in July, the Atlanta *Journal* reported that Smith's legislative friends had returned to the capitol more confident than ever that their man would be elected. But Gray's paper would not predict his election, pointing out that Terrell was a strong candidate and noting that some Smith men were inclined to feel that their leader's duty was to remain as governor. Senator Emmett R. Shaw was quoted as saying: "If there is any place on earth we need the heaviest weight man we have got, at this time, it is in the governor's chair—a man with nerve and backbone—and Hoke Smith will make the mistake politically of his life if he receives the senatorship."[8]

The election in the General Assembly occurred on July 11 and 12. On the first day Smith received a majority of 107 to 71 in the house of representatives, but he lacked 2 votes of having

[6] Watson to W. A. Covington, January 26, 1911, in Watson Papers; Atlanta *Constitution*, June 11, 20, 25, 27, July 1, 1911; *Watson's Magazine*, XIII (June, 1911), 178-79.

[7] Atlanta *Journal*, June 20, 1911; Savannah *Morning News*, July 2, 1911; Atlanta *Constitution*, July 8, 1911.

[8] *House Journal* (1911), 253; *Senate Journal* (1911), 223-24; Atlanta *Journal*, June 20, 29, July 3-9, 1911; Atlanta *Constitution*, June 25, 1911.

a majority in the senate.[9] This made it necessary to hold a joint session of the two houses on the following day, when Smith was elected on the first roll call by a vote of 155 to 65 for his opponents.[10] He won without publicly announcing himself as a candidate, apparently letting things move along "without any open interference one way or another." Some observers noted, however, that Commissioner of Agriculture Thomas G. Hudson had served as a capable behind-the-scenes champion of the governor.[11]

No sooner had Smith been elected than he involved the state in excited political discussion by announcing that he intended to remain governor until December.[12] Senator Terrell was indignant. He sent his resignation to Smith and the United States Senate, and in two letters to the governor vigorously asserted that his term expired when the legislature elected Smith. The position "belongs to you," he wrote Smith, and no "fine spun reasoning" would induce him to continue in the office.[13]

Smith first tried persuasion with Terrell. He requested him to withdraw his resignation, declaring that legislation was pending before the General Assembly "of great importance to the state to which I have given careful study, and I regard it as imperative that I should continue to co-operate with that body as governor during its present session." He cited precedents to support his contention that he was governor of Georgia and Senator-elect, and that he would not become a Senator until his commission was presented to the Senate. He reminded Terrell that he was unfamiliar with much of the legislation before Congress and that he could do little more than vote during the few remaining weeks of the session.

Senator Terrell was in no mood to be persuaded to do any-

[9] The vote in the house was: Smith 107, Terrell 36, Stovall 17, Covington 10, Watson 5, and Brantley 3. In the senate Smith received 21, Terrell 17, Covington 4, and Stovall 2 votes. *House Journal* (1911), 378-83; *Senate Journal* (1911), 300-301.

[10] *House Journal* (1911), 398-403; *Senate Journal* (1911), 308-310.

[11] Atlanta *Journal*, July 11, 12, 1911; Savannah *Morning News*, July 13, 1911.

[12] Atlanta *Journal*, July 12, 1911; Atlanta *Constitution*, July 13, 1911.

[13] Atlanta *Georgian*, July 12, 1911; Atlanta *Constitution*, July 15, 16, 1911.

thing for the man who had recently defeated him. He wrote the
governor that if he would not assume his new duties the General
Assembly should elect someone who would; he lashed out at the
state executive committee for having failed to call a primary
election; and he suggested that Smith had promised the patronage
at his disposal as governor to influence legislators to vote for
him, and that he now wished to continue in office so that he
could dispense the appointments. He contended that Smith was
not essential to the governorship, and he bitterly noted " that
habitual arrogance and domination and disregard of principles
which has characterized him, under the banner of exalted
patriotism. . . ." [14]

Hoke Smith's reply was a mixture of sarcastic rejoinders to
Terrell's charges and insinuations, and of an indignation that
scorned the Senator's " manifestation of ill-temper." He observed
that Terrell had not been in Washington for weeks, and he
categorically denied having used patronage in a single case to help
win the Senate seat. At the same time, Smith refused to accept
Terrell's resignation; he treated the matter as settled and steadfastly ignored the widespread criticism he encountered, some of
it from his own faction. In the meantime Terrell had his name
stricken from the Senate roll.[15]

The anti-Smith politicians, confident of placing " Little Joe "
Brown back in the governor's office, were anxious for Smith to
leave the state as soon as possible, in part to prevent him from
disposing of all the state patronage. When it became evident that
Smith would not give up the governorship at once, hostile legislators introduced resolutions urging him to assume his Senate
duties and proposing not to confirm his appointments.[16] Opposition newspapers belabored him for not going immediately to
Washington to assist other Democrats. Both factions quoted
Senators in Washington to prove that Smith was or was not
needed to help the Democrats. Everybody could agree with

[14] Atlanta *Journal*, July 12, 1911; Atlanta *Constitution*, July 15-17, 1911.
[15] Savannah *Press*, July 13, 1911; Atlanta *Constitution*, July 14, 16, 1911.
[16] Anti-Smith legislators failed in their efforts to pass resolutions urgently
requesting the governor " to repair " to Washington at once. *House Journal*
(1911), 497, 823; *Senate Journal* (1911), 574; Atlanta *Journal*, July 14, 16,
23-26, August 2, 4, 1911.

Daniel A. Tompkins, who wrote from North Carolina, "It is not often that a man is gove[r]nor and senator at the same time." [17]

Although the fifty-day session of the General Assembly in 1911 failed to enact as many important measures as did the Smith legislatures of 1907 and 1908, its achievements were considerable and in decided contrast to the previous two sessions under Joseph M. Brown. The house of representatives proved to be more amenable to Smith's will than did the senate. In the house the governor's friend, John N. Holder, was elected speaker and Hooper Alexander stood out as a strong progressive leader; but in the upper house John M. Slaton, the president of the senate, and other Brown spokesmen frequently were able to dominate proceedings.

An old progressive proposal that was approved during this session was the antilobbying bill. It required any agent employed "to aid in or oppose" state legislation to file with the secretary of state a sworn statement giving full details as to his employer, compensation, expenses, and the legislation with which he was concerned. The terms of the act banished lobbyists from the legislative chambers and provided that no person or corporation could hire an agent to aid or oppose a measure on a contingent basis.[18]

The General Assembly established a department of commerce and labor with an elective commissioner to collect labor and industrial statistics, to investigate the operation of employee-safety and child-labor laws, and, if it chose, to inquire into labor-management disagreements. Organized labor in Georgia had long demanded this legislation, and both Smith and Brown had endorsed it in 1910. The legislature of 1911 also passed a measure to reduce the maximum hours of textile-mill employees from sixty-six to sixty per week, but despite Smith's recommendation and a strong effort by Representative Alexander, a stronger child-

[17] Tompkins to Smith, July 19, 1911, in Daniel A. Tompkins Papers (Southern Historical Collection, University of North Carolina Library).

[18] *House Journal* (1911), 583, 612, 1218-20; *Senate Journal* (1911), 215, 351, 996; *Georgia Acts* (1911), 151-54.

labor law was not enacted. Not until 1914 were the progressives able to push through a stricter child-labor bill.[19] Other laws of some importance enacted in 1911 included a comprehensive bill to regulate insurance companies in the state, a measure sponsored by Senator Joseph H. Felker and recommended by Smith to allow superior court judges to change the venue for trials in criminal cases to avoid the threat of lynching, and an amendment to the registration act of 1908 providing for the qualification of voters in special elections.[20]

Several administration bills failed to win the approval of the legislature. These included the highway commission bill, a measure to create a state board of tax equalizers, Smith's proposals that the governor be inaugurated in January and that the election of state officials be held at the same time Congressmen were elected, and his recommendation that the state pay the managers of primaries. A number of progressive bills which had not received Hoke Smith's endorsement also failed, among them measures to initiate woman suffrage, to adopt the initiative and referendum, and to institute a preferential Senatorial primary.[21]

The difficulties Smith had encountered during his first administration in managing Georgia's cumbersome financial system and the controversy in which he became involved with respect to the status of the treasury convinced him that several changes should be made in the state's machinery for collecting and expending its revenue. He proposed a five-point plan to improve the situation: (1) to increase the governor's borrowing power to $500,000 annually, in order that all current obligations could be met; (2) to advance the time public service corporations paid their taxes to September 1; (3) to establish a finance board composed of the governor, the comptroller-general, and the treasurer, " with a general supervision over the collection of taxes, the deposit of money in banks and the borrowing of money when that is necessary "; (4) to create a state audit department; and (5) to

[19] *Georgia Acts* (1911), 65-66, 133-37; Davidson, *Child Labor Legislation in the South*, 205-209.

[20] *Georgia Acts* (1911), 74-75, 149-51, 167-69, 174-79, 1681-82; Atlanta *Journal*, August 18, 1911.

[21] Atlanta *Journal*, May 30, June 7, 29, July 3, August 1, 18, 1911.

inaugurate the governor and state house officers in January, thereby making their terms coterminous with the fiscal year.[22]

The first two parts of this program were approved by the legislature in 1911 and later ratified as amendments to the state constitution. The General Assembly also passed a bill providing for a state auditor, but the governor decided to veto the measure because it was poorly drafted. The recommendation for the establishment of a finance board was not acted on, and although the house passed a bill authorizing a January inauguration for the governor and state house officials, it failed to come to a vote in the senate.[23]

During the session Smith warned the legislature that a deficit was in prospect, and when the house approved a bill appropriating more than the anticipated revenue, he urged it to reduce the special appropriations, to increase certain taxes, and to carry over some allocations until the next year. His concern was lessened somewhat when a portion of his finance program was enacted, but in his opinion the final appropriations exceeded the estimated revenue by three hundred thousand dollars. He was determined not to spend more than the state's current income, however, and announced that he would postpone the payment of certain special appropriations authorized by the General Assembly.[24] The progressives had discovered that they could not have their cake and eat it too, at least not until they could obtain greater revenues.

During the campaign of 1910 and in his inaugural address, Hoke Smith had urged several educational reforms, including the remodeling of the state's school laws, a proposal long advocated by leading Georgia educators. The legislature of 1911 passed a comprehensive reorganization bill which created a state board of education, composed of the governor, the state superintendent, and four others to be appointed by the governor and confirmed by the senate for four-year terms. These men were

[22] House Journal (1911), 211a-216a.

[23] Georgia Acts (1911), 49-53; Smith to the General Assembly, August 23, 1911, in Smith Collection.

[24] House Journal (1911), 533-38, 1237-43, 1309-13; Georgia Acts (1911), 20-21; Atlanta Journal, August 11, 13, 18, 24, 1911.

to be educators or men with practical teaching experience, a requirement that Smith had often urged. The act spelled out the duties of the county boards, made normal-school instruction compulsory in each district, and provided for supervisors of schools and normal institutes.[25] This legislation, plus the increase in education appropriations, pleased educational reformers; but the compulsory education bill, which some progressives fought for but which Smith failed to endorse, did not pass during this session.

Smith continued to take an active part in the work of the Peabody Board of Trustees. He accepted the board's decision to award a large sum of money to Peabody College, but he held out for wider distribution of a portion of the fund. As Joseph H. Choate wrote in 1911, "Governor Smith stoutly combats the giving of any more money to Nashville, on grounds that are strongly put." [26] The Georgian, who opposed "a teachers' college for all Southern teachers in Nashville," urged the use of Peabody money to erect "commodious buildings" at some of the state universities in the South. During his first administration as governor Smith co-operated with the trustees of the University of Georgia in the establishment of the Peabody School of Education. An agreement was prepared, with his help, for the appropriation necessary to maintain the school, provided the Peabody Fund would grant fifty thousand dollars for the construction of a building in which to locate it. Smith, more than any other person, was responsible for the forty thousand dollar award the Peabody trustees finally gave the University for this purpose.[27]

"Progress must be the watchword for agriculture," Smith declared in his opening campaign speech of 1910. Successful farming, he frequently said, "does not depend upon manual labor" alone; "it is a pursuit which offers the widest field for scientific investigation, and which requires the very best of trained minds." It was this belief that led Smith to foster "corn

[25] *Georgia Acts* (1911), 94-108; Atlanta *Journal*, August 18, 19, September 5, 1911.

[26] Joseph H. Choate to Richard Olney, January 30, 1911, in Peabody Papers.

[27] Smith to Choate, January 23, 1909, January 27, 1911, and to Olney, January 29, 1911, *ibid.*

clubs " for boys and domestic science clubs for girls throughout
Georgia during these years.[28] Smith's inaugural address was an
illuminating discussion of the state's agricultural prospects. The
time was psychologically right, declared the new governor, to
"revolutionize the farming of Georgia." To assist in this revolution, he proposed a series of measures to stimulate rural education and recommended a liberal increase of expenditures in
support of the state agricultural college. He wanted the college
to undertake more extension and demonstration work, to co-
operate with Federal workers in making soil surveys, to improve
plants and distribute seeds, to encourage livestock, poultry, and
dairying industries, and to promote industrial clubs for boys and
girls. In addition Smith urged the college to foster agricultural
research, to make available correspondence courses, and to become
"a co-operative clearing house of agricultural information." He
also proposed the creation of a special commission of agriculture,
preliminary surveys of swamps and overflow lands in the state,
and the use of convicts to improve public roads.[29]

Smith recommended that the General Assembly increase the
appropriation to the state agricultural college by fifty thousand
dollars to be used for the special services he had outlined. But
when the legislature appropriated special sums for most of these
proposals and added certain projects of its own without an
adequate increase in revenue, he felt compelled to request that
most of the special appropriations lie over until the next legislature
increased the revenue or reduced the appropriations. Other agricultural measures enacted in 1911 included a bill to regulate more
adequately the sale of commercial fertilizer, the provision for
a full-time drug inspector in the department of agriculture, the
establishment of a department of game and fish, with hunting and
fishing restrictions, and appropriations to be used in fighting
cotton diseases and hog cholera. The General Assembly also memo-

[28] Late in 1910, for example, the newspapers reported that Joseph Stone,
an eleven-year-old boy, had won the boy's corn grower's prize for Georgia,
and that Smith had entertained him in Atlanta, urging the press to publicize
the boy's feat. Atlanta *Journal*, December 28, 1910.

[29] Atlanta *Journal*, September 1, 1910, February 4, July 4, 1911; *House
Journal* (1911), 222a-227a.

rialized Congress to enact a rural parcel-post act and passed an ambitious measure for the purpose of draining the swamp lands of the state. Unfortunately, the legislature failed to appropriate the $5,000 needed to match a like Federal sum which would have given the elaborate plan some chance of success.[80]

Smith managed to avoid becoming involved in one of the most controversial measures before the General Assembly in 1911— an unsuccessful proposal to abolish the so-called near-beer allowed under the prohibition legislation. But he had a major tug of war with the senate, which refused to confirm some of his appointments. It was frustrating indeed for the opposition day after day to watch the hated governor hand out the prized appointments that went with the governorship. Early in the session the senate adopted a resolution providing that only those executive appointments that became effective before Smith resigned the governorship would be considered. Despite the efforts of Smith's lieutenants, this policy was followed throughout the session. Near the end of the sitting the senate refused to go into executive session to consider two sealed communications from the governor, presumably containing appointments, and returned them unopened to his office. This was " BABYISH POLITICS," exclaimed the Atlanta *Journal*. Smith made the appointments anyway, subject to the confirmation of the next legislature.[81]

At the beginning of his second administration Smith had suggested that the General Assembly investigate the port rates, but neither the Assembly nor the railroad commission took any action in the matter. The legislature did pass a measure providing for a commission to consider the question of a new leasing contract for the Western and Atlantic Railroad and to look into the problem of terminal property in Chattanooga. For a time near the end of his governorship, Smith showed once more some of his old-time vigor in dealing with the railroads. During the Brown administration the charge had been made, and the railroad commission verified it, that the Nashville, Chattanooga, and St. Louis Railroad was violating its agreement in leasing the Western

---

[80] *House Journal* (1911), 1237-43; *Georgia Acts* (1911), 21-23, 41-45, 56, 108-32, 137-46, 170-74, 1677-79, 1694.

[81] *Senate Journal* (1911), 968, 992; Atlanta *Journal*, June 28, August 17, 18, 1911.

and Atlantic, by charging rates higher than the intrastate rates in effect in Georgia. Governor Smith ordered the matter investigated, heard the railroad's argument, and demanded that the N. C. & St. L. abide by the letter of its contract. Unfortunately, Smith resigned before the question could be settled, and the succeeding administration showed no enthusiasm for his approach.[32]

Among the several bills Smith vetoed in 1911 was one which would have authorized railroad companies to give transportation to newspaper employees in exchange for advertising space. Hooper Alexander described this proposal as a "start toward emasculating the free-pass rule." Hoke Smith agreed. "For years we have fought the pass system in Georgia," he declared in his veto message. "For years we have fought to stop railroad companies and other public service companies from granting special privileges. We know that when they grant special privileges to a few in return they place extra burdens on the many."[33]

In the fall of 1911 Smith made a number of speeches reiterating his constant themes of education, diversified farming, and better marketing methods. In mid-September he attended the governors' conference at Spring Lake, New Jersey, where he had an opportunity to discuss such common state problems as railroad regulation and divorce laws, as well as to talk national politics and to meet many prominent political leaders. He supported the East coast highway being promoted by the Atlanta *Journal* and other newspapers and in October participated in an organized tour of the road. He entered his Maxwell automobile in the tour at New York and drove south to Winston-Salem, where he left the group of travelers. Accompanied by his chauffeur and his two oldest daughters, he spent five days on the road. There was a festive atmosphere about the whole affair, and the genial Smith enjoyed it to the utmost. As he humorously put it, "I've taken the bounces, swallowed whole mouthfuls of rain and eaten the dust for many miles."[34]

[32] Atlanta *Journal*, July 24, September 19, 20, October 21, 1911.

[33] Atlanta *Constitution*, August 18, 1911; *Governor Smith's reasons for vetoing the State Auditor Bill, the W. & A. Commission Bill and the Newspaper Bill*, pamphlet in Smith Collection.

[34] Atlanta *Journal*, August 24, October 11, 12, 16, 19, 20, 23, November 10, 1911.

Following the adjournment of the General Assembly in August, Smith began to make plans for his retirement from the governorship. His enemies hopefully reported that he would resign before October 15, but he continued in office until November 15.[35] On that date President of the Senate John M. Slaton took over as acting governor.

Shortly before relinquishing the governorship, Smith issued an executive order discontinuing the work of ex-Governor William J. Northen as compiler of the state records. Smith based this action on the grounds that the Colonial, Revolutionary, and Confederate records were almost complete, that the remaining work was primarily clerical, and that Northen had refused to visit the governor's office for conferences about his work. Smith also emphasized the expense involved in the project. The governor's critics, on the other hand, charged that he was evening old political scores by punishing Northen for his support of Brown in 1908 and 1910.[36] Smith's motives are not readily apparent, but by this action he set off one of the periodic flare-ups in the state's political cauldron.

Meanwhile, the primary campaign to nominate Smith's successor had already begun. The anti-Smith faction had long before settled on "Little Joe" Brown, and in October he issued a statement strongly criticizing Smith. "Without a precedent in Georgia for such a thing," declared Brown, "he remained on to mingle in state affairs, and to control and to justify this executive committee, and this condition is facing the people now and against this regime my candidacy is a protest." Pope Brown and Richard B. Russell also entered the race.[37]

Smith partisans seemed unable to agree on a candidate. A Savannah newspaper noted early in August that "Gov. Smith's time is largely taken up in seeking a gubernatorial candidate who can carry the Smith faction colors to victory."[38] There were

[35] Atlanta *Constitution*, August 3, 21, 1911; Atlanta *Journal*, August 21, October 12, November 9, 1911.

[36] Smith to Northen, August 30, October 12, 1911, and undated press release (1911), in Northen Collection; Macon *Telegraph*, November 4, 15, 1911.

[37] Atlanta *Constitution*, May 11, July 9-12, October 11, 1911.

[38] Savannah *Morning News*, August 1, 1911.

indications for a time that Commissioner of Agriculture Thomas
G. Hudson would represent the Smith wing, but a legislative
investigation of his department during the summer of 1911 made
him unavailable. Smith leaders, for some reason, appeared strangely unreceptive to Pope Brown's candidacy, perhaps because of
Brown's closeness to Watson. Brown made a trip to the capital
to see the governor but did not obtain an open endorsement.
For whatever reason, the Smithites virtually surrendered to the
opposition by default. Perhaps the choice from among so many
ambitious lieutenants was too difficult to be made without causing
dissension.[39] At any rate, "Little Joe" won the primary on
December 7, although he received only a plurality of the votes,
approximately 43,000 to his two opponents' 67,000.[40]

On the day Hoke Smith left office, an Atlanta *Journal* editorial
reminded Georgians of some recent history. Smith's governorship
would be remembered "as the most progressive in the annals of
Georgia," declared the *Journal*. Its results were "cut deep in the
tablets of history." [41] The state convention of 1910 had proudly
enumerated the accomplishments: the railroad commission law,
the registration and primary acts, the corrupt-practices legislation,
the abolition of the convict-leasing system, the ending of free
passes, reduced passenger rates and partial adjustment of freight
schedules, increased appropriations for public education, and
prohibition. The legislature of 1911 had added the antilobbying
act, a comprehensive education law, and several agricultural
measures.

Anti-Smith spokesmen always entered a caveat. The good
would have come anyway, they said, and without the strife and
upheaval. Moreover, they argued, the reform laws were largely
"meaningless," to which the *Journal* replied: "If the laws that
were placed upon the statute books were meaningless bluffs, the
reactionaries have wasted a deal of their precious time in vainly
striving to remove them." [42]

Smith's progressivism was limited in many respects. But for

[39] Smith finally advised his friends to support Pope Brown.
[40] Atlanta *Journal*, October 1, December 8, 11, 1911.
[41] *Ibid.*, November 15, 1911.
[42] *Ibid.*, July 28, 1912.

a moment his leadership caught the spirit of the progressives in Georgia. Through the vigor of his personality and astuteness of his politics, he translated a portion of it into reality. As far as state reforms were concerned, Smith's election to the Senate at the very outset of his second term was unfortunate, for it turned his attention away from Georgia and weakened his influence in the legislature of 1911. The work was far from finished, but Smith's road now led to Washington, where he could match his leadership in a different arena.

1912

Veterans of Georgia politics called 1912 "a political year." For the new Senator from Georgia, who took his seat when the second session of the Sixty-second Congress convened on December 4, 1911, the year brought its full share of political activities. While he was eagerly immersing himself in his Senate work, a movement was taking shape in Georgia and throughout the country that was to give him and like-minded Democrats a marvelous opportunity. The success of that movement made Woodrow Wilson President of the United States.

Hoke Smith was already well known when he entered the Senate. His service in Cleveland's Cabinet, his colorful campaigns and reform politics in Georgia, and his support of humanitarian endeavors had given him a national reputation. Recent articles about him had appeared in periodicals and newspapers beyond the borders of his own state. Alexander J. McKelway, for instance, had written a substantial article for *Outlook* entitled "Hoke Smith: A Progressive Democrat." McKelway described the Georgian as "the most conspicuous figure in the Progressive Democracy of the South, if not in the Nation . . . [and] the only Southern man with successful executive experience both in his State and in the National Cabinet." [1] Another national magazine referred to Smith as the "La Follette of Georgia," and John Temple Graves called him "the most powerful man in Georgia if not in the South—the most fiercely hated and the most idol-atrously admired." Do away with Georgia, was the facetious admonition of the New York *Sun*, "and let the new state of

[1] *Outlook*, XCVI (October 1, 1910), 267-72.

Hoke Smith enter the Union. Georgia is Hoke, just as Hoke is Georgia." [2]

Never a man to hide his light under a bushel, Smith showed no reluctance to express himself on a wide range of questions during his first session. At his request he was made a member of the committees on Agriculture and Forestry, and on Post Offices and Post Roads. In Janury, 1912, he demonstrated his progressive inclinations by supporting the measure to establish a Children's Bureau in the Department of Commerce and Labor. According to Senator William E. Chilton of West Virginia, the magic word "progressive" was "already being whispered in these Halls as the mascot which shall land this bill safely on the side of the majority." Chilton was right, for the bill was approved. During the debate Smith said: "The bill appeals to me; the purpose of the bill appeals to me. The truth is, I believe in appropriating public money for work of this kind; and I had rather see the National Government appropriating the money . . . than to depend upon the charity of some one who has accumulated his millions and in his old age concludes perhaps to make atonement for the way in which he accumulated them." [3]

Smith delivered his first major speech in the Senate early in March, during the final disposition of the general arbitration treaties which the Taft administration had negotiated with Great Britain and France in 1911. The treaties had been subjected to strong criticism, and Secretary of State Philander C. Knox was anxious to win the support of as many Senators from both parties as possible. Knox contacted Smith and took pains to send him some information about the arbitration treaties, but the Georgian was noncommittal. [4] The reason was soon apparent. He was opposed to the very provision of the treaties that Taft and Knox considered most vital, the famous third article, by which

[2] "Hoke Smith, Georgia's New Heavy-Weight Senator," in *Current Literature*, LI (September, 1911), 263-65; Graves, "Hoke Smith of Ga.," *loc. cit.*, 48; New York *Sun*, quoted in Atlanta *Constitution*, July 27, 1911.

[3] *Cong. Record*, 62 Cong., 2 Sess., 1532-33. See also *ibid.*, 1531, 1579.

[4] John Temple Graves to P. C. Knox, December 10, 1911; Knox to Smith, December 13, 1911, January 23, 1912, and Smith to Knox, February 10, 1912, in Department of State Papers (National Archives).

a joint high commission was authorized to decide whether or not a disputed question was "justiciable."

The Georgia Senator agreed with his colleague, Augustus O. Bacon, who secured the adoption of an amendment excluding from arbitration questions involving immigration, alien admission to American schools, Federal or state territorial integrity, and the Monroe Doctrine. In his lengthy discourse on March 7, Smith asserted that the arbitration arrangements were too broad in their application. "Is there any subject of dispute between the two contracting parties," he asked, "that might not honestly be held, with such language used in the proposed treaty, to be covered by its terms?" He criticized the joint high commission that was to decide which questions were "justiciable," and urged his colleagues to announce in unmistakable terms just what they wanted to withhold from arbitration. Smith professed to be a warm friend of universal peace, but he felt that a more constructive approach would be to invite the major powers "to join with us in reducing the size of standing armies and in stopping the construction of battleships." He supported all of the limiting amendments and then joined with an overwhelming majority of the Senators in approving the meaningless treaties.[5]

On March 8, when Senator Porter J. McCumber called up the first of a large number of special pension bills, Smith began a vigorous attack upon them that kept him on the floor for many hours during the following weeks. In view of the criticisms he had received for his pension policies as Secretary of the Interior, Smith might have been expected to approach this subject with caution, but the very fact that he knew something about the pension system probably led him to assume the role of pension expert. He disclaimed any intention to examine the special pension measures in detail or "to resist them to the extent they could be resisted." But he was eager, he declared, to show "the utter impossibility of any real consideration of these measures by the Senate," and he stressed the fact that the Sixty-first Congress had enacted no less than 9,649 special bills.[6] It was

---

[5] Cong. Record, 62 Cong., 2 Sess., 2944-50, 2954-55; Atlanta Journal, January 18, 21, 1912.

[6] Cong. Record, 62 Cong., 2 Sess., 1177, 3013-17, 3078-80.

easy for Smith to demonstrate how inefficient such a system was, but it was impossible for him to force any serious consideration of his complaints. The Republican defenders of the special pensions soon brought up the question of patriotism and changed the direction of the debate by attacking Smith's policies as Secretary of Interior.[7]

A little later the Southerner participated in the final debate preceding the passage of the general pension bill. The House of Representatives had already passed a bill sponsored by Representative Isaac R. Sherwood, which would increase the annual pension expenditures by an estimated $75,000,000. The Senate committee had reported a substitute for the Sherwood bill somewhat less liberal than the House measure. Smith offered several limiting amendments, and appealed for a businesslike appraisal of the government's financial obligations. "Being a new member," he observed, "I am not so thoroughly initiated as to understand the propriety of passing appropriations here and relying upon the House to kill them." He admitted the difficulty of maintaining one's "legislative reason" after listening to the "just tributes" to the old soldiers, but someone had to consider the status of the treasury, he asserted. Smith and several other Southerners voted against the McCumber substitute, but it was passed easily.[8]

The Georgia Senator won no concessions in his vigorous attack on the pension legislation, although one Georgia newspaper claimed that his offensive had forced the adoption of the McCumber substitute instead of the Sherwood bill.[9] The debate had at least given Smith some valuable experience on the Senate floor, which was perhaps his real objective.

The question that aroused Smith's greatest interest in the spring of 1912 was the workmen's compensation bill, sponsored in the Senate by George Sutherland of Utah. Based upon the report of a special commission appointed by President Taft, the Sutherland bill would have eliminated the doctrine of negligence, assumption of risk, fellow servant's rule, and contributory fault and would have established a schedule of compensation benefits for the

[7] *Ibid.*, 3081-85, 3090, 3136-37, 3474-78, 3674-84, 3723-33.

[8] *Ibid.*, 3995-98, 4010-12, 4015.

[9] Athens *Tribune*, in Atlanta *Journal*, June 15, 1912.

employees of interstate railroads. Smith, who was thoroughly at home in any discussion of the rights of injured employees and the legal liabilities of employers, aggressively opposed the bill. On one occasion he was on his feet almost continuously for six hours.

The heart of the Senator's opposition to the measure was the proposal to make the law the "exclusive remedy for injuries" suffered by railroad workers. Smith argued that injured workers could expect greater compensation under the liability acts of 1908 and 1910 and the recent safety-appliance laws than under the proposed legislation. He described the schedule of benefits authorized in the bill as "trifling" and "utterly inadequate." He also disliked the provision that designated special Federal court masters to make the compensation awards. This arrangement would leave the worker "without a chance for representation somewhat commensurate to the representation which will be on the other side," asserted the Georgian. Damage suit lawyer that he was, Smith disliked the fact that juries were not to serve with the Federal adjusters. "I do not think the counsel for railroads are fond of juries," he declared.[10]

Ranging far and wide over the legislative and legal history of workingmen's problems in the United States and Europe, Smith constantly embroidered upon his theme of opposition to the "exclusive" feature of the compensation bill. A note of sarcasm crept into his voice when he talked of the measure's "tenderness" to the employer, and when he declared that it contained everything "that the ingenuity of a trained railroad lawyer could put into it to facilitate defense. . . ." He delivered an eloquent description of the legal difficulties and handicaps confronting workingmen in meeting the railroads in the courts. He also told of his own experiences with railroad employees: "I can not forget that when, almost a boy, with practically nothing, I came to a great city they were my first friends and gave me my first small fees that helped . . . me to meet my monthly expenses, and if they are ground down and if the burdens of this bill are placed upon them, I can grieve with them, and only regret that I did not have the capacity to bring . . .

[10] Cong. Record, 62 Cong., 2 Sess., 4405-4407, 4786-90, 5860-63, 5874.

Senators . . . [to] realize what they were doing." [11] Smith's arguments followed closely those contained in a recent article in the Raleigh *News and Observer* attributed to Chief Justice Walter Clark of the North Carolina supreme court. Clark, observed the Senator in the course of his remarks, was " one of the greatest judges upon the bench of any State in the Union." [12]

Late in April Smith offered a long list of amendments to the Sutherland bill. They were designed to liberalize the compensation features of the plan in a striking fashion, to increase the period of compensation to the worker's dependents in case of death, to allow common law or statutory right of action for compensation, and to guarantee the employee's legal rights in numerous other ways. One of Smith's amendment was less generous to the employee: It provided that the compensation scale would apply " to those employees whose injuries occur without contributory negligence on their part." Other workers would receive only one half of the compensation fixed in the bill. Accidents did not just happen, said the Senator from Georgia; somebody had to be at fault. This was the weak point in his defense of the workingman. As Senator Coe I. Crawford of South Dakota pointed out, " You will still have a class of worthy men who go out maimed, halt, blind, and some of them to their deaths, who can not be helped under the employers' liability act of 1908, and who are absolutely remediless at common law or under the laws of the several States." [13]

Smith admitted that many labor leaders had endorsed the Sutherland plan, but he contended that the rank and file of the railroad men would oppose it. As evidence of this sentiment he inserted in the *Record* a number of memorials and petitions from local railroad unions opposing the bill. On one occasion during the final debate on the measure, Elihu Root of New York, who was supporting the bill, looked across the aisle at the Democrats and remarked that he could understand how lawyers who had been bringing suits against railroad companies would oppose the compensation bill. In reply Henry F. Ashurst of Arizona de-

[11] *Ibid.*, 5876, and 5859-62, 5871-79.
[12] *Ibid.*, 5735-38, 5926-28.
[13] *Ibid.*, 4788-90, 5521, 5797-98, 5878.

clared, "I can and do well understand why attorneys who have
been active as representatives for railroad companies and vested
interests all their lives can consistently try to pass this bill."[14]

If Hoke Smith made any converts to his position as a result
of his long argument, they were few indeed. Only two or three
of his amendments, and those of secondary importance, were
accepted by the Senate. He seemed to be the leader of a group
of kindred spirits that included James A. Reed of Missouri and
several Southerners; but this little band could not prevent Sutherland and Crawford from steering the bill through the upper
house on May 6, by a vote of 64 to 15. Both Georgia Senators
voted against the bill.[15]

The House of Representatives failed to act on the compensation measure in 1912. But during the third session of the Sixty-
second Congress, early in March, 1913, the bill was passed by the
lower house. In the House debate Thomas W. Hardwick and
others made use of Smith's arguments in opposing the bill. When
the measure was returned to the Senate, Sutherland tried to
persuade that body to accept the House amendments, but Smith
prevented further action by threatening to discuss the amendments until the end of session.[16] Thus he killed the bill as far
as the Sixty-second Congress was concerned.

Smith had received considerable support from his own labor
constituents for the position he took. Representatives of three
of the four great railroad organizations in Georgia had informed
the Georgia Senators that they opposed the Sutherland bill.[17]
The remarkable success Smith had enjoyed as a lawyer for injured
railroad workers undoubtedly predisposed him to adopt a critical
attitude toward railroad companies in liability cases and to feel
that compulsory compensation legislation should not become the
exclusive remedy for those killed or injured in railroad work.
Nevertheless, it is difficult to reconcile Smith's old-fashioned views
on the nature of industrial accidents with the attitude of most
progressives in supporting workmen's compensation laws.

[14] *Ibid.*, 5945.
[15] *Ibid.*, 5873, 5876, 5948-59; Atlanta *Journal*, May 5, 1912.
[16] *Cong. Record*, 62 Cong., 3 Sess., 4547, 4562-63, 4673-77.
[17] *Ibid.*, 62 Cong., 2 Sess., 5924, 5935; Atlanta *Journal*, April 13, 15, 1912.

When the Senate began to vote on the various tariff bills in 1912, Hoke Smith joined with most of the other Democrats in an effort to keep the duties somewhat in line with the reductions made in the House.[18] He also supported a corporation tax, although he opposed Senator William E. Borah's amendment to provide for an income tax, on the ground that it would be impolitic at the time.[19] Near the end of the session Smith took part in the lengthy debate on the bill providing for the operation of the Panama Canal. He opposed the suggestion by the Senate committee that American shipping in foreign commerce be allowed free passage through the canal, pointing out the obligations the United States had accepted in the second Hay-Pauncefote Treaty and voicing his distaste for " the disposition which seeks an opportunity to make the eagle screech whenever our relations with a foreign country are involved." Yet by a complicated explanation he sought to distinguish between coastwise and foreign shipping. In supporting free transit for coastal vessels, he seemed to feel that water transportation would be encouraged and that competition with transcontinental railroads would be increased.[20]

One of Smith's principal interests during his first session in the Senate was agricultural legislation. "If you asked me what I think has been the greatest deficiency in the work of State and National government to this country during the past century," he declared in 1911, "I should unhesitatingly reply that it has been neglect of the farmer and the farm." [21] To relieve "the hard conditions of farm life " and to encourage better farming, Smith and other Congressmen were urging the enactment of at least four important measures in 1912: a parcel-post system, a Federal program of road construction or assistance, a system of agricultural extension, and the establishment of a division of

[18] *Cong. Record*, 62 Cong., 2 Sess., 7310, 7320, 7370-73, 9637-38, 11069.

[19] Smith expressed his devotion to the idea of a general income tax. The Borah amendment was rejected and the corporation tax approved. *Ibid.*, 9681-85, 9708-9709.

[20] Smith secured the insertion of the word "exclusively " in the phrase "engaged in coastwise shipping." *Cong. Record*, 62 Cong., 2 Sess., 9169, 10300-10301, 10390-92, 10446-47, 10451-52, 10457-60, 10578-79, 10590.

[21] New York *Times*, September 17, 1911.

markets. The first bill Smith introduced in the Senate provided for a system of agricultural extension work. He spent many hours in committee, working on parcel-post rates, and joined with other Senators in a successful effort to obtain a graduated scale of rates which would help farmers and merchants interested in short hauls.[22]

At the request of the Farmers' Union, Smith introduced a bill in February to establish a Bureau of Markets in the Department of Agriculture. Its functions would be to investigate systems of marketing, to estimate the consumption of and demand for farm products, and to facilitate the distribution of farm goods. The measure was reported favorably by Smith from committee early in April, but when it appeared that the House would not approve it, the Senator managed to get it adopted as an amendment to the agricultural appropriations bill. Subsequently, the amendment was twice abandoned in conferences between the two houses, but late in the session the Georgian got it through the Senate as a separate bill, only to have it fail in the House.[23]

For a freshman Senator, Hoke Smith took an active part in the debates on the floor. By the time Congress adjourned late in August, he had expressed himself on a variety of issues and had demonstrated that he was likely to have more than ordinary influence in Senate affairs.

Meanwhile, important political developments had taken place in Georgia. After some hesitation, the Smith-dominated State Democratic Executive Committee had issued a call for a Presidential primary to be held on May 1, 1912.[24] The Smith wing of the party soon decided to support Woodrow Wilson in the primary. The Brown-Howell faction, after some delay, threw its support to Congressman Oscar W. Underwood of Alabama, and the two Democratic groups were once again locked in a bitter primary fight.

[22] *Cong. Record*, 62 Cong., 2 Sess., 9946-47, 10660-61, 10817-18, 10821-24, 10830.

[23] *Ibid.*, 2041, 4232, 6333, 7447-49, 7451, 10340-41, 11432.

[24] Apparently Smith advised the committee not to hold a primary, possibly feeling that in the absence of a primary the committee could dominate the selection of delegates to the national convention.

The Atlanta *Journal* and the Savannah *Press*, long-time Smith newspapers, had endorsed Wilson many months before the primary campaign began. Hoke Smith, of course, was aware of the striking victory Wilson had won in New Jersey in 1910—the same year his own campaign for "progressive democracy" had triumphed—and as the New Jersey governor began to succeed with his progressive program, the Georgian quickly saw, as did others, that Wilson might make a good Presidential candidate. The first public indication of Smith's attitude came in March, 1911, on the occasion of Wilson's visit to Georgia to speak to the Southern Commercial Congress. Smith was host at a luncheon in honor of the visitor, and he and his advisers were prominent in the round of festivities given for him. Smith and Wilson conferred at length, and a few weeks later the Georgia politician indicated that he favored Wilson for the Democratic nomination in 1912, calling him "one of the brightest figures in the Democratic party to-day." Arthur S. Link describes this announcement as "the first declaration of an important political figure in support of Wilson's candidacy." [25] Nevertheless, Smith waited until early 1912 to begin a campaign for Wilson's nomination in Georgia.

In almost every Southern state the Wilson campaign elicited the support of the more progressive element in the Democratic party, whereas the Underwood movement generally received the strong backing of the more conservative factions, which seized upon the Underwood candidacy not alone because of their attraction to Underwood's position and their dislike of Wilsonian liberalism but also as a means of countering the progressive movements of earlier origin throughout the South. This was true in Georgia. "I find the same old lines are drawn here," wrote a South Georgian in April—"the Hoke Smith men on one side and Joe Brown's on the other." [26]

The Underwood campaign gathered momentum rapidly in March and April. Underwood leaders opened headquarters in

[25] Arthur S. Link, "The Democratic Pre-Convention Campaign of 1912 in Georgia," in *Georgia Historical Quarterly*, XXIX (September, 1945), 144-46; Atlanta *Journal*, March 9, 10, 1911; Nashville *Banner*, April 6, 1911.

[26] F. C. Roberts to Neyle Colquitt, April 17, 1912, in Neyle Colquitt Papers (Duke University Library).

Atlanta, and the newspaper phalanx, under the aggressive leadership of the *Constitution*, the Macon *Telegraph*, and the Augusta *Chronicle*, began a vigorous campaign for the Alabama candidate. Several of Georgia's Congressmen gave him their support and such out-of-state Underwood men as James K. Vardaman and John H. Bankhead entered the state to speak for their candidate. Tom Watson, who had developed a bitter hostility toward Woodrow Wilson and who was subtly encouraged by Joseph M. Brown and Clark Howell to use his influence for the anti-Smith candidate, soon added his voice in the *Jeffersonian*. Underwood's supporters emphasized his " genuine " Southernism, his reform views on the tariff, and his work as majority leader and chairman of the House Ways and Means Committee. "Georgia must be carried," wrote an Underwood spokesman from Washington; ". . . we believe that with the prestige of victory over Mr. Wilson in that State our campaign will have an impetus not otherwise obtainable." [27]

One cause for concern among Wilson supporters in Georgia was a mistake in strategy which was turned to good advantage by the opposition. The state committee announced that the county-unit system would not apply in the Presidential primary and that a plurality of popular votes would win the state's delegation to the Baltimore convention. Then the committee decided that the names of Champ Clark and Judson Harmon, who had not entered the primary despite earlier speculation, would appear on the ballot, apparently assuming that this would lead to a division of Wilson's opposition. This decision played into the hands of the Brown-Howell-Watson combination, which for years had rallied the farmers and rural counties against an alleged threat by the large cities under Hoke Smith's guidance to dominate Georgia politics. Governor Brown and Tom Watson denounced the committee's action, and Clark Howell stormed in the *Constitution* against such a "machine" scheme to destroy minority representation.[28]

One of the most decisive weapons in the armory of the Under-

[27] Thomas M. Owen to Colquitt, April 5, 1912, *ibid.*; Macon *Telegraph*, April 22, 1912; Atlanta *Constitution*, April 28, 30, 1912.

[28] Link, " The Democratic Pre-Convention Campaign of 1912 in Georgia," *loc. cit.*, 153-54; Savannah *Morning News*, March 14, 1912.

wood camp was the support of the rural press. Perhaps the man most responsible for this support was William Neyle Colquitt, erstwhile publicity worker for Judson Harmon in Georgia and subsequently publicity manager for the Underwood campaign in the state. He worked indefatigably throughout March and April, interviewing prominent politicians, writing feature articles, and touring the state. When the Wilson men sent out a page of free plate to 104 newspapers early in April, for instance, he sat down and wrote to each of the editors, advising him that he was forwarding Underwood plate with a check for publishing the material. The Underwood managers used a large amount of money in this way and, according to Colquitt, this policy "created a panic in the ranks of the opposition." [29]

Woodrow Wilson aroused a good deal of enthusiasm in Georgia. Most of the state's large evening papers endorsed him, and many teachers and students, ministers, and prominent civic leaders and businessmen supported him. Numerous Wilson clubs were organized, and a host of speakers went out to promote his cause. Wilson leaders in Georgia chose to emphasize their candidate's Southern background and that of his Georgia wife. But much was said about the general subject of Wilsonian progressivism. As for the Underwood campaign, observed the Atlanta *Journal*, it was "a series of shams and falsities," a "mock campaign" designed to deliver Georgia's delegation to another candidate. [30]

The Underwood leaders were confident of victory, but one of them noted early in April that the Wilson men "have an inning that will cause us some concern, when Wilson, Smith and Hardwick come here on the 16th." Smith found it necessary to come to Atlanta two weeks before Wilson's invasion of the state, probably to confer with other Wilson leaders about an embarrassing shortage of campaign funds. [31] While in his home city the Senator addressed a conference of Wilson workers in a speech described as "the beginning of the real fight for Mr. Wilson in this state." In an interview released a few days earlier,

[29] Colquitt to Owen, April 3, 5, 1912, in Colquitt Papers.
[30] Atlanta *Journal*, April 2, 3, 5, 11, 30, 1912.
[31] Colquitt to Owen, April 3, 5, 6, 1912, in Colquitt Papers.

Smith gave his reasons for supporting Wilson: he was without
a superior in ability among the Democratic candidates; he had
the best prospects for election if nominated; and he was a
Southerner with Georgia connections. The Senator also noted
Wilson's "thoroughly sound" position on the tariff and his
"progressive work in behalf of government by the people and
human rights" in New Jersey. If Georgians really wanted a
Southerner for President, he advised them to "quit wasting
support on a man who is not really in the race." [32]

The high point of the Wilson campaign occurred in mid-April
when Governor and Mrs. Wilson visited the state. The faithful
were all in attendance on the night of April 16, when Wilson
opened his Georgia tour with a thrilling address before nine
thousand enthusiastic people in Atlanta. He was introduced by
Georgia's new Senator, who was given a "tremendous personal
ovation." Two weeks later, on the eve of the primary, Smith
issued another interview in which he declared that Wilson had
"caught the popular imagination." He conceded that Underwood
was a good Congressman, but "I tell you candidly," he stated,
"he is not seriously counted as a candidate." Turning to the
Republicans the Senator declared: "If they nominate the colonel
we want somebody that can talk against him and write against
him, and I promise you he will make Teddy sorry if he runs
against him." [33]

But Woodrow Wilson did not win in Georgia. Underwood
won the primary with 71,410 votes to 57,261 for Wilson. The
Wilson managers could feel some satisfaction in having carried
Fulton County by a decisive majority, but that was small conso-
lation for the Smith faction's once-splendid dreams of capturing
the state for Wilson—and for Smith Democrats. [34]

[32] Smith felt that Taft would be renominated by the Republicans and
that Wilson was the only Democrat who would attract the dissident liberal
Republicans. If the Democrats chose a conservative, "Taft would get
the conservative vote and the third Republican ticket would get the progressive vote." Atlanta *Journal*, March 31, April 6-8, 1912.

[33] Atlanta *Journal*, April 17, 18, 29, 1912.

[34] Wilson also carried Augusta, Macon, Savannah, and Rome, which
is some indication of the attraction he had for middle-class, urban folk.
Atlanta *Constitution*, May 2, 1912.

The Wilson movement appeared to be crumbling everywhere before Champ Clark's campaign. Smith partisans could find little to be optimistic over when the state convention met in Atlanta on May 29 to ratify the Underwood victory and to select the delegates to the national convention. Wilson leaders had to content themselves by urging that Wilson receive the votes of the Georgia delegation if Underwood should lose.[35]

In the gubernatorial primary that followed in Georgia the Smith faction fared no better than in the Presidential contest. The candidate of the Brown-Howell wing was John M. Slaton, one of the state's most popular politicians, and against him the Smith men seemed lethargic and directionless. Two Smith leaders —Thomas G. Hudson and Hooper Alexander—entered the race against Slaton, but Hudson soon withdrew, and Alexander implied that Hoke Smith had abandoned the progressive movement in Georgia. It was true that Smith had disclaimed any intention to interfere in local politics, and the Smith organization did seem to be disintegrating. The *Journal* felt called upon to deny that "the progressive forces are disbanding simply because they do not attack every windmill, as though it were a giant." [36]

The summer brought one bright spot for Smith and his political friends in Georgia. That was Wilson's triumph at Baltimore. Smith, who was in Washington, immediately wrote the Democratic nominee "to say that I believe all the Democrats in the Senate are ready to give you the most loyal support, and to give their time in the way that it can be most serviceable." [37] Smith kept in touch with Wilson during the remainder of the summer. In mid-July he offered to make the trip to Seagirt to present "several suggestions," but the pressure of Senate business prevented him from going. "Of course," he observed, "I have been giving close observation to conditions since your nomination." Later the Georgian wrote to urge Wilson to say nothing in his letter of acceptance that would prevent his serving a second

[35] Atlanta *Journal*, May 29, June 29, 1912.

[36] *Ibid.*, March 31, June 27, July 28, August 4, 21, 28, September 4, 15, 1912.

[37] Smith to Wilson, July 3, 1912, in Woodrow Wilson Papers (Division of Manuscripts, Library of Congress).

term and to advise him to avoid giving the impression that the Democrats were in favor of a stringent tariff-for-revenue-only measure. "If you have no objections," he wrote, "whenever anything occurs to me which I think may be of service to you, I will bring it to your attention. . . ." [38]

At the end of the session Smith returned to Atlanta, planning to attend to some personal business and to spend a brief period with his family before starting the campaign circuit. Late in September he joined other Democratic leaders in Chicago, where he spent about three weeks alternating between working in the party headquarters and making speeches in the Midwest. Subsequently, he delivered several addresses in New Jersey, New York, Connecticut, and Massachusetts. The Princeton University boys greeted the Southerner with a "Princetonian roar," after which the Senator regaled them with an analysis of the issues of the campaign for an hour and a half. He made a hit with the students with at least one point: He described Roosevelt's Bull Moose Party as the "Loose Bull" Party. [39]

Ordinarily Smith stressed his party's progressivism, identifying it with the campaign "to bring the government back to the people, and to break the grip of the agents of special privilege. . . ." He attacked the Republican position on the tariff, which he discussed in "all its phases," and the Progressives for being soft toward the trusts. He quoted Taft and "T. R." on each other. A Peoria, Illinois, newspaper—undoubtedly Democratic—presented this interesting description of Smith's address in that city:

> The distinguished southerner was in a genial mood throughout his address and carried his auditors right along with him by a wonderful chain of arguments that were logical and convincing. . . .
>
> Sturdy and rugged, gifted with the power to drive his arguments home to the hearts of the hearers, the brilliant statesman showed repeatedly that he could "deliver the goods." He was repeatedly interrupted by applause. . . .
>
> While he was genial and entertaining, yet he was intensely

---

[38] Smith to Wilson, July 11, 22, August 17, 1912, *ibid*.
[39] Atlanta *Journal*, August 26, 28, September 23, 25, October 20, 25, 1912.

earnest, making an appeal, that was entirely devoid of personal attack or bitter invective. His southern accent gave additional force to his argument.[40]

Woodrow Wilson's election in November appeared to enlarge Hoke Smith's opportunities in national politics and to strengthen his position at home. All things considered, 1912 had been a good year for Smith, even though it had proved disappointing in many ways to the fortunes of his faction in Georgia.

[40] Peoria *Journal*, quoted in Atlanta *Journal*, October 19, 1912.

The New Freedom

"For fifty years Georgia and her sister Southern States patiently submitted to an ignoble and degrading station in this Union," declared Hooper Alexander in 1910. "Her sons have been born, have grown to manhood, and have served their country, and many of them have been gathered to their fathers, all of them conscious always of a power and prejudice that barred them from one high and honorable ambition to which it would be whole-some for the Republic if every citizen might aspire. . . . If this nation is ever to be reunited in spirit and in fact, the time has come."[1] The "high and honorable ambition" Alexander had in mind, of course, was the Presidency of the United States. In Woodrow Wilson, Hooper Alexander and millions of other Southerners found a President whom they could claim as their own. Wilsonian liberalism—the New Freedom—elicited Southern support not only because of Wilson's leadership but also because of the progressive ferment that had been at work in varying degrees for a decade within almost every Southern state.

Hoke Smith, the leader of the reform movement in Georgia, appeared in the Senate at an ideal time to take advantage of his earlier association with progressive politics. Having such a record and having early identified himself with the Wilson movement, he was in position to exert considerable influence in the organiza-tion of the new Senate and in the formulation of the New Freedom legislation. Had a discerning observer of the political scene in 1912 been able to foresee the evolution of Wilsonian progressivism, he might have predicted some disagreement be-

[1] Atlanta *Journal*, September 1, 1910.

tween such a man as Smith and the new administration. In many ways the Georgian was a good example of the so-called Southern progressive, for he symbolized the strength and the limitations of the more aggressive Southern liberals.

During the interim between the Democratic victory in November, 1912, and the inauguration of Woodrow Wilson on March 4, 1913, Hoke Smith concerned himself with a variety of legislative matters and with the plans being developed for the reorganization of the Senate. The Senator returned to Washington shortly after the November elections, and the Smith family moved into a newly purchased house on California Avenue. After the third session of the Sixty-second Congress convened on December 2, Smith tried without success to secure the passage of his agricultural extension bill.[2] He was one of the leaders in the Democratic effort to prevent the confirmation of President Taft's postelection nominations to Federal positions, and when the annual appropriations were being considered, he became a veritable gadfly to the Republican majority.[3]

Meanwhile Wilson was deciding upon his Cabinet members and preparing his legislative program. Among the Democratic leaders the President-elect consulted were Smith and Senator Thomas P. Gore of Oklahoma, who traveled to Trenton on January 8 and talked with Wilson for three hours. Smith recommended William Jennings Bryan, Josephus Daniels, and James R. Gray for the Cabinet.[4] There had been rumors, especially in Georgia, that the Senator himself might be appointed to the Cabinet. William Jennings Bryan had written Wilson late in 1912, "Every one praises Brandies [*sic*] for Attorney General but I would regard Hoke Smith as the ideal man for that place if he could accept." [5] Apparently Wilson gave no serious consideration to the selection of Smith, who preferred to remain in the Senate in any event.

The lack of aggressive leadership on the part of the senior

[2] *Ibid.*, November 13, 17, 1912; *Cong. Record*, 62 Cong., 3 Sess., 1659-64.
[3] Atlanta *Journal*, December 12, 1912, January 5, February 27, 1913; *Cong. Record*, 62 Cong., 3 Sess., 3244-46, 4031-34, 4050, 4055-56.
[4] Edward M. House to Wilson, November 28, 1912, and Smith to Wilson, January 3, 1913, in Wilson Papers; Atlanta *Journal*, January 7, 9, 1913.
[5] Bryan to Wilson, December 30, 1912, in Wilson Papers.

Democrats in the Senate had disturbed Hoke Smith from the time he first entered Congress. With the inauguration of a progressive Democratic President just over the horizon, the Georgian joined several other progressive Democrats during the third session of the Sixty-second Congress in an effort to prevent the conservative Senators, whose seniority normally would ensure their selection to the best committee positions, from dominating the new Senate. Thus Colonel House wrote Wilson late in November, 1912, "Senator Smith is trying to get on the Finance Committee and he is arranging with Gore and others to control that Committee so that the reactionaries, like [Thomas S.] Martin, will not be able to block progressive legislation." [6]

According to the progressives, the committee system needed to be made "more democratic." But there was some suspicion that the reformers, who were mainly new men in the Senate, had their own axes to grind. At any rate Smith proposed a five-point plan of reorganization which provided the basis for the progressives' action: first, the Democratic Senatorial caucus rather than the chairman of the caucus should select a committee on committees to make committee assignments; second, the committee thus chosen should not assign any Senator to more than one of the five most important committees until every Democrat had been offered a place on one of those committees; third, the members of each committee should elect the chairman of their committee on the basis of fitness; fourth, the chairman of the caucus should change with each Congress; and fifth, selection of Senate conferees should be made by the committee concerned and not restricted to the three senior committee members customarily designated. [7]

A few months later Smith described the success of the reorganization plans:

> With several other Senators early last December, I determined to seek the overthrow of the old rule of seniority, and the establishment of a form of organization more Democratic in its character, and more serviceable in its results. After full

---

[6] House to Wilson, November 28, 1912, *ibid*.

[7] Atlanta *Journal*, December 30, 1912, January 5, 7, 9, 14, February 6, 1913.

conference we determined to accord the Chairmanships of the various committees to Senators based upon length . . . of service, but not to concede second places upon any committees to Senators simply on account of their length of service. The plan which we adopted prevailed in the Democratic Caucus, and those of us who advocated this plan named the new officers of the Caucus, and elected the new steering committee, which in turn assigned the various Senators to committee positions. The old Senators were given the most prominent chairmanships, but new Senators were placed upon all the leading committees with a disregard to the rule of seniority never before known in the Senate.[8]

The Senator from Georgia was a bit extravagant in his claims, but the reformers did achieve some of their objectives.

John W. Kern, an Indiana progressive, was elected chairman of the caucus, and a steering committee of nine men, including Smith, was chosen to name the Democratic committee members and to assume supervision of the party's program in the upper house.[9] The steering committee violated the seniority rule in the selection of committee chairmen in only one instance, the choice of Thomas S. Martin instead of Benjamin R. Tillman to head the Appropriations Committee. Nevertheless, Smith was substantially correct in saying that new members had received better assignments than ever before; and the progressives obtained some concessions in the caucus for their demands that new committee members be given greater influence in committee business.[10]

When the work of the steering committee was completed, it was obvious that Hoke Smith had received the committee positions he wanted. He was named chairman of a new Committee on Education and Labor; he retained his place on the Agriculture and Forestry, and Post Office and Post Roads committees, and in addition was named to the important Finance

[8] MS. Address (1913), in Smith Collection.

[9] The other members of the steering committee were Kern, ex officio chairman, George W. Chamberlain, Robert L. Owen, James A. O'Gorman, Luke Lea, Charles S. Thomas, Thomas S. Martin, and James P. Clarke. Atlanta *Journal*, March 6-9, 15, 1913.

[10] *Ibid.*, March 10, 15, 1913; Burton J. Hendrick, "The New Order in Washington," in *World's Work*, XXVII (January, 1914), 317-18.

Committee. Few of his colleagues could boast of better assignments.

One act of the Democratic caucus brought Smith a moment of acute embarrassment. Unexpectedly, the caucus chose James P. Clarke of Arkansas as the Democratic nominee for President pro tempore of the Senate, rather than Augustus O. Bacon, whose unanimous selection had been confidently predicted and whose name Smith had presented to the caucus. Bacon was the senior Democratic Senator in point of service, having entered the Senate in 1895. Eminently respectable and far above average in ability, he had served his party well and could scarcely understand the refusal of his colleagues to honor him with this position. It was true that he was a conservative and was slated to head the important Foreign Relations Committee—and thus would have held two major posts. Smith was so chagrined at the defeat of his colleague that he immediately offered to resign from the steering committee, although he failed to do so when Senator Bacon importuned him to retain the position.[11]

As if Bacon's surprising defeat in the caucus were not enough, Benjamin R. Tillman, angered at the progressives for failing to name him chairman of the Appropriations Committee, gave a special interview to an Atlanta *Constitution* reporter in which he spoke of a "conspiracy" against his good friend Bacon and of Smith's disloyalty to the senior Senator from Georgia. The *Constitution* seized upon this choice item with alacrity to feed the anti-Smith fires in Georgia. Meanwhile, "Pitchfork Ben" dropped a line to Joseph P. Tumulty for the President's ear. The progressives "have played the Devil in the caucus," he wrote. "They are like the wild asses mentioned in the Bible, 'who were athirst and trampled down the green corn.' Hoke Smith's treatment of Senator Bacon was simply infamous. . . ."[12]

What actually happened is not easy to unravel. In a special statement Smith declared that his colleague's defeat had come

[11] Atlanta *Journal*, November 13, 1912, March 9, 1913.
[12] Memorandum by Tillman, March 8, 1913, in Wilson Papers. Tillman's implication that the progressives defeated Bacon was scarcely borne out by the vote, which was 27 to 14. Several progressives voted for Bacon, whereas a number of conservatives, including Martin, supported Clarke.

as "a great surprise" and disappointment to him. He referred
to his part in the movement to reform the committee system and
observed that a proposal had been made several weeks before
to include the position of President pro tempore in the reorganization, so that one man would not be able to hold that position
in addition to a major chairmanship. Smith had opposed this
suggestion and it was subsequently voted down in the Democratic
caucus. Smith also took the floor at a caucus meeting to defend
himself against Tillman's charge. He declared that at no time
had any of the Senators who voted against Bacon indicated to
him any intention of opposing the Georgian, and he invited those
who voted for Clarke to tell the caucus if this were not the case.
James A. O'Gorman, a leader in the Clarke movement, gave some
support to Smith's contentions by stating that he had not finally
decided to nominate Clarke until ten minutes before the caucus
election. Several Senators expressed the opinion that the same
man should not serve as President pro tempore and chairman of
the Foreign Relations Committee. A New York *Times* article
explored another possibility: that the election was in reality a
show of strength between Smith and O'Gorman for the honor
of serving as administration spokesman.[13]

Benjamin R. Tillman felt better after getting the chairmanship
of the Naval Affairs Committee. He apologized to the caucus
and withdrew his charges. Where the term "conspirators" had
appeared in his *Constitution* interview, explained the South Carolinian, he had really meant "progressives." Having since learned
that Smith had supported him rather than Martin for the Appropriations Committee chairmanship, he now praised the Georgia
Senator for having "battled manfully" for his cause. "We need
in the Senate a man of his brains," he declared. When Smith
visited Atlanta a little later for a few days rest, he again voiced
his disappointment over Bacon's defeat and proclaimed a new
reign of harmony in Democratic ranks.[14]

Hoke Smith's political enemies in Georgia were not so sure
that peace and good will dominated the party's ranks, at least

[13] New York *Times*, March 8, 1913; Atlanta *Journal*, March 9, 15, 16,
1913.
[14] Atlanta *Journal*, March 15, 16, 24, 1913.

not in Georgia. In the summer of 1913 anti-Smith newspapers
gleefully reported that relations between the Senator and other
Georgia Congressmen, including Augustus O. Bacon, were "becoming exceedingly strained." The Macon *Telegraph* warned
that Senator Bacon's nominations might be turned down on the
ground that "Underwood men need not apply." Smith and
Bacon did seem to be on the point of an open clash over the
question of dividing Federal offices in Georgia. But the two
Senators reached an agreement whereby Bacon would make the
appointments to positions in South Georgia and Smith those in
North Georgia.[15] The trouble was that some positions, such
as the internal revenue collectorships, were not easily classified
on such a basis; but with some difficulty the two men handled
these questions, and their relations remained cordial.

The original Wilson men in Georgia naturally felt that they
should be given preference for Federal appointments over those
who had opposed Wilson in 1912. Anti-Smith spokesmen argued
that Underwood supporters should not be penalized for old
loyalties and denounced what they termed a policy of "pro-
scription." Yet when the new administration's patronage began
to be distributed, there were also complaints from the Smith
faction. Pleasant A. Stovall, who became the new minister to
Switzerland, wrote to protest against certain appointments in
South Georgia which, he felt, would "demoralize and estrange"
some of Wilson's best friends. Another Wilson man opposed
the nomination of Joseph S. Davis of Albany to be marshal of
the Southern district on the ground that he was "a reactionary
of the boldest type" and an anti-Wilson man during the Georgia
Presidential primary of 1912. "It is a shame," he asserted, "for
a man like this to come in and secure office from a man whom
he did not support."[16]

Hoke Smith unquestionably looked upon Democratic control
in Washington as a means of bolstering his position in Georgia

[15] Savannah *Press*, July 11, 1913; Atlanta *Constitution*, July 13, 1913;
Macon *News*, July 13, 14, 1913; A. O. Bacon to Wilson, June 9, 1913, in
Wilson Papers.
[16] P. A. Stovall to Wilson, March 19, 1913, and L. J. Ballard to Wilson,
June 18, 1913, in Wilson Papers; Macon *Telegraph*, July 12, 1912; Atlanta
Journal, March 16, 1913.

politics. " I have always felt that this being a Democratic administration," he was reputed to have written an office-seeker, " appointees should be Democratic. What I wish to know from you
candidly is how you have voted in national politics." [17] He might
have added that applicants from Georgia needed to bear the
stamp of the Smith faction's approval.

Before the advent of the new administration, Smith had disclaimed any desire to have a hand in dispensing post-office
patronage, declaring that his "unbroken policy as a member of
the post office committee " had been to secure the approval of the
Representative in whose district the vacancy existed. Yet at
the very beginning of the Wilson administration the Senator
was drawn into a patronage wrangle involving a post-office
appointment at Gainesville. Congressman Thomas M. Bell of
that city was eager to replace Mrs. Helen D. Longstreet, the
Republican postmistress of Gainesville, with a political supporter.
Smith agreed to a number of people Bell suggested, but he would
not approve the Congressman's first choice, an old political enemy
of the Senator.[18]

When the position was finally filled, it was widely interpreted
as a victory for Smith. Congressman Bell was furious. He issued
a statement criticizing Smith for not aiding him in securing the
appointment of his own choice. Smith released a statement of
his own, replying to Bell and indicating his approach to patronage
matters:

> I have endeavored at all times to recognize the rights and
> obligations of my colleagues in both houses. There has been
> absolutely no disposition or purpose here, so far as I know,
> on the part of anyone to exclude from recognition those
> Georgia democrats who saw fit to oppose the president in the
> recent primary in an honorable and proper manner. . . .
>
> I have, however, insisted, and shall continue to insist, that
> nowhere in Georgia [should] men be discriminated against
> because they have been supporters of the president or myself,

---

[17] William Dudley Foulke, *Fighting the Spoilsmen: Reminiscences of
the Civil Service Reform Movement* (New York, 1919), 237.
[18] Helen D. Longstreet to Wilson, March 8, 1913, in Wilson Papers;
Atlanta *Journal*, November 13, 1912.

and I think it but my simple duty to see that they have a fair and just proportion of the appointments.[19]

The Sixty-third Congress convened in extra session on April 7 to begin work on President Wilson's legislative program. When Congress assembled, Hoke Smith remained only briefly before hurrying home to be with Birdie, who had been seriously ill for several days. She had been in wretched health all winter and had overtaxed her slender resource of strength, finally collapsing completely. Smith was especially attentive to her, despite the heavy pressure of his work. Gradually she improved, but she remained a semi-invalid the rest of her life.[20]

The first session of the Sixty-third Congress proved to be one of the longest and most fruitful in the nation's history. Smith was interested in the tariff and currency legislation, which dominated the session, but he also devoted a great deal of time to his proposals for a program of agricultural extension and the establishment of a division of markets. In addition, the Georgia Senator gave considerable attention to the proposed vocational education bill and to certain labor questions which came before his Education and Labor Committee.

Wilson had decided that the administration's first task should be a thoroughgoing reduction of the tariff. During the campaign of 1912 Smith, like other Democratic orators, had said a good deal about tariff reform. More recently, he had insisted that the Finance Committee, which would have charge of the tariff bill in the Senate, should have several progressives, including himself, among its members. But Smith felt that the party should not sponsor a drastic measure—he undoubtedly remembered the fiasco of the Wilson-Gorman tariff.[21] He stated his position in a letter to Woodrow Wilson in 1912:

I believe, myself, thoroughly in a tariff for revenue only, but

---

[19] Atlanta *Constitution*, July 13, 1913; Atlanta *Journal*, July 13, 1913.

[20] Atlanta *Journal*, April 2-4, 1913.

[21] It was on Smith's motion that several members of the Senate Finance Committee held a series of conferences with members of the House Ways and Means Committee prior to the convening of the extra session. *Ibid.*, November 13, 1912, January 20, March 24, 25, 30, April 2-4, 1913.

it would be utterly impracticable to undertake at this time, in good faith, to pass a tariff bill which sought to avoid anything but revenue.

. . . Industrial enterprises have been built up for so many years under a protective tariff that to pass legislation removing entirely, and at once, the protection, would cause many of these enterprises to suspend business, throw many men out of employment and bring on a general panic. The country would probably at once return to another high protective tariff and the chance for just tariff reforms of a permanent character would be destroyed.[22]

The Senate Finance Committee began its consideration of the tariff on April 4, and a few weeks later Oscar W. Underwood started the debate on the administration's bill that led to its passage by the House of Representatives on May 8. During April and May the Senate committee often devoted ten hours a day to the measure. The committee, under the direction of Furnifold M. Simmons of North Carolina, was divided into three subcommittees to work on different sections of the Underwood bill. Smith was chairman of the subcommittee to which was assigned Schedule A (chemicals), Schedule I (cotton manufactures), Schedule M (pulp, paper, and books), and Schedule N (sundries). When the Republicans attempted to force the Finance Committee to hold public hearings on the bill, Smith was one of the leaders defending the Democrats' decision to hold the hearings in closed session.[23]

Smith could provide no definite information about organized lobbying when he appeared before the subcommittee of the Senate Judiciary Committee which was investigating lobbying activities in connection with the tariff measure.[24] But among the names of those who appeared before Smith's subcommittee on the cotton schedule was Fuller E. Callaway, a cotton manufacturer from Georgia who had long been on friendly terms with the Senator, and one or two other textile men. Smith was careful to emphasize the correctness of his relations with these Southern

---

[22] Smith to Wilson, July 22, 1912, in Wilson Papers.
[23] *Cong. Record*, 63 Cong., 1 Sess., 1593-95, 1608, 1654-57.
[24] *Ibid.*, 1817; Atlanta *Journal*, June 5, 1913.

cotton-mill owners, perhaps because some Republicans had already
hinted that he had promised to prevent the reduction of tariff
levies on Southern cotton goods. This the Georgian emphatically
denied in an interesting colloquy with Reed Smoot of Utah.
"Not a suggestion of a raise of a rate on cotton manufactured
goods has come to me from Georgia," Smith asserted.[25] Nevertheless, he had earlier received some protests from Southern
industrialists,[26] and there is good reason to believe that Simmons,
especially, and Smith were sympathetic with the Southern textile
owners.

The Finance Committee was not ready to submit its work to
the Senate caucus until early July. After the caucus approved
it, with a few changes, Simmons reported the bill back to the
Senate on July 11, and a week later the upper house began to
debate it. Smith defended the changes the Senate committe had
made in the Underwood bill and endeavored to prove that the
measure would in no way harm the farmer.[27]

When the cotton schedule was taken up early in August,
Smith represented the committee on the floor. Many of the
provisions in this section of the bill were extremely technical—
concerning such things as yarns, dyes, rates, and the like—but
the Georgian demonstrated a remarkable mastery of the schedule's
details, and under his guidance most of the committee amendments were adopted. Senator Gallinger, an old antagonist on the
pension question, complimented Smith for the "industry, the
courtesy, and the intelligence" he brought to the consideration
of these problems. Another Republican, Senator Henry F. Lippitt of Rhode Island, was more critical of Smith's role. He contended that the cotton schedule was "made by Southerners," and
that its effect would be to leave unchanged "nearly every coarse-
yarn fabric made in the South" while reducing the duties on

[25] *Cong. Record*, 63 Cong., 1 Sess., 1594-95.

[26] Daniel A. Tompkins, for instance, had written: "Our representatives
have been so long advocating free trade, that it is hard for them to refuse
to acquiesce in a cut on southern products towards a free trade basis, but
meanwhile northern representatives get the highest tariff possible and hold
to it." Memorandum prepared for Smith by Tompkins, January 31, 1913,
in Tompkins Papers (Division of Manuscripts, Library of Congress).

[27] *Cong. Record*, 63 Cong., 1 Sess., 3088, 3377-79.

the finer cotton goods produced in New England. The Georgia Senator denied that sectionalism had entered into the preparation of the schedule, pointing out that his subcommittee had included among its members a Senator from Maine and a Senator from New Jersey. He also noted Lippitt's "own personal interests in the manufacture of many of these articles about . . . which he complains. . . ." [28]

Smith gave his support to the income tax feature of the Underwood-Simmons bill. The Finance Committee proposed a surtax of 3 per cent on incomes over $100,000, but at a party caucus near the end of the summer James K. Vardaman of Mississippi and three other Democratic Senators refused to abide by this recommendation and endorsed Senator Robert M. La Follette's proposal for a maximum rate of 10 per cent. Smith then suggested a compromise plan of 7 per cent. The caucus accepted this proposal, and it became a part of the Underwood-Simmons Act. [29]

Two features of the tariff bill caused Hoke Smith some irritation. He assumed complete responsibility for his subcommittee's recommendation that the duty on wild bird feathers be removed; this led to accusations by various people outside of Congress that the Georgian had no interest in protecting the country's birds. The other case was more serious. The Finance Committee proposed that the House bill be amended to allow the appointment of various internal revenue officials and clerks without complying with the civil service rules. Smith defended the committee proposition and somewhat laboriously attempted to differentiate between regular civil service positions and the internal revenue jobs being considered. Senator Henry Cabot Lodge chided him for abandoning his earlier loyalty to civil service reform, referring to him as "one of the most ardent civil-service reformers that I have ever met." [30]

When Senate Democrats were marshaling their forces for the final action on the tariff bill early in September, the junior Senator from Georgia contributed his part to the floor action. In a

[28] *Ibid.,* 3150-51, 3518-19, 3522-23, 3536-47, 4305-4308.

[29] New York *Times,* September 2, 6, 1913.

[30] *Ibid.,* August 28, 1913; *Cong. Record,* 63 Cong., 1 Sess., 3431-32, 3744-45, 3873-83.

speech on September 6, he spoke of Republican efforts to conjure
up a dark picture of "financial distress," which they argued
was certain to follow the enactment of the tariff reform bill.
Smith gave a long historical account of previous tariffs, citing
the prosperity that followed the tariff of 1846. "We believe in
this bill," he declared. "It is an honest revision of the tariff
downward, free from all favoritism." [31]

By the time the Underwood-Simmons bill was enacted, the
House of Representatives, under the leadership of Carter Glass,
had completed work on the second important reform sponsored
by the administration in 1913—the banking and currency bill.
Hoke Smith had followed banking and currency developments
with a keen eye for many years. He could scarcely forget how
the free-silver issue had forced him into political exile in 1896,
nor was he likely to forget the monetary stringency that led to
the panic of 1907 and afterward contributed to his defeat in the
primary of 1908. Shortly after entering the Senate, Smith sent
to friends some pamphlets prepared by the economist J. Laurence
Laughlin, observing that one of the most important problems
confronting Congress was the need to provide "some elasticity
to the currency." Early in 1913 he declared that some means
must be found for "converting credits into cash in time of
necessity." He predicted that the Wilson administration would
enact a wise and "conservative" currency law.[32]

But Colonel House, with whom the Georgian discussed the
problem after Wilson's election, was not so sure that Smith was
conservative on the money question. House found the Senator's
mind "in a very nebulous condition," he wrote Wilson. "He has
no conception of what a sound economic measure is and rather
admitted it before I finished with him. He went off into almost
as many vagaries as Mr. Bryan but I hauled him back and when
I left I believe that his mind was in a receptive condition for
any measure which you might approve." [33] Early in May, 1913,

[31] *Cong. Record*, 63 Cong., 1 Sess., 4302, 4387-89; Atlanta *Journal*, May 29,
June 27, September 7, 1913.

[32] Smith to Warren A. Candler, December 20, 1911, in Warren A. Candler
Papers (Emory University Library); Atlanta *Journal*, January 7, March 24,
1913.

[33] House to Wilson, November 28, 1912, in Wilson Papers.

Smith outlined his ideas to the legislative committee of the American Bankers' Association. He proposed the establishment of a number of regional reserve banking associations, which would have the power to issue currency on the basis of approved personal collateral and which would be supervised by a Federal board.[34]

Meanwhile, the House was working on the currency legislation and in mid-August the Senate Democrats agreed to consider the bill during the current session. In September the Senate Banking and Currency Committee began a series of hearings which continued until late October. The committee was so sharply divided that when it finally reported to the Senate on November 22, it presented two reports. In order to settle upon a definite plan, the Democrats took up the question in the Senate caucus, and eventually Chairman Robert L. Owen's bill was approved with some modifications. It was on Smith's motion that the caucus changed the gold reserve required in the bill from the proposed $33\frac{1}{3}$ per cent to 40 per cent.[35] He vigorously supported Owen's proposal for the establishment of at least eight regional banks, and he offered an amendment to extend the provisions of the Aldrich-Vreeland Act and to fix more reasonable interest rates on the currency authorized by that law.[36] Smith urged the approval of agricultural mortgages as acceptable collateral and joined with other agrarian radicals in the successful movement to empower the new reserve banks to rediscount agricultural paper for six months.[37]

The Owen bill was passed by the Senate on December 19, and the conference report was adopted four days later. During the Senate debate Smith's principal concern seemed to be the movement to secure a regional bank for Atlanta, and for the next three months this campaign claimed much of his time. " I secured the

[34] Atlanta *Journal*, May 4, 1913.

[35] Undated memorandum, in Smith Collection; Atlanta *Journal*, October 12, 18, 1913.

[36] Smith's amendment was adopted by the caucus and later approved by the Senate. Atlanta *Journal*, December 19, 28, 1913.

[37] *Ibid.*, January 5, August 4, 1914.

location of the Federal Reserve Bank in Atlanta over the insistent claims of Birmingham, and New Orleans," he later asserted.[38]

Smith argued that Atlanta's claim to one of the regional banks was irrefutable, and he undertook to make sure that nothing went amiss. During the midst of the Christmas season of 1913, he appeared at the office of the Secretary of the Treasury William G. McAdoo, a member of the committee to organize the Federal Reserve districts, "armed with a pocket full" of documents on all phases of Atlanta's business. He addressed the members of the Atlanta Clearing House Association and of the Atlanta Chamber of Commerce in an effort to rally them to the city's cause. He co-operated with a local committee of businessmen in the movement for an Atlanta bank. He urged Georgia banks to join the reserve system, declaring that the new law would prove especially helpful to the South. The Georgia Senator conferred with President Wilson and sent a long statement to Secretary of Agriculture David F. Houston, who was also a member of the organizational committee.[39] He appeared before the Federal Reserve committee when it was holding hearings in Atlanta and a few weeks later disregarded his doctor's orders— having suffered a severe case of "grippe"—to make a second appearance before the committee.[40]

In a feature story of April 3, 1914, the Atlanta *Journal* told the story of the successful campaign to win a reserve bank for Atlanta. Its praise of Hoke Smith was unstinted. In the meantime Smith was deluged with congratulatory messages from all over the state.

During the summer of 1913 Smith had appeared before the Georgia legislature to give an account of his "stewardship" in the Senate. Characteristically, he gave a comprehensive address, describing in a straightforward manner his own work and the

[38] *Cong. Record*, 63 Cong., 2 Sess., 690, 698, 847; undated memorandum, in Smith Collection.

[39] "Facts Showing Why There Should Be a Southeastern Region with a Reserve Bank at Atlanta," in Department of Agriculture Papers (National Archives); Atlanta *Journal*, December 26, 27, 1913, January 5, 9, 19, 1914, October 26, 1916.

[40] Atlanta *Journal*, February 15, March 1, 8, April 3, 1914; *Cong. Record*, 63 Cong., 2 Sess., 6329, 6379-82.

program of the Wilson administration. He told of his position on such questions as workmen's compensation, the parcel-post bill, and his own measures for agricultural extension and a marketing division. He discussed the reorganization of the Senate and the status of the tariff and currency legislation. In conclusion he mentioned his conception of the New Freedom: "Out of this Democratic administration much good will come for the entire country, but especially for our section, reinstated and rehabilitated, great in the past, and to be far greater in the future."[41]

About the time Smith completed his second year in the Senate, late in 1913, the Macon *News* took note of that fact in a long editorial listing the Senator's accomplishments. "We cannot recall an instance in which any man has ever in so short a time attained so forceful a position in that body of distinguished statesmen," declared the *News*, "nor more completely won public confidence by a clear, strong grasp of great public questions."[42] There was, of course, a strong element of local pride in such statements as this, but it was true that the first two years of Smith's Senate tenure had been successful ones. The next year promised to be even more rewarding.

[41] MS. Address (1913), in Smith Collection; Atlanta *Journal*, July 9, 20, 1913.

[42] Macon *News*, quoted in Atlanta *Journal*, November 28, 1913.

Agricultural Extension and Vocational Education

The first year of the New Freedom brought the enactment of an important tariff law and the creation of a new banking and currency system. The second year resulted in the passage of two significant measures designed to regulate business more adequately and the adoption of several acts to benefit farmers, including Hoke Smith's agricultural extension bill. This period in Smith's Senate career can be compared to his political experiences during the palmy days of 1906-1907. The years after 1914 were less successful for the Senator, but they did bring the passage of his vocational education bill and the enactment of other Federal aid measures which he sponsored.

Although Smith was chiefly interested in agricultural and educational legislation during the Senate's consideration of the antitrust proposals in 1914, he devoted considerable time to the Clayton bill following his appointment to the Judiciary Committee early in the year. He was especially interested in the exemption of farm organizations from the penalties of the antitrust laws.[1] Earlier in 1914 the Senator from Georgia had opposed an administration bill providing for a government-owned railroad in Alaska. During the debate on the measure he criticized the broad authority the legislation would give the President and spoke of an "abandonment of legislative responsibility." Smith also challenged the size of the appropriation included in the bill, but

---

[1] *Cong. Record*, 63 Cong., 2 Sess., 13317-19, 14318, 14364-67; Atlanta *Journal*, June 12, 1914.

his amendment to reduce the amount was defeated. When he saw that the bill would pass, he expressed the hope that the President would lease the railroad rather than allowing the government to operate it.[2]

In the spring of 1914 Smith took an active part in the administration's fight to secure the repeal of the Panama Canal tolls exemption clause. The House passed the repeal resolution within a few weeks, but a stubborn fight occurred in the Senate, with such Democrats as James A. O'Gorman siding with the Republicans in opposing the administration. Smith had voted for exemption in 1912, but now he did all he could to aid the repeal forces, conferring with President Wilson and assisting other administration leaders on the floor.[3] On May 12, following weeks of debate on Wilson's proposal, Smith made a long speech in reply to O'Gorman's denunciation of the repeal plan. The Georgia Senator presented an historical survey of canal diplomacy that filled ten pages of the *Record*. He asserted that owners of coastwise shipping should pay "a fair part of the cost" of building and operating the canal. He declared that the United States should honor its obligations under the Hay-Pauncefote Treaty. Effectively led by Senator Simmons, the upper house finally repealed the exemption clause on June 11. Smith was at Simmons' elbow throughout the fight, helping all he could.[4]

Woodrow Wilson's decision to ask for the repeal of the tolls exemption provision was related to the growing crisis in the relations between the United States and Mexico. Hoke Smith supported the President's tortuous diplomacy throughout the Mexican crisis.[5] One of the influences Wilson missed was the steady hand of Augustus O. Bacon, who had passed from the scene in February, 1914. Smith and Bacon were never close friends, but they respected each other and the younger man referred to his departed colleague as "a great senator."

[2] *Cong. Record*, 63 Cong., 2 Sess., 2154, 2173, 2228-31, 2247-50.

[3] *Ibid.*, 5025, 5644-45, 6218-19, 7191-92; New York *Times*, March 12, 29, April 5, 1914.

[4] *Cong. Record*, 63 Cong., 2 Sess., 7192, 7248, 8428-38, 9734-45, 10158-59, 10247-48; New York *Times*, May 13, June 6, 1914.

[5] *Cong. Record*, 63 Cong., 2 Sess., 7007-7008, 7014; New York *Times*, November 4, 1913, April 19 (III), 1914.

The demand for a Federal program of agricultural extension grew out of a long period of earlier work. The effect of Theodore Roosevelt's Commission on Country Life, the participation of the General Education Board in farm demonstration work, the influence of the Department of Agriculture's work for the establishment of such a program, and the strong support of business firms and associations throughout the country contributed to the adoption of the legislation. The particular character of extension work provided for in the Smith-Lever Agricultural Extension Act was an outgrowth of the spectacularly successful farmers' co-operative demonstration projects undertaken by Seaman A. Knapp in Texas, Oklahoma, Mississippi, and other states.[6]

Eventually the Association of American Agricultural Colleges and Experiment Stations endorsed the new demonstration system and agreed upon a Federal assistance bill, which was introduced in the House of Representatives by James C. McLaughlin of Michigan in 1909. Jonathan P. Dolliver of Iowa presented a similar measure in the Senate. A few years earlier Representative Charles R. Davis of Minnesota had introduced a bill providing for Federal aid in the teaching of agriculture, mechanical arts, and home economics in public secondary schools. This proposal, which was endorsed by President Roosevelt, the National Grange, the American Federation of Labor, and other groups, was finally combined with the Dolliver bill, thus making an agricultural extension and a vocational education measure. Following Senator Dolliver's death in October, 1910, Carroll S. Page of Vermont, a member of the Senate Committee on Agriculture and Forestry, presented a slightly revised version of the Dolliver bill. In June, 1911, Representative Asbury F. Lever of South Carolina introduced a measure similar to the McLaughlin bill, providing for a Federal system of agricultural extension through the land-grant colleges.[7]

[6] Grant McConnell, *The Decline of Agrarian Democracy* (Berkeley and Los Angeles, 1953), 24-30; Alfred C. True, *A History of Agricultural Extension Work in the United States, 1785-1923* (Washington, 1928), 50-65; Joseph C. Bailey, *Seaman A. Knapp: Schoolmaster of American Agriculture* (New York, 1945).

[7] True, *History of Agricultural Extension Work*, 103-109; McConnell, *Decline of Agrarian Democracy*, 25-26, 33.

In December, 1911, representatives of the National Soil Fertility League, the agricultural colleges, and the Department of Agriculture revised the Lever bill, and in mid-January, 1912, it was introduced by Hoke Smith in the Senate and Representative Lever in the House.[8] What the Senator from Georgia failed to contribute to the early formulation of the Smith-Lever bill, he made up in his ardent advocacy of the measure in the Senate. Smith placed himself in the center of the forces working for the extension act, and in so doing he remained true to an old interest and at the same time revealed his determination to appropriate to himself a measure of Congressional power.

The House first passed the Lever bill in August, 1912. In the meantime, Smith found it difficult to get action on the bill in the Senate, which was controlled by the Republicans and which seemed inclined to approve the Page plan for a combined vocational education and agricultural extension program.[9] On the first day of the short session that convened in December, 1912, the Georgia Senator presented a memorial adopted by the colleges' association and portions of about forty communications from agricultural colleges and other institutions favoring the passage of his bill. A few days later he presented a favorable report on the measure from the Committee on Agriculture and Forestry.[10]

In describing the bill to his colleagues, Smith explained that it provided for the establishment and maintenance of extension departments within the land-grant colleges to give instruction and demonstration work in agriculture and home economics to farmers in their own homes and on their own land. Each state would be granted an initial appropriation of ten thousand dollars for this work, if it would agree to match it, and subsequent increases would be made on the basis of rural population until the total annual expenditure by the Federal government was about three million dollars. General supervision of the program would be charged to the Department of Agriculture, but the colleges would enjoy a large amount of independence in carrying out the extension work. An opportunity was available at last, declared Smith,

[8] Bailey, *Seaman A. Knapp*, 259-65; *Cong. Record*, 62 Cong., 3 Sess., 831.
[9] *Cong. Record*, 62 Cong., 2 Sess., 10646-48, 10784-86, 11273.
[10] *Ibid.*, 3 Sess., 15-17, 627; Atlanta *Journal*, January 24, November 13, 17, 1912.

"to carry to the farmers at their homes the valuable information which has been and will be obtained by the work of the colleges and experiment stations."[11]

In January, 1913, the Senator made a vigorous effort to secure the passage of the bill. At the same time, he criticized the Page bill on the grounds that it authorized a much greater appropriation than the Smith-Lever bill, that it was poorly prepared, and that the House would not accept it. In a long speech on January 24, the Georgian repeated his criticisms of the Page bill and reiterated his arguments in support of his and Representative Lever's plan.[12] Smith's attack disturbed Carroll S. Page, who reminded the Democratic Senator of a number of conferences in which they had discussed a possible compromise between the Smith-Lever and the Page bills. Plaintively, Page said that he had understood a "meeting of minds" had resulted from his conferences with Smith, but the Southerner denied that he had approved a compromise, contending that he had merely pointed out what he considered to be the defects of the Page plan. The Vermont Senator suggested that in view of the changes he had made at Smith's suggestion the measure might be called the "Smith-Page" bill.[13]

When Page offered his bill as a substitute for the Smith-Lever bill, which the Senate had been considering section by section, John R. Thornton of Louisiana voiced the dilemma that confronted many Democrats in choosing between the two measures: "If I vote for the Page bill as a substitute for the Smith bill," he declared, "I assist in eliminating from further consideration entirely the Smith bill, which, while it is not of such general scope in its application, yet will bring material benefit to every State in the Union."[14] At this point Hoke Smith professed a willingness

[11] *Cong. Record*, 62 Cong., 3 Sess., 831-32.

[12] *Ibid.*, 913, 1659-64, 1763, 1955-56.

[13] *Ibid.*, 1957-58, 1961-63.

[14] *Ibid.*, 2088-91, 2093-96, 2107, 2109, 2111. A fierce struggle as to the merits of the Page and Smith-Lever bills had been going on for some time among education and labor groups. The Association of American Colleges and Experiment Stations and the National Soil Fertility League strongly supported the Smith-Lever bill, while the National Society for Industrial Education, the American Federation of Labor, the National Grange, and

to accept the Page bill if certain changes were made in it. But when he offered several amendments, they were all rejected and the Page substitute was then approved, first by the committee of the whole and then by the Senate.[15] The House refused to accept the Page bill, as Smith had forecast, and the conference of the two houses was unable to reach an agreement during the remainder of the session. Smith, who was one of the Senate conferees, attempted without success to have the Senate discharge its conferees and give up the Page substitute in favor of the Smith-Lever bill.[16]

During the extra session of the Sixty-third Congress, which convened in April, 1913, Smith again introduced his extension bill as well as a measure to provide Federal aid for training vocational teachers and a joint resolution authorizing an investigation of the entire question of vocational education. While Congress was absorbed in the tariff legislation and before the Smith-Lever bill could be reported from the agricultural committees of the two houses, Secretary of Agriculture David F. Houston took the lead in an effort to strengthen the co-operative features of the proposed bill. In the spring and summer of 1913, Houston, Smith, and Lever conferred several times with representatives of the colleges' association. The result was a revised version of the Smith-Lever bill, which the two Congressmen introduced in their respective houses on September 6, 1913.[17]

Shortly after the second session of the Sixty-third Congress began, Smith reported the bill from the Committee on Agriculture and Forestry with a unanimous recommendation that it be passed. He explained that it was essentially the same measure as the original Smith-Lever bill, with the notable exception of the

the Farmers' Union supported the Page bill. The National Soil Fertility League claimed that 500 chambers of commerce and other organizations, 1,088 newspapers, and a large number of banks were actively working for the Smith-Lever plan. True, *History of Agricultural Extension Work*, 109-10.

[15] *Cong. Record*, 62 Cong., 3 Sess., 2211-12, 2215-18, 2222.

[16] *Ibid.*, 2228, 2684, 4136, 4426, 4589, 4840; Atlanta *Journal*, March 30, 1913.

[17] *Cong. Record*, 63 Cong., 1 Sess., 52, 57, 4330, 5478-80, 5663, 5928; David F. Houston to Smith, May 28, 1913, and Assistant Secretary of Agriculture to Smith, July 31, 1913, in Department of Agriculture Papers.

"co-operative" features. Whereas the original plan had given
control of the extension work to the agricultural colleges, the
new proposal specified that the Department of Agriculture must
approve the projects submitted by the colleges. Smith admitted
soon afterward, "The truth about it is that the real object this
bill had in view was to prevent the diversion of the money to the
college. It was to force it away from the college, and to the
country." [18]

The bill came up on the Senate calendar on January 17, 1914,
exactly one year after Hoke Smith had begun the struggle in
the third session of the previous Congress. The Georgian discussed the measure at length, emphasizing the accomplishments
of Seaman A. Knapp with the demonstration method and the
success of similar work in Europe. Federal assistance in the field
of agricultural extension was but one of a series of steps needed
to relieve the farm problem, declared Smith. But it would bring
benefits "in the line of more prosperous farmers, better schools
in the country, better roads, and largely increasing farm population. . . ." [19]

The House passed the revised Smith-Lever bill on January 19,
after which the House bill was introduced in the Senate and
reported favorably by Smith from the Senate committee, with a
motion that it be substituted for the Senate bill. This was done,
and the Senate, acting as a committee of the whole, began a
ten-day debate of the measure, with Smith in charge. [20]

As the debate proceeded in the Senate a number of criticisms
were leveled at the bill. Senator John D. Works of California
described it as "class legislation." Senator McCumber called it
a "sop" to the American farmer after the Democrats had robbed
him of his American market through the Underwood-Simmons
tariff. [21] More important were the strictures of Senator Cummins,
directed at the plan of allocating Federal funds which the bill
contained. Cummins proposed that the basis for making such
allocations should be "acres of improved land in farms," rather

[18] *Cong. Record*, 63 Cong., 2 Sess., 623, 1827-28, 7623.
[19] *Ibid.*, 1822-26, 1830-40.
[20] *Ibid.*, 2288, 2426-29.
[21] *Ibid.*, 2427-29, 2511-20, 2572-78.

than rural population. The Senator from Iowa pointed out that although the population of his state was almost as large as that of Georgia, and although Iowa had over twice as much improved land as the Southern state, under the Smith plan it would receive less money than Georgia. Broadening his illustration, the Iowan declared that twelve Southern states would receive more Federal money than twelve Northern states which produced almost twice the value of farm products grown by the Southern states.

The South was not without its defenders, as Bacon, Simmons, Williams, and others spoke for the bill. During the spirited debate on the Cummins amendment, Smith observed that in making rural population the basis for the extension appropriations, he and other advocates of the measure were thinking ahead to the time when Federal aid to vocational education would be provided, with the nation's urban population receiving primary consideration. He disclaimed any sectional motivation and contended that the colleges' association had unanimously agreed upon rural population as the basis for the Federal allotments. Smith noted that 83 per cent of the farm land in Iowa was " improved," as compared to the national average of 25 per cent; he also shrewdly pointed out that if the Cummins proposal were adopted, Iowa, with a population of 2,225,000, would receive as large an appropriation as New York, Pennsylvania, and New Jersey, with a total population of 19,300,000. When the vote came on the Cummins amendment early in February, it received only sixteen ayes, mainly from Western Senators.[22] It was an important victory for Hoke Smith.

Even before the defeat of the Cummins amendment, an attack from another angle threatened Smith's bill. Senator McCumber had noted that under the Smith-Lever plan the state legislatures were empowered to decide which agricultural college in their respective states would receive the Federal money in those cases where more than one college existed. In the South, McCumber contended, this would mean that Negro agricultural colleges would not receive any Federal support. This feature of the bill led Senator Wesley L. Jones of Washington to sponsor an amend-

[22] *Ibid.*, 2525, 2580-82, 2649-55, 2659, 2731-36, 2740, 2744; Atlanta *Journal*, February 4, 1914.

ment providing that Federal funds for extension purposes must be "equitably divided" between white and Negro colleges in states that had separate institutions. Several other Senators joined Jones and Cummins in attacking this section of the Smith-Lever bill.[23]

The Negro question, of course, was grist for the Southerners' mill. James K. Vardaman, arch defender of the South, resorted to some of his most rhetorical periods in answering Jones, asserting that the Senator from Washington did not understand the "racial peculiarities of the negro." The race issue soon dominated the debate, and charges of sectionalism by both sides rang through the Senate halls. Smith assumed the responsibility of justifying the allocation scheme contained in the extension bill. He attempted to show that Negro colleges in the South were not prepared to send out trained demonstrators, and that Negroes evinced little interest in agricultural education. In the white colleges, on the other hand, "the highest class of scientific work is done, for men who are capable of receiving the instruction and who are seeking it." The Senator joined Vardaman in blaming the backwardness of Southern agriculture on the black man, but he claimed that there was no lack of desire on the part of Southern white leaders to see the Negro make progress.[24]

When the vote on the Jones amendment came, it was rejected 23 to 32. But Senator John F. Shafroth of Colorado secured the adoption of an amendment directing the governors and the Secretary of Agriculture, rather than the state legislatures, to determine which colleges in the various states would receive the extension money. Senator Gilbert M. Hitchcock managed to insert in the bill a clause stating that extension work should be conducted "without discrimination as to race." Smith successfully opposed Senator Thomas Sterling's substitute to remove all of the "cooperative" features of the measure. He then accepted certain minor amendments, and the bill was reported to the Senate from the committee of the whole, read the third time, and passed. Senator Page, the Georgian's erstwhile rival for the honor of steering an agricultural extension bill through the Senate, compli-

[23] Cong. Record, 63 Cong., 2 Sess., 2519-20, 2929-30, 2932, 2947, 3119.
[24] Ibid., 2936-37, 2943-48, 3031-32, 3034-41, 3118-19.

mented Smith on his good work, and Elihu Root referred to his conduct as " altogether admirable." [25]

Hoke Smith and Asbury F. Lever headed the conferees from the two houses who worked earnestly during the following weeks in an effort to reconcile the differences between the bills passed by the House and the Senate. The chief bone of contention, apparently, was the Shafroth amendment. The House conferees steadfastly refused to accept this provision, and finally the Senate members agreed to abandon it; the House made certain concessions to the upper house, and a compromise was reached on the total appropriation authorized by the bill.[26] Smith secured the approval of the conference report by the Senate on April 27, but two days later Senator Reed Smoot protested the adoption of the report and managed to have it recalled. Senator Jones was particularly critical of the Senate conferees' surrender of the Shafroth amendment, but a motion to reconsider the Senate's approval of the conference report was voted down, and Smith had carried the day. Meanwhile, the House had agreed to the report, and President Wilson signed the bill on May 8.[27]

The Smith-Lever Act received a large measure of praise. " It has become increasingly clear," Secretary Houston declared sometime later, " that no more important extension machinery has ever been created." [28] During the following years the act demonstrated its merit by the rapid progress made in the use of the demonstration method. It resulted in a remarkable three-level integration of Federal, state, and county governmental machinery, and its matching features set the pattern for much subsequent Federal legislation.

Hoke Smith always considered the Smith-Lever Act the most important Federal legislation he ever sponsored. He could neither claim to have originated the bill nor to have provided an indis-

---

[25] *Ibid.,* 3119-21, 3123-29.

[26] The ultimate sum expended annually by the Federal government was to be $4,580,000. *Cong. Record,* 63 Cong., 2 Sess., 3877, 4717-18, 7309, 7421-22.

[27] *Ibid.,* 7417-18, 7421-28, 7493-94; Atlanta *Journal,* May 13, 1914. Wilson signed the bill with two pens, giving one to Lever and one to Smith.

[28] David F. Houston, *Eight Years With Wilson's Cabinet, 1913 to 1920, With a Personal Estimate of the President* (Garden City, 1926), I, 204-205; undated MS. Address, in Smith Collection.

pensable influence in its enactment, but he recognized its importance as a constructive piece of legislation, and in the course of its passage he stamped his personality on its provisions in more ways than one. As Secretary Houston said, " he introduced and was the real promoter of the bill in the Senate." Smith was not a modest man, but he was right when he declared of the bill, " It was justly called the Smith-Lever bill." [29]

Smith's long interest in vocational training and his chairmanship of the Committee on Education and Labor during the Wilson period gave a certain logic to his sponsorship of a vocational education bill. The proposal for a Federal vocational education program had been discussed for many years in Congress. Senator Page's bill, which failed in the Sixty-second Congress, represented the most important of these early plans. In 1913 Smith introduced a joint resolution providing for the creation of a nine-man commission to consider the question of Federal aid to vocational education and to report a plan to Congress. This resolution was approved by both houses.[30]

Early in 1914 President Wilson appointed the members of the commission authorized by Smith's resolution. The Georgia Senator had definite ideas about the composition of the commission, and he attempted to influence the selection of its members. The secretary of the National Society for the Promotion of Industrial Education wrote to Secretary of Commerce William C. Redfield late in January, for instance, to report that Smith desired " a preponderance of Southern representatives " on the commission and to say that his organization feared such " sectional control." [31] In addition to Smith, who was named chairman, three other Congressmen were appointed to the commission: Senator Page; Representative Dudley M. Hughes of Georgia, the chairman of

[29] Houston to Tumulty, May 7, 1914, in Wilson Papers; Atlanta *Journal*, August 4, 1914.

[30] *Cong. Record*, 63 Cong., 1 Sess., 57, 1838-39, 2238; Atlanta *Journal*, July 23, August 1, 1913.

[31] Charles A. Prosser to Redfield, January 28, 1914, in Wilson Papers. See also Wilson to Redfield, February 2, 1914, *ibid*.

the House Committee on Education; and Representative Simeon D. Fess of Ohio.[32]

In April, following the organization of the Commission on Industrial Education, Smith made arrangements for a series of hearings as one phase of the commission's work, and the hearings were held in late April and early May. On June 1 the Georgian presented the commission's report to the Senate. It was a comprehensive document that explored the need for vocational education, the types of such training in which the Federal government should participate, the conditions under which Federal support should be given, and other factors. The report pointed out that there was "a great and crying need" for vocational education.[33]

In presenting the report Smith analyzed the provisions of the plan recommended by the commission, pointing out that it provided for the same type of dollar-matching program as that contained in the Smith-Lever Act. It would attempt through Federal grants and some degree of Federal supervision to promote training in agricultural, industrial, and domestic arts in the secondary schools, with an ultimate appropriation of seven million dollars per year. It also provided for the training of vocational education teachers. A Federal vocational education board would supervise the program.[34]

The Smith-Hughes bill, as the commission plan came to be called, aroused considerable attention in 1914, but it was not acted on by Congress during that year. The brevity of the third session of the Sixty-third Congress prevented action on the measure in 1915, but Smith and Hughes reintroduced the legis-

[32] The non-Congressional members of the commission were: John A. Lapp, secretary of the Indiana Commission on Industrial Education; Agnes Nestor, president of the American Federation of Labor's Committee on Industrial Education; Charles A. Prosser, secretary of the National Society for the Promotion of Industrial Education; Florence M. Marshall, principal of the Manhattan Trade School for Girls; and Charles H. Winslow, an expert on labor and industrial problems. *Cong. Record*, 63 Cong., 2 Sess., 9503.

[33] *Report of the Commission on National Aid to Vocational Education Together with the Hearings Held on the Subject Made Pursuant to the Provisions of Public Resolution No. 16, Sixty-Third Congress (S. J. Res. 5)* (Washington, 1914).

[34] *Cong. Record*, 63 Cong., 2 Sess., 9503-9505.

lation when the first session of the Sixty-fourth Congress convened in December, 1915. The plan was endorsed by the National Association of Manufacturers, the United States Chamber
of Commerce, the National Society for the Promotion of Industrial Education, and a number of labor organizations. Such
progressives as Charles McCarthy of Wisconsin and educators
like Charles R. Van Hise of the same state also approved the
measure. In the Senate the bill was favorably reported from
Smith's Education and Labor Committee early in 1916 and placed
on the Senate calendar. By this time, however, Congress was
involved in the preparedness debate, and Smith was forced to
delay until summer.[35]

It was not until July that Hoke Smith was able to have the
vocational education bill considered by the upper house. Smith
and Page made the only notable speeches on the measure. The
Vermont Senator stressed the "fast-growing and persistent demand" for Federal aid. The Southerner carefully outlined the
provisions of the bill and noted that Congress "might well give
some preparation for peace" as well as for war. Apparently
there was little or no opposition to the bill, and following the
adoption of some committee amendments, it was passed without
a roll call.[36]

The House failed to pass the measure in 1916. Smith observed
in the fall that there was little opposition to the bill in Congress,
and this proved to be true, for the House passed the bill under
Representative Hughes's guidance early in 1917.[37] There was no
such conference wrangle as had occurred over the Smith-Lever
bill, and the two houses soon agreed to compromise the disputed
points. The bill was then approved by both houses.[38]

[35] *Ibid.*, 64 Cong., 1 Sess., 92-93, 1781, 2681, 7622, 9350-51; New York
Times, September 27 (IV), 1914; Smith to Wilson, about June 1, 1916, in
Wilson Papers.

[36] *Cong. Record*, 64 Cong., 1 Sess., 4178, 6479-80, 11275, 11464-72, 11873-78.

[37] *Ibid.*, 64 Cong., 2 Sess., 1189, 1321; Atlanta *Journal*, November 22, 1916;
"Hoke Smith on Education," in *Journal of Education*, LXXXIV (September
14, 1916), 232.

[38] The most important point at issue in the conference was the makeup
of the Federal vocational education board. Smith, with President Wilson's
endorsement, secured the Senate's approval of a board to be made up of

Hoke Smith sponsored the Smith-Hughes bill with all of his customary energy, and after the bill's passage he followed the Federal work in vocational education with keen interest. One of his main objectives during the debate on the preparedness legislation in 1916-17 was to provide for vocational training in the armed forces. A principal concern of the Georgia Senator during and immediately following the war was vocational rehabilitation for veterans. Perhaps Smith's understanding of the problems involved in an adequate program of vocational education was limited, as some of his critics implied, but he saw clearly enough the need for such Federal assistance, and he appreciated the fact that vocational training was a natural complement to the extension work provided for in the Smith-Lever Act.

Cabinet officers, whereas the House provided for a board of representatives from the fields covered by the Smith-Hughes bill. Smith played a leading part in the eventual compromise, which provided for a board including the Commissioner of Education, three Cabinet members, and three outsiders. *Cong. Record*, 64 Cong., 2 Sess., 3262-65, 3481-83.

An Election and a Crusade

While Hoke Smith was laboring so hard early in 1914 to complete the passage of the Smith-Lever bill and to make certain that
Atlanta received a Federal Reserve bank, he was not unaware of
the fact that he must face the voters in his bid for renomination
in the summer primary. With the Underwood victory in the
Presidential primary of 1912 and the subsequent election of
John M. Slaton as governor, the Howell-Brown wing of the
party had assumed control of the party machinery in the state.
Nevertheless, the Smith faction advanced a kind of proprietary
claim to the Wilson administration, which seemed to be confirmed
by Smith's importance as an administration leader. Thus both
elements of the party could point to some successes, and a
momentary calm settled over the Georgia political scene.

There was not, of course, a complete cessation of the old
quarrels between the two factions. Smith's newspaper critics, for
instance, lost no opportunity to put him in an unfavorable light.
Furthermore, the primary campaign for the Senate seat left vacant
by the death of Augustus O. Bacon in February, 1914, soon
precipitated a vigorous political struggle. One of the candidates
was Governor Slaton. To the amazement of many Georgians two
of Smith's supporters—Attorney General Thomas S. Felder and
Congressman Thomas W. Hardwick—entered the contest. Political discussion immediately turned to the significance of this
development. Was it a shrewd scheme to outmaneuver the powerful Slaton in the state convention? What was Hoke Smith's
attitude? Hardwick seemed to realize that the situation might

be a delicate one for Smith; he declared that he intended "to hoe his own row and to tote his own skillet." [1]

Smith managed to avoid any public statement about the Senate race to nominate Bacon's successor, but in May he released a statement with respect to the campaign for governor. He stated that it was his "intention to have no part in anybody's race for governor." [2] This, it should be noted, came before any opposition had appeared to his own re-election.

For months the Atlanta *Journal* had been engaged in a campaign to publicize Smith's services in the Senate. In 1913 and 1914 the Senator was mentioned in practically every issue of the *Journal*. He was the subject of innumerable articles, interviews, and predictions, not only in the Atlanta paper but in newspapers all over the state. Some of the old anti-Smith papers were even beginning to praise him. The Augusta *Chronicle*, for example, ran an editorial early in April, 1914, entitled "Let Hoke Smith Remain on the Job in Washington." According to the *Chronicle*, Smith was far and away the most "influential, energetic and effective" Senator Georgia had sent to Washington in a generation. [3]

By late May, however, reports were circulating in Georgia that Joseph M. Brown was considering the possibility of opposing Smith in the 1914 primary. Smith chose this time to come home, ostensibly to introduce Vice-President Thomas R. Marshall to an Atlanta audience, but more likely to confer with his Georgia friends about Brown's course. As soon as he returned to Washington the Senator formally announced his candidacy for re-election. "It has hardly seemed necessary," Smith declared in his announcement, "for me to make any formal statement of my candidacy for the nomination in August to succeed myself in the senate." He pointed out that many of his supporters had written him to promise their support, and he alluded to the long factional struggle within the state, expressing regret that it had led to "some acute differences and even estrangements." He

[1] Savannah *Morning News*, March 2, 1914; Atlanta *Journal*, March 8, April 25, 1914.

[2] Atlanta *Journal*, May 19, 1914.

[3] Augusta *Chronicle*, Apirl 3, 4, 1914.

anticipated greater harmony in the Georgia Democracy, he said, and promised to continue to serve all Georgians.[4]

Joe Brown's candidacy could not be headed off, and early in July the former governor announced that he would oppose Smith in the primary. Brown's announcement caused Smith partisans to denounce the opposition for establishing an anti-Smith junto to plot a campaign for revenge and personal ambition. The theme of scores of newspapers sympathetic to Smith, and of a goodly number of old Brown papers, was that "Little Joe's" decision was ill-advised. Many agreed with the Columbus *Ledger*, which asserted that Brown had been misled by "those who are unfriendly to Mr. Smith." Others agreed with the Savannah *Press*, which contended that Georgians were "heartily sick of the political feud between Smith and Brown" and predicted that the latter would not find the "old animosities so easy to use in a political way."[5]

Although Brown's campaign seemed to be less formidable than his earlier election efforts, it was not without support. The Atlanta *Constitution* naturally lent its assistance, though it appeared less vigorous in Brown's behalf than in former campaigns, probably because of its more serious attention to Slaton's fight for the short-term seat. The Macon *Telegraph* was as active as ever in its denunciation of Smith. Several strong anti-Smith political leaders spoke for Brown, including a promising young politician named Hugh M. Dorsey, who had risen to prominence as the prosecutor of Leo Frank. Tom Watson, who hated Hoke Smith as bitterly as ever, attacked the Senator as a Negrophile, an enemy of white supremacy, and a truckler to Rome.[6]

The major factor in Joseph M. Brown's campaign was Brown himself. He wrote a series of cards, as was his custom, which were published in newspapers throughout the state. Long critical of organized labor, and particularly so after some serious labor disturbances during his second administration, Brown concen-

---

[4] Atlanta *Journal*, May 25, 28, 29, June 1, 1914.

[5] Columbus *Ledger*, Savannah *Press*, and numerous other newspapers, quoted in Atlanta *Journal*, July 4, 12, 14, 1914.

[6] Macon *Telegraph*, July 2, 10, August 2, 4, 8, 1914; Woodward, *Tom Watson*, 433-34.

trated much of his fire on the alleged threat of radical labor. He presented elaborate statistics in an effort to prove that "labor unionism is a foreign importation into this country," and he filled his cards with examples of violence, destruction, and "anarchistic practices." He pointed out that Samuel Gompers had referred to Smith in 1911 as a "dependable friend" of labor, and he asserted that every labor leader in Georgia was supporting Smith. "Which do you prefer," queried Brown, "Hoke Smith or the law?"

But it was soon apparent that Brown was without a good issue. The opposition to Smith was not developing as the anti-Smith leaders had hoped; there was no "uprising of the people." The former governor then shifted his attack. He paraded through the long columns of his statements all of the hoary charges of the old Smith-Brown controversy. One of "Little Joe's" sharpest barbs was his charge that Smith was a patronage dictator. "He interferes with every congressman in naming even the minor postmasters throughout the state," declared Brown. He ridiculed what he termed the exaggerated claims for Smith made by some newspapers. The challenger accused organized labor, and inferentially Smith, of trying to organize the "hordes of negroes" in Georgia. "What farmer's home or wife or daughter will be safe during a strike by negro union members in the country?" demanded Brown. He also accused his opponent of being lukewarm in his opposition to Negro officeholders.[7]

Early in July the Smith campaign was formally begun, with the opening of headquarters in the Kimball House in Atlanta and the announcement that Henry Y. McCord, an Atlanta businessman, would serve as state manager. Smith clubs were organized, a series of speakers was obtained, and the Atlanta *Journal* rallied the newspaper brigade. Encouraging news poured into Smith headquarters from all over the state. Smith leaders emphasized the Senator's role as a spokesman of the Wilson administration. They publicized Smith's efforts to provide relief for the cotton farmers when the war in Europe closed the foreign markets late in the summer. The following resolution adopted by a group

[7] For the Brown campaign cards see Atlanta *Journal*, July 16, 22, 30, August 4, 11, 14, 17, 1914.

of Emanuel County farmers is an indication of the effectiveness
of this approach: " We wish to express to you our sincere appreciation of the manner in which you are. handling the cotton
situation, and of other work you are doing in behalf of the
farmers of the South. . . . We have the utmost confidence in
your willingness and ability to do all that can be done to protect
our interest. We also wish to assure you that we . . . are doing
what we can to protect your interest while you are absent
serving us." [8]

Hoke Smith's active contribution to his own cause was less
than in any of his previous campaigns. He informed his constituents that he was so preoccupied with his Senate work that
he would be unable to come to Georgia for a speaking tour,
although rumors were circulated about the state that he would
make a personal appearance. Smith was indeed busy, but the
fact that he took little part in Senate debate during the campaign
—which was not like him—indicates that he was probably more
concerned with his campaign than he revealed. In various interviews with the *Journal*'s Washington correspondent and in two
printed statements, he struck out at what he called "a most
inexcusable campaign of slanders" by his political enemies. He
defended himself against the criticisms of his handling of patronage, demonstrated that he had supported the immigration-restric-
tion legislation, and praised Georgia labor leaders as "splendid
law-abiding men." [9]

Smith saw to it that his persistent opposition to Negro officeholders was publicized. In July he received a letter from a
Georgian which read: "This is to advise you that a number
of your opponents in south Georgia are trying to arouse prejudice
against you in rural districts and among the voters by repeating
to them a great story about your having voted to keep a negro
in office over a white man, having reference to a negro judge
in Washington." The Georgia Senator at once had all the
references to the appointment in the *Congressional Record*
brought together and the vote in executive session made public.[10]

[8] Atlanta *Journal*, July 3-5, 7, 8, 12-14, 19, August 3, 5, 10, 11, 14-18, 1914.
[9] *Ibid.*, August 4, 7, 9, 11, 17, 1914.
[10] The Negro referred to by Smith's opponents was Robert H. Terrell,

Smith's followers also showed that the Senator had seen the President on several occasions to protest against Negro appointments. In the heat of the campaign they were no doubt proud of Oswald Garrison Villard's recent characterization of the Georgia leader as one of those "reactionary demagogues" who had "risen on Negroes' backs." [11]

The primary returns on August 19 gave Smith a sweeping victory. He received 135,000 votes to approximately 69,000 for Brown, and carried 138 counties to Brown's 10.[12] Among the letters of congratulations Smith received was this one from President Wilson: "I know I need hardly tell you the deep gratification I feel at your success, and at the scale and emphasis of it." [13]

A few days after the primary Smith announced that he would attend the state Democratic convention in Macon on September 1, to receive his nomination in person. He arrived in Macon on the afternoon of August 31 to find an enthusiastic crowd of 1,500 people gathered at the station to receive him.[14] Thronged about by admiring Georgians, the Senator was in his element—the political sage had come to show himself to his people!

After the preliminary organization of the convention on the following day, the nominations of Smith and Nathaniel E. Harris, the successful gubernatorial candidate, were formally ratified by the convention. In his address of acceptance Smith thanked the delegates and the people of Georgia for his impressive victory; he spoke of the great Democratic record and dealt at some length with the economic crisis in the South.[15] The convention then turned to its major task, that of nominating a Senator for Bacon's

who had been confirmed as a municipal court judge of the District of Columbia. *Cong. Record*, 63 Cong., 2 Sess., 7621, 12003-12004; Atlanta *Journal*, May 1, July 27, August 2, 1914.

[11] New York *Times*, May 6, 1914; Atlanta *Journal*, May 18, June 12, July 27, 1914.

[12] Atlanta *Journal*, August 19-23, 1914.

[13] Wilson to Smith, August 20, 1914, in Wilson Papers.

[14] Atlanta *Journal*, August 25, 31, 1914.

[15] *Ibid.*, September 2, 1914; Nathaniel E. Harris, *Autobiography: the Story of an Old Man's Life with Reminiscences of Seventy-Five Years* (Macon, Ga., 1925), 345-46, 349.

seat, since none of the candidates had obtained a majority of the county-unit votes in the primary.[16]

It was evident that the convention was a Smith body and that if the Hardwick and Felder delegates ever combined, the contest would be over. This fact made the anti-Smith forces especially sensitive about Smith's presence near the convention. A noisy argument was precipitated early in the meeting when J. E. Sheppard announced in " stentorian tones " that he was authorized to name Senator Smith's nominee for chairman of the convention. G. R. Hutchens, himself a candidate for the Senate seat, called it " an insult to the Democracy of this state for a man to sit off in some room and by sending messages here attempt to dictate the actions of this convention." [17]

Although Slaton obtained a plurality of the convention votes on the first ballot, he lost ground as the balloting proceeded.[18] But if Slaton could not get a majority, neither could Hardwick or Felder. The weary delegates took ballot after ballot on through the night. A contemporary historian has described that futile night: "Dawn found the convention still in session. With bedraggled looks but eyes still flashing defiance, the rival factions faced each other in gray morning watches. There was no longer the orderly decorum of the day preceding. Wilted collars— disheveled locks—passionate gesticulations—violent outbursts of temper. . . ." [19] At 7:15, after thirteen unsuccessful ballots, the delegates agreed to adjourn until noon.

When the convention reassembled, Thomas S. Felder appeared to request that his name be withdrawn, declaring that he and Hardwick were friends and that he was " not willing to jeopardize the interests of progressive democracy." Slaton was allowed to

[16] Slaton had led in popular votes with almost 70,000 and 140 unit votes, while Hardwick trailed by a few thousand popular votes and a few unit votes. Felder was third with a substantial vote, and G. R. Hutchens carried only a few counties.

[17] Atlanta *Journal*, September 1, 1914.

[18] The vote on the first ballot was Slaton 130, Hardwick 124, Felder 91, and Hutchens 18.

[19] Lucian Lamar Knight, *A Standard History of Georgia and Georgians* (Chicago, 1917), II, 1156-57.

plead his cause, but the fight was over. Thomas W. Hardwick was nominated on the fourteenth ballot.[20]

The anti-Smith press was sure that Smith had finally chosen between his two lieutenants. It was an "abject surrender of manhood" to an "arrogant and selfish political 'boss,'" stormed the Macon *Telegraph*.[21] There is little doubt that Hardwick was Smith's choice and that it was his word that finally settled the question. Quite likely the Senator had decided on Hardwick long before but had hesitated to interfere until it was obvious that the convention was hopelessly deadlocked. That some kind of understanding existed between Smith and the two candidates is certain. Soon after the convention Smith and Hardwick began sponsoring Felder for a Federal appointment.

For a long time it had been almost second nature to Hoke Smith to emphasize the importance of agriculture. "With us in Georgia," he reminded the state legislature in 1913, "it furnishes the chief source of prosperity. When the farmer prospers every occupation and every line of industry in Georgia prospers. When the farmer fails to make a profit from his crop money is scarce in the State and the complaint of hard times is heard on all sides."[22] Smith was convinced that an agricultural revolution was taking place in the South, and for a generation he had devoted himself to the "rural uplift" of his state and section. Furthermore, he had learned from experience the influence of the farmers in Georgia politics. The fact that he was a city man and a lawyer forced him to make certain compensations.

From the time he entered the Senate Smith identified himself with the principal legislation designed to aid the farmer. He believed that there were "practical and sane ways" of assisting farmers, not "in a sense of taking from them their own responsibilities," but to stimulate individual initiative and to "open the door of hope to many a struggling farmer and encourage many a tenant farmer to become the owner of the land he tills."[23]

[20] The vote gave Hardwick 235, Slaton 133, and Hutchens 4. Atlanta *Journal*, September 2, 1914.

[21] Macon *Telegraph*, September 3, 1914.

[22] MS. Address (1913), in Smith Collection.

[23] *Cong. Record*, 64 Cong., 1 Sess., 7391.

Smith had assumed the leading role in the passage of the Smith-Lever Act in 1914. His bill to create a bureau of markets failed to pass, but he and other Congressmen secured appropriations for this work beginning in 1912 that soon reached large sums and made it possible for the Department of Agriculture to establish the Office of Markets and Rural Organization. Along with Representative Lever and Senator Clarke, Smith attempted unsuccessfully to amend the Underwood-Simmons tariff bill in 1913 to provide for Federal regulation of cotton exchanges, and in 1914 he was one of the leading advocates of the bill introduced by Lever and Senator Ellison D. Smith.[24] The Georgian supported the movement for Federal co-operation with the states in the construction of roads, especially rural roads. He heartily approved a long-term credit system based on agricultural land, although he was not altogether happy with some of the provisions of the Federal Farm Loan Act, being a little dubious of the magnitude of the plan and of its constitutionality. But he supported the measure, and when Wilson signed it in 1916, he was present at the President's invitation.[25]

Throughout his Senate career Hoke Smith made it a practice to serve his constituents to the maximum of his and his staff's resources. He employed clerks at his own expense to assist in meeting the requests of his fellow-Georgians. Many of these requests were from farmers asking Federal aid of one kind or another, and the Senator carried on a continual correspondence and had frequent interviews with Department of Agriculture officials about such diverse matters as the eradication of cattle ticks, experimentation with new crops, and the opportunities for cattle production in Georgia.[26] An example of this kind of service was Smith's aid to southeastern naval-stores men. He

[24] *Ibid.*, 63 Cong., 1 Sess., 4415-16; 2 Sess., 5078-79, 5158, 5339, 5591-92, 12655, 13661; Atlanta *Journal*, May 25, June 7, 29, July 11, 26, August 14, 1914.

[25] *Cong. Record*, 62 Cong., 3 Sess., 2971; 63 Cong., 1 Sess., 5941; 63 Cong., 3 Sess., 2940, 5325-26; 64 Cong., 1 Sess., 2050, 2054-55, 2330-32, 6842, 7377-79, 7390-93, 7412.

[26] See, for example, Smith to David F. Houston, May 28, June 19, July 9, October 8, 1913, May 18, 1914, November 17, 1915, August 19, 1916, in Department of Agriculture Papers.

secured an appropriation for an investigation of the industry and encouraged an attempt to standardize certain of its aspects.

A more striking illustration of Smith's devotion to the agricultural interests of his constituents was his long fight for the cotton farmers, following the temporary disruption of the cotton market abroad caused by the war in Europe. With a surplus crop predicted and the sudden prospect of losing the foreign market, the price of cotton dropped to six or seven cents per pound.

Smith began to make plans to protect cotton as soon as the war came. On August 1, 1914, he conferred with a number of his colleagues from the South about the situation, and they decided to call a conference of Southern Congressmen to explore the entire problem. When the conference convened at the capitol on the evening of August 3, it quickly elected Smith chairman, and he appointed three committees to investigate various aspects of the problem. A few days later the Congressmen issued a report, emphasizing the importance of cotton to the South and calling on government officials and Southern leaders to co-operate in the emergency. The Southern political leaders stressed the need for adequate transportation, new markets, additional farm credit, and the "most cordial and unselfish cooperation" by farmers, merchants, and bankers in meeting the cotton depression.[27]

Smith and his associates then proceeded to seek concrete steps by which Congress might assist the cotton producers. One plan they proposed was an amendment to the Aldrich-Vreeland Act, to allow a portion of the emergency currency authorized by that law to be loaned directly to the holders of cotton warehouse receipts. On August 11 Smith introduced a joint resolution empowering the Secretary of the Treasury to advance currency on such notes, and three days later he presented to the Senate a comprehensive bill prepared by the cotton Congressmen in co-operation with Department of Agriculture officials to enable the Secretary to license cotton warehouses and thus facilitate borrowing against agricultural receipts. In mid-August Smith appeared before a cotton congress meeting in Washington, confidently predicting that Congress would provide assistance to

[27] *Cong. Record*, 63 Cong., 2 Sess., 13140, 13518; Atlanta *Journal*, August 2-6, 8-10, 1914.

the farmers. He also became a strong supporter of the "buy
a bale of cotton" movement, and he urged farmers to reduce their
next cotton crop by one half.[28]

The first problem mentioned by the Southern Congressmen
in their statement of early August, that of shipping facilities, did
not occupy much of their time. Congress soon passed a bill
amending the ship-registry law, in order to encourage foreign
ships to seek American registration. Speaking of ships, Smith
declared: "We will see to it that the American flag is floating
upon vessels prepared to carry our agricultural and manufactured
products . . . even though it be necessary for the government
to own the vessels." The bill to license agricultural warehouses
was the subject of more extended treatment. Smith called it up
in the Senate on August 18, and managed to get it passed a week
later. But the House failed to pass the measure during the second
session.[29]

September appeared to bring some improvement in the cotton
situation. Secretary McAdoo had agreed to issue Aldrich-Vreeland currency to national banks on the basis of short-term notes
secured by warehouse receipts for cotton. Smith appeared before
the Federal Reserve Board and conferred with the Comptroller
of the Currency about a scheme to allow state banks to issue
emergency currency under the Aldrich-Vreeland Act. He pointed
out that state banks were far closer to the farmers than were
the national banks, and that unless the state institutions could
obtain additional currency, the farmers would suffer. Early in
September the Georgia Senator offered an amendment in the
Senate that would extend the provisions of the Aldrich-Vreeland
Act to state banks, and a few days later it was adopted by the
upper house. Meanwhile, the "buy a bale of cotton" campaign
seemed to be making some progress, and other voluntary movements were being pushed in the South.[30]

[28] *Cong. Record*, 63 Cong., 2 Sess., 13571-72, 13734-35, 13840; Atlanta
Journal, August 11, 13, 14, 17, September 2, 1914.

[29] *Cong. Record*, 63 Cong., 2 Sess., 13902-13906, 14128-38, 14156-57, 14161-
69; Atlanta *Journal*, August 17, 20, 24, September 2, 1914.

[30] *Cong. Record*, 63 Cong., 2 Sess., 14721-32, 14894-96, 14903-14904, 14906,
14909-15, 14963, 14967-70, 14973, 14979; Atlanta *Journal*, August 26-30,
September 2, 10, 11, 13, 16, October 8, 1914.

Hoke Smith had never been busier. He attended endless conferences with members of both houses. Late in September the governors and other representatives of the Southern states met in Washington to confer with Southern Congressmen about the cotton crisis, and Smith was chosen temporary chairman of the group. The Senator from Georgia received an astonishing amount of mail from all over the South telling of a mounting crisis: "Farmers being compelled to sacrifice their cotton around 6 cents. . . . Many women and children in the South will suffer the coming winter for lack of food and clothing. . . . Conditions are infinitely worse than press finds expedient to publish. . . . The cotton market is now flat and approaching the 5-cent-per-pound level in the interior. . . . If something is not done soon we are ruined here. . . ." [31] So the letters went.

Early in October the cotton leaders decided to offer a bill in the House providing for $500,000,000 in greenbacks to be deposited in Southern banks by the Secretary of the Treasury for the purpose of making loans to cotton farmers at an interest of 3 per cent. This was good Populist legislation, but the Southerners were getting desperate. A short time later, a group of Senators meeting at Smith's home agreed to sponsor a more drastic measure based on a proposal of the Farmers' Union. It called for an issue of $250,000,000 in 4 per cent bonds with which to purchase five million bales of cotton at ten cents per pound. In mid-October Smith introduced the new cotton plan as an amendment to the revenue bill. "The whole business fabric of this section rests for its conduct upon a market for this crop," Smith reminded his Senate colleagues. The cotton farmers' plight was a question of the general welfare, "a war situation," he asserted, "as distressing and as serious as has ever been brought on by a flood in Ohio or a fire in Salem, Mass." The Southerners did not come as "mendicants," declared the Senator, but they needed credit, just as the reclamation work in the West and a railroad in Alaska needed Federal aid.[32]

[31] *Cong. Record*, 63 Cong., 2 Sess., 16504-16505, 16565.

[32] Smith's amendment also proposed a special excise tax of two cents per pound on cotton produced in 1915 in excess of 50 per cent of a farmer's crop in 1914. *Cong. Record*, 63 Cong., 2 Sess., 16594-95, 16633-39, 16695; New York *Times*, October 14, 15, 1914.

The administration was critical of the Smith amendment and of a similar plan sponsored in the House by Robert L. Henry. Senator McCumber voiced the feeling of many members of the upper house when he described Smith's proposal as a "mighty advance" toward paternalism. When the Southerners had finished their speeches, the amendment was rejected by a vote of 21 to 40. Smith was inconsolable. He impulsively moved to table the administration's tax bill. Senator James E. Martine of New Jersey called Smith's motion "unpatriotic," and Senator Williams declared that six or seven men should not be allowed to "stultify the party and to starve the Treasury." James K. Vardaman remained defiant, announcing that he would vote against the revenue bill. Smith would not go that far; he called the tax measure "wise and necessary" and said he would vote for its passage.[33]

The Southerners turned their attention to the House. Representative Henry made a stubborn fight, but in the end the various proposals for assisting the cotton farmers were defeated or buried in committee, and on October 22, the House passed a resolution to adjourn.

But Smith and his cohorts in the Senate had not given up. A "coterie" of Southern Senators, led by the Georgian, decided to resist adjournment until they obtained some of their legislative proposals. When the conference report on the revenue bill reached the Senate on the same day the House decided to adjourn, there was more discussion of the cotton crisis than of the conference report. "I am ashamed to go home," Smith declared. Unless Congress acted, "the speculator will get the cotton, and six or eight months hence it will be selling at 9 or 10 cents a pound . . . and the men who got it from the men who made it will earn a rich harvest . . . and we great statesmen will have the gratification of knowing that we did nothing!"[34]

The conference report was adopted on October 22, but Smith and a few other extremists prevented the Senate from adjourning

[33] *Cong. Record*, 63 Cong., 2 Sess., 16639-48, 16707-13, 16715, 16787, 16791, 16793-97, 16801; New York *Times*, October 15, 17, 1914.

[34] *Cong. Record*, 63 Cong., 2 Sess., 16909-15; Atlanta *Journal*, October 21, 22, 1914.

sine die until 6 P. M., the time fixed by the House resolution. On
the following day the filibuster continued. "Senator Hoke Smith
and his filibustering abettors," reproached the New York *Times*,
"seem determined to hurl back the foul imputation that the
Democratic Party has at last become a sane, coherent, and orderly
organization. . . ." By the time the Senate convened on October
24, the rebellious Southerners had agreed to cease their opposition
to adjournment. Smith again presented the cotton bond plan,
but it was obviously hopeless. "I have no apology and no regret
for the action which I have taken," he declared. ". . . My own
personal judgment would be to stay here, but I am almost alone
in that opinion." [35]

The relief measures in Congress failed, but Hoke Smith won
one point. Having been informed by cotton exporters that no
cotton was being shipped to North Europe because of the likeli-
hood that the ships would be seized by the British, the Georgia
Senator secured the approval of a resolution providing for the
appointment of five Senators to consult executive department
officers about shipping impediments. Smith was one of those
appointed, and he and the other four Senators conferred with
State Department officials who in turn took the matter up with
the British. Within a few days Foreign Minister Sir Edward
Grey had given his assurance that cotton was not on the British
contraband list and would not be seized.[36]

As Smith relaxed in Atlanta following the long and arduous
work of the first two sessions of the Sixty-third Congress, he had
less cause to feel expansive than he had during his triumphal
trip to the Macon convention only two months earlier. There
were whisperings and nodding of heads about his recent conduct.
Outside newspapers like the New York *Times* called his leadership "foolish" and described the recent filibuster as an inglorious
ending to the "unprecedented record" the Democratic Congress
had achieved. The Atlanta *Constitution* declared that Smith was

[35] *Cong. Record*, 63 Cong., 2 Sess., 16915-27, 16959-62, 16968-73; New York
Times, October 23-25, 1914.
[36] *Cong. Record*, 63 Cong., 2 Sess., 16904-16905; Atlanta *Journal*, October
26, 29, 1914; Smith to Robert Lansing, October 24, 1914, and Lansing to
Smith, October 26, 28, 1914, in State Department Papers.

maligning the South. Even the Atlanta *Journal* seemed unen-
thusiastic over the Senator's various proposals for Federal aid
during the latter part of the session.[37]

But Hoke Smith would not be deterred. He worked constantly
to improve the means of shipping cotton abroad, badgering the
State Department about all kinds of cotton problems. He introduced cotton merchants " to the German and Austrian ambassa-
dors " and " obtained clearances for vessels from the German
ambassador to German ports." Between December 1, 1914, and
March 1, 1915, Smith claimed, almost three million bales of cotton
were exported to German ports.[38]

The extent of Smith's preoccupation with the cotton situation
was revealed in his decision to oppose the La Follette seaman's
bill to improve the working conditions of American seamen. The
Georgia Senator had taken little part in the debate preceding
the measure's passage but suddenly, on February 27, 1915, after the
upper house had approved the conference report, he moved to
reconsider the Senate's action in agreeing to the report. It was
soon obvious that cotton was at the bottom of Smith's hostility
toward the bill: he thought the standards established by the legislation would interfere with foreign shipping in American ports
and make it more difficult for cotton to be exported. Everything
must give way to cotton. Senator La Follette replied to Smith's
criticisms of his bill and moved to table the Georgian's motion,
which was done.[39]

The chief incident in the third session was the struggle over
the ship-purchase bill, which occupied almost all of the Senate's
time in January and February, 1915. Because the war in Europe
had placed ships at a premium, President Wilson urged Congress
to provide the country with a fleet of government-owned vessels.
In the Senate caucus Smith opposed making the shipping bill a

[37] Atlanta *Journal*, August 17, October 14, 1914; New York *Times*, October
24, 25 (III), 1914; Atlanta *Constitution*, November 10, 1914.

[38] Smith to Lansing, November 10, December 22, 1914, and to Cone
Johnson, December 16, 1914; William Jennings Bryan to Smith, December
18, 1914; and F. M. Butt to Smith, December 20, 1914, in State Department
Papers; *Cong. Record*, 63 Cong., 3 Sess., 633, 962, 1013-14; Atlanta *Journal*,
February 22, 24, 1915.

[39] *Cong. Record*, 63 Cong., 3 Sess., 4811-17.

party measure. He offered an amendment to the administration plan, which he presented in the Senate on the following day, providing that ships acquired by the government should if possible be leased to private concerns at an interest rate of 4 per cent on the government's investment and an annual depreciation charge of 5 per cent.[40]

On February 1, Senator James P. Clarke, expressing concern that the rural credits bill and the appropriations bills had not been passed, startled his colleagues by moving to recommit the shipping bill to committee. Senator Duncan U. Fletcher, the measure's leading sponsor, raised a point of order against Clarke's motion, and the Vice-President upheld Fletcher. Clarke then appealed from the Vice-President's ruling, and the Senate refused to sustain the presiding officer. Smith and eight other Democrats voted with the majority. While the Democrats sought to re-form their battered lines, Smith and Nathan P. Bryan of Florida rejoined the party caucus; but seven of the Democratic recalcitrants refused to attend.[41]

Smith was embarrassed by his vote against Vice-President Marshall's ruling. Aware of the disappointment many of his friends in Georgia felt over his course, he issued a statement to the press and also spoke on the Senate floor in an effort to explain his position. The report that he opposed the shipping bill was "unfounded," asserted the Senator. "I have co-operated with the Democratic caucus in every way to support this measure, and I expect to continue to do so and I earnestly desire the legislation passed." As for his vote on the Clarke motion, he contended rather weakly that the rules of the Senate expressly provided that a motion to recommit a bill was in order at any time before the final action on the measure. This led the Macon *Telegraph* to observe that Smith cared little for "the niceties of parliamentary tangles." When the Senator realized what his vote meant, declared the *Telegraph*, "Hoke's tail dropped between his legs and he scuttled back home as fast as he could. . . ."[42]

[40] *Ibid.*, 1840, 2539-40, 2542; New York *Times*, January 19, 23, 1915.

[41] *Cong. Record*, 63 Cong., 3 Sess., 2786-87; Atlanta *Journal*, February 2, 1915.

[42] Atlanta *Journal*, January 17, February 2, 4, 1915; Macon *Telegraph*, February 6, 1915; *Cong. Record*, 63 Cong., 3 Sess., 2988.

When the Democrats finally reorganized their attack, the Republicans once more filibustered. Smith was steadfast in his support of the administration, although he admitted that he was sympathetic with some of the limiting amendments being offered. The bill failed to pass the Senate, and for the time being the administration's shipping plan was dead.[43]

Economic conditions in the cotton belt improved after the fall of 1914. The increased domestic consumption of cotton and the heavy sales to belligerents on both sides forced prices up. Then early in March, 1915, the British announced their blockade of the North European ports and began to seize cotton as conditional contraband. Hoke Smith soon began to receive information like this: "We are advised that Greek vessel SYYROS VALLIANOS sailing March 10 from Savannah to Rotterdam is being detained at Falmouth, England, cargo 14,000 bales cotton, cargo owned by Georgians, contracts all made for shipments prior to March 1 . . . ; will appreciate . . . investigation and cooperation to get release. . . ." [44] Smith was shocked. He gave up his plans to spend a vacation in Georgia following the adjournment of Congress on March 4, and held conferences with State Department officers and the British ambassador, pointing out Lord Grey's promise of the previous October. A few weeks later he warned the British and French to cease their infringements of his country's rights as a neutral. On March 30, the State Department sent a strong protest to the British.[45]

Momentarily, in April, Smith was optimistic. Then, early in May, the British seized several hundred thousand bales of cotton. Smith conferred at once with the President and Secretary Bryan. In a long letter to Bryan he reviewed the history of the British interferences and protested particularly against the detention of cargoes during March. Cotton exporters, relying on Grey's promise, had made contracts before March to ship large amounts

[43] *Cong. Record,* 63 Cong., 3 Sess., 3713-14, 4008-4009, 4011, 4015-17; Atlanta *Journal,* March 5, 29, 1915.

[44] Smith to the Secretary of State, April 8, 1915, in State Department Papers.

[45] Smith to Bryan, March 19, 1915, Bryan to Smith, March 26, 1915, and Lansing to Smith, April 10, 1915, in State Department Papers; Atlanta *Journal,* March 9, 29, April 28, 1915.

of cotton abroad.[46] During the weeks and months that followed, Smith and other Southern Congressmen repeatedly condemned the Allied blockade as a violation of international law. When the British delayed their answer to the American note of March 30, Smith issued a long statement, warning that "Unless this order is modified when Congress meets, the exportation of munitions of war will be stopped, and the action of Congress may go much further." [47]

Meanwhile, the rising tide of indignation in the United States at the German submarine campaign overwhelmed the protests of cotton spokesmen. Smith described the sinking of the *Lusitania* as one of "the most inhuman acts" of the war, but at the same time he noted that "It was an English vessel carrying munitions of war." If Great Britain "had given more attention to fighting German submarines and less to seizing vessels carrying cotton to neutral ports, some of the submarine attacks might have been avoided." [48]

In June Smith returned to Atlanta to spend the summer, but he did not cease his vigil on behalf of his cotton constituents. In numerous speeches, interviews, and communications to the State Department he complained about British interference with American shipping. Early in June he addressed a long letter to Postmaster General Albert S. Burleson, pleading with him to use his influence to secure vigorous action against the British interferences. "For two months past," Smith wrote, "I have given most of my time to the burdens placed upon the cotton growers and cotton exporters of the United States by the action of Great Britain and her Allies." This action was preventing the sale of over a million bales of cotton, contended the Senator, and was keeping the price low. He voiced a growing feeling of helplessness:

---

[46] Smith to Bryan, May 6, 1915, and Lansing to Smith, June 11, 16, 1915, in State Department Papers.

[47] Smith to the Secretary of State, May 13, July 22, 1915, to Cone Johnson, June 1, 1915, to Wilbur J. Carr, June 23, 1915, and to Lansing, July 26, 27, August 24, 1914, and Lansing to Smith, June 11, 1915, all in State Department Papers; Atlanta *Journal*, May 23, 1915.

[48] Atlanta *Journal*, May 8, 9, 1915; New York *Times*, May 9, 16 (II), 1915.

I am discouraged by my inability to obtain any real action from our Government. I am finally laying these facts before you as a representative in the Administration of the greatest cotton growing State in the Union. I cannot but feel that the apparent indifference is due to a failure by those in authority to grasp the gravity of the situation. . . .

It would be so easy for our Government to force Great Britain to recognize our neutral rights. Great Britain and her Allies are receiving to-day, I am assured, more than one-half of their munitions of war from this country. We need but to notify Great Britain these shipments will cease so long as Great Britain prevents shipments by citizens of the United States legal at the time the war began.[49]

Late in June, Smith addressed the General Assembly of Georgia in a long speech on the achievements of the Wilson administration and the British violations. "Every time Great Britain seizes a shipment of raw cotton from America to a neutral European port," he asserted, "she violates the rights of this nation. And she doesn't deny it."[50] Throughout the summer the Senator smarted under the administration's refusal to take a stronger stand against the Allies. He reminded Georgians that the President had done nothing since dispatching the March note of protest. He told a convention of merchants in New York, "I have determined that the only thing to do is to tell Great Britain to revoke the blockade order, or she can have no neutral trade with us."[51]

One development during the summer of 1915 must have caused Hoke Smith to consider the probable consequences of the course he was pursuing so vigorously. This was the open break between the Senator and the Atlanta *Journal* over the cotton question in particular and the international situation in general. The *Journal*, which had been Smith's pilot for so long and which had carried favorable articles about his every move for years, reduced its news about him drastically, following the filibuster in October,

[49] Smith to Burleson, June 7, 1915, in Albert Sidney Burleson Papers (Division of Manuscripts, Library of Congress).

[50] Atlanta *Journal*, June 30, July 1, 1915.

[51] *Speech of the Honorable Hoke Smith . . . at a meeting of Importers and Exporters held . . . at the Hotel Biltmore, New York City, August 11, 1915* (n. p., n. d.), in Smith Collection.

1914. The Atlanta paper's open opposition to Smith's campaign against the British came in a long editorial on August 13, 1915, under the heading "Senator Smith's Mistake." The immediate impetus for the editorial was Smith's forceful address two days before in New York. "In their views on most matters of State and national concern," began the *Journal*, "Senator Hoke Smith, and The Journal have been in hearty accord. It is, therefore, with distinct regret but with emphatic conviction that we demur to the Senator's present attitude toward the issues arising from European encroachments upon American sea rights, and toward the Administration's treatment of those issues." More than dollars and cents was involved, asserted the *Journal*: The European war was "a life and death struggle between democratic government and Prussian autocracy." The *Journal* chose "English liberty."

In August the British decided to classify cotton as absolute contraband. Smith issued a strong protest; the British order was an "act of lawlessness to be expected from a nation which for nearly six months has blockaded neutral ports." [52]

Meanwhile, early in August, the editor and the owner of the Providence, Rhode Island, *Journal* made a startling statement to Colonel House while discussing German propaganda. "They said," House wrote in his diary, "Hoke Smith was undoubtedly in the pay of the German embassy. They do not dare publish this until they can get positive proof of money being passed, because they fear criminal prosecution and damages." [53] These rumors of Smith's financial involvement in the cotton fight were never published, and there is no evidence of their validity. Some years later the Georgian's name came up in connection with the work of the American Embargo Conference, the statement having been made in 1915 that the conference had the "moral support of such men as Senators HITCHCOCK, WORKS, AND HOKE SMITH." In 1918 Smith denied ever having had any "relations, dealings, or communications of any character with it or its members." He had known of the rumors that he was trying "to help the Germans," asserted Smith, but he "was entirely in-

[52] New York *Times*, August 25, September 13, 18, 1915.
[53] Edward M. House diary, August 2, 10, 1915, in House Collection (Yale University Library).

different to the Germans." He "was moved solely" by his conviction that the rights of American citizens "were being illegally disregarded," and especially by the suffering of his "constituents who raised cotton." [54]

The agitation of men like Smith probably persuaded the English that some concessions must be made to the cotton men. In August, 1915, the British reached an informal understanding with American authorities whereby they promised to maintain the price of cotton at ten cents a pound. They arranged to buy large quantities of the staple on the exchange.[55] Smith was immediately aware of the English strategy, but he continued to demand that they revoke their Orders in Council.

Smith had awaited impatiently the convocation of the first session of the Sixty-fourth Congress in December, 1915, having several times implied that the legislative branch would take decisive action against the British restrictions if the executive would not. "There is no limit to what Congress can do to meet this blockade," the Senator told reporters on the first day of the session. On the following day he inserted in the *Congressional Record* a list of the ships and cargoes seized or detained by the British. He also introduced a resolution citing the action of the Allies in "virtually blockading the neutral ports of northern Europe" and requesting the Senate Committee on Foreign Relations "to investigate the subject and to suggest to the Senate the action, if any, they may deem advisable." [56]

The Smith resolution precipitated a sharp debate in the Senate on December 10. In speaking for his resolution, the Georgia Senator emphasized the steady encroachment of the British orders on the rights of neutrals. He indicted the British by citing their own learned writers and court decisions. Smith contended that the English were selling goods similar to those seized from American vessels to the very ports they were blockading, and he argued that there was no rule of international law to justify the doctrine

[54] *Cong. Record*, 65 Cong., 3 Sess., 444-45.

[55] Arthur S. Link, "The Cotton Crisis, the South, and Anglo-American Diplomacy, 1914-1915," in J. Carlyle Sitterson (ed.), *Studies in Southern History* (Chapel Hill, 1957), 137-38.

[56] *Cong. Record*, 64 Cong., 1 Sess., 71-73, 94; New York *Times*, December 7, 8, 1915.

of continuous voyage. He said that Germany had always "been a friend of the United States" and that many good Americans "love their Fatherland only second to . . . our own country."[57]

Henry Cabot Lodge took the floor to offer an amendment to Smith's resolution providing that the committee should also investigate the sinking of the *Lusitania* and six other German submarine attacks. "The body of an innocent child, floating dead on the water, the victim of destruction of an unarmed vessel, is to me a more poignant and a more tragic spectacle than an unsold bale of cotton," declared Lodge. Smith answered by charging that some Americans had sought for months to divert attention from Great Britain's commercial violations by "holding up the *Lusitania* and the horrors of certain losses of life." He had no objection to the Massachusetts Senator's amendment, said Smith, though he objected to the effort to "load it down with a sentimentalism which appeals to every man with a drop of blood in his veins." Senator Thomas J. Walsh of Montana, who spoke against the British interference with copper exports, declared that Smith was "entitled to the thanks of the country for the lucid exposition" he had presented.[58]

Smith's resolution was adopted with Lodge's amendment. On the following day Lodge wrote Theodore Roosevelt that several men "were good enough to say that in five minutes I had killed a speech on which Smith had spent eight months."[59]

The Senator from Georgia denounced British "lawlessness" again in an address before the Southern Commercial Congress in mid-December, and he continued to urge the State Department to adopt more aggressive tactics in dealing with the British. His last major effort in the cotton crusade came in a Senate debate on January 20, 1916, when he repeated the long argument he had made so many times before and presented an elaborate discussion to prove that the Germans were no longer using cotton

[57] *Cong. Record*, 64 Cong., 1 Sess., 138-43.

[58] *Ibid.*, 144-45.

[59] Henry Cabot Lodge (ed.), *Selections from the Correspondence of Theodore Roosevelt and Henry Cabot Lodge: 1884-1918* (New York, 1925), II, 467.

in the manufacture of explosives.[60] For a short time early in 1916 Smith seemed to toy with the idea of an embargo—the New York *Times* referred to him as "that ululant Georgian Cotton Democrat and boiling embargoist"—but it was soon apparent that there was no real chance to pass such a resolution. He continued to insert an occasional protest in the *Record*, and he delivered a robust attack on the British blacklist announced in the summer of 1916.[61] But by early 1916 Smith's long battle was over.

Smith realized, apparently, the futility of further struggle. Few of his proposals had been adopted, yet the price of cotton rose steadily in the wake of increased Allied purchases and greater domestic demand, and by the fall of 1916 he no longer seemed concerned about commercial restrictions. The Senator was aware of the opposition his aggressive campaign had brought in Georgia. The Augusta *Chronicle*, for instance, said of Smith early in 1916: "He is disloyal to the American people from whom he comes in that his voice has been raised only for money, never a word as to the right or wrong of this way, never a word as to any obligation on our part to set our faces against the butchery of innocents on the high seas—only that we must move heaven and earth to get our cotton into Germany."[62] The fact that 1916 was an election year probably led Smith to moderate his criticisms of the administration's diplomacy. Furthermore, he was anxious to secure the passage of the vocational education bill, and he needed the support of the administration and of Congress to be successful.

For eighteen months—from August, 1914, until January, 1916—Smith made the cotton crusade his major concern. He was but one of many Southern Congressmen who criticized the British restrictions, of course, and the movement he led formed a part of a broader protest by Americans against the Allied treatment of neutrals and of the hostility toward the British by Irish-

---

[60] Smith to Lansing, January 10, 15, 1916, in State Department Papers; *Cong. Record*, 64 Cong., 1 Sess., 1187-88, 1295-1311; Atlanta *Journal*, December 18, 1915.

[61] *Cong. Record*, 64 Cong., 1 Sess., 1621, 2196, 11517; New York *Times*, February 5, March 8, August 9, 1916.

[62] Quoted in New York *Times*, February 5, 1916.

Americans and others. But it is clear that Smith was primarily motivated by his anxiety about the distress in the cotton belt. Perhaps he was sorry in after years that the struggle had been followed with such single-minded purpose. For it disrupted his work along other lines in the Senate and undermined old friendships and political loyalties, not to mention the irritation it caused in his relations with the administration. But Hoke Smith was not a man to look back; if he had any regrets he did not publicize them.

Preparedness and Politics

When the first session of the Sixty-fourth Congress convened at noon on December 6, 1915, Hoke Smith formally began the six-year term to which he had been elected in 1914.[1] The Senator's attention was focused on the British trade violations but a different, though related, issue had arisen to dominate Congressional proceedings. This was the administration's preparedness program. During the following fifteen months military measures and neutrality problems became increasingly important. During this period, moreover, a national election occurred, and the final domestic reforms sponsored by the Wilson administration were enacted.

Before the administration's preparedness legislation could be acted upon, Woodrow Wilson's leadership was challenged by a strong movement in Congress to prevent Americans from taking passage on the armed ships of belligerents. Resolutions warning American citizens against traveling on armed belligerent ships were introduced in the House of Representatives by Jeff: Mc-Lemore and in the Senate by Thomas P. Gore. A great debate was soon under way in both houses. Hoke Smith took little part in this debate, but there is reason to believe that he sympathized with the proposal of his friend Gore. In February, when relations between the United States and Germany deteriorated further as a result of the unsettled *Lusitania* negotiations, Smith declared: "I regret deeply that law heretofore has not provided against

[1] Smith asked to be replaced on the Democratic steering committee, but he retained his position on the following standing committees: Education and Labor, Agriculture and Forestry, Finance, Judiciary, and Rules.

the carrying of human life and death dealing ammunition on one and the same ship and that, therefore, our citizens had the right to travel on the ill-fated Lusitania." [2]

It was soon apparent that the situation in Congress imperiled the President's diplomacy, and he acted swiftly to counter the Gore-McLemore movement. In an open letter to William J. Stone, chairman of the Senate Committee on Foreign Relations, Wilson reiterated his determination to keep the nation out of war, but he declared that he would not consent to " any abridgement of the rights of American citizens." With the publication of the President's letter, the support for Gore and McLemore began to wane, and Wilson soon felt strong enough to risk a vote on the resolutions. When the Gore resolution was tabled on March 3, Smith was one of the Senators who upheld the administration. [3]

In the meantime, the administration's fight to enact its preparedness measures had begun. The President's program called for a substantial increase in the regular army, the strengthening of the National Guard, the creation of a reserve army of 400,000 men, and an equally ambitious expansion of the navy. A number of Congressional leaders soon made known their opposition to the preparedness program, and one of the great crises in Wilson's leadership had arisen.

Smith was critical of several features of the defense legislation, but he announced his faith in preparedness early in the debate. [4] He urged that the regular army be increased to 250,000 men. While Senators like Vardaman referred to the proposed army increase as the possible " tombstone of republicanism in America," the Georgian saw no " serious danger of militarism " in the military plans. He joined five other Southerners in voting for the 250,000 men decided upon by the Senate. [5] The administration's proposal to strengthen the National Guard also elicited Smith's endorsement. But he insisted that National Guard troops were

[2] New York *Times*, February 12, 1916.

[3] *Cong. Record*, 64 Cong., 1 Sess., 3464-65; Atlanta *Journal*, March 5, 1916.

[4] *Cong. Record*, 64 Cong., 1 Sess., 4005, 4370-71, 4374-75, 4377-78, 5217, 5227, 9992, 9994; New York *Times*, March 16, 1916.

[5] *Cong. Record*, 64 Cong., 1 Sess., 6334, 6342-45, 6356-57, 6359.

primarily state troops and that the recommended "Federaliza-tion" plan would not change this fact. He opposed Senator James W. Wadsworth's amendment designed to clarify the mean-ing of this feature of the National Defense bill, and he lashed out at the provision requiring soldiers in the Guard to agree to serve outside of the United States. This was an effort to make such troops "contract in disregard of limited power conferred on Congress by the Constitution," contended Smith.[6] In the end the Georgia Senator and other critics of this section of the bill were defeated, and the measure authorized the War Department to supervise the enlistment, equipping, and training of the National Guard.

Hoke Smith's strongest fire was directed at Secretary of War Lindley M. Garrison's proposal for a large reserve force to be known as the Continental Army. The opposition to this part of the administration's program was so strong in the House that President Wilson had been forced to accept Garrison's resigna-tion and to agree to a House bill without the reserve army provision. Smith had no faith in reserve soldiers, referring to them on one occasion as "30-day excursionists." In spite of the opposition of Smith and others, however, the Continental Army plan was approved by the Senate. After a long controversy between the two houses, a compromise was finally worked out whereby the Senate gave up the Continental Army scheme, a concession that pleased Smith.[7]

One reason for Smith's interest in preparedness was his desire to commit the Federal government to the support of vocational education; he saw in the administration's defense legislation an opportunity to advance the principle of vocational training. On February 17, he introduced an amendment to the army reorgani-zation bill, providing for an educational program of ninety-six hours per month "not directly connected with military service, and preparatory to their [the soldiers'] return to civil life." After the House passed the army bill on March 23, and its version was sent to the Senate, Smith moved to amend it by adding his

[6] *Ibid.*, 6132-34, 6187, 6203, 6212, 6374-75.
[7] *Ibid.*, 5161, 5232, 5355, 5358, 5360, 6034-35; New York *Times*, April 4, 1916.

vocational training plan. "There is no question of greater importance for our national life," he asserted, "than the better preparation of our young men for the work in which they will engage." [8]

Smith claimed "no novelty" for his proposal. He cited the fact that such army leaders as General Leonard Wood had endorsed vocational education for soldiers, and he called attention to the success of a limited training program in the Coast Artillery. Early in April the Senator modified his amendment to provide for seventy-five hours of educational instruction per month, and Senator George E. Chamberlain, who was in charge of the army bill, then agreed to accept it. As finally worked out in the conference between the two houses, Smith's provision was watered down to a general requirement that vocational instruction would be available for enlisted men in the regular army in accordance with rules devised by the Secretary of War. But Hoke Smith's principle had been adopted—to enable soldiers "to return to civil life better equipped for industrial, commercial, and general business occupations." [9]

Another aspect of the national defense bill that interested Smith was the authorization of a government plant to manufacture synthetic nitrates. The Georgian had earlier demonstrated an interest in Federal legislation to provide some supervision of the allocation of interstate water-power sites, and he had discussed the "potash situation" with Senate colleagues and with Department of Agriculture officials. [10] Although Smith could see the need for constructing a nitrate plant, he was disturbed by the prospect of government ownership and operation of the proposed plant. The charge that the measure was "socialistic" did not worry him, he said; it was not "a question of principle, but a question of business." He supported both a limiting amendment offered by Hardwick and Underwood's effort to amend the bill

[8] *Cong. Record*, 64 Cong., 1 Sess., 2683, 4181, 4427, 5164, 5227; Atlanta *Journal*, February 17, 1916.

[9] *Cong. Record*, 64 Cong., 1 Sess., 5227-30, 5359-62, 5624-28; New York *Times*, April 8, 1916.

[10] Smith to David F. Houston, April 3, 1916, and Houston to Smith, April 4, 1916, in Department of Agriculture Papers; *Cong. Record*, 64 Cong., 1 Sess., 3180-83, 3758, 3998.

by providing for the leasing of the nitrate and power facilities
in time of peace, but neither was successful. After that he supported the nitrate plant provision as it passed the Senate. Whatever would benefit the farmer " as a broad proposition of national
statesmanship," Smith averred, would receive his backing.[11]

In March, 1916, the Senator from Georgia joined most other
Southern Senators in supporting Benjamin R. Tillman's bill for
the construction of a government armor-plate plant. When the
Senate finally got around to considering the naval features of
the administration's preparedness program, Smith voted for the
big-navy bill that eventually passed both houses. He also lent
his support to the administration's new merchant marine bill,
which was introduced early in 1916 as a part of the preparedness
program. The Senator approved of the point emphasized by the
measure's sponsors that the merchant ships would be useful as
auxiliary vessels for the navy in case of war. " The whole scheme
involves an effort to broaden the commerce of the United States,"
he declared, " to give it a chance to go to the world." [12]

Another question closely related to the preparedness legislation
was the revenue bill of 1916, which in many ways marked a
dividing line between older, more conservative tax policies and
newer, progressive demands that taxes be apportioned in accordance with ability to pay. As a member of the Senate Finance
Committee, Smith spent considerable time working on the new
revenue bill. When it reached the Senate floor in late summer,
he was in charge of those sections dealing with special taxes,
documentary stamp taxes, and the proposed tariff commission.[18]

Smith's advocacy of the tariff commission, which was eventually
incorporated in the Revenue Act of 1916, led him into a spirited
debate with Senator Underwood, who accused his party of having
accepted the Republican philosophy on the tariff. Underwood
also opposed the imposition of a tariff on dyestuffs, which Smith
defended. The Alabama Senator referred to his colleague from

[11] Cong. Record, 64 Cong., 1 Sess., 5711-12, 5932-34, 5967, 6035-37, 6108-
6109.
[12] Ibid., 4553, 11384, 12627-31.
[18] Ibid., 13273, 13408-10, 13413, 13748-50; Arthur S. Link, Woodrow Wilson
and the Progressive Era, 1910-1917 (New York, 1954), 192-96.

Georgia as the "leader of this sentiment in his party" and criticized him for writing "on the statute books a high protective tariff." Smith replied that the party should not be "tied down to past tariff bills," and that the creation of the tariff commission was "one of the many proofs that the Democratic party is today progressive, ready to meet wisely any emergency that may come upon the country." [14]

At about the same time that he was criticizing certain parts of the administration's preparedness program, Hoke Smith came close to voting against Wilson's choice for a Supreme Court vacancy. The President had selected Louis D. Brandeis to replace Justice Joseph R. Lamar, who had died in January, 1916, and the forces opposed to "the people's attorney," including the business community and some of the most respectable men in public life and in the legal profession, immediately began a campaign of opposition. As a member of the Judiciary Committee, the Senator from Georgia was drawn into the bitter controversy surrounding the nomination of Brandeis. Not only were the Republicans on the committee against the appointment, but according to newspaper reports, Democratic Senators Smith, Reed, O'Gorman, and John K. Shields were also hostile to the selection.

The Judiciary Committee began consideration of the Brandeis appointment late in January, but a special subcommittee held lengthy hearings, and even after this group's favorable recommendation to the full committee the proceedings dragged on. Senator Lee S. Overman informed the Senate late in April that some committeemen were still investigating "three or four serious charges" against Brandeis. "I say frankly for myself," Hoke Smith declared at the same time, "that there never has been a time that I have been ready to vote for a report favorable to Mr. Brandeis." [15]

Smith and Hardwick had earlier voted against the confirmation of George L. Rublee as a member of the Federal Trade Commission when Senator Gallinger invoked the time-honored Sena-

[14] *Cong. Record*, 64 Cong., 1 Sess., 13415-16, 13864-68; New York *Times*, August 15, 16, 27, 1916.
[15] *Cong. Record*, 64 Cong., 1 Sess., 6972, 9032.

torial courtesy. Smith seemed to have genuine doubt as to Brandeis' fitness for the court. Furthermore, he harbored some resentment against the President for having grown cool toward him during the course of the cotton crusade. " Smith feels keenly that you did not consult any of the democratic members of the Judiciary Committee about the nomination . . . ," Henry Morgenthau wrote Wilson in mid-May. " He also stated that since January he has not been at the White House for conference." According to Morgenthau, who had recently talked to Smith, the Georgian and " some of the other Senators have been nursing their discontent so long that it may become chronic—while now— a few soothing words from you will produce a prompt cure." [16] Wilson was " willing to do anything " within reason, but he was doubtful about Smith. " I think the matter goes deep with him," wrote the President sorrowfully, " and is uncurable, having been born with him. . . ." [17]

Wilson had already made a move calculated to get action in the Judiciary Committee. Early in May he wrote a forthright and vigorous letter to Chairman Charles A. Culberson defending his appointment. Wilson's letter, the approaching national elections, and the status of some legislation he was sponsoring caused Hoke Smith to hesitate, as did the support for Brandeis from Georgia and other states. The Atlanta *Journal*, for instance, urged the lawyer's confirmation, describing it as a " test of the loyalty and statesmanship" of the Democratic Senators. Labor unions in Georgia also recommended that Brandeis be confirmed. By May 22, Smith was " much mollified," having had an opportunity to talk to Brandeis. He even promised to use his influence to carry Senator Shields along. " My investigation has convinced me that Mr. Brandeis is an honest, conscientious, able lawyer," the Georgia

---

[16] Henry Morgenthau to Wilson, May 18, 1916, in Wilson Papers.

Late in 1921, in an article in *World's Work*, Morgenthau claimed that he had been requested by Wilson to talk to Smith about the Brandeis confirmation. In a letter to the editor of this magazine, Smith denied having discussed the matter with Morgenthau, calling the latter's article " interesting but imaginative." Henry Morgenthau, " All in a Life-Time, Chapters From an Autobiography, V. The Campaign of 1916," in *World's Work*, XLIII (December, 1921), 140-41; Smith to editor of *World's Work*, December 30, 1921, in Smith Collection.

[17] Wilson to Morgenthau, May 19, 1916, in Wilson Papers.

Senator declared, "and that his great purpose in public service has been to do good." The Judiciary Committee voted to recommend Brandeis' confirmation on May 24, by a vote of 10 to 8, and a week later the Senate confirmed the appointment.[18]

During the early years of the New Freedom Hoke Smith had little difficulty in reconciling his liberal professions and the Wilson administration's moderate progressivism. But as the administration began to translate its progressive ideals into social welfare and labor legislation, the Georgian's inner conservatism seemed to assert itself more emphatically and to make him more and more critical of advanced industrial reforms. This was particularly the case with respect to labor legislation.

Although Smith had been one of those most responsible for the failure of the Sutherland compensation bill in 1913, he supported the liability act of 1914. In July, 1916, Smith himself reported another compensation measure—the Kern-McGillicuddy bill—from the Committee on Education and Labor with a recommendation that it be enacted. But he had persuaded the committee to accept an amendment to provide "some lessening of the compensation to the man whose own negligence brings on the casualty." Senators Kern, Cummins, and Walsh all sought to demonstrate the backwardness of the "contributory negligence" principle. But Smith announced that his views had "matured" on the subject; there should be "some stimulus and some reward" for vigilance and care. As he said: "I think we are drifting in our philanthropic purpose to serve humanity into the danger of a failure entirely to recognize the differences between men. In our public schools our greatest trouble is that we mass the pupils and give little chance for the brighter to advance more rapidly. . . . I think the danger lies in disregarding the opportunities of men. . . . There is a humanitarian side to this view, but there is also a dangerous side to it." The Senator realized that his amendment had no chance, and following its defeat he expressed his "entire sympathy" for the bill and joined with Kern in pushing it through the upper house.[19]

---

[18] Atlanta *Journal*, May 16, 22, 1916; Alpheus Thomas Mason, *Brandeis, A Free Man's Life* (New York, 1946), 503-504.

[19] *Cong. Record*, 64 Cong., 1 Sess., 12166-67, 12887-96, 12900, 12902, 13670, 13739.

In 1914 and 1916, Smith revealed his opposition to the United
States Commission on Industrial Relations when he criticized
the commission for investigating matters over which it had no
jurisdiction and for presenting distorted information about conditions in the South.[20] In spite of his earlier work for child-labor
legislation in Georgia, he also opposed the administration's child-
labor bill in 1916.

Smith seemed to agree with a resolution adopted by the Georgia
Manufacturers' Association which condemned the proposed Federal child-labor act as a "strained interpretation" of the Constitution and a threat to "State jurisdiction over local enterprises."
The Senator was afraid that if Congress interpreted the commerce
clause so broadly as to prohibit the production of goods in which
child labor was used, "practically anything produced in a State"
could be similarly regulated. Following a conference with President Wilson on July 24, the Georgian was quoted as saying
that he was inclined to support the measure, but a few days later
he expressed his determination to vote against it. Yet he had
opposed dilatory tactics in the recent Senate caucus, and it was
on his motion that the caucus was polled and found to be strongly
for the child-labor bill. He regarded obstruction as futile and
felt that "the Democratic party should reap whatever political
benefit it could." The Senate passed the bill early in August,
but Smith joined several other Southerners in voting against it.[21]

When faced with the prospect of a breakdown in the nation's
rail system because of a threatened strike by the railroad brother-
hoods late in the summer of 1916, the Wilson administration
sponsored the Adamson bill, which imposed an eight-hour day
for all workers engaged in interstate railroad work. Smith had
earlier endorsed the eight-hour principle, and he now gave his
support to the Adamson plan. Pointing to his long record of
service to railroad laborers, he declared: "Mr. President, for
more than 30 years my relations with the men in my State who
operate railroad trains have been most intimate. They have been

[20] *Ibid.*, 63 Cong., 2 Sess., 11681-84, 11687-90, 11700-11701; 64 Cong., 1 Sess.,
6274-77.

[21] *Cong. Record*, 64 Cong., 1 Sess., 2680, 12089-90, 12313; Atlanta *Journal*,
July 24, 30, 1916; New York *Times*, August 9, 1916.

my personal friends at my home, my clients, my political supporters. I think I have drawn or helped prepare practically every
amendment to our laws in Georgia for the past 25 years intended
to better their conditions." Yet no matter "how rightful might
be their claims against managers of the roads," asserted the
Senator, "when the 90 per cent of the people . . . who are
disconnected with the railroads, feel the grinding heel of suffering
that this strike will bring, they will not forgive the men who
bring it on them." [22]

Among the factors that persuaded Hoke Smith to make a
determined effort to co-operate with the administration was the
approaching election. During the summer of 1916, the Southerner
became one of the arch defenders of the Democratic record and
a constant tormentor of his Republican colleagues in the Senate.[23]

When it was reported in March, 1916, that the German-American Alliance intended to use its influence in the coming elections
and that certain Congressmen had already been used by a German
lobby, Smith was careful to state publicly that he knew nothing
about any German lobby.[24] A few weeks later a group of dissident
Democrats in California, evidently influenced by Irish-American
and German-American organizations in that state, indicated their
intention to use the Georgian's name as a Presidential candidate
in the election of delegates to the National Democratic Convention. Smith immediately sent the California secretary of state a
telegram declaring that "No individual or political organization
has authority to use my name for this purpose. Am supporting
the renomination of President Wilson." But in Georgia the
Senator's enemies set up a hue and cry about his alleged perfidy
to the party. "Hoch der Hoke!" exclaimed the Macon *Telegraph*. According to the *Telegraph*, Hoke Smith was the "high
priest and prophet" and the ideal embodiment of "the treason-
able, treacherous attacks being made within his party on the
President of the United States." [25]

[22] *Cong. Record*, 64 Cong., 1 Sess., 13402-13403, 13655; New York *Times*,
August 31, September 2, 3, 1916.
[23] *Cong. Record*, 64 Cong., 1 Sess., 11159-61, 12423-25, 12523-24, 13084-88,
13504-10.
[24] New York *Times*, March 8, 1916.
[25] Atlanta *Journal*, April 11, 1916; Macon *Telegraph*, April 11, 12, 1916.

In mid-September, following the adjournment of Congress, the Smiths visited Atlanta. After delivering a few addresses in Georgia, the Senator went to Chicago to work in the party's Western headquarters and to make campaign speeches in Missouri, Indiana, and Ohio. Late in October he returned to complete the campaign in his own state. Smith presented an elaborate review of the Democratic record, emphasizing the New Freedom legislation and calling particular attention to the long list of agricultural and educational measures recently enacted. He painted a glowing picture of a Southern future undergirded by shipping, diversified agriculture, and industry, pointing out the relationship between a prosperous South and the Wilson legislation.[26]

Smith praised Woodrow Wilson as the "greatest leader who has occupied the White House in fifty years." He admitted that he had not always agreed with the President, "but at no time," he declared, "have I ever failed to appreciate his sound judgment and foresight." Like other party stalwarts on the election line across the country, the Southerner made much of the President's "peace with honor" diplomacy. It was "Wilson's pen" that had "kept the country out of war," declared Smith, who said Americans would "understand that Wilson kept their sons at home instead of sending them to the war as food for cannon." [27]

Hoke Smith could feel some satisfaction in the Democratic victory of 1916, but he had less cause to be pleased with the election results in Georgia. The truth was that the Smith faction had been unable to present a strong leader to replace Smith within the state, and apparently the Senator had allowed his organization to deteriorate as he concerned himself with Congressional matters. In 1916 the governorship was captured by Hugh M. Dorsey, a vigorous young representative of the anti-Smith element. Dorsey was supported by Tom Watson, who was bitterly opposed to President Wilson. Yet at the state convention Dorsey endorsed Wilson and significantly attacked Smith for not giving the President "the co-operation and support he deserves." [28]

[26] Atlanta *Journal*, September 17, 21, 29, October 19, 21-26, 1916.
[27] *Ibid.*, September 17, 29, October 25-27, 1916.
[28] *Ibid.*, September 8, 26, 29, 1916.

During the second session of the Sixty-fourth Congress, which convened in December, 1916, Smith helped pass the Burnett immigration bill, providing for a literacy test, over the President's veto. A consistent Senate advocate of Federal prohibition legislation, he gave vigorous support to the District of Columbia prohibition bill which passed the upper house in January, 1917.[29] Smith was particularly interested during this session in a bill proposing a radical change in the retirement system for Federal judges and in the adoption of a cloture resolution.

Following his appointment to the Judiciary Committee in 1914, Smith began to give more attention to legislation affecting the courts. In December, 1914, he introduced a bill recommended by the Justice Department that would authorize the President to appoint an additional district and circuit court judge for every such incumbent judge who, having reached the retirement age of seventy, failed to retire.[30] The Georgia Senator reported the bill favorably from the Judiciary Committee in February, 1915, but he was unable to secure its passage until late 1916.

In the Senate debate on the measure at that time and subsequently, the Republicans vigorously attacked the plan and challenged its constitutionality, referring to it as an administration scheme to pad the Federal courts. Smith and other supporters of the bill contended that it would improve the efficiency of many Federal courts and enable some judges of retirement age to continue on a part-time basis. It was neither a constitutional nor a partisan question, asserted Smith, who endeavored to prove by citing numerous precedents that it would be a proper delegation of Congressional authority to the President. He also emphasized the fact that several attempts to provide an additional judge for the Fifth Circuit, "where a judge had been bedridden for five or six years," had failed.[31]

In December, 1916, after agreeing to accept Senator Cummins' amendment to authorize the President to appoint additional judges

[29] *Cong. Record*, 63 Cong., 3 Sess., 851-55, 1623; 64 Cong., 2 Sess., 1054-56, 1065-66, 1166-70.

[30] James C. McReynolds to Smith, July 24, 1913, in Department of Justice Papers (National Archives); *Cong. Record*, 63 Cong., 3 Sess., 490, 2839, 4395.

[31] *Cong. Record*, 63 Cong., 3 Sess., 4394-97; 64 Cong., 1 Sess., 2684-88, 3844-45, 4675-80, 4999-5000, 5093-98, 11274-75; 64 Cong., 2 Sess., 42-46, 89-90.

only "If he finds that any such judge is unable to discharge the duties of his office by reason of mental or physical ailments of permanent character," Smith was able to get the bill passed by a vote of 33 to 25. But the House failed to approve the measure.[32] A modified version of the Smith bill finally passed both houses in 1919.

After the fiasco over the shipping bill early in 1915, Democratic Senators began to consider the possibility of adopting a cloture rule, but they found it difficult to reach any agreement on the subject. Nothing happened until a proposal by Hoke Smith in March, 1916, revived the question. Smith had long been irritated at certain Senate rules, particularly some of the practices concerning unanimous-consent agreements. In mid-March, 1916, he proposed the following amendment to Senate Rule XXII:

> If 32 Senators present to the Senate, before the reports of standing and select committees provided for in the order of business during the morning hour, a signed motion to bring to a close the debate upon a bill which is the unfinished business, thereupon, at the hour of 2 o'clock, the Chair shall, without debate, put the question to the Senate:
> "Is it the sense of the Senate that the debate shall be brought to a close?"

If two thirds of those present voted in the affirmative, the bill would be in order, and thereafter no Senator could speak more than one hour on the measure.[33]

Two months later Smith reported a substitute cloture proposal from the Rules Committee, announcing that the committee had "harmonized on this rule." But the Senate took no action on the resolution during that session. In December, 1916, the Georgian again urged the adoption of the cloture resolution, but it was

---

[32] Smith's enemies in Georgia assiduously tried to promote friction between Federal Judge William T. Newman and the Senator, alleging that Smith's bill had been aimed at Newman. The Senator denied this in a public statement, pointing out that Newman had first suggested the need for some such legislation. *Cong. Record*, 64 Cong., 1 Sess., 307, 317, 489; 2 Sess., 18-19, 90-92, 94, 99; Atlanta *Journal*, January 15, February 13, 18, 1917.

[33] *Cong. Record*, 64 Cong., 1 Sess., 4051, 4111; Atlanta *Journal*, March 19, 1916.

not until after the armed-ship filibuster that the Senate acted.[34]
In March, 1917, during the special session of the Senate, Thomas
S. Martin introduced a resolution on behalf of a bipartisan committee and with President Wilson's support that provided for
a cloture rule along the same lines as the resolution reported by
Smith the previous May. Smith, who opposed "a majority
cloture," was a member of the group that sponsored the Martin
resolution, and he called it "a splendid rule." After some perfunctory debate, the resolution was approved by a vote of 76
to 3.[35]

During the early months of 1917, a sharp struggle between the
two Georgia Senators and the Wilson administration was taking
shape behind the scenes. The differences between Thomas W.
Hardwick and the administration—and to some extent those between Hoke Smith and the administration—were fundamental in
origin, having their roots in disagreements over domestic legislation and certain features of the President's preparedness program
and diplomacy. But the immediate cause of the dispute in 1917
was the appointment of a Federal judge for the Southern district
of Georgia.[36]

Senator Hardwick considered it to be his prerogative to recommend a successor to Judge William Wallace Lambdin, who died
in December, 1916, and he soon decided upon John T. West
of Thomson, Georgia, a vigorous opponent of Tom Watson.
Smith was inclined to favor the selection of Thomas S. Felder,
whom Hardwick had defeated for the Senate in 1914, but he
acquiesced in the choice of West. Meanwhile, early in 1917, the
two Senators were "being deluged with letters and telegrams
concerning the judgeship." Smith and Hardwick conferred
several times with Wilson and Attorney General Thomas W.
Gregory to urge West's appointment, but the administration
finally decided not to appoint him, ostensibly because of his
advanced age but more likely because of the strong pressure

[34] *Cong. Record,* 64 Cong., 1 Sess., 8023, 9222-23, 9637-38; 2 Sess., 17-18;
Atlanta *Journal,* March 2, 5, 8, 1917.

[35] *Cong. Record,* 65 Cong., Special Sess., 19, 26-27, 32-35, 38, 45.

[36] Smith had sponsored a bill in the Senate, enacted in 1915, providing
for the appointment of an additional judge for this district. *Cong. Record,*
63 Cong., 3 Sess., 1487, 4681-82, 4837, 4843.

from other directions for the selection of Congressman Frank Park.[37]

The reports that Park would be appointed provoked a strong reaction from the Smith-Hardwick faction in Georgia, primarily on the ground that it would give aid and comfort to Tom Watson. Two Augusta leaders sent Smith and Hardwick this urgent telegram: "We sincerely trust and urge that you will find it possible to defeat confirmation of this appointment, which is not only a direct slap to you but will be considered a virtual victory for Thomas E. Watson and all of the vicious things he stands for in the public life of Georgia. This not so much on Parks account personally as from the fact that Watson is so bitterly opposed to West. Your friends and supporters in Georgia will stand by you to a man in overcoming this inexcusable blunder of the Department of Justice."[38] When Park asked Smith and Hardwick what their position would be if he were appointed, they informed him that they would oppose his confirmation. Park had not previously mentioned the matter "to either of the senators from Georgia, and seems utterly indifferent as to their views or wishes about the matter," wrote Hardwick.[39] Under the circumstances Park withdrew his name from consideration.

The Georgia Senators' prestige in their home state was involved, it seemed, as well as their personal pride. According to William J. Harris, who was on friendly terms with Representative Park and the President, "The contest is most bitter on account of Senator Hardwick having informed several of the House Members that he would control this appointment and that he resented their even endorsing one of their colleagues."[40] As February passed and the administration took no action, Smith and Hardwick continued to support John T. West. On March 10, James R. Gray wrote a long letter to President Wilson, urging him to make no appointment that would "discredit your personal and

[37] Atlanta *Journal*, January 3-7, 10, February 1, 2, 1917.

[38] Thomas W. Loyless and J. C. McAuliffe to Smith and Hardwick, February 1, 1917, in Wilson Papers.

[39] Atlanta *Journal*, February 12, 1917.

[40] Harris to Wilson, February 12, 1917, in Wilson Papers.

political friends." He summed up the Smith faction's position this way:

It is difficult for you to realize that in this as in every other political matter of importance in this state, the friends and supporters of the administration are opposed, denounced, and attacked in every conceivable way by Thomas E. Watson and his large following, aided and abetted by the old machine newspapers and politicians, whom we have so frequently whipped to a frazzle and who truckle to Watson in the hope that they can defeat the wishes of those who are supposed to have, by reason of their friendship, some little influence with the administration.[41]

Meanwhile, a new name entered the lists in the person of U. V. Whipple of Cordele, Georgia. For a moment Smith appeared ready to accept Whipple, but Hardwick was adamant and his colleague stood by him. March passed with the appointment still undecided. But in April, despite a last-minute appeal by Smith and Hardwick, Wilson appointed Whipple to the vacant position. The President wrote Smith that it troubled him "not a little that my judgment should not go with yours in the matter. . . ." He had "gone over the field of choice not once but many times," Wilson declared, "and with an interest and concern heightened by my interviews with you, and by my knowledge of and interest in Georgia." [42]

Smith was distressed. "The nomination causes me great embarrassment," he confessed to the President. He criticized Gregory, declaring that the Attorney General "desired to select some one in disregard of the advice of the Senators." Feelingly, the Georgia Senator declared: "I regret exceedingly that a fight on the nominee will be made at this time when I had so much hoped for united support of all acts of the Administration, and when I know the comfort it will give those in Georgia opposing the important measures now pending." Woodrow Wilson replied at once. He called Whipple's appointment "a personal choice on my part" and assured the Senator that Gregory could be exon-

---

[41] Gray to Wilson, March 10, 1917, *ibid.*

[42] Memorandum prepared by Joseph P. Tumulty, March 13, 1917, and Wilson to Smith, April 7, 1917, in Wilson Papers.

erated "of any desire to act contrary to the preferences either
of yourself or of Senator Hardwick." [43] Smith answered in an
aggrieved tone, expressing "genuine surprise" that Wilson himself had selected Whipple and pointing out that newspapers were
reporting that the appointment was intended as recognition of
Governor-elect Dorsey's faction in Georgia. "I am not aware
of anything in my course which should have caused a desire
for such a result," he wrote.[44]

Whipple's nomination was referred to the Senate Judiciary
Committee and in turn by that committee to a three-man subcommittee of which Hoke Smith was a member. Hardwick
immediately announced that the selection was "objectionable and
offensive" to him, and he arranged to appear before the subcommittee. The Judiciary Committee recommended that Whipple
not be confirmed, and the Senate voted to that effect. The conduct of the Georgia Senators was "past understanding," declared
Wilson.[45]

More than two months passed before the administration made
another appointment, this time selecting William E. Thomas of
Valdosta. Hardwick again objected, and Smith's subcommittee
initiated the same process of defeating the confirmation. Wilson's
patience was wearing thin. "The trouble with the Senators from
Georgia," he wrote John Sharp Williams, "is that they have
practically taken the position that I have no right to name anyone
whom they have not suggested." [46] Just before sending in
Thomas' name, the President addressed a brief letter to Smith
as "My dear Sir," acknowledging a recent letter from the
Georgian in opposition to the new appointment. "You did not
state any reasons or any objections to Judge Thomas," said
Wilson, "and I write in order to omit no courtesy and to inform
you that I am today sending in the nomination. . . ." In forwarding Smith's reply to Gregory, Wilson revealed the depth of his

[43] Smith to Wilson, April 10, 1917, and Wilson to Smith, April 11, 1917,
in Wilson Papers.
[44] Smith to Wilson, April 14, 1917, and Wilson to Smith, April 17, 1917,
ibid.
[45] Atlanta Journal, April 12, 13, 22, 1917.
[46] Wilson to Williams, July 5, 1917, in Wilson Papers.

disgust: "What do you think of the enclosed? Please do not reply in writing because I know it would involve profanity! " [47]

A solution was already in sight, but, unfortunately, it came too late to repair Smith's sagging relations with the administration. Hardwick submitted a list of seventeen names of South Georgians acceptable to him and Smith, and when one of these men—Beverly D. Evans of Sandersville—was appointed, his nomination was quickly confirmed by the Senate.[48]

Meanwhile, during the months preceding American entry into the war, Hoke Smith strongly supported the President's diplomacy. He endorsed Wilson's peace note of December 18, 1916, and described the famous peace-without-victory address on January 22, as "simply magnificent"—"a masterful expression of the highest ideals of international relations." When William E. Borah proposed a resolution reaffirming the Senate's endorsement of the Monroe Doctrine, Smith reassured the Idaho Senator that Wilson had not advocated a departure from that venerable doctrine.[49]

Smith played a mediating role in the framing of a Senate resolution adopted on March 1, following the disclosure of the Zimmermann Note, requesting information from the President about the German message. Senator Lodge was quick to see an opportunity to "widen the breach with Germany and drive us toward the Allies." In order to demonstrate the authenticity of the Zimmermann Note, therefore, he introduced the resolution asking the President about its genuineness, but he shrewdly decided not to ask Wilson about the message's origin, realizing that this information might embarrass Great Britain's friends. It was Hoke Smith's rather than Lodge's wording that was adopted.[50]

[47] Wilson to Smith, July 11, 1917, *ibid.*; Smith to Wilson, July 12, 1917, and Wilson to Gregory, July 13, 1917, in Thomas W. Gregory Papers (Division of Manuscripts, Library of Congress).

[48] Wade H. Cooper to Tumulty, August 1, 1917, in Wilson Papers; Atlanta *Journal*, July 10, August 11, 1917.

[49] *Cong. Record*, 64 Cong., 2 Sess., 792, 897, 1885; New York *Times*, January 4, 23, 27, February 4, 1917.

[50] *Cong. Record*, 64 Cong., 2 Sess., 4571, 4601, 4605; New York *Times*, March 2, 1917.

Smith had little to say during the debate on the armed-ship proposal, but he remained loyal to the administration.[51]

The Senator from Georgia also supported the war resolution early in April. Like other observers, he had seen the war coming during the past few weeks, and while in Atlanta on March 22, he delivered an address to a large audience, sounding a note of "patriotic pride." During the discussion of the war declaration in the Senate, Smith had nothing to say. But he voted for war and, according to the Atlanta *Journal*, was "a member of the steering committee in charge of the president's war program."[52] In Washington, meanwhile, all was excitement. The war lay ahead.

[51] *Cong. Record*, 64 Cong., 2 Sess., 4381, 4583, 5019; Atlanta *Journal*, February 29, March 22, 1917.

[52] Atlanta *Journal*, April 3, 1917.

War Senator

Questions of war and peace dominated the Congressional scene during the remaining years of Hoke Smith's Senate service. American participation in the war brought Smith an opportunity to share in the formulation of important military legislation and to serve the interests of his constituents in numerous more specific ways. But the war proved to be a stern test of the Georgian's willingness to adjust to the requirements of complete mobilization, and of his loyalty to the Wilson administration.

Smith's disagreement with President Wilson over the Federal judgeship during the first half of 1917 was reflected in his criticisms of the administration's military program. Yet the Senator was by no means completely unco-operative with respect to this legislation. In speaking for the five-billion-dollar bond bill in April, he declared: "I have been intensely for peace; but from the time that the German Government issued its last notice . . . I have seen no escape from war unless Germany abandoned her announced purpose." On the following day he informed the President that he would support the necessary war measures.[1]

But the Georgia Senator raised pointed questions about most of the emergency legislation requested by the administration in 1917. When the conscription bill was taken up in the spring, he was one of those who wanted to define the "emergency" referred to in the measure as the "existing war" with Germany. "Many of us are utterly unwilling to give these powers except as incidents of the war with Germany," he explained, "and in voting for the

[1] *Cong. Record*, 65 Cong., 1 Sess., 757-58, 769; Atlanta *Journal*, April 18, 1917.

bill we put that language into it and sent it to conference with
that language in it." Smith voted for the conference report
without the proposed limitation but he was not happy about it.
He did secure the adoption of an amendment to the army and
navy appropriations bill embodying his "period of the war"
proposal, although the form in which it was passed was suggested
by Kenneth D. McKellar of Tennessee.[2]

The Senator from Georgia voted for the administration's
espionage bill, but he was sharply critical of some of its provisions,
including the section relating to newspapers. "It is a time when
the door should be left wide open for the fullest criticism," he
asserted.[3] The crux of Smith's criticism was his opposition to the
broad delegation of power to the President; this proved to be
the key to his position on numerous other administration proposals
for increasing the Chief Executive's authority during the war.

The Georgian contended, during the debate on the embargo
section of the espionage bill, that there was no need "to transfer
our entire export business to the control of any officer of the
United States": "I would be utterly unwilling to permit the
President or anybody else to determine just what can be exported
from the United States. To reach such a view, of necessity,
I think, requires almost a feeling of hysteria with regard to present
conditions. It seems to me that, while we have declared war and
while we are preparing to do our full part in it, we should
interfere with the general business of the country and with normal
conditions just as little as possible." Senator Overman, who was
responsible for the bill on the floor, asked: "Does not the Senator
think that we have got to trust the President in this day and
time to do things that are right and honorable and just?" To
which Smith replied: "Yes, but I believe in preserving some
respect also for ourselves by not putting into a bill an authority
to the President that would be unconstitutional if he exercised
it." Smith disclaimed any personal opposition to Wilson. "Is
there a man on the floor," he asked, "who has given the President
for the past four years more intense support than I have or who

[2] *Cong. Record*, 65 Cong., 1 Sess., 1500-1501, 1613, 1625, 2437-39, 2454-57,
2501, 2504; Atlanta *Journal*, May 18, 1917.

[3] *Cong. Record*, 65 Cong., 1 Sess., 837-38, 849; New York *Times*, April
17, 18, 1917.

has admired him more than I do? I doubt it. But if I could combine Col. Roosevelt and Col. Bryan and Mr. Taft and the President all in one, and get all that was best in each of the four, and take out of that composite man all that was objectionable in either of the four and put him in the White House, I would not vote for the provision. . . ." [4]

Senator Simmons and others defended the committee provision, chiding Smith for an "attempt to alarm the farmers" by posing the threat of an Executive embargo. But Overman finally accepted the Georgia Senator's proposals to limit the embargo powers to "the present war" and to stipulate that no preference should be given to the ports of one state over those of another.[5]

The administration-sponsored bill authorizing the President to establish priorities and preferences in railroad transportation, which was enacted in June, 1917, also provoked complaints from Hoke Smith. He described the priorities plan as "inconceivable" and an "astounding proposition." Rather than transferring "the entire control of the transportation system of the country" to the Chief Executive, declared the Southerner, "we should settle in detail some of the policies and manner of operation." During the long debate on the measure Smith, Reed, Hardwick, and a few other Senators constantly harped on the broad delegation of power the bill provided. "I am utterly opposed to legislation which adds to the unrestricted power of one man," exclaimed Smith.

In addition to his strictures against the scope of the bill and the "legislative abdication" it would involve, the Senator contended that it would "wipe out every liability of the railroad companies to shippers," leaving the latter with no means of securing redress of their grievances against the carriers. He offered an amendment providing for the appointment of a five-man "transportation priority board" to handle priorities and spelling out the duties of the board, the Council of National Defense, and the President in dealing with transportation questions.[6]

---

[4] *Cong. Record*, 65 Cong., 1 Sess., 1686-88, 1728, 1733, 1782-90.

[5] *Ibid.*, 1783-92, 1796-97, 1896, 2165, 2270-71; New York *Times*, May 5, 1917.

[6] *Cong. Record*, 65 Cong., 1 Sess., 3258, 3347-53, 3397-3401, 3440.

Woodrow Wilson opposed such a scheme, and in the end he had his way, but only after Smith had delivered a long harangue in the Senate in mid-June and after some modifications of the administration bill had been made. The Southern Senator reiterated his earlier criticisms. "I am tired of being frightened by Germans, or hearing talk about Germans when I am not frightened," he cried. "I am tired of that nightmare being brought out to scare the children and the women." But after the Senate had amended the bill by providing that priorities should be limited to the transportation of commodities essential to the prosecution of the war, Smith appeared satisfied. He blandly announced that he would vote for the measure.[7]

Hoke Smith's attack on the priorities proposal was linked with his interest in a pending railroad application for an increase in freight rates. He introduced various evidence in the Senate designed to show how prosperous the country's railroads had been in previous years, offered two resolutions directing Senate investigations of railroad conditions, and proposed that the Interstate Commerce Commission be required by law to allow rate increases only after hearings had been held. He managed to secure the adoption of an amendment to another bill making hearings before the ICC mandatory "upon complaint or protest." He tried to amend the army and navy appropriations bill in such manner as to authorize a hundred-million dollars for the purchase of railroad freight cars, and thus ease the demand for rate increases and provide badly needed equipment. This amendment failed, but the Council of National Defense soon completed plans for the government to buy a hundred thousand freight cars to relieve the shortage.[8]

Meanwhile, Smith had assisted in the passage of the so-called "first food-control" bill, a measure concerned with various means of stimulating food production and providing for relatively modest food-control provisions. The Senator was especially enthusiastic about the ten-million-dollar appropriation for nitrates to be distributed to farmers at cost in order to increase food

[7] *Ibid.*, 3643, 3645-50, 3707, 3711, 3714.
[8] *Ibid.*, 871, 896-99, 901-902, 1564-65, 1670-72, 2531-32, 2577-78, 2581-85, 3317; Atlanta *Journal*, April 22, May 16, 1917.

production.[9] He was much less enthusiastic about the administration's comprehensive plan to establish a food administration. In June, while the House was debating this bill, newspapers linked Smith with Thomas W. Hardwick and James A. Reed as "the nucleus of intensive opposition to the bill" from Senate Democrats.[10]

Smith insisted, as he said in a commencement address at the University of Georgia late in June, that the first food bill provided all the controls that were needed. He was particularly upset by the price-fixing implications in the Lever bill and in an interview declared that it was "a part of the program to fix a maximum price on cotton, and as we had been able to secure no help towards fixing a minimum price on cotton in 1914, when we needed it, I was opposed to fixing a maximum price at this time." Gradually, the Georgian came around to the bill's support, but as he admitted, "it has been hard for me to satisfy myself that I should vote for this bill. . . . One of its features that shocked me in its original shape was a little section which would have allowed special agents to go into any man's house and count his eggs, or count his potatoes, or weigh his meat, and say whether he had too much." [11] When the Senate finally passed the bill on July 21, Smith deserted his erstwhile fellow-critics, Reed and Hardwick, to vote for the measure, although as one of the Senate conferees he held out to the end for a three-man food-control board.[12]

One reason Hoke Smith had assumed a more moderate attitude toward the administration's food bill was the strong opposition his attacks on the war legislation had precipitated in Georgia. Despite the criticisms of war measures by such men as Tom Watson, most Georgians rallied to the support of the war program. "The storm is coming!" declared Clark Howell's *Constitution*, which warned that the "few recalcitrants" who opposed

[9] *Cong. Record*, 65 Cong., 1 Sess., 1635-36, 2651-53, 2875-76, 2985, 3054-55.

[10] New York *Times*, June 1, 1917; Atlanta *Journal*, June 16, 21, 1917.

[11] *Cong. Record*, 65 Cong., 1 Sess., 3754, 4480, 4619-20, 4627-28; Atlanta *Journal*, June 18, 21, 22, July 3, 1917.

[12] *Cong. Record*, 65 Cong., 1 Sess., 4600, 4628-31, 4688, 4775, 4952-54, 5028, 5251-52, 5273, 5364, 5367.

"patriotism" would soon be overcome. This warning was repeated with greater effect at a huge war rally in Athens on July 4,
when Andrew J. Cobb, a relative of Smith by marriage and a
judge on the state supreme court, strongly condemned "delay
in the halls of congress on these war measures." Continuing,
Cobb declared: "Not long ago the senior senator from Georgia
had a talk with us from the rostrum of this University and I
tell you in all frankness we did not like the way he talked. It
was not necessary for him to warn us not to get outside the
constitution in the conduct of this war." There was no middle
ground, the Athenian told the cheering crowd; a man was either
a patriot or he was a traitor.[13]

Cobb's attack immediately became the subject of statewide
discussion and press comment. The Macon *Telegraph* was
especially outspoken, condemning what it called a "Copperhead
Cabal" and expressing alarm at "a campaign of sedition" by
hitherto irreconcilable elements in Georgia politics, all "urging
the same things and—at last—pulling cover in the same bed."
According to the *Telegraph*, these new allies included Hoke
Smith and Thomas W. Hardwick, Joseph M. Brown, who had
opposed the conscription act, and Tom Watson, "the heart and
soul, the master of the movement in Georgia."[14]

In the face of this outburst Smith could not remain silent.
On July 10 he issued a statement from Washington defending
himself against Cobb's attack and declaring that the judge had
"no right to create the impression that I uttered a view disloyal
to my country or the president in connection with the conduct
of the war." He had supported "every measure to strengthen
our nation and the president in the war," asserted Smith. He
pointed out that the war legislation had contained "many provisions calculated to unnecessarily annoy and distress our citizens."
It was no criticism of the President "to stop immature provisions
in legislation," the Senator had written a constituent a few days
earlier. To demonstrate his loyalty he soon requested that

[13] Atlanta *Constitution*, July 1, 5, 1917.

[14] Macon *Telegraph*, July 5, 7, 29, 1917; Savannah *Morning News*, July 2,
August 5, 1917; Atlanta *Constitution*, July 6, 22, 26, 1917; Atlanta *Journal*,
July 6, 1917.

Wilson's recent appeal to businessmen be placed in the *Congressional Record*; he described it as a "powerful call . . . to substitute patriotism for profits." [15]

But the attack from Georgia continued. Lucian Lamar Knight and other officers of the Georgia Historical Association directed a circular to the association's members calling for co-operation in the war effort and criticizing the Georgia Senators for their obstruction. Smith answered this criticism in a public letter to Knight, reiterating his contention that he had supported the war program and denouncing the historical association's circular as "deceptive and misleading." [16] Alexander J. McKelway, a long-time admirer of Hoke Smith and the legislative agent of the National Child Labor Association, reminded Knight that "Senator Smith voted for the declaration of war, voted for the selective draft measure, voted for the Espionage bill, including the embargo act, though he opposed the censorship clause of that bill, to which both the Senate and House majority were opposed. In the matter of the food regulation bill, I am convinced that its passage today in the Senate is due as much to the influence of Senator Hoke Smith as that of any other man." According to McKelway, Smith was "a Senator who thinks for himself and who votes for or against measures according to his own views of his duty to his state and to his nation." [17]

Lucian L. Knight stuck to his guns. He replied to Smith's public letter by writing: "Granting that what you say is true . . . it nevertheless remains that before the final vote was taken [on the war bills], you found hills to climb and rivers to cross, all of which delayed the march, if it did not comfort the foe." Smith was coldly furious. "Now I am confident," he wrote the historian, "that you have acted in the entire matter after con-

[15] Smith to C. Strickland, July 6, 1917, and pamphlet statement entitled *Senator Hoke Smith Replies to the Speech of Judge Andrew J. Cobb* (July 10, 1917), in Smith Collection; *Cong. Record*, 65 Cong., 1 Sess., 4995.

[16] Pamphlet entitled *Senator Hoke Smith Replies to the Georgia Historical Association* (July 20, 1917), in Smith Collection; Atlanta *Journal*, July 23, 1917.

[17] McKelway to Knight, July 21, 25, 27, 1917, and Knight to McKelway, July 23, 1917, in Alexander J. McKelway Papers (Division of Manuscripts, Library of Congress).

ferences with the political coterie of my enemies who occupy
the offices of the newspaper in which your publications appear."
Sarcastically, he observed, " You assume the role of an historian.
You pretend to be a teacher and seeker after truth. Teaching
history is a high and worthy calling. Do you think you live
up to it? " If he had, declared Smith, he would have stated
" which of the amendments I offered were wise and which were
unwise." [18]

One outside newspaper that took note of the controversy was
the New York *Times*, which contended that the two Georgia
Senators had done much to impede the prosecution of the war.
" The anti-British attitude of Mr. Smith and his persistent
subordination of American rights to cotton is of old date and
too familiar," declared the *Times*. Smith immediately wrote the
New York paper, pointing to his support of the war program
and detailing his reasons for opposing certain aspects of it. The
Times then apologized to the Senator and referred to him as a
" thoroughly good. American." Smith had given " earnest and
effective support to the measures by which Congress must confer
upon the Executive the authority, power, and means to carry
on the war." [19]

During the three months prior to the adjournment of Congress
on October 6, 1917, Hoke Smith's attitude toward war legislation
differed markedly from that of the first half of the year. The
early summer furor in Georgia must have had its effect; for the
moment the Senator was chastened, apparently willing to lean
over backward to prove his Americanism. He worked hard on
the new revenue bill and assisted in the passage of the war credits
bill and the war risk insurance legislation.[20] In the fall he told
Georgians: " We should not be critical of those in authority,
but should give them loyal support." He issued a lengthy statement urging the purchase of war bonds, made a special trip to
inspect Camp Wheeler, the " beautiful camp " near Macon,

[18] Knight to Smith, July 24, 1917, in Atlanta *Constitution*, July 25, 1917,
and Smith to Knight, July 27, 1917, in McKelway Papers.

[19] New York *Times*, July 26, 28, 1917.

[20] *Cong. Record*, 65 Cong., 1 Sess., 6319-20, 6420-25, 6609-10, 7755-56;
Atlanta *Journal*, June 5, September 16, 1917.

Georgia, and in an address to a large Atlanta audience in mid-November admonished the people to have courage in the face of the Allied disasters in Russia and Italy.[21]

By the time the second session of the Sixty-fifth Congress convened in December, 1917, the country was caught in the throes of a severe fuel shortage. As the Atlanta Chamber of Commerce reported early in January, 1918, "Situation daily growing worse. . . . Everybody crying for coal. Distress is appalling." Smith had begun to receive such complaints weeks before; he had conferred with Harry A. Garfield, the fuel administrator, and with other Washington officials in an effort to secure additional coal for Georgia cities. He remained in the capital during the Christmas holidays to devote his time to relieving his state's distress.[22]

In mid-January Garfield announced that factories would be closed for five days in order to relieve the fuel shortage, and that thereafter manufacturing plants and business and professional offices in the territory east of the Mississippi River would be closed on Monday of each week. This order precipitated a storm of criticism. Smith joined with an overwhelming majority of the Senators in adopting a resolution requesting modifications of the Garfield order, but the administration stood firm. The Senator from Georgia did have some success with the fuel administration in obtaining exemptions for certain plants in his state.[23]

Hard on the heels of the fuel controversy, Senator Chamberlain proposed the establishment of a ministry of munitions, and Republican critics like Theodore Roosevelt increased the tempo of their attacks on Wilson. Hoke Smith was one of the loyal Senators who conferred with the President about the Congressional situation late in January, 1918. The Georgian also gave

[21] *Cong. Record*, 65 Cong., 1 Sess., 5423; Atlanta *Journal*, August 20, October 23, November 15, 22, 1917.

[22] Atlanta *Journal*, November 29, December 21, 1917, January 2, 3, 6, 1918.

[23] New York *Times*, January 17, 19, 1918; *Cong. Record*, 65 Cong., 2 Sess., 687, 918, 936, 1001-1002, 1311, 1407.

his support to the creation of the War Finance Corporation, which was established by an act passed in March to facilitate the mobilization of credit for the war effort.[24]

Smith was much more critical of certain other administration proposals. Following the President's seizure of the railroads, he questioned some features of the legislation to spell out the government's operation of the roads. He preferred to limit government operation to the war period and expressed alarm at the possible violation of shippers' rights and at the "abandonment of legislative responsibility" in the railroad bill. He reluctantly voted for the measure, but only after a futile effort to circumscribe the President's powers in operating the railroads.[25] The Senator also criticized certain sections of the administration's sedition bill which was passed in the spring. He suggested a number of changes in the bill's provisions and supported an unsuccessful amendment which explicitly stated that nothing in the measure should be construed " as limiting the liberty or impairing the right of any individual to publish or speak what is true, with good motives and for justifiable ends." But, as in the case of the railroad bill, he voted for the measure in the end.[26]

The legislation with which Hoke Smith found most fault was the Overman bill to delegate to the Chief Executive extensive powers to consolidate and reorganize executive departments and administrative agencies. During the three months before the Senate passed this bill, late in April, 1918, Smith attacked it again and again in committee and on the floor. He voted for an unfavorable report in the Judiciary Committee and proposed a substitute for the administration plan to limit the President's powers to those executive offices directly concerned with the army and navy. Wilson refused to compromise, and ultimately, on March 21, the Overman bill was favorably reported. "We have no desire to filibuster or delay this bill," Smith declared at

[24] Atlanta *Journal*, January 24, 25, 29, 1918; *Cong. Record*, 65 Cong., 2 Sess., 2791-94, 2839-41, 2857-59, 3085-86, 3100, 3135-36.

[25] *Cong. Record*, 65 Cong., 2 Sess., 2437-38, 2440, 2444, 2491-97, 2505-2506, 2519.

[26] *Cong. Record*, 65 Cong., 2 Sess., 4826, 4829-30, 4833-34, 4885, 6051, 6053-54, 6057.

that point. "If Congress wants to enact it, all right, but it will not do it until I and some others have had a chance to say our say upon it." [27]

During the following weeks Smith had his "say" and more. He joined Reed and several Republicans in a vigorous assault upon the bill, stressing the point that the administrative departments and agencies were "all established and guarded as to their duties" by acts of Congress. He contended that the Overman bill would remove "every branch of the government from the safeguards thrown around them by law." He professed a special concern for the Interstate Commerce Commission and the Federal Reserve Board. Referring to the President he said:

I am aware of the fact that he is the idol of the American people. I am aware of the fact that in my own State many of my best friends would have me follow anything without amendment that had administration approval. . . . A vast majority of the people are devoted to the President, and many of them think Congress should do anything he suggests or adopt anything with administration approval without change. . . . That would be the easy course, to do nothing to serve my country but to serve myself. But are we here simply to seek the retention of office? [28]

As the debate proceeded in April, Smith threw caution to the winds. He indulged in long defiant harangues filled with repetition and lacking his customary logic and good temper. Like a wounded animal he lashed out at the multiplying force and demands of the executive branch, referring on one occasion to action by Wilson that might be "impeachable." "I do not know how far Congress can go in abdicating its responsibilities without passing unconstitutional legislation," he exclaimed. "I only know that for one I will not vote for such a measure, constitutional or unconstitutional." [29] The Senator was rapidly burning his bridges behind him.

[27] Atlanta *Journal*, February 9, 10, March 12, 20, 21, 1918; New York *Times*, March 21, 1918.

[28] *Cong. Record*, 65 Cong., 2 Sess., 3815, 4945-52; Atlanta *Journal*, March 24, April 12, 1918.

[29] *Cong. Record*, 65 Cong., 2 Sess., 4952-54, 5019, 5251-62, 5504-5505, 5604-5605, 5609-10.

Smith fought the Overman bill to the end. His amendment to exclude the Federal Reserve Board was narrowly defeated, by a vote of 37 to 41; a similar amendment which he proposed to exclude the Interstate Commerce Commission lost by a vote of 35 to 42. Smith supported several Republican amendments in the same vein, but they also failed of adoption. He hesitated when the final vote came, but finally voted for the Overman measure, pointing out that the Senate was ready " to back the President and stand to the last man for everything that will help conduct the war with force and power." [30]

Fortunately for Hoke Smith's peace of mind, he found it necessary to devote much of his time to the immediate service of his constituents. There were innumerable petitions of a military nature, ranging from applications for a commission " to inquiries as to the fate of some boy in France." Smith was the leader among Georgia Congressmen in the efforts to secure the location of army cantonments and war plants in Georgia. He spent considerable time early in 1917 pressing the claims of Rome for a government armor-plate plant and in seeking to obtain a nitrogen plant for Cartersville.[31]

During these years Smith was probably the Congressman who did most to meet the requests of the administrators of the agricultural extension and vocational education programs.[32] He was also interested in certain new educational measures that assumed importance because of the war, including a bill he sponsored to establish a program of vocational rehabilitation for disabled servicemen. By late 1917 Smith had begun to study the operation of vocational rehabilitation programs in other countries, and early in 1918 he secured the passage of a resolution directing the Federal Board for Vocational Education to provide additional information on the subject.[33]

[30] *Ibid.*, 5688-5700, 5703, 5747, 5757, 5759-61, 5766.

[31] Atlanta *Journal*, February 11, March 5, April 8, July 5, 1917; Theodore Tiller, *Busy Days For Hoke Smith*, undated pamphlet in Smith Collection.

[32] See for instance Prosser to Smith, November 7, 1917, and memorandum prepared by Prosser, November 25, 1917, in Bureau of Education Papers (National Archives); *Cong. Record*, 65 Cong., 2 Sess., 17, 60, 220-25.

[33] Charles H. Winslow to Smith, January 8, 1918, and Smith to Winslow,

By the spring of 1918 several measures had been introduced to authorize some form of vocational rehabilitation. Smith's bill, which grew out of a series of conferences and suggestions by Cabinet officers, the Vocational Education Board, the Public Health Service, the Council of National Defense, and other Federal agencies and private organizations, was introduced on April 8, 1918. The Smith-Sears bill, as the measure was called, was for all practical purposes an administration plan. It provided for a program to be supervised by the Federal Board for Vocational Education, with an initial appropriation of $2,000,000.[34]

In April and May, 1918, Smith pressed the rehabilitation bill along the road to enactment. As a result of the hearings held by a joint meeting of the education committees of the two houses, a number of minor changes were made in the bill, but the only important modification was the decision to strike out the provision placing the injured men under military discipline while undergoing vocational training.[35] On the Senate floor Smith emphasized the need for such a program and called attention to the success other countries had achieved, particularly Canada. It was an inspiration, the Senator declared, to think of the possibilities of doing so much "for the men who had risked their lives for their country."[36]

It soon developed that the question of jurisdiction over the disabled serviceman was the thorniest issue confronting the Senate in its consideration of the bill. Senators Joseph E. Ransdell and James W. Wadsworth led a movement to have the rehabilitation work done by the medical department. Smith made a powerful reply to the bill's critics. He conceded the right of the medical authorities in the army and navy to initiate some training while the servicemen were still in military hospitals, but if that was all

January 11, 1918, in Bureau of Education Papers; *Cong. Record*, 65 Cong., 2 Sess., 1333.

[34] *Cong. Record*, 65 Cong., 2 Sess., 4428, 4754-57; Atlanta *Journal*, April 9, 1918.

[35] Smith to Lansing, April 20, 1918, and Lansing to Smith, April 23, 1918, in State Department Papers; Prosser to Smith, May 2, 1918, and T. B. Kidner to Smith, May 3, 1918, in Bureau of Education Papers; *Cong. Record*, 65 Cong., 2 Sess., 6764-65, 6822, 6910.

[36] *Cong. Record*, 65 Cong., 2 Sess., 6952-53, 6957.

Congress had in mind, he advised it to forget all about real vocational rehabilitation. In Canada, he pointed out, the rehabilitation
program included training in 194 different lines. Obviously such
an extensive arrangement could not be undertaken by the medical
services, and the efforts to amend the bill in line with the suggestions of Ransdell and Wadsworth failed.[37]

The Senate passed the bill on May 25 with no opposing votes
recorded. The House approved the measure two weeks later.
According to one of the officials of the Vocational Education
Board, who praised Smith for his " devoted zeal and consummate
skill " in steering the rehabilitation bill through the upper house,
"numerous and active agencies" were opposed to the Smith-
Sears plan.[38] Soon after the enactment of his bill, the Senator
from Georgia released a long statement outlining his hopes for
the new legislation. No effort and no expense would be spared,
he declared sometime later in an article for *Forum*, "to fit
disabled fighters for self-sustaining positions, and to aid them
in securing such positions."[39] Smith was right. By June, 1920,
Congress had appropriated $129,000,000 for this work.

Smith devoted a good deal of time during the war years to
the defense of cotton. One of his constant fears was that the
government would seize control of the staple, especially by fixing
the price of raw cotton. He struggled unrelentingly in 1917 to
prevent cotton from being directly involved in any of the war
legislation. He and other Southern Congressmen managed to
exclude cotton from the list of products affected by the Lever
Food Act.[40] They were able also to prevent its inclusion in the
first embargo list, despite the claims by Northeastern cotton
manufacturers and others that cotton was reaching Germany
in large amounts.[41]

[37] *Ibid.*, 6953, 6958-62, 6965, 7001-7026, 7070-79; New York *Times*, May 25,
1918.

[38] James P. Munroe to Smith, June 11, 1918, in Bureau of Education
Papers; *Cong. Record*, 65 Cong., 2 Sess., 7790-91.

[39] Hoke Smith, "Rebuilding the Injured Soldier," in *Forum*, LX (November, 1918), 572-80; Atlanta *Journal*, June 11, 14, 1918.

[40] Atlanta *Journal*, February 24, 1918.

[41] *Ibid.*, September 18, 1917, February 24, 1918; *Cong. Record*, 65 Cong.,
1 Sess., 7065-67.

Early 1918 brought an "active agitation" for fixing the price of cotton, precipitated, according to Hoke Smith, by the textile manufacturers' fear that unless such prices were regulated they would reach impossible levels. Smith and "a conference of determined" Southern Congressmen warned that if cotton prices were fixed, they would attempt to have every other commodity and manufactured item, as well as wages, controlled. Whether or not as a result of this threat, cotton prices escaped direct regulation.[42]

The most serious effort to regulate cotton prices came late in the summer of 1918. In July W. P. G. Harding of the Federal Reserve Board wrote President Wilson to warn him that a large surplus of cotton was likely to exist after the fall harvesting, and to suggest the advisability of fixing cotton prices.[43] Rumors that cotton prices would soon be regulated spread rapidly in August and September, and they increased after Bernard Baruch announced that the War Industries Board might find it necessary "to stabilize" the situation. Late in September the WIB appointed a cotton distribution committee to handle all government and Allied purchases and to make allocations to domestic and foreign consumers. Following this development, Ellison D. Smith and Asbury F. Lever took the lead in the organization of a conference of Southern Congressmen, including Hoke Smith, to guard the rights of cotton producers.[44]

Smith was extremely uneasy about the situation. He reassured Southerners that their Congressmen were "earnestly defending the rights and interests of cotton growers." The cotton defenders pointed out to the President, the War Industries Board, and other agencies that cotton prices were not too high in view of the cost of producing the staple, that high prices were being received for other products, and that there was no occasion or authority for price-fixing. Momentarily, the outlook for cotton brightened. The cotton committee of the WIB announced that the prices

[42] *Cong. Record*, 65 Cong., 2 Sess., 3186, 3188; New York *Times*, February 2, 1918.

[43] Harding to Wilson, July 17, 20, 1918, in Wilson Papers.

[44] Atlanta *Journal*, September 22, 24, 25, 1918; Josephus Daniels, *The Wilson Era: Years of War and After, 1917-1923* (Chapel Hill, 1946), 244-46.

of raw cotton were not to be controlled, at least not for the
present. Smith, who had received thousands of "cotton letters
and telegrams" from all over the South and who had "devoted
practically all his time to the cotton price controversy," was
elated.[45]

During the final stages of the Congressional campaign of 1918,
Republicans attacked the Wilson administration for having fixed
wheat prices while leaving cotton "untouched." Smith deprecated "this appeal to sectional prejudice" and seized the opportunity on the Senate floor to defend cotton. He painted a graphic
picture of the difficulties confronting cotton farmers over the
past few years. He argued that cotton had been affected by
government action, and affected adversely. When the War Industries Board announced in September the "desirability and feasi-
bility of effecting a stabilization of [cotton] prices," Smith
declared, the price of cotton had dropped drastically, leaving the
cotton region in a depression.[46]

By the time the war ended the cotton situation was "chaotic."
Southern Congressmen blamed "price fixing agitation and dearth
of shipping" for the cotton slump. Hoke Smith called a meeting
of Congressmen from the South to consider what action might
be taken. He and other Southerners wrote the President to urge
that the embargo against Germany be lifted and that the War
Trade Board suspend the requirement of licenses for cotton shipments.[47] The Georgian also introduced a resolution in the Senate
directing the War Trade Board to report what restrictions remained on the export of cotton, the reasons for such regulations,
and when they would be removed. The board soon relaxed the
restrictions on cotton exports, but Wilson informed the Southerners that the blockade against Germany could not be raised.[48]

Hoke Smith argued that Germany and Austria should be

[45] Atlanta *Journal*, September 26, 28, 1918, April 4, 1920.

[46] *Ibid.*, October 29, November 9, 1918; *Cong. Record*, 65 Cong., 2 Sess.,
11507-11509.

[47] James Young and others to Wilson, November 18, 1918, Smith and
Morris Sheppard to Wilson, November 20, 1918, and Wilson to Vance
McCormick, November 22, 1918, in Wilson Papers.

[48] *Cong. Record*, 65 Cong., 2 Sess., 11578, 11611-14; Atlanta *Journal*,
November 19, 24, 1918.

allowed to import all the raw materials they needed. In answer to the Senator's inquiry, Bernard Baruch, who was attending the Paris Peace Conference, replied: "Sympathize with your desires but at present removal is impossible." Vance McCormick was no more encouraging.[49] The Southerners continued to protest against the restrictions on cotton shipments to Europe, but they got no relief during the early months of 1919.[50]

The last year of the war found Hoke Smith increasingly concerned with war problems—ranging from the support of Federal housing for defense workers to opposition to the conscription of farm workers. In the summer of 1918 he was appointed chairman of a subcommittee of the Finance Committee charged with handling all war insurance legislation. When the Democratic steering committee, of which the Georgian was a member, decided to enlarge the Military Affairs Committee, he was chosen one of the new members. He spent much of his time in military conferences and on tours of army camps, and he revealed a keen interest in ordnance problems and in the production of "flying machines." Soon after his appointment to the military committee, he acted as a "peacemaker" in the committee when certain members launched an assault on the War Department because of its alleged mistakes in dealing with the question of aircraft production.[51]

Eventually, overwork forced the Georgia Senator to bed, feverish and attended by two doctors. He had caught cold while returning in an open car from addressing a flag-raising ceremony at Camp Meigs. Late summer and early autumn brought Smith some respite; he and Birdie spent ten days in Atlanta, where they got some rest. In September they rented their large home and took an apartment in the Brighton Hotel. All of the girls had married, and the house on California Avenue was simply too large.

[49] Smith to Baruch, January 20, 1919, and to McCormick, February 5, 1919, and McCormick to David F. Houston, February 14, 1919, in State Department Papers.

[50] *Cong. Record*, 65 Cong., 3 Sess., 2280-81, 2730, 2797-98, 4441-48; Atlanta *Journal*, February 4, 7, 14, March 3, 1919.

[51] *Cong. Record*, 65 Cong., 2 Sess., 3480-89, 3838-39, 5972-73, 6429-30, 7994-95, 9521-22; Atlanta *Journal*, May 9, 16, June 9, 19, July 7, 1918.

During the early fall of 1918, Smith remained in Washington, although Congress was engaged in the most perfunctory proceedings. Most Congressmen were vitally concerned with the fall elections. Smith worked with the Finance Committee on the new revenue bill and served as a kind of acting Democratic floor leader during those last days of the war. " I have been engaged for the past ten days each morning in the amusing occupation of adjourning the Senate and preventing the Republicans from giving expression to their partisan harangues," he wrote a friend in November.[52]

Meanwhile, the Senator was giving renewed evidence of his support of the administration. He approved of the President's request for the election of a Democratic Congress and applauded Wilson's course during the peace negotiations with Germany. "In this hour of joy at the cessation of bloodshed," he declared on the day after the armistice was signed, ". . . all fairminded men should be ready to concede that the diplomacy of President Wilson, criticized by some during the past 60 days, has really saved the world from 12 months more of war and sacrifice." [53] Strong words from one who had vigorously resisted several administration measures during the war and who had implied that Woodrow Wilson had gone power-mad!

The past eighteen months had proven a severe trial to Smith. He had demonstrated his ability to act as a constructive leader by championing the vocational rehabilitation bill and by his conscientious work on the Finance, Military Affairs, and Agricultural and Forestry committees. By dint of considerable compromise he had brought himself in line with most administration policies. But despite his best efforts, he could not bring himself to accept with equanimity the vast changes ushered in by the war, particularly in the role of the Chief Executive. Smith's irritation at Wilson and other administration officers might have prompted some of his criticisms, but he believed sincerely that some of the wartime legislation was a threat to individual liberties and to the Constitution, and he spoke out against such measures. This made

[52] Smith to John S. Cohen, November 7, 1918, in Smith Collection.
[53] *Cong. Record*, 65 Cong., 2 Sess., 11172, 11544; New York *Times*, September 16, 17, October 13, 24, November 5, 1918.

him *persona non grata* at the White House. Inevitably, his enemies in Georgia, and many of his old supporters, criticized his course, and explosive reactions like that started by Andrew J. Cobb in the summer of 1917, added to his defiance and bafflement. The war years did not form a happy chapter in Hoke Smith's life. He himself anticipated a happier time in the peaceful years ahead.

The Politics of Peace: 1919

The year following the armistice in November, 1918, failed to bring Hoke Smith the satisfaction he awaited so hopefully. There was no return to the halcyon prewar days; instead, 1919 brought additional stresses and strains. Prosperity among cotton producers deteriorated and the embargo continued, while in politics the struggle over the Treaty of Versailles resulted in the final, irrevocable break between Smith and Woodrow Wilson. Worst of all, the death of the Senator's wife left him without one of the greatest stabilizing influences in his life.

Cotton, of course, received much of Smith's attention. Although he continued to demand the removal of restrictions on the movement of cotton abroad, he realized that the problems confronting cotton farmers were more fundamental in nature than the German blockade or European commercial barriers. Like some other Southern political leaders, the Georgia Senator sought to attack these problems on a broad front. Thus he prodded the Department of Agriculture to be more zealous in its supervision of the cotton exchanges, and he was one of the sponsors of an amendment to the cotton-futures act designed to define cotton classifications more clearly.[1] In the fall of 1919 he helped secure the passage of a measure authorizing a more liberal discount rate on commercial paper backed by cotton. He urged Southern farmers to diversify their products and to co-operate in the marketing of their cotton. If they would produce more cattle

[1] Charles J. Brand to Smith, May 31, 1918, and Smith to Brand, June 13, 1918, March 15, 1919, in Department of Agriculture Papers (National Archives); Atlanta *Journal*, June 18, 1918, February 7, July 14, 1919.

and hogs, more corn and peanuts, if they would "stand together collectively" in disposing of their cotton, they would be far more prosperous, asserted Smith. For his own part, he energetically championed the program of the American Cotton Association, which hoped to promote co-operation among cotton producers in the production and sale of the staple.[2]

The guns had scarcely ceased firing before Hoke Smith was thinking in terms of normalcy. He wanted to demobilize the armed forces rapidly, reduce taxes sharply, abolish government controls, and let the American free enterprise system pick up its old pattern. In the Senate Finance Committee he was one of the most insistent advocates of a six-billion-dollar tax bill for 1919, instead of an eight-billion-dollar measure.[3] Almost as soon as the third session of the Sixty-fifth Congress convened, in December, 1918, the Georgian introduced a bill to return the rate-making authority to the Interstate Commerce Commission, and a short time later he offered a measure to repeal part of the Espionage Act of 1917.[4] He urged that the railroads be returned to private control as soon as possible. The Plumb plan, to have the government purchase the roads and to have them operated by a board of directors representing the operating officials, the railroad employees, and the public, seemed to him "worse than socialism."[5]

The Southern Senator did support a bill to prohibit rent profiteering and a measure to provide transportation for government workers no longer needed in the capital. He also expressed concern about the high cost of living and seemed interested in some of the proposals for a public works program to relieve unemployment. But legislation was not the real answer, said

[2] J. S. Wannamaker to Smith, October 21, 1919, and Smith to Wannamaker, November 18, 1919, in Smith Collection; *Cong. Record*, 66 Cong., 1 Sess., 4909, 4971, 5289-93, 5452-56, 5770-71, 5893, 6263-64; Atlanta *Journal*, September 5, 6, 21, 29, October 3, November 25, 1919.

[3] Smith to John S. Cohen, November 11, 1918, and to Reuben Arnold, November 16, 1918, in Smith Collection; *Cong. Record*, 65 Cong., 3 Sess., 739-42, 780, 784, 792-93, 820.

[4] *Cong. Record*, 65 Cong., 3 Sess., 68-69, 1080, 1527.

[5] *Ibid.*, 4971, 4976; 66 Cong., 1 Sess., 4440-41; Atlanta *Journal*, January 1, August 28, 1919.

Smith. If "all the people engaged in labor in the United States would work a few more hours each day, whether upon the farm or in the cities and towns, and increase production, and in the meantime economize in expenditures," he declared, "we would be following a course more likely to bring about beneficial results than from legislation seeking to interfere with normal courses in trade." [6]

The violence and alleged radicalism in connection with the strikes in 1919 disturbed Smith; indeed, he seemed to become a victim of the very hysteria he had so deprecated during earlier days. He expressed the opinion that Congress might find it necessary to outlaw any labor arrangement or agreement interfering with interstate commerce. As a leading member of the Committee on Education and Labor, he participated in the investigation, in September and October, 1919, of the great steel strike. Although the Georgian took little part in the hearings, the questions he asked indicated concern about radicalism and "alien agitators and organizers." [7]

In other postwar legislation Smith backed the prohibition enforcement measures and opposed the woman suffrage amendment. He had indicated hostility toward woman suffrage several years earlier, but it was not until May, 1918, that he discussed the question in the Senate. According to the Senator, it was a very different thing " to insist upon the right to determine by the votes of your State what shall be the requirement for suffrage of your own State and to insist upon forbidding in an adjoining State the production of intoxicating liquors which may be shipped into your State, to the detriment of your people." [8]

When Congress convened in extra session on May 19, 1919, the Democrats in the Senate were in a minority for the first time

[6] *Cong. Record*, 65 Cong., 3 Sess., 2879-80; 66 Cong., 1 Sess., 3623, 5296-98, 5304, 6721-22.

[7] U.S. Congress, *Investigation of Strike in Steel Industries. Hearings Before the Committee on Education and Labor United States Senate Sixty-Six Congress First Session* . . . (Washington, 1919), 14-15, 23-25, 940-45, 953-64; *Cong. Record*, 66 Cong., 1 Sess., 4503, 4832-33, 7793.

[8] *Cong. Record*, 65 Cong., 2 Sess., 6306-6307, 11039-40, 11580; 66 Cong., 1 Sess., 226-31.

in six years. Hoke Smith lost the chairmanship of the Committee on Education and Labor, as well as his position on the Finance and Military Affairs committees. He became the ranking minority member of the Education and Labor Committee and retained his place on the committees on Agriculture and Forestry, Judiciary, and Rules. He was also reappointed to the Democratic steering committee.

Smith's interest in education continued to be a major theme of his Senate work. In the summer of 1919, for instance, he joined Senator William S. Kenyon in opposing efforts to whittle down the appropriation for vocational rehabilitation work. " I do not know what we would have done without your splendid championship of this work from the very beginning," one of the officials of the vocational education board wrote the Southerner. " It has been magnificent." [9]

In September, 1918, Smith had introduced a bill to provide for Federal assistance in the vocational rehabilitation of persons disabled in industry. A similar measure was sponsored in the House by Representative William B. Bankhead of Alabama. Although the proposal received a favorable report from the Senate Committee on Education and Labor, it failed to pass during the Sixty-fifth Congress. Reintroduced in May, 1919, the bill received another favorable report from the Senate committee and was called up for consideration by the Senate early in June under the direction of Senator Kenyon, the new chairman of the Committee on Education and Labor.[10] For the first time in years Hoke Smith was absent during the Senate debate on an important education bill. He was in Atlanta, where Birdie was desperately ill, but he was back at his desk before the measure was disposed of, eager to aid in its passage. He addressed the Senate at some length, reviewing the bill's origin and the need for industrial rehabilitation. Under the guidance of Kenyon and Smith the bill was passed on June 21, but the House did not approve it

[9] James P. Munroe to Smith, August 2, 1919, in Bureau of Education Papers; *Cong. Record*, 66 Cong., 1 Sess., 155, 2826-27, 4325.

[10] *Cong. Record*, 65 Cong., 2 Sess., 6956, 6959-62, 10170; 3 Sess., 842; 66 Cong., 1 Sess., 54, 509.

until 1920. It authorized a modest appropriation of about three million dollars to be granted to the states on a matching basis.[11]

Sometime in 1917 Smith conferred with a group of educators who urged the creation of a Federal Department of Education. Out of this conference and several others emerged a bill to create a Department of Education and to provide a large Federal appropriation to aid the states in the improvement of their educational facilities. The bill was introduced in the Senate by Hoke Smith and in the House by Horace Mann Towner. Meanwhile, following the recommendations of Secretary of the Interior Franklin K. Lane and the Bureau of Education, the Georgia Senator introduced a bill to authorize a small Federal program to combat illiteracy.[12] Neither of these measures was approved by Congress in 1918. The illiteracy bill received a favorable report from Smith's Education and Labor Committee in the spring of 1918, but several Senators attacked it on the floor as " an indictment of the educational systems of the States" and as evidence of "paternalism." In defending the proposal Smith asserted: "It is simply along the line of work which the Government has been doing for years." He also advanced the patriotic argument that it would be an " Americanizing measure." [13]

In January, 1919, Smith and William B. Bankhead introduced an Americanization bill prepared by a committee representing an Americanization conference called by Secretary Lane in 1918. But this comprehensive Federal-aid measure died with the Sixty-fifth Congress. Smith and Bankhead reintroduced the Americanization bill in May, 1919, but by this time a new measure—the Kenyon-Vestal Americanization bill—had pushed the Smith-Bankhead bill into the background.[14] The new bill received a favorable report from the Senate committee in the fall of 1919, and was considered by the upper house early in 1920. The senior

[11] Ibid., 66 Cong., 1 Sess., 1381-83, 1451-55, 1458, 1497-1502; 2 Sess., 5536; United States Statutes at Large, XLI, Pt. I, 735-37.

[12] Cong. Record, 65 Cong., 2 Sess., 3637, 11169; 66 Cong., 1 Sess., 351, 3236-38.

[13] Ibid., 65 Cong., 2 Sess., 3999, 4004-4005, 4363-73, 4427, 4429-30, 4476-82, 4501-4503, 5237, 6196, 6409, 6433-34.

[14] Ibid., 66 Cong., 1 Sess., 351, 3238; New York Times, February 23 (III), 1919.

Senator from Georgia lent strong support to Senator Kenyon in urging the measure's approval. The Senate passed it late in January, but the House committee failed to report it during the Sixty-sixth Congress.[15]

In the meantime, Hoke Smith was concentrating his attention on the Smith-Towner bill. Although considerable support developed for the proposal in 1919, it provoked a strong opposition movement, particularly on the part of certain Roman Catholic leaders and organizations. The bishop of the Catholic diocese of Burlington, Vermont, for example, wrote a Vermont Congressman in June, 1919, declaring that the bill was "dictated not by patriotism or education but by socialism and State paternalism." He referred to "intimidation from Washington," and spoke darkly of "a malicious attempt to deprive parents of a God-given right, inherent in parenthood itself." Besides, if the bill was passed, Vermont "would be taxed in the futile attempt to educate the Southern Crackers." [16]

Smith carefully defended the measure against such attacks, declaring that criticisms of this nature could not represent the "mature views of any considerable number of our citizens." The proposed legislation would not centralize the control of education in Washington, he asserted, and he cited one of the provisions which specifically provided for the retention of control by the states.[17]

The Georgia Senator continued until the end of his Senate career to work for the enactment of the Smith-Towner bill. "I have completed my educational legislation," he wrote in the summer of 1920, "with the exception of one bill—the greatest of all—the Smith-Towner Bill. . . ." As one would suspect, the Senator was particularly interested in Federal support for rural schools. But there was no doubt in his mind about the necessity

[15] *Cong. Record*, 66 Cong., 2 Sess., 1663-66, 1876-77, 1943-44, 1947, 1949-50, 1985; Edward George Hartmann, *The Movement to Americanize the Immigrant* (New York, 1948), 231-33.

[16] Joseph J. Rice to Frank L. Greene, June 4, 1919, and Greene to Rice, June 13, 1919, in Frank L. Greene Papers (Division of Manuscripts, Library of Congress); *Cong. Record*, 65 Cong., 3 Sess., 3905-3908, 4391-92.

[17] Smith to Dr. W. P. Smith, October 29, 1919, in Smith Collection; *Cong. Record*, 66 Cong., 1 Sess., 3236-42.

and the justification for Federal aid. " The national government now having the power to collect an income tax," he said, " it is only fair that the wealth derived from incomes should contribute toward the development of the children of the entire country." [18]

The Smith-Towner bill received strong support from the National Education Association, but there was much opposition to it, partly on the ground of the expense it would involve. Smith made a lengthy speech in favor of the measure in mid-February, 1921, but while he managed to get a favorable report from the Committee on Education and Labor the bill died with the session.[19]

In March and April, 1919, the Smiths spent several weeks in Atlanta before the Senator returned to Washington for the extra session in May. Those days in the spring of 1919 proved to be almost the last that Hoke and Birdie Smith spent together, for Smith had scarcely settled down to the work of the new session before word came from Atlanta that his wife was seriously ill. When he reached Atlanta she seemed considerably better, and the members of the family were encouraged. But within a few days her condition grew worse, and at 1:45 A. M. on Saturday, June 7, she died. Birdie had suffered from poor health for years and had never really recuperated from a severe attack of bronchitis and pneumonia in September, 1917.[20]

Mrs. Smith was a gentle person whose life was bound up with the " ministries of home." Her " goodness, gentleness and beauty," declared the Atlanta *Journal*, made her " a woman in whose life the tenderest and most beautiful traditions of the South found expression." Apparently the bitter political feuds in which Smith was involved cost her heavily, but she subordinated her own life to the interests of her husband and children. She brought out the best in Hoke Smith. Her frail condition had long been a source of concern to him and she was the object of his constant

[18] Smith to Sam L. Olive, May 29, 1920, to Amelia D. Irving, January 4, 1921, to W. Carson Ryan, Jr., January 29, 1921, and numerous other letters, in Smith Collection.

[19] *Cong. Record*, 66 Cong., 3 Sess., 2183, 2359-61, 2890, 3038-45.

[20] Atlanta *Journal*, March 27, April 23, June 7, 1919; Smith to Marion Smith, December 18, 1918, and to Mrs. Alston Simpson, December 27, 1918, in Smith Collection.

solicitude. During his busiest years he found time to write her a tender note of greeting almost every day when she was away. As a family friend said years later, " I recall with vivid recollection how tender and devoted you were to her during her illness." [21] For over thirty-five years Birdie Smith had been the center of Hoke Smith's world; he would miss her greatly in the years ahead.

The most momentous question that faced the Senate in 1919 was the Treaty of Versailles and the League of Nations. Smith's disagreement with President Wilson on the League was profound, though the Senator's position was revealed only gradually as the year passed.

Like most Democrats, the Georgian endorsed Wilson's decision to attend the Paris Peace Conference, but a few weeks later, after Senator Philander C. Knox introduced his sweeping resolution calling for the postponement of the League by the peace conference, Smith was not so sure that Wilson's trip was wise. In a letter to John Temple Graves in mid-December, 1918, he opposed the idea of attaching the proposed League to the treaty with Germany. A few days later he endorsed the President's statement that the League would be " enforced by collective moral force," but he remarked that " we may not be willing to surrender any of the sovereignty of our country to a new constitutional government embracing the nations of the world that would have the right to dictate for us governmental policies." [22]

A number of Southern Senators made prepared speeches in the Senate during the first half of 1919, but Hoke Smith was not one of them. When the details of Wilson's League became known in February, 1919, Smith was quoted as saying, " I cannot believe for a moment that the President has advocated or would advocate any such impracticable [and] impossible theory of a League of Nations." In his Georgia speeches, following the ad-

[21] Oliver Orr to Smith, October 18, 1923, in Smith Collection; Atlanta *Journal*, June 8, 1919.

[22] Smith to Graves, December 18, 1918, *ibid.*; New York *Times*, November 19, December 4, 1918; Atlanta *Journal*, January 1, 12, 1919; *Cong. Record*, 65 Cong., 3 Sess., 858-59.

journment of Congress on March 4, 1919, the Senator urged that the League be amended to allow the United States as many votes in the assembly as any other nation and to provide for withdrawal from the organization.[23]

Between May 19, when Congress assembled in extra session, and November 19, when the treaty was finally voted on, the Democrats, led by Gilbert M. Hitchcock of Nebraska, ranking Democrat on the Foreign Relations Committee, fought an increasingly uphill fight for the treaty Wilson officially presented to the Senate on July 10. Not all Democrats co-operated with the Wilson supporters. James A. Reed of Missouri, who had always been close to Hoke Smith, was irreconcilably opposed to the League. Hardwick and Vardaman, as long as they remained in the Senate, approached the same position.

Smith's first remarks on the League in the new session were delivered on June 30. He reminded the Republicans that many of them had declined to support the reservations made by the Senate to the arbitration treaties in 1911-12. Some of the Georgian's colleagues interpreted this to mean that he favored similar reservations to the League, but when questioned by reporters Smith would only say that he was " opposed to Oriental immigration." In a Chautauqua address in August, the Senator preferred to discuss the war and such current domestic problems as the high cost of living, although he made some passing references to the treaty. Nevertheless, by September he was listed in the press as a reservationist.[24]

Meanwhile, Lodge was directing the committee hearings on the treaty, and the slow strangulation of the League was taking its course. The treaty became the regular business of the Senate on September 15. A few days later Smith issued a statement announcing that he had prepared certain reservations which he planned to offer to the League. " The United States must not submit to the imposition of any moral or legal obligation to send its troops anywhere," he declared, " and Congress must be left

[23] New York *Times*, February 16, March 28, 1919; Atlanta *Constitution*, February 21, 1919; Atlanta *Journal*, March 27, April 16, 1919.

[24] *Independent*, XCIX (September 27, 1919), 432; New York *Times*, July 1, 9, September 6, 7, 1919; *Cong. Record*, 66 Cong., 1 Sess., 2186.

absolutely free to decide when and in what conflicts we shall participate...." Henry Cabot Lodge wrote Elihu Root: "There are seven or eight votes on the Democratic side for reservations. Hoke Smith has prepared some of his own, but we shall find them to 'Hoax Smith' (Ha-Ha)...."[25]

On October 2, the very day Woodrow Wilson collapsed in the White House following his illness in the West, Smith offered seven reservations to the League covenant. Taking the floor, the Senator read his reservations, observing at the outset that the framers of the Constitution had given the Senate a guarantee against treaties not "maturely considered and overwhelmingly approved." Smith's reservations provided for equality of nations in the League; the right of the United States to withdraw by concurrent resolution of Congress; the exclusion of any question involving the Monroe Doctrine or such domestic questions as immigration from the League's jurisdiction; the right of the United States to refuse to join in League action involving military force or economic measures, including the right to accept or reject mandates, unless Congress approved; a guarantee that the reparations commission would not interfere with commerce between the United States and Germany unless the former approved; and the provision that American representatives on any League agency must be appointed by the President and confirmed by the Senate. Smith also indicated that he desired changes in that part of the covenant dealing with the international labor organization.[26]

The Senator from Georgia admitted that his reservations were similar to those already suggested by several Republican Senators. During the past two weeks he had conferred with reservationists from both parties, evidently hoping to take the lead in a compromise movement. He asserted that the treaty could not be ratified "in its present form." His strong feeling that the executive branch in recent years had usurped Congressional prerogatives found expression in his position on the League. Here was a power

[25] Lodge to Root, September 29, 1919, in Lodge Papers (Massachusetts Historical Society); New York *Times*, September 23-25, 1919.

[26] *Cong. Record*, 66 Cong., 1 Sess., 6271-72; New York *Times*, October 3, 1919.

even more remote—and a foreign one at that—which could
threaten the rights of the Senate. Moreover, the possible consideration by the League of such questions as immigration disturbed Smith because of his belief in white supremacy, and the
alleged radicalism of European labor made him suspicious of an
international labor organization. There was also the effect that
the treaty and the League might have on cotton. The President
of the American Cotton Association wrote Smith to warn of
this danger: "For God's sake protect us in the treaty with
Germany." [27]

During October and early November all of the direct amendments to the treaty were defeated. Several times during this
period Smith repeated his desire for reservations to the League
covenant. He made a long statement of his position on November
7, the day the voting on the Lodge reservations began. Declaring
that he would vote for most of the reservations, the Georgia
Senator exclaimed: "I believe one of the most valuable things
the Senate can do to-day is to help bring the country back to
congressional responsibility." He disliked most of all Article X—
a pledge "of guns, or armies and battleships," he called it.[28]

When the treaty was reported from the committee of the
whole, fourteen reservations had been attached to the League
covenant.[29] Hoke Smith and John K. Shields accounted for
twenty-three of the twenty-eight Southern votes cast for the
reservations. The Georgian voted for reservations on withdrawal,
Article X, mandates, the exemption of domestic questions, the
appointment of representatives, the reparations commission, arma-
ments, covenant-breaking states, the international labor organization, and dominion votes.[30] No doubt he still hoped to play the

[27] Wannamaker to Smith, October 21, 1919, in Smith Collection; *Cong.
Record*, 66 Cong., 1 Sess., 6271, 7805-7806.

[28] *Cong. Record*, 66 Cong., 1 Sess., 7540, 7542, 8058-62, 8276-78; Atlanta
Journal, October 19, 1919.

[29] Smith's proposal for withdrawal by concurrent resolution of Congress,
a resolution not subject to the President's veto, was incorporated in the
first reservation.

[30] *Cong. Record*, 66 Cong., 1 Sess., 8139, 8547, 8560-71; New York *Times*,
November 9, 14, 16, 1919.

compromise role, but even if the President had been willing to compromise he would not have turned to the Georgia Senator.[31]

The Lodge resolution of ratification was rejected by a vote of 39 to 55. Almost all of the Democrats stood firm in their loyalty to Wilson; only Smith and Shields joined the Republican reservationists. When the treaty was voted on without the reservations, it was defeated by a vote of 38 to 53, with Smith opposing it. "The Lodge-Smith combination did the work! " declared the Atlanta *Constitution*. On the other hand, eighty Georgia veterans of the recent war wrote Tom Watson's Columbia (S. C.) *Sentinel* to commend Smith for having helped defeat the "Wilson-Lloyd George British League." [32]

From Atlanta Smith issued two long statements late in November, urging immediate ratification of the League of Nations but reiterating his demand for reservations. He warned of the dangers involved in his country's accepting a mandate, of the radicalism of European labor leaders, of the threat by a reparations commission, "with power to cut off a 3,000,000 bales market annually from our cotton," of a world organization in which white men would not be in the majority, and of the obligations under Article X. But the Georgia politician professed to believe that a compromise might soon be arranged. "All that is needed," he said, "is for the extremists on each side, who really desire the treaty ratified, to understand that the treaty can not be ratified without concessions." When Congress convened in December, Smith became one of the most active supporters of a movement seeking a compromise.[33]

By early January, 1920, the compromise talk pervaded the

[31] When Colonel House had urged Wilson to be more deferential to the Senate—and even to Hoke Smith—the President had angrily referred to the Georgian as an "ambulance-chaser." He would "receive him, of course, as the senator from Georgia, if he calls, but, House, no nosegays, no olive branches in that direction." Thomas A. Bailey, *Woodrow Wilson and the Great Betrayal* (New York, 1945), 13.

[32] Columbia (S. C.) *Sentinel*, November 14, December 12, 1919; Atlanta *Constitution*, November 16, 21, 1919; *Cong. Record*, 66 Cong., 1 Sess., 8802-8803.

[33] Atlanta *Journal*, November 24, 30, December 19, 21, 23, 24, 1919, January 1, 1920; *Cong. Record*, 66 Cong., 2 Sess., 62-64, 738.

Senate, and both moderate Republican and Democratic Senators were showing a desire for quick ratification of the treaty. Smith conferred with George E. Chamberlain, William H. King, and Park Trammell about compromise possibilities; he also participated in a meeting called by Robert L. Owen. The major bipartisan conference, of which Smith was not a member, met several times during the last half of January, but it proved abortive in the end, when Lodge and the Democrats could not agree.[34]

On February 9, the Senate voted to begin reconsideration of the treaty, and on the following day the debate on the question of ratification was resumed. Between February 21 and March 18 the Lodge reservations, now numbering fifteen, were voted on and approved. Hoke Smith adhered substantially to his earlier position, voting for a majority of the Lodge amendments. In several clashes with Senator Hitchcock, the Georgian contended that some Democrats were irreconcilables themselves in their unwillingness to accept reservations to the covenant. There was one final effort at compromise. Senator Simmons led a movement in March, in which Smith participated, in an attempt to obtain an agreement on Article X. But the President remained steadfast in his opposition to such a compromise.[35]

Smith took the Senate floor on March 12 and again on March 19 to urge ratification with reservations. He opposed the idea of carrying the League issue into the Presidential campaign of 1920, and in a final " impassioned speech " he defended his course and criticized Wilson's claim that the reservations would nullify the League's effectiveness. When the final vote came he again supported the Lodge resolution, although eighteen other Southerners voted against it.[36]

There is no indication that Hoke Smith ever doubted the wisdom of his position on the treaty. Throughout the remainder

[34] New York *Times*, December 18-21, 24, 27, 1919, January 3, 4, 1920.

[35] Smith to John B. Young, February 19, 1920, and to Thomas J. Hamilton, August 20, 1920, in Smith Collection; *Cong. Record*, 66 Cong., 2 Sess., 3242, 3515, 3520-21, 3579-82, 3741, 3748, 3857, 3864, 3894, 4007, 4067; New York *Times*, February 26, March 3, 6, 9-11, 13, 15, 1920.

[36] *Cong. Record*, 66 Cong., 2 Sess., 4222-23, 4588-93, 4599; Atlanta *Journal*, March 21, 1920.

of his life he classed himself as a League man, but he blamed Woodrow Wilson's "obstinacy" and refusal to accept "proper reservations" for the failure of the League in the United States. For all his arguments to the contrary, Smith was really an opponent of the League, or at least of any organization that resembled Wilson's League. The Senator would not have been unhappy had the covenant never been drafted.

The record of Smith's career in 1919 reflected the unsettled conditions within the Democratic party that resulted from the Democratic losses in 1918, Wilson's intense preoccupation with the Treaty of Versailles, and the President's illness and loss of control in the fall of 1919. It reflected even more the extent of Smith's personal disagreement with the administration and his growing conservatism. With the exception of his work for educational legislation, his Congressional interests were becoming more and more provincial. The irritations, the doubts, and the growing frustrations of the war years continued after the armistice and hardened into a permanent pattern in the Georgian's thinking. But there was little time for remorse or idle speculation about past developments. Hoke Smith's final political test was already looming over the horizon of 1920.

Defeat: 1920

The opposition to Hoke Smith's re-election in 1920 had been apparent for a long time. "It is well known here," wrote one of the Senator's old supporters late in 1917, "that the Howells, Joe Brown, Dorsey & Harris are agreed—Dorsey is to tackle Smith two years hence." [1] During the war the Howell-Dorsey faction, which had long maintained an informal alliance with Tom Watson, emerged as a clear-cut champion of the Wilson administration. Governor Dorsey became an enthusiastic supporter of the President's policies and William J. Harris, one of the Howell-Dorsey leaders and an ardent defender of Wilson, defeated Thomas W. Hardwick for the Senate in 1918.

Characteristically, Smith was optimistic about 1920. "I am not at all disturbed about the situation," he wrote one Georgian in the fall of 1918; he informed another man at the same time that he would be a candidate for re-election in 1920 "regardless of opposition." Smith seemed to feel that the alliance between Dorsey and Watson would dissolve, in view of Dorsey's strong support of the Wilson administration and Watson's belligerent opposition to it. [2] John S. Cohen, who had become editor of the Atlanta *Journal* when James R. Gray died in 1917, did not underestimate the opposition to Smith. But as he surveyed the political scene in the autumn of 1918, he felt that the Senator was "infinitely stronger" than he had been six months earlier. This was true,

[1] C. Murphy Candler to McKelway, December 5, 1917, in McKelway Papers.

[2] Smith to John S. Cohen, October 10, 1918, to Frank U. Garrard, October 21, 1918, to Stiles Hopkins, October 30, 1918, and to J. F. Crawley, November 9, 1918, in Smith Collection.

the *Journal* editor wrote, for two reasons: first, there had been "no apparent friction" between Smith and the Wilson administration for several months, and, secondly, the people had come to understand what "really great and useful services" their senior Senator was rendering in Washington.[3]

Emphasizing Cohen's second point, Smith did his best during the following eighteen months to demonstrate to Georgians how completely devoted he was to their interests. He continued to work unceasingly for the cotton farmers. He was an energetic leader of the movement to have the War Department retain Camp Gordon and Camp Benning as permanent army installations. He revealed a keen interest in the improvement of Southern ports and spent considerable time seeking to obtain larger appropriations for the development of Savannah and Brunswick.[4] The Senator tried to make sure that these services were widely publicized in Georgia. He employed the Gilreath Press Syndicate to distribute copy to Georgia newspapers and encouraged his Atlanta *Journal* friends to take the lead in rallying the rural papers to his banner. If the people could only be told of his long fight for cotton, of his efforts to locate war industries and army camps in the state, of his work for education, and of his innumerable services to individual Georgians in connection with the war, he did not see how they could fail to re-elect him.[5]

Meanwhile, Smith was watching developments in Georgia more closely than he had in former years. When Federal Judge William T. Newman retired, for instance, the Senator was careful to avoid the kind of patronage controversy he and Hardwick had with the administration in 1917. The question that excited most discussion among Smith's constituents in 1919 and 1920 was the League of Nations. The League was endorsed by many leaders of both factions in Georgia, but it was vigorously opposed by Tom Watson and his followers. It was a little difficult, perhaps, to ascertain the real direction of the shifting winds of opinion

[3] Cohen to Smith, November 9, 1918, *ibid.*

[4] Atlanta *Journal*, January 4, July 3, December 18, 21, 1919, January 1, 19, 24, 1920; *Cong. Record*, 65 Cong., 3 Sess., 857-58, 3428-32; 66 Cong., 1 Sess., 1071-72, 1639-41, 2186-88, 2190-95, 7866-67, 7873-75; 2 Sess., 2432-33.

[5] Atlanta *Journal*, March 27, 30, April 23, May 18, 1919; Smith to Frank C. Gilreath, October 7, November 6, 1918, in Smith Collection.

in view of such divergent attitudes, particularly if one's own emotions got involved. Perhaps there was some middle ground between the advocates and the opponents of the League.

The first round in Hoke Smith's campaign for re-election was the Presidential primary of 1920. The exact route by which he entered the primary as a favorite son is difficult to retrace, but it seems likely that he was maneuvered into the race by the astute plotting of Clark Howell and other anti-Smith men, who saw more clearly than did the Senator the probable outcome and the bearing it would have on the Senatorial primary during the following summer.

Smith's name first entered into the speculation about the Presidential primary when reports began to circulate that Oscar W. Underwood would enter the contest, with the backing of the Howell-Dorsey faction. Since Underwood was at this time engaged in a struggle with Senator Hitchcock for the party leadership in the Senate, Smith refused to vote for Underwood in the caucus until the Alabaman had promised not to allow the use of his name in the Georgia primary. The Senator from Georgia then wrote one of his constituents, "I do not think it will be necessary for me to have my name mentioned in the primary." [6]

Many of Smith's friends thought that it would be a "serious mistake" for him to become involved in this election. The managers of the *Journal* wanted the primary to develop into a contest between leading candidates for the Democratic nomination. Indeed, the Atlanta paper had launched a vigorous campaign for Herbert Hoover which came to an end only with Hoover's refusal to permit his name to be used and the decision of the State Democratic Executive Committee to abide by his wishes. In an effort to embarrass Smith, the Atlanta *Constitution* implied that he would bolt the party if Hoover were nominated, but the Senator denied this. "I am taking no part in the presidential primary contest in Georgia," he declared, "and I would appreciate it if the papers of the state would let the public so understand." But it was very hard not to become involved. Some of

[6] Smith to Thomas J. Shackleford, February 25, 1920, and to R. L. Shipp, February 23, 1920, in Smith Collection; Atlanta *Journal*, February 12, 20, 1920.

his supporters warned him to "Keep Reed out of Georgia," a reference to Senator James A. Reed's candidacy. Others urged him to repudiate reports that he was supporting Attorney General A. Mitchell Palmer, who had entered the Georgia primary as a defender of the Wilson administration.[7]

It was into the position between Palmer's strong endorsement of the Wilson program and Reed's thoroughgoing opposition to it that Smith allowed himself to be led. By the time the treaty was defeated the second time, on March 19, 1920, and it was clear that Wilsonian ideals were to face severe criticism throughout the country, the Georgia Senator was seriously considering the possibility of entering the Presidential primary in his home state. Felix Jackson, a Smith supporter from Gainesville, filed a petition with the state committee requesting that the Senator's name be placed on the ballot. Many people in Hall County were satisfied with neither Palmer nor Reed, asserted Jackson. "Neither of these extreme views," he wrote Smith, "in our judgments, represents the real opinion of thousands of progressive, forward-looking Democrats." After a round of conferences with political friends in Atlanta, Hoke Smith issued a formal announcement on March 25 indicating that he would run. He stressed the point that the voters had been faced with only the two extreme views on the League represented by Palmer and Reed. Both positions, he said, would be "injurious to our country." He would be "derelict" in his duty if he failed to make the fight for a middle position.[8]

Senator Reed withdrew from the Georgia primary when requested to do so by his friend Hoke Smith. But if the Georgia politician lost an opponent in Reed's leaving, he soon gained one in the unexpected entry of Tom Watson into the race. Some anti-Smith men urged Governor Dorsey to enter the campaign, and Dorsey considered doing so for a time after Smith's announcement; but it was apparent that the governor could invoke no

[7] Rogers Winter to Smith, February 15, 1920, and Jesse E. Mercer to Smith, February 23, March 8, 1920, in Smith Collection; Atlanta *Journal*, February 26-29, March 1, 8, 12, 18, 1920.

[8] Atlanta *Journal*, March 18, 19, 21-25, 1920; New York *Times*, March 26, 1920.

new issue and that he could not endorse President Wilson any more strongly than had Palmer.

Smith had little time to prepare for the campaign. Headquarters were opened at the Piedmont Hotel in Atlanta, with Henry Y. McCord and J. R. Smith in charge. Ex-Congressman William Schley Howard directed a corps of Smith speakers, and a great quantity of literature was spread over the state.[9] The Senator began his campaign in Savannah on March 25, with a two-hour address devoted largely to the League. During the first three weeks of April he made speeches in fifteen or twenty other Georgia towns.

Smith's long and vigorous addresses were mostly concerned with questions of war and peace—and with the usual personalities in Georgia politics. He denied that he had obstructed the war effort but refused to endorse " every phase " of the Wilson program. If the people wanted "a senator to be led around by the nose," declared Smith, "they certainly will be obliged to get them another man, and they will not have to wait very long. . . ." He defended the reservations he had proposed to the League and denounced Article X, asserting that it " puts upon you and your children and your children's children the obligation to participate in the wars of the world." He made light of Palmer's candidacy while adopting an ambivalent attitude toward Woodrow Wilson, praising the President's leadership on the one hand and condemning his one-man government on the other.

One theme that found expression in Smith's campaign speeches was his alarm at the threat of recent radicalism. He was opposed to " public ownership of industry, equal distribution of all industrial profits, and numerous other forms of radical socialism." He favored state rights, individual initiative, and " America first." The Senator did not fail to remind his fellow-Georgians of his many services in their behalf. He also attacked his enemies, lashing out at the *Constitution* for charging that he had made a deal with Reed and Hardwick and had urged Watson not to enter the primary. " Malice has never inspired a black heart to

[9] Smith to Andy Smith, November 24, December 1, 4, 1919, and to the Public Printer, June 9, 1920, in Smith Collection; Atlanta *Journal*, March 28-31, 1920.

lie more infamously than Clark Howell has lied about me," he exclaimed.[10]

The Senator's two opponents were much less active on the hustings. Attorney General Palmer made a few speeches in the state, calling for unqualified endorsement of Wilson's leadership and of the League of Nations. He referred to Smith as one of the "bitter enders" whose purpose was to discredit the administration. Tom Watson had almost no organization, and he made no speeches. In his newspaper he denounced many of the war restrictions, attacked Palmer's anti-Red activities, and ridiculed Hoke Smith as "Straddle-bug Smith." The old Populist leader called the Senator a "colossal Yankee," a "blend of Wilsonism and William Howard Taft." [11]

The anti-Smith papers, led by the Atlanta *Constitution*, the Macon *Telegraph*, and the Savannah *Morning News*, attacked Smith as pro-German, as an obstructer of the war effort, and as the real author of the Lodge reservations. They sought to embarrass him further by asserting that he had exonerated Germany in the sinking of the *Lusitania* and that Bernstorff had said: "He can be useful to us!" Most newspapers contended that the vital issue in the campaign was the League, but as the Columbus *Enquirer-Sun* observed, issues had been swallowed up in the bitterness of the contest.[12] The leading Smith papers were the Atlanta *Journal*, the Macon *News*, and the Columbus *Enquirer-Sun*. They emphasized their candidate's middle-of-the-road position on the League and his long record of fruitful public service.[13]

On the eve of the balloting Smith predicted that he would carry over a hundred counties. But the results disclosed the shocking fact that he had won only forty-six counties and 45,344 popular votes out of more than 145,000. He failed even to carry Fulton County.[14]

[10] Atlanta *Journal*, March 26, April 1-20, 1920.

[11] *Ibid.*, April 11, 13, 16, 18, 1920; Columbia (S. C.) *Sentinel*, April 12, 1920; Woodward, *Tom Watson*, 466-68.

[12] Macon *Telegraph*, April 3, 12, 13, 15, 19, 1920; Atlanta *Constitution*, April 10-15, 1920; Atlanta *Journal*, April 16, 18, 19, 1920.

[13] Atlanta *Journal*, March 21, 26, 30, 31, April 1, 4, 13-16, 19, 1920.

[14] Palmer carried 53 counties (144 county-unit votes) and received 48,041

The April contest did not end the controversy over the Presidential primary. The state convention in mid-May had to ratify the results of the primary and select the delegates to the national convention in San Francisco. The Palmer managers contended that on the basis of the attorney general's plurality of county-unit votes, he had the right to name the entire Georgia delegation to the national convention. This claim was based on Rule 10 of the regulations governing the primary, but the Smith and Watson men refused to accept this interpretation, calling it an "unfair and ridiculous suggestion." Smith spent most of the month between the primary election and the state convention in Georgia, conferring with his advisers and making plans for the convention. He let it be known that he favored an unin-structed delegation to San Francisco, divided among the three candidates on the basis of their county-unit votes.[15]

When the convention met in Atlanta on May 18, a combination of Smith and Watson men dominated the meeting. The manner in which the Smith-Watson entente was arranged was never satisfactorily explained. Each of the three groups appears to have made overtures to the other two. The Smith and Palmer delegates certainly discussed the possibility of an alliance against Watson, although each side later asserted that the other made the first proposal. There was strong support for such an agreement among Palmer and Smith men, but the leaders of the two factions, long at odds, were unable or unwilling to work together.[16] Having won a plurality of the county-unit votes, the Palmer managers felt that compromise was unnecessary.

The Smith-Watson combination did its work with dispatch. It chose the convention officers and selected a slate of Smith and Watson men to go to the national convention. A motion by the Palmer spokesmen to endorse the Wilson administration and the "principles" of the League was voted down. The convention expressed "unalterable opposition" to "the League of Nations

popular votes; Watson had 55 counties (130 county-unit votes) and 52,129 popular votes. Smith had 110 county-unit votes.

[15] Atlanta *Journal*, April 22-25, May 4, 5, 7, 12-18, 1920.

[16] John W. Bennett to Smith, July 31, 1920, in Smith Collection; Atlanta *Journal*, May 18, 21, June 17, 1920.

brought back from Versailles," urged the repeal of the war measures, and opposed a third term for President Wilson. Feeling, perhaps, that he had gone too far, Smith sent a resolution to the convention stating, "We indorse the splendid achievements of the Democratic congress and administration, and confidently predict overwhelming Democratic victory in the fall." But Watson secured the adjournment of the convention before the resolution could be acted on.[17]

Tom Watson was satisfied; he had obtained "a straightout condemnation of the League, and a straight defeat of endorsement of Wilson." Smith also expressed approval, although in a letter to the New York *Times* he called himself a friend of Wilson and of the principles of the League. The New York paper had thought it "a curious whimsicality" that Smith should "sit silently by and see a Democratic Administration assassinated by a Georgia Democratic Convention." And Clark Howell smugly declared, "We really thought Hoke Smith had more political sense than to form an open alliance with Tom Watson to vent his spleen toward the democratic administration. . . ."[18]

Following the adjournment of the state convention, the Palmer followers had chosen a slate of their own delegates to the national convention, basing their action on the ground that the rules of the state convention had been violated. Both sides then prepared their cases to be presented at San Francisco. The national committee, of which Clark Howell was an influential member, voted unanimously to seat the Palmer delegation, and the credentials committee approved this decision by a vote of 43 to 4. Smith deplored the rejection of the " regular " delegation, but he would not bolt the ticket—" we Georgians must support the ticket."[19]

Hoke Smith's poor showing in the April primary made it clear that he would have great difficulty in being re-elected to the Senate. Reports spread in late spring and early summer that he

[17] Atlanta *Journal*, May 19, August 3, 1920.

[18] Smith to the editor of the New York *Times*, May 24, 1920, in Smith Collection; Atlanta *Journal*, May 19-21, 26, 1920.

[19] Smith to T. S. Hawes, June 23, 1920, in Smith Collection; Atlanta *Journal*, May 19, 27, June 19, 26-30, July 6, 14, 1920.

would not run in the Senate primary. Meanwhile, several Georgia leaders, including Hooper Alexander and Commissioner of Agriculture J. J. Brown, were mentioned as possible candidates. Smith was watching the political situation closely, hoping no doubt that either Dorsey or Watson would not enter the race. "I think it quite possible," he wrote in mid-July, "that neither Dorsey [n]or Watson will be a candidate. . . ." He received encouraging news from various parts of the state, though some of his supporters in earlier years wrote him critical letters.[20]

By late July the Senator had made up his mind: he would run. On July 27 he mailed his entrance fee to the secretary of state and announced that he would stand squarely on his record and on the Democratic national platform. After being "undecided" for several weeks, Watson also announced his candidacy. This was not unexpected by political observers; the old agrarian leader had spared neither Smith nor Dorsey in the recent issues of his newspaper. Governor Dorsey dispelled any illusions the Smith element had about his position when he declared a few days later that he would be a candidate.[21]

The following campaign was a hectic six-week affair as bitterly fought as any during the past decade. During the first two weeks of the campaign Smith confined his activities largely to the creation of a statewide organization. His staff distributed great quantities of campaign literature, and the Senator wrote hundreds of personal letters to people all over the state. He insisted that his "personal inclination was to stay out of the race," but he was willing to serve "if the people want me." He tried desperately to explain his position on the League and his actions during the recent state convention. A typical explanation went like this:

> I am disposed to agree with you that I made a mistake in entering the race in Georgia, and also in not having gone in person to the State Convention and handled my side of the question on the floor. I favored a resolution endorsing the

---

[20] Charles L. Bartlett to Smith, July 7, 1920, J. E. Carter to Smith, July 13, 1920, Roger D. Flynt to Smith, July 14, 1920, B. H. McLarty to Smith, July 20, 1920, and Smith to Roger D. Flynt, July 21, 1920, in Smith Collection.

[21] Smith to Hiram L. Gardner, July 27, 1920, *ibid.*; Atlanta *Journal*, July 25, 28, 29, August 1, 7, 1920.

splendid work of the Administration and of Congress, and when I heard the character of platform which had been reported, I sent such a resolution to the Convention. . . . [But] Watson secured an adjournment of the Convention, preventing action. The truth is that some of the Palmer leaders had been so abusive and so offensive that the state of mind of the Convention was unfortunate.[22]

"You were once my friend," was his plaintive note in many letters; "I want to reason with you a little." [23]

Beginning about August 10 and continuing for the next month, Smith conducted one of the most energetic speaking campaigns of his career. He spoke in every section of the state, making a particularly strong appeal in those counties Palmer had carried in the April primary. By the last week in August he was delivering two and three addresses a day. A South Georgia newspaper described one of the Senator's speeches: " Senator Smith's address for the most part was unimpassioned. It lacked bitterness except on occasional references to those who have been most bitter and unfair with him. It was not an attempt at fine oratory to carry the crowd by the spell of words, although the senator possesses this power, but a face-to-face, man-to-man discussion of affairs of importance to every citizen." [24]

It was soon apparent that Smith had moderated his position with respect to the Wilson administration and the League in order to appeal to the Palmer men and to many of his old followers who had turned against him because of his truculent attitude. He seemed eager to demonstrate that he was in accord with James M. Cox and the Democratic platform, although he still insisted that the League required modification. " All of us are human," he declared. " I have made mistakes. I am free to admit them." [25]

[22] Smith to H. J. Davis, August 7, 1920, and numerous other letters, in Smith Collection.

[23] For examples, see Smith to William H. Hosch, July 31, August 2, 1920, to John Collins, August 1, 1920, to T. C. Hughes, August 3, 1920, and to George I. Teasley, August 15, 1920, in Smith Collection.

[24] Americus *Times-Recorder*, quoted in Atlanta *Journal*, September 5, 1920.

[25] Smith to Thomas J. Hamilton, August 20, 1920, and undated memo-

Smith also defended himself against the charge that he had deliberately made an agreement with Tom Watson in the state convention. The Howells and their faction, now so critical of his combination with Watson, had constantly worked with the Populist leader during the past twelve years, the Senator charged, while he himself had not spoken to Watson during all those years. Smith described Dorsey as a "tame, gentle, inexperienced man" who had mismanaged the state's finances and collected "false" tobacco taxes from Georgia merchants. As for Tom Watson, "He hates everybody. He slanders everybody. He preaches no doctrine but bitterness and strife. He is radical and dangerous. If you follow him to the end, he will lead you out of the Democratic party. I beg you not to let the Watson hydrophobia get into your system." [26]

As the campaign tempo quickened, Smith resorted to some demagoguery himself. He hinted darkly that the Republicans might reduce the number of Federal Reserve banks and restrict farm credit, and he spoke increasingly of the "ignorant and purchaseable negro vote," reminding his audiences that a resolution was pending in Congress designed to bring about an investigation of state election laws. [27]

Governor Dorsey's managers advertised their candidate as an "able, sincere and courageous Democrat with a record of 100% loyalty to the party, the administration and the State." His entrance fee was paid by the American Legion, from which he received strong support. The governor criticized Tom Watson but he concentrated his attack on Hoke Smith, denouncing his war record and his position on the League. After Dorsey called him a "squelcher, welcher and squirmer," Smith invited the governor to debate with him, but Dorsey refused to rise to the bait, despite a second invitation from the Senator. [28]

Dorsey waited until after the legislature adjourned to begin his campaign addresses, but Watson toured the state three times

randum for speech (1920), in Smith Collection; Atlanta *Journal*, August 11, 13, 19, 23-27, September 2, 3, 7, 1920.

[26] Atlanta *Journal*, August 13, 16, 23-28, September 1, 7, 1920.

[27] *Ibid.*, August 26, 27, 29, September 2, 5, 1920.

[28] Smith to Dorsey, August 29, 30, 1920, in Smith Collection; Atlanta *Journal*, July 30, 31, August 5, 12, 18, 23-29, September 2, 3, 1920.

and carried out a vigorous editorial campaign. He denounced the newly organized American Legion and lashed out at the League, compulsory military training, Palmer's Red raids, and the alleged mistreatment of privates in the army. Of Smith he scornfully declared: "He's been for reservations, and he's been against them. He's been against the whole d——— thing and he's been for it." [29]

The controversy among Georgia newspapers was, if anything, even more intense than that among the three candidates. Governor Dorsey received the support of a majority of the papers, while Smith was backed by ten or twelve daily newspapers and twenty-five or thirty weeklies. Watson apparently received little newspaper support. Despite Watson's growing strength, the Dorsey and Smith papers preferred to attack each other rather than Watson. Smith and his newspaper advocates contended that Dorsey had been forced into the Senate race by a "coterie of politicians with axes to grind." Some Dorsey papers, such as the Savannah *Press* and the Augusta *Chronicle*, approached the primary contest on a relatively impersonal basis, but many journals were more abusive of Smith. "In the retirement of Senator Smith," declared the Macon *Telegraph*, "Mr. Lodge will be deprived of one of the best reservation writers, office boys and listening posts he ever stole from the Democratic party." [30]

The illusion that he was winning the race died hard with Hoke Smith. He desperately wanted to win. "Of course this is the most important race of my life," he told one man. It was true that there were hopeful signs. Complimentary letters flowed into Smith's headquarters praising his speeches, several prominent businessmen and industrialists endorsed him, the Jews and Catholics seemed to favor him, and he was informed that he would obtain many of the Palmer votes. [31] But mixed in with the opti-

[29] Columbia (S. C.) *Sentinel*, October 18, 1920; Woodward, *Tom Watson*, 471-72.

[30] Macon *Telegraph*, May 19, 24, July 31, August 4, 13, 19, September 7, 1920; Atlanta *Constitution*, September 1-8, 1920; Thomas J. Hamilton to Smith, August 16, 1920, in Smith Collection.

[31] Smith to Thomas J. Loyless, August 15, 1920, to W. D. Kirkland, August 17, 1920, to Hoyt Brannon, August 27, 1920, and to W. T. Nicholson, September 1, 1920; Roger D. Flynt to Smith, August 30, 1920, and numerous

mistic reports was a strong current of warnings and qualifying statements. "It seems that your stand on the treaty has aroused resentment," wrote many local leaders to the Senator. "You cant get anywhere fighting the League and belittling Woodrow Wilson," asserted another Georgian. "Dorsey is splitting up your vote," was another refrain. Even more disturbing was the growing evidence that Tom Watson might win the primary.[32]

Smith and his advisers did their best, but they must have known before the end of the campaign that they were whistling in the dark. They made a strong effort to appeal to organized labor, but labor condemned the Senator for some of his antilabor votes in the Senate. The Smith managers vigorously advertised a scheme to persuade Dorsey followers to combine with them in supporting Smith so that Watson could be defeated. But, to their dismay, the Dorsey men were attempting the same strategy.[33]

Whatever lingering hopes Hoke Smith may have had were smashed by Tom Watson's sweeping victory. Watson received 111,723 popular votes to 72,885 for Dorsey and 61,729 for Smith.[34] This was certainly a "political upheaval" in Georgia, declared the Macon *Telegraph*, which found the "psychology" of Watson's nomination to be "the general discontent that prevails throughout the world." "Who Killed Cock Robin?" asked the Atlanta *Constitution*. "The truth is," said Clark Howell's paper, with vast satisfaction, "nobody but Senator Smith is responsible for his defeat. . . . Robin killed himself."[35]

In a sense this was true. Smith realized only too late that his

other letters, in Smith Collection; Atlanta *Journal*, August 24, 26-29, September 5-7, 1920.

[32] L. J. Sharp to Smith, August 2, 1920, E. R. Lockridge to Smith, August 12, 1920, Bowdre Phinizy to Smith, August 16, 1920, Louis L. Brown to Smith, August 18, 1920, I. J. Bussell to Smith, August 21, 1920, and O. B. Bush to Smith, August 26, 1920, in Smith Collection.

[33] Murray Stewart to Smith, July 27, 1920, and J. S. Lewis to Smith, September 4, 1920, in Smith Collection; Atlanta *Journal*, August 7, 1920; Savannah *Morning News*, August 11, 1920.

[34] Watson carried 102 counties with 247 county-unit votes, whereas Dorsey won 38 counties with 103 county-unit votes and Smith carried only 14 counties with 34 unit-votes. Atlanta *Journal*, September 10, 11, 1920.

[35] Macon *Telegraph*, September 10, 1920; Atlanta *Constitution*, September 10-12, 1920.

entrance into the Presidential primary had been a mistake of the first order. There was an independence and vanity about him that made it difficult for him to foresee the results of such political decisions. Having joined forces with Tom Watson in the state convention, Smith probably hoped against hope that Watson would not enter the Senatorial primary. His chances would have been improved considerably had either Watson or Dorsey not entered the contest. But more fundamentally the Senator's defeat was largely personal; the voters had lost confidence in him, despite the widespread acknowledgment of his abilities and his service to his state. Furthermore, the middle ground he cultivated so assiduously proved highly barren and left him open to attack from both sides. An editorial in the Macon *Telegraph* was about right: " Senator Smith straddled and evaded on big issues, losing a great deal of his support to Watson, and by flirting with him in the Atlanta convention, the Senator brought into being a monster that consumed . . . him." [36]

" The pygmies of personal and factional hate may draw such satisfaction as they can from knowing that at last, after years of harassing and misrepresenting him, they have deprived the State of Hoke Smith's services," declared the Atlanta *Journal* in an editorial reminding Georgians of Smith's many contributions. As for the Senator, he took his defeat in stride, accepting the results of the election with " little mental disturbance." But the outcome baffled him. " I stayed in Washington the whole time for nine years practically," he wrote one man, " working for the people, but the bulk of them never really understood it." [37]

Following the primary, Smith remained in Atlanta for a few weeks. He wrote personal letters of thanks to many of his supporters in the recent primary and returned some campaign contributions, " being unwilling to burden my friends with any part of my campaign expenses." During the Senate campaign he had carefully refrained from getting involved in the guberna-

---

[36] Macon *Telegraph*, September 10, 1920.

[37] Smith to Thomas P. Gore, September 14, 1920, to J. M. Byrd, September 18, 1920, to Joseph W. Wells, October 1, 1920, and to M. M. Allen, October 5, 1920, in Smith Collection; Atlanta *Journal*, September 9, 10, 1920.

torial race, in which Hardwick, John N. Holder, and Clifford Walker were the candidates, but in the runoff primary between Hardwick and Walker he supported the ex-Senator. He did not take an active part, however. "What I wish now," he said, "is to be let alone so far as political contests are concerned, and to contribute what I can to the welfare of my fellow citizens from the standpoint of a private citizen." [38]

In the fall and winter Smith joined other cotton Congressmen in another effort to save the prosperity of the cotton belt. The South's chief staple had fallen on evil days. Prices had declined steadily since the war, there was a large surplus, and thousands of farmers struggled under a heavy indebtedness contracted during the booming days of the war. The Senator participated in the conference held in Washington in October, conferred with the Federal Reserve Board about liberalizing the requirements for discounting agricultural paper, and acted as host in Atlanta at a conference of the Georgia Congressmen which convened to discuss the cotton problem. At his suggestion, the Congressmen endorsed a scheme for the establishment of an export finance corporation to ship cotton to Germany. When Congress reassembled in December, 1920, Smith took a leading part in the passage of the War Finance Corporation bill and in the support of other farm bloc measures. [39]

The third session of the Sixty-sixth Congress—Hoke Smith's last —found him as busy as ever. In addition to his support of the efforts to assist cotton producers and to secure the passage of the Smith-Towner education bill, he devoted much time to the agricultural appropriations bill. He defended the emergency tariff bill of 1921, being determined to see that Southern products were ade-

[38] Smith to Theodore Tiller, September 20, 1920, to J. D. Strickland, September 25, 1920, to F. L. Dyar, September 27, 1920, and to George D. Rucker, October 1, 1920, in Smith Collection; Atlanta *Journal*, September 15, 18, 26, 1920.

[39] Smith and others to W. P. G. Harding, October 13, 14, 1920, Georgia Congressmen to Woodrow Wilson, October 19, 1920, and Smith to G. Arthur Gordon, December 4, 6, 1920, in Smith Collection; Atlanta *Journal*, October 14, 19, 23, 29, December 22, 1920, January 5, 1921; *Cong. Record*, 66 Cong., 3 Sess., 18-19, 27, 112, 160-68, 557-58, 1028-29, 2895-96, 4113.

quately protected, and approved Republican plans to hurry the nation back to normalcy.[40]

Meanwhile, Smith had decided upon his future work. He had made up his mind to practice law in Washington and had "purchased five beautiful offices in the Southern Building." He planned to retain his assistant, Major O. H. B. Bloodworth, Jr., and his secretary, Miss Mazie Crawford. "I may not get any business," he wrote his daughter Mary Brent, "but on the other hand, there is a chance that I may get some very large paying cases, and my sole object in opening offices here is to see if I can make a very substantial amount of money by staying a year or two." He needed to make a large amount of money, for he owed nearly $150,000.[41] As the end of the session approached, the Senator grew increasingly enthusiastic about his future work. He was always a man who faced the future; the past was something to live by but not to live for.

During the final days of the term the Georgia Society of Washington gave Smith a farewell reception, and Senator Harris was host at a farewell luncheon for his colleague. Smith issued a statement on the eve of his retirement, bidding his constituents good-bye and expressing his "intense appreciation for the generous support they have so often given." "Whatever differences of opinion may exist as to my public work," he declared, ". . . I have never cast a vote, or done an official act, moved by any influence other than an earnest purpose to promote their welfare. . . ." Faithful to the last, the Atlanta *Journal* sounded a final note of praise in a long editorial entitled "A Senator Who Has Served." [42]

The long political struggle was over for Hoke Smith. In May, 1921, he canceled his subscription to the Atlanta *Constitution*, a certain sign that the political fires in his career were burning out. The Senate years had brought their share of success to the Georgia politician. He had left his name on some important legislation, and he had contributed substantially to the shaping of the Wilson administration's reform program. But the Senate

[40] *Cong. Record,* 66 Cong., 3 Sess., 1961-62, 3250, 4060-61.
[41] Smith to Mary Brent Ransom, January 20, 1921, in Smith Collection.
[42] Atlanta *Journal,* February 4, March 2-6, 1921.

years had also brought misfortune and ultimate defeat. Frequently at odds with the administration over cotton diplomacy and occasionally over patronage matters, abhorring the vast war powers given the President, and suspicious of the League of Nations, Smith's increasing conservatism forced him more and more to adopt a negative role during his final years in the Senate. Perhaps the voters sensed the fact that obstruction was not his best role.

Peaceful Decade: 1921-31

The final ten years of Hoke Smith's life brought him greater freedom and more real satisfaction than had his last years in the Senate. He remained in Washington for more than four years following his retirement from office, engaged in some of the most lucrative legal work of his career. He returned to Atlanta in 1925 to spend the remainder of his life amid the surroundings he loved so well. When political temptation came, as it did with powerful insistence on two or three occasions in the 1920's, Smith found the strength to resist.

In Washington business came with a rush. Major O. H. B. Bloodworth, who was a member of the Smith firm, described the nature of their work:

> . . . we do general practice of all kinds, with particular attention to income tax matters, matters pending before the various Departments and Congress. So far as legislation is concerned, we are interested in a number of claims which are pending before various committees; we have represented . . . wholesale grocers associations, newspaper associations, turpentine associations, watermelon growers associations, importers, etc. . . . in looking after legislation, adverse to their interests, or the passage of which they desired, and have constantly appeared before committees of both houses in connection therewith.[1]

During the first half of the twenties Smith devoted considerable time to an elaborate scheme, in which his brother Burton was a leading participant, designed to persuade Congress to authorize

[1] Bloodworth to M. J. Witman, February 17, 1923, in Smith Collection.

the return of certain taxes that allegedly were illegally collected by the Federal government during Reconstruction.

Much of Smith's work was essentially lobbying, and in this sphere he found his Congressional contacts extremely useful. "I have sought to keep in constant touch with the Bureau," he wrote John S. Cohen in connection with a tax case, "and to reach such other influences here as might be potential. Confidentially," he continued, "I have even brought [about] conferences with the President. . . ."[2] The Georgia lawyer had lost none of his old enthusiasm for his profession. If people understood how fully he was enjoying his "present work," he wrote soon after leaving the Senate, they would not want him "again in official position."[3] Smith could well be pleased as far as the firm's earnings were concerned. He did not seek "any employments which do not bring a certainty of at least $2,500," he wrote in June, 1923. By the fall of that year he had received over $23,000 from the Chestatee Pyrites and Chemical Corporation and had won an award of almost $500,000 for the company from the government.[4]

Several of Smith's most important cases were alien property claims. Through George F. Parker, an official in Cleveland's second administration, and J. Lyman Pratt, Smith's son-in-law, he came into contact with Ludwig Nissen and other German-Americans, mostly in New York. He had discussed the possibility of forming a cotton export corporation with F. A. Borgemeister even before leaving the Senate and through him met Carl Schreiner, who employed the Southerner to aid him in securing the return of the funds of the Swiss National Insurance Company. Smith also represented the Bank fuer Handel und Industrie, Henry Blattmann and Company, John H. Volkmann, and others in efforts to recover property seized during the war. Some of these cases were taken to the Federal courts, and in other instances Smith tried to get direct Congressional action.[5]

In 1923 Smith was employed to assist several other lawyers

[2] Smith to Cohen, September 3, 1921, ibid.
[3] Smith to M. B. Wellborn, March 24, 1921, ibid.
[4] See the correspondence on this case in Smith Collection.
[5] For the alien property cases, see the extensive correspondence between Smith and F. A. Borgemeister, Carl Schreiner, A. W. Lafferty, Henry Blattmann, Ludwig Nissen, and Charles Nagel, in Smith Collection.

in representing the government of Peru in an attempt to settle the long-standing Tacna-Arica dispute between Chile and Peru. In 1922 Secretary of State Charles Evans Hughes had brought the two nations together in Washington, and they finally agreed to arbitrate the question, with the President of the United States being designated as arbiter.

Hoke Smith's association with the Peruvian case lasted from the late summer of 1923 until 1926. He assisted in the preparation of the first argument in the fall of 1923 and in the countercase against Chile's claims. The Southerner's ideas as to the direction Peru's arguments should take and his tendency to assume the lead in the development of the case provoked Professor Edwin M. Borchard of Yale University, who regarded himself as the leading American lawyer in the case.[6] The two Latin-American countries finally accepted a compromise plan in 1929. Meanwhile, as long as he was a member of the Peruvian counsel, Smith had received $1,000 a month "together with other payments to be made as a result of the success obtained for Peru."[7]

With such handsome retainers, Hoke Smith was able to pay or refund his debts and to invest in other business enterprises. He bought and sold securities on the stock market, often to the extent of twenty-five or thirty thousand dollars. He began once more to purchase Atlanta property. By September, 1924, he owned about $250,000 worth of improved real estate in the city and $100,000 worth of suburban property, in addition to his holdings in the Piedmont Hotel and the Fulton National Bank. "In thirty days," he wrote, "I could turn my property into cash, over and above liabilities, at substantially more than $500,000."[8]

[6] Smith to Edwin M. Borchard, September 26, October 2, 20, 1923, and Borchard to Smith, September 29, October 11, 18, 21, 1923, January 24, April 14, 1924; Meliton F. Porras to Smith, October 19, 1923; and Smith to Porras, October 20, November 3, 1923, in Smith Collection. See also briefs and other correspondence concerning this question, *ibid*.

[7] Edwardo Higginson to Smith, February 7, July 8, August 1, November 15, 1924, January 20, 1925, in Smith Collection.

[8] Smith to Ronald Ransom, January 2, April 7, 1923, and to Riggs National Bank, September 6, 1924, in Smith Collection. For Smith's operations on the stock exchange, see records, *ibid*.

Had Smith been a millionaire he would have played the game
of organized philanthropy with enthusiasm. As it was, he gave
generously of his time and money. As the agricultural depression
deepened over the South during the 1920's, he received hundreds
of letters every year asking for help of some kind. " I am writing
you out of habit," one man informed him, " as you are the natural
one I have always turned to when anything was needed in Washington." [9] The ex-Senator contributed to innumerable worthy
causes and individuals, particularly for educational purposes. He
assisted many young people in furthering their education and
was especially generous to the large number of " Hoke Smiths "
who made up his " Namesakes " book.

In his addresses at educational rallies, business conventions,
and civic gatherings the lawyer expressed a philosophy that fitted
in well with the dominant political ideas of the decade. Americans, he said, should " depend upon the maintenance of individual
initiative, free from unnecessary Government interference, supported by a spirit of co-operation extended to every legitimate
occupation." A case in point was the disposition of Muscle
Shoals, which he felt would stimulate agricultural production
and help bring prosperity to the Southern farmer. But the power
facilities and the nitrogen plants must be operated by private
enterprise, declared the Southerner, who appeared before a Congressional committee to support the Ford offer to lease the Muscle
Shoals facilities.[10]

The recurrent crises in the cotton belt led Smith to devote
much of his time to agricultural problems. He continued to
preach the doctrine of diversified farming, urged a more liberal
extension of agricultural credit, and supported the movement to
have farmers reduce their cotton acreage. Arranging to operate
a " one-horse farm " in Jones County, Georgia, where the ravages
of the boll weevil were especially severe, he employed an
overseer to demonstrate the effectiveness of Hill's mixture, a liquid
poison composed of calcium arsenate, molasses, and other ingredi-

[9] Robert H. Jones, Jr., to Smith, April 1, 1921, and many other letters,
in Smith Collection.
[10] Typescript copy of address delivered at Muscle Shoals, May 22, 1922,
in Smith Collection; New York *Times*, May 18, 1922.

ents. "What I want to do is to have the satisfaction of contributing something towards the return of normal conditions in
Jones County," he declared.[11]

In 1922 Smith was unofficially offered the presidency of the
Georgia School of Technology, but he refused to consider the
position. Nathaniel E. Harris, chairman of the board, was disappointed. "You have done more for technical education in
the Nation than any man who has lived since the War," he wrote.
"It would have been a fitting conclusion to a magnificent career
if you could have come to the State that has honored you. . . ."
When Smith's name was mentioned in the Georgia capitol, added
Harris, "there was a spontaneous, enthusiastic response."[12]

Such reports of approbation by his fellow-Georgians provided
a frequent reminder to the ex-Senator of the possibility of returning to political life. He did not expect "to return to public
life," he had said several times, but he could not divorce himself
completely from politics. Because of his friendship for President
Harding and other members of the administration, many Georgians
turned to him for assistance in obtaining Federal appointments,
and he took the lead in persuading the President to visit Atlanta.
In 1922 he endorsed Governor Hardwick's bid for re-election,
denouncing his opposition as an "unholy alliance" and praising
the governor for attacking the Ku Klux Klan. Meanwhile, many
of his correspondents urged him to run again for political office,
and when Senator Watson died in September, 1922, his name was
immediately brought to the fore. "From all parts of the state,"
reported the Atlanta *Journal*, "come the news that former Senator
Hoke Smith's name is everywhere being mentioned in connection
with the senatorial primary."[13]

For a week or more Smith pondered the question. A large
number of encouraging letters and telegrams "from all parts of

[11] Smith to Ransom, January 6, 1923, to J. R. Middlebrooks, March 6,
August 13, 1923, to Frank Barrett, March 28, April 13, 1923, and to R. L.
McKinney, February 11, 1924, in Smith Collection.

[12] Marion Smith to Nathaniel E. Harris, July 6, 1922, and Harris to Smith,
July 7, 1922, *ibid.*

[13] Matthew C. Bennet to Smith, October 25, 1921, Pearson Ellis to Smith,
February 20, 1922, and Hooper Alexander to Smith, September 30, 1922,
in Smith Collection; Atlanta *Journal*, October 1, 3, 1922.

the state" gave him confidence. But he could not bring himself
to enter the race. After contacting Marion Smith, Walter F.
George announced his candidacy and in the following primary
defeated Governor Hardwick for the position. "Under ordinary
circumstances," Smith wrote, "I should have entered the race,
for I really know that I am in a position to render valuable service
to the state, but I had assumed obligations to a number of clients
involving large amounts of money. . . ."[14]

Unfortunately for his complete peace of mind, Smith could
not close the door to the possibility of an eventual return to the
Senate. Long urged by friends in Georgia to challenge Senator
William J. Harris' re-election in 1924, he allowed the thought
of such a step to play around the edges of his mind throughout
1923 and into 1924. Marion Smith was keenly aware of the
situation and constantly urged his father to make a decision with
respect to the race.[15] But the older man evinced a curious reluctance to make up his mind.

Publicly Smith would not admit that he was considering the
race. Reports of his renewed hold on the people of Georgia
continued to reach him. "I find your name to be still a magic
word in Georgia," Helen Dortch Longstreet wrote after a tour
of the state. It would be pleasant, Smith admitted to his son,
to retire undefeated, but he was "content" with his present work.
"If you and my other children are satisfied for me to remain
in private life," he wrote Marion, "it pleases me."[16] Smith was
enjoying his work, he was deeply involved in some of his largest
law cases, and he was under some obligation to Senator Harris,
who had co-operated with him in a few of his recent legislative
interests. He was no longer held up to the scourge of public

---

[14] Marion Smith to Walter F. George, October 2, 1922, and to Smith,
October 2, 3, 14, 1922, in Marion Smith Papers (in possession of Hoke
Smith II, Atlanta, Georgia); Smith to Hooper Alexander, October 6, 1922,
in Smith Collection.

[15] Marion Smith to Smith, January 10, 1923, in Marion Smith Papers;
id. to id., February 9, 1923, in Smith Collection.

[16] Smith to Clarence H. Levy, May 15, 1923, to Charles E. Brown, June
22, 1923, and to Marion Smith, September 8, 1923; Helen Dortch Longstreet
to Smith, May 28, July 21, 1923, and Marion Smith to Smith, August 30,
September 12, 1923, in Smith Collection.

criticism but instead was praised on all sides for his long record of service and for his humanitarian spirit.

Despite his busy schedule Hoke Smith found time for social diversions. He belonged to numerous Washington professional and fraternal organizations and served as president of the Georgia Society in the capital. There was nothing threadbare about the ex-Senator's life. He lived at the Shoreham Hotel, maintained a car and chauffeur, and spent a great deal of money on his family. Always a large eater, he relished huge meals. He enjoyed doing many things, liked the company of both men and women, and was a good traveler. In August, 1924, he married Mazie Crawford, his secretary, from Cordele, Georgia. He had not consulted the children, and except for Callie, who attended the wedding, they were reluctant to approve their father's remarriage. But Smith was happy. The new Mrs. Hoke Smith, many years younger than her husband, was described as a "woman of great charm and attractiveness." [17]

Smith had long dreamed of returning to Atlanta to spend his old age. He began to make plans for the move early in 1923, but it was not until the summer of 1925 that he and his wife left Washington for home. Hoke Smith felt like Ulysses coming home. "I may take a law case every now and then," he told newspapermen, "if it is offered to me and it interests me, but I want to spend most of my time . . . doing things for Atlanta and for Georgia. . . ." [18]

Smith's law practice declined after he came back to Georgia, although it remained fairly heavy for two or three years. He employed a young lawyer named F. M. ("Buster") Bird to assist him, and the younger man proved a great help in preparing briefs, helping with the correspondence, and running the office during the older man's frequent absences. Smith made numerous public appearances, often speaking on the state's "splendid resources" and its industrial possibilities. He also liked to discuss historical subjects in a patriotic vein.

By the time he returned to Georgia to live, Hoke Smith was

---

[17] Atlanta *Journal*, August 27, 1924.
[18] *Ibid.*, July 13, August 2, September 4, 1925.

almost seventy years old. Having failed to oppose Senator Harris in 1924, he had apparently given up all thought of re-entering political life. But almost before he had settled in Atlanta people began to urge him to run for governor in 1926, and when the state began a vigorous debate over a proposed highway construction program the interest in his possible candidacy increased. Hundreds of people wrote him. "The hope that Senator Smith will decide to make this race is often heard on the streets," reported the Savannah *Press* in the autumn of 1925. As one man wrote Smith, "we dont need no young lawyer for that office we need a man like you . . . and i think the pepple has found it out." [19]

From late fall, 1925, until late spring, 1926, there appeared to be a chance that Smith would enter the race. "If I felt that Georgians really wanted me, and I could be of service to the state," he said in the fall, "I would consider the matter very seriously." But he could not decide what he "ought to do." Early 1926 brought additional evidence of the support for the old political war horse. But Smith continued to delay, just as he had done in 1922-23. He was "carefully considering" the question, he wrote many correspondents, adding that he did not "really desire the place." He appeared before a joint legislative committee to urge the approval of a bond program for roads and education, but he simply could not make the decision to enter the contest, although it was not until June 22 that he definitely took himself out of the race.[20]

Marion Smith and others close to the ex-Senator probably discouraged him from entering the campaign because of his advanced age. Moreover, Smith himself was genuinely reluctant to become entangled in a bitter political fight.

There was one additional moment of political excitement in Hoke Smith's life. He gave vigorous support to Alfred E. Smith

[19] W. S. Trent to Smith, October 1, 1925, John K. Dykes to Smith, November 10, 1925, Jere M. Pound to Smith, March 5, 1926, and large number of similar letters, in Smith Collection.

[20] Atlanta *Journal*, June 23, 1926; Smith to T. L. Pickren, December 23, 1925, to Ben A. Neal, January 30, 1926, to R. E. Trussell, March 12, 1926, to J. P. Rushing, April 13, 1926, and to G. S. Cobb, June 15, 1926, in Smith Collection.

in the election of 1928, despite the denunciation of the New Yorker by many Georgia leaders. He made several addresses for the Democratic nominee and sponsored a rally of Democrats in Atlanta in an effort to stamp out the growing party disloyalty.

Smith enjoyed the attention these political interludes brought him. When some local newspaper described him as "the Nestor of Georgia politics," he was as pleased as a boy. When Warren P. Hunnicutt, one of his secretaries while he was in the Senate, wrote two or three magazine articles about his career, he purchased hundreds of copies for distribution in Georgia. He especially liked to be pointed out as a member of Cleveland's Cabinet, and during these last years he often spoke on Grover Cleveland, delivering one address in New York to the Cleveland Association.

Smith's grandchildren were a source of constant delight to the old man. He was always interested in their aches and pains, in their youthful triumphs and failures. His correspondence contains many of his letters to them and reveals how completely he indulged in his grandfatherly prerogative of buying them what they wanted.[21] Smith was equally interested in his children. When the two younger daughters separated from their husbands, their father cheerfully provided for them, advised them, and tried constantly to assist them in adjusting to their new lives. There were other family disappointments. Burton, who had been forced to leave Atlanta after succumbing to alcoholism and getting into other difficulties, never quite succeeded in New York. He turned to his brother for help again and again. The many financial burdens that Hoke Smith assumed for various members of his family and some losses he suffered as a result of investments in Florida real estate in 1926-27 cost him heavily.

Hoke Smith doted on his wife. He liked to have her accompany him everywhere, and he consulted her about most of the small threads that were woven together to make up his final years. During the late twenties the Smiths devoted themselves to the plans for the home they were having built on a portion of

[21] See, for example, Smith to Barbara Ransom, December 29, 1920, September 21, 1923, to Mary Brent Ransom, April 7, 1922, to Hoke Smith Simpson, June 9, 1922, and to Birdie Cobb Pratt, June 2, 1926, *ibid.*

Smith's Howell Mill Road property. Unfortunately, the plans were held up for a time, and the house was not completed until 1930.

"My doctors in Washington went over me a few months ago," Smith wrote in 1925, "and Xrayed me from my head to my heels. As a result of this examination they advised me that I have no physical defects." In 1927 John T. Boifeuillet could still detect the ex-Senator's "quick and springy step, his deep and sonorous voice, his alert and forceful brain." [22] Yet that wonderful physical machine was running down. There were heavy lines in the old man's face, the corners of his mouth sagged, and his hair was white and thinning. He complained in 1928 that a client had sent him "such an enormous amount of matter" that he could not digest it—a complaint that he had never made before. His speeches became rambling, and in some of his last courtroom appearances he was rather pathetic.

Death came peacefully to Smith at 11:40 on Friday morning, November 27, 1931.[23] The funeral was held on Sunday afternoon at the North Avenue Presbyterian Church; the simple but impressive services were conducted by Smith's old pastor, Richard Orme Flinn, and his long-time friend, Bishop Warren A. Candler. The church overflowed with people, including Governor Richard B. Russell and such old Smith lieutenants as Henry H. Cabaniss, Reuben Arnold, and Hooper Alexander. "So many old timers, some bent with age, others almost too feeble to be about," wrote the *Journal*'s Ralph Smith. "Through many a stirring campaign they'd followed the senator, and now they were gathered in reverence and respect to do homage to his memory." [24]

Messages of condolence and tribute poured in from all over the country. Governor Franklin D. Roosevelt of New York recalled that, as a boy, he had first known Hoke Smith when the Southerner was a member of Cleveland's Cabinet. Numerous

[22] Smith to Louis Moore, November 2, 1925, *ibid.*; Atlanta *Journal*, March 3, 1927.

[23] Smith's health had declined rapidly during the past year. A week before his death his condition suddenly became much worse, and two days before the end he sank into a coma from which he never aroused. Atlanta *Journal*, November 27, 1931.

[24] Atlanta *Journal*, November 27, 29, 30, 1931.

Southern political leaders and many of Smith's old colleagues in the Senate praised him as " an outstanding southern statesman." He was " a veritable lion of a man," declared the Atlanta *Journal*. " The Journal mourns his going hence, as a friend of long years and deeply cherished associations." Clark Howell wrote a final word for his old enemy: " In going Senator Smith leaves an indelible imprint upon the history of the state, which he served long and well." [25]

Hoke Smith's political career might have been more fortunate, but as one newspaper noted, it was sometimes difficult for a Georgia politician " to keep either his head or his office." Smith had an insatiable yearning for public acclaim, but he had none of the " professional suaveness which flatters every comer." Indeed, there was an independence and an egoism about the man that caused other politicians to regard him with suspicion, and he was never a person whom businessmen could trust completely. " He had a certain radicalism," declared the New York *Times*, " innate or bred of environment and of the time-spirit, which made him thunder against the corporations." [26]

A bold and imaginative politician, Smith thought in large terms and dreamed great dreams for the progress of the people of his state and section and for himself. He had a gift for sensing the vital issues that brought him into contact with the most important developments of his day. His administrative success in the Cabinet, his numerous reforms as governor, and his work for education and agriculture in the Senate marked him as a constructive political leader. Yet there was far greater promise than fulfillment. Hoke Smith wanted to be a reformer; the pity was that in his zeal to succeed in politics his vision often became distorted, and he was willing to use means that were unworthy of his ideals.

[25] *Ibid.*, November 29, 1931; Atlanta *Constitution*, November 28, 1931.
[26] New York *Times*, November 28, 1931; Atlanta *Journal*, November 29, 1931.

Critical Essay on Authorities

Manuscript Materials

The Hoke Smith Collection in the University of Georgia Library contains the principal manuscript sources available for a study of Smith's public career. Unfortunately, the bulk of Smith's vast accumulation of correspondence and public papers was destroyed soon after his death, and the correspondence in the collection is complete only for the last year or two of his Senate career and for the decade that followed his retirement from politics in 1921. But these papers are often relevant to his earlier activities and are extremely rich for the election of 1920. In addition to this correspondence, the Smith Collection includes important biographical memoranda, most of Smith's legal letterbooks for the years 1880-1910, about 50 volumes of newspaper clippings, approximately 375 letters dealing with Smith's appointment to the Cabinet, and a large number of printed pamphlets and speeches.

The most useful manuscripts relating to Hoke Smith's service in the Cabinet are the Department of Interior records in the National Archives. A large amount of material having to do with appointments, land questions, Indian affairs, pensions, and patents may be found in the various divisions of the archives, much of it purely routine but quite valuable in throwing light on the operation of the department and its most important decisions. Several collections in the Manuscripts Division of the Library of Congress are valuable for the Georgian's Cabinet career, especially the papers of Grover Cleveland, Richard Olney, Daniel S. Lamont, William C. Whitney, and Josephus Daniels.

A very important collection of manuscript materials for Smith's governorship and Georgia politics during the first decade of the twentieth century is the Thomas E. Watson Collection in the Southern Historical Collection of the University of North

372

Carolina Library. The Joseph M. Brown Collection, a small accumulation of papers relating to Brown's governorship, and the William J. Northen Collection of correspondence, scrapbooks, and pamphlets, both located in the Georgia Department of Archives and History, are useful. The Neyle Colquitt Papers in the Duke University Library are indispensable for the election of 1912 in Georgia, and the Alexander J. McKelway Papers in the Library of Congress are particularly helpful for the child-labor movement in Georgia and the South. It is a regrettable fact that the papers of such men as Clark Howell, John M. Slaton, Alexander S. Clay, and Hugh M. Dorsey are not available.

For Smith's Senate service the Woodrow Wilson Papers in the Library of Congress are extremely important. Other useful manuscript materials for this phase of the Southerner's public life are the Daniel A. Tompkins Papers in the Southern Historical Collection and the Thomas W. Gregory Papers in the Library of Congress. There is a wealth of material relevant to the Georgia leader's Senate career in the National Archives, particularly in the State Department, Department of Agriculture, Bureau of Education, and legislative records papers. The Marion Smith Papers, in the possession of Hoke Smith II of Atlanta, are useful for the 1920's.

Government Documents: State and National

A record of the General Assembly's proceedings during Smith's governorship is provided in the *Journal of the House of Representatives of the State of Georgia* (Atlanta, 1907-1909, 1911) and the *Journal of the Senate of the State of Georgia* (Atlanta, 1907-1909, 1911). The *Acts and Resolutions of the General Assembly of the State of Georgia* for the years 1900-12 (Atlanta, 1900-12) are invaluable for the legislation enacted during the period. Other useful state publications for Smith's governorship include the annual reports of the state treasurer, comptroller-general, department of education, and railroad commission.

The annual *Report of the Secretary of the Interior* (Washington, 1892-97), usually in five volumes, is a convenient source for the Secretary's recommendations and the varied activities of the department. The *Congressional Record* for the Sixty-second Congress through the Sixty-sixth Congress (Washington, 1911-21) provides a valuable record of Hoke Smith's lengthy remarks and his recorded votes on a great many issues. The *Official Congressional Directory* for the same Congresses gives committee assignments and biographical sketches of all Congressmen. For the legislation enacted during Smith's Senate years, *The Statutes at Large of the United States of America* (Washington, 1912-21) is very useful.

Newspapers and Periodicals

In the absence of manuscript sources for much of Hoke Smith's public activities, the Atlanta *Journal*, which he controlled for thirteen years and which was afterward edited by his friend and supporter, James R. Gray, provides an indispensable record of Smith's actions and opinions, as well as a convenient reflection of reform sentiment in Georgia during the progressive era. The Atlanta *Constitution* (for the years 1873-1921), a consistent opponent and critic of Smith, is a valuable corrective to the *Journal* in studying Smith and Georgia politics. Other useful anti-Smith newspapers in the state include the Macon *Telegraph* (1890-1921), the Augusta *Chronicle* (1883-1921), and the Savannah *Morning News* (1892-1921). Pro-Smith papers of most value, in addition to the Atlanta *Journal*, are the Augusta *Herald* (1900-21), the Macon *News* (1900-21), and the Savannah *Press* (1900-21). Also important for the progressive period are Thomas E. Watson's various publications: the *Weekly Jeffersonian*, the Columbia (S. C.) *Sentinel* (1918-21), and *Tom Watson's Magazine*.

The following periodical articles have useful information on Smith: Woodrow Wilson, "Mr. Cleveland's Cabinet," in *Review of Reviews*, VII (April, 1893), 286-97; "The New Secretary of the Interior," unsigned article in *American Law Review*, XXVII (March-April, 1893), 263-66; John C. Reed, "The Recent Primary Election in Georgia," in *South Atlantic Quarterly*, VI (1907), 27-36; Herbert Quick, "Hoke Smith and the Revolution in Georgia," in *Reader*, X (August, 1907), 241-48; and Alexander J. McKelway, "Hoke Smith: A Progressive Democrat," in *Outlook*, XCVI (October 1, 1910), 267-72. Valuable articles written by Hoke Smith include "The Disastrous Effects of a Force Bill," in *Forum*, XIII (August, 1892), 686-92; "The Resources and Development of the South," in *North American Review*, CLIX (August, 1894), 129-36; "The Duty of the People in Child Protection," in *Supplement to the Annals of the American Academy of Political and Social Science*, XXXII (July, 1908), 97-100; and "Rebuilding the Injured Soldier, How Uncle Sam Will Give Back to Society the Disabled Heroes," in *Forum*, LX (November, 1918), 572-80.

Correspondence, Autobiographies, and Memoirs

Published correspondence of help in the preparation of this biography include Elting E. Morison (ed.), *The Letters of Theodore Roosevelt*, 8 vols. (Cambridge, 1951-54); Ray Stannard Baker, *Woodrow Wilson, Life and Letters*, 8 vols. (Garden City and New York, 1927-39); and Charles Seymour (ed.), *The Intimate Papers of Colonel House*, 4 vols. (Boston and New York, 1926-28).

Mrs. William H. Felton, "*My Memoirs of Georgia Politics*" (Atlanta, 1911), is revealing on Georgia politics in the 1880's. Josephus Daniels, *Editor in Politics* (Chapel Hill, 1941), contains an account of Smith's career as Secretary of the Interior. Other autobiographical accounts of value for this study are Nathaniel E. Harris, *Autobiography: The Story of an Old Man's Life with Reminiscences of Seventy-Five Years* (Macon, 1925); George F. Parker, *Recollections of Grover Cleveland* (New York, 1909); Gifford Pinchot, *Breaking New Ground* (New York, 1947); and James M. Cox, *Journey Through My Years* (New York, 1946).

Biographies

Especially important for the Georgia phases of Hoke Smith's public career is C. Vann Woodward, *Tom Watson: Agrarian Rebel* (New York, 1938), brilliantly written by a writer with a flair for interpretation. Raymond B. Nixon, *Henry W. Grady, Spokesman of the New South* (New York, 1943), is a good biography of a significant Georgia leader. Two biographies that give a first-rate coverage of the second Cleveland administration are James A. Barnes, *John G. Carlisle, Financial Statesman* (New York, 1931), and Allan Nevins, *Grover Cleveland, A Study in Courage* (New York, 1932). Joseph C. Bailey, *Seaman A. Knapp: Schoolmaster of American Agriculture* (New York, 1945), and Arthur S. Link, *Wilson: The Road to the White House* (Princeton, 1947), and *Wilson: The New Freedom* (Princeton, 1956), are very helpful.

Studies in Georgia History

The best short history of Georgia is E. Merton Coulter's *Georgia, A Short History* (Chapel Hill, 1947). The fullest account of Georgia during the period covered by this study is Lucian Lamar Knight, *A Standard History of Georgia and Georgians*, 6 vols. (Chicago and New York, 1917), but it is extremely patriotic and often unreliable. The following monographs are important: Alex Mathews Arnett, *The Populist Movement in Georgia, A View of the "Agrarian Crusade" in the Light of Solid-South Politics* (New York, 1922); Enoch Marvin Banks, *The Economics of Land Tenure in Georgia* (New York, 1905); Robert Preston Brooks, *The Agrarian Revolution in Georgia, 1865-1912* (Madison, Wis., 1914); and Lynwood M. Holland, *The Direct Primary in Georgia* (Urbana, 1949).

An excellent study of the Bourbon period in Georgia is Judson Clements Ward, Jr., "Georgia Under the Bourbon Democrats, 1872-1890" (Ph. D. dissertation, University of North Carolina, 1947). Other valuable unpublished studies are Frances Beach Hudson, "The Smith-Brown Controversy" (M. A. thesis, Emory University, 1929); Randolph L. Fort, "History of the Atlanta Journal" (M. A. thesis, Emory University, 1930); Jim David Cherry, "The Georgia Railroad Commission, 1879-1888" (M. A. thesis, University of North Carolina, 1941); A. Elizabeth Taylor, "The Convict Lease System in Georgia, 1866-1908" (M. A. thesis, University of North Carolina, 1940); and J. Chalmers Vinson, "Hoke Smith, Cleveland's Secretary of the Interior" (M. A. thesis, University of Georgia, 1944).

General Works and Monographs

A sparkling study of the post-Reconstruction generation is C. Vann Woodward's *Origins of the New South, 1877-1913* (Baton Rouge, 1951), while Wilbur J. Cash, *The Mind of the South* (New York, 1941), is one of the most provocative books on the region. More specialized works dealing with the South during the period covered by this biography include the following: Paul H. Buck, *The Road to Reunion, 1865-1900* (Boston, 1937); Charles W. Dabney, *Universal Education in the South*, 2 vols. (Chapel Hill, 1936); Maxwell Ferguson, *State Regulation of Railroads in the South* (New York, 1916); Elizabeth H. Davidson, *Child Labor Legislation in the Southern Textile States* (Chapel Hill, 1939); Paul Lewinson, *Race, Class, & Party, A History of Negro Suffrage and White Politics in the South* (New York, 1932); and V. O. Key, Jr., *Southern Politics in State and Nation* (New York, 1949).

Two valuable articles on Southern politics during the progressive era are Daniel M. Robison, "From Tillman to Long: Some Striking Leaders of the Rural South," in *Journal of Southern History*, III (August, 1937), 289-310, and Arthur S. Link, "The Progressive Movement in the South, 1870-1914," in *North Carolina Historical Review*, XXIII (April, 1946), 172-95.

Index